Options

Founded in 1807, John Wiley & Sons is the oldest independent publishing company in the United States. With offices in North America, Europe, Australia and Asia, Wiley is globally committed to developing and marketing print and electronic products and services for our customers' professional and personal knowledge and understanding.

The Wiley Finance series contains books written specifically for finance and investment professionals as well as sophisticated individual investors and their financial advisors. Book topics range from portfolio management to e-commerce, risk management, financial engineering, valuation and financial instrument analysis, as well as much more.

For a list of available titles, please visit our Web site at www.WileyFinance.com.

Options

Trading Strategy and Risk Management

SIMON VINE

John Wiley & Sons, Inc.

Published by John Wiley & Sons, Inc., Hoboken, New Jersey.
Published simultaneously in Canada

Library of Congress Cataloging-in-Publication Data:

Vine, Simon.
Options : trading strategy and risk management / Simon Vine.
p. cm.—(Wiley finance series)
Includes bibliographical references and index.
ISBN 0-471-69128-3 (cloth)
1. Options (Finance) 2. Risk management. I. Title. II. Series.
HG6024.A3V56 2005
332.64'53—dc22
2004016488

Printed in the United States of America.

10 9 8 7 6 5 4 3 2 1

This book is dedicated to my mother Lilia Vine
whose love, support, and sacrifice
were the reasons it became possible.

Contents

Foreword

Over the last 30 years, the options industry has been transformed from one-time deals into the market with daily trading volumes measured in billions of dollars. Due to high profitability of the new sphere of trading and risk management, many institutions spent hundreds millions of dollars on building businesses in derivatives of all types.

The book summarizes material of seminars the author has given in the United States, Europe, and Latin America. The conclusion from the questions asked by practitioners is that they prefer explanations of derivatives that contain minimal financial mathematics. This book is oriented to this group of readers.

It covers a broad gamut of themes such as trading and hedging, other types of derivatives, credit and market risks, psychological aspects of trading, and many others. Thus, the book provides an overview of derivative markets as a whole. Hedging, credit, and market risks are discussed in semiautonomous blocks, which contain summaries of relevant information presented in earlier chapters.

Chapters 1–10 and 19–21 can be useful for marketing professionals, Chapters 1–21 may be helpful to investors and traders. Parts 6 and 7 target credit and market risk managers. To all specialists, the author recommends Part 8 on the psychological aspects of financial markets.

The book has a few special moments. To reflect practical reality as much as possible, the author sometimes uses different terminology regarding the same financial operations. This is necessary since the options world is populated with duplicate terms.

The author gives thanks to Philip Halperin for valuable ideas, to Gena Ioffe for recommendations in preparation of publication, and to Aleksey Baykov for technical assistance.

Introduction

ABOUT DERIVATIVES

The word *derivatives* comes from a mathematical function that derives its value from a data series. The term may scare someone who does not deal with math daily. However, we are talking about a commonly used class of financial instruments. Terms that ordinary people use should not be very difficult to understand. Imagine that you enter a conference hall and the host wants to prepare you for something you have never seen before. He takes you on a tour. The walls of the first room are covered with mathematical formulas. The walls of the second one are covered with design blueprints. You are at a loss. What's all this about? The curtain rises, and there is a car behind it! All the formulas and design drafts were the plans for a car. You may not understand the calculations or drafts, but you will have no problem driving the car. The same is true of derivatives—although they are based on complex calculations, they are easy to use.

Financial instruments are called *derivatives* because their prices depend on the prices of other assets such as oil, gold, stocks, interest rates, or currencies. For example, if oil prices change, the prices of the derivatives on oil change as well. That's why we say *derivative on* such and such an asset, meaning that the given derivative's price depends on the performance of the asset. Assets that serve as the basis for calculation of derivatives are referred to as *underlying assets*.

Derivatives are divided into three groups of instruments: futures/forwards, options, and swaps. The future/forward contracts depend on future prices of the underlying assets. Swaps depend on the relative changes of the current and future prices of the asset. The prices of option contracts also depend on the future prices of assets, but not one for one as in the case of futures.

Futures contracts on commodities appeared in the middle of the nineteenth century. The commodity exchanges allowed farmers to sell their future harvests, enabling the mills to secure their supply. The transactions would settle on standard dates set by contracts. The seller was obliged to deliver to one of the sites specified in the contract a commodity of quality, which was also defined in the contract. Since the delivery was to take place in the future, the contracts were called *futures*.

The main difference between futures and forwards is that the former are quoted on exchanges, and the latter in the interbank market (also known as over-the-counter market (OTC)). The rules of exchanges are standard in terms of contract size and settlement dates. The interbank market, in contrast, offers more flexibility because terms can be dictated in part by client needs. In terms of pricing and business objectives, futures and forwards are as similar as twins. Although the term *forward* has appeared recently, the instrument has existed for millennia ever since peasants started preselling their crops to finance themselves between harvests.

Unlike buyers of futures and forwards, options buyers have the right *but not the obligation* to deliver or take delivery on dates set in contracts. Therefore, sellers of options, although they assume the obligation to honor the orders of buyers, are not certain until the settlement date that the delivery will take place. The option is a financial market equivalent to insurance. Let's say, for example, that you were in a car accident and your car was insured. The car insurance is equivalent to buying an option to sell at a price that is higher than the current one. You can decide whether or not it is worth it to file an insurance claim. This is not very different than an oil producer who sees oil prices fall, and feels a similar pain from the loss in the value of an asset. An option contract that gave the producer the right to sell oil at a stipulated price higher than the current market price would not really be all that different than insurance against a car accident.

The option is a very old instrument. Aristotle was first to mention it. Option contracts on herring have been found in Dutch commercial records from the twelfth century. Warrants, or stock options, have been very popular since the eighteenth century.

Swaps appeared at the end of twentieth century. They are the newest financial instruments. Swaps constitute exchanges of a sort. They are not settled physically, only in cash. The most utilized are asset swaps, in which one party has to pay a floating price and the other has to pay a fixed price. For example, our farmer sold contracts on a product for future delivery and bought it for today's delivery. Although the product will not be delivered to him (only a cash settlement), in a way he borrowed the product (e.g., grain) at today's price and sold the future harvest at today's price for delivery on the future date. The farmer's opportunity profit/loss will depend on the change of the price differentials of the bought and sold contract prices.

APPLICATION OF DERIVATIVES

Futures, forwards, swaps, and options exist on practically every underlying asset (corn, gold, stocks, to name just a few). Like an insurance policy, they can be issued on almost any event. There are derivatives on agricultural production, currency exchange rate, indexes linked to stock prices and baskets of commodities, the results of sports events, and electricity. Among the latest innovations are weather derivatives, which are used by utilities to cope with the uncertainty of weather conditions and their impact on any utility company's bottom line. Suppliers and users of fuel oil know the length of any winter and the underlying temperature of this season can have a huge impact on how much energy they sell or consume. In other words, derivatives cover every side of economic activity: production companies, service companies, financial companies, and governments can all potentially manage price uncertainty and risk through their use.

One interesting caveat is that derivatives are used for very different purposes. For insurance, for example, the producers and users protect themselves from price fluctuations in the financial markets (the process known as a hedging). At the same time, banks and mutual funds actively use derivatives for speculation and investment transactions. Even though there is such a variety of users, the same contract serves as an instrument of hedging for the buyer (such as a production company) and as an instrument of speculation for the seller (such as a financial company).

Volumes of derivative transactions rise steadily. According to BIS, more than $24 trillion of foreign exchange (FX) derivatives were outstanding as of December 2003. The outstanding exchange-traded options contracts reached $29 trillion for the same date.

Options are popular because of their flexibility and relative cheapness. Those who cannot afford to buy the underlying product (a stock, for example), as a rule have enough to buy an option on the stock. Options may have a variety of terms. For example, options with different execution prices will have different probabilities of making a profit. Due to such varying probabilities, options attract a variety of users. Each user adapts this instrument to his forecast and risk preference.

FUNCTIONS INVOLVED IN DERIVATIVES OPERATIONS

Although simple and popular, derivatives carry substantial risk and are based on complex mathematical models.

Models are developed by physicists and mathematicians. They are used by traders and investors—also called front offices—the decision makers.

Not every trader or investor understands the models they use, any more than users of calculators understand how they are made.

Traders and investors are controlled by market and credit risk managers. The market risk managers set up limits for traders' portfolios. Since the risks of derivatives are long-term, credit risk managers evaluate customers' credit and set up client/counterparty limits. Lawyers draft agreements to reduce credit risks.

Mid-office specialists control the front office (traders) to make sure that traders act within the limits that are permitted by market and credit risk managers. Back offices process trades at the end of this chain.

All this adds up to the following picture of interaction: top managers decide to develop derivatives. Mathematicians work out the models, which make it possible to value instruments. Market risk managers determine the types and the boundaries of the allowable risk. Credit risk managers define counterparties allowed for trading. Traders try to make money under constant monitoring of middle office risk managers. Back offices conclude the process.

Options have received a lot of bad publicity because of managerial flaps. Banks suffered losses because of mistakes in models (UBS in 1998 on stock options), because of traders' misfortunes (Société Génerale in 1992), because of accounting mistakes (Kidder Peabody in 1994), and so forth. Weak control processes led to the bankruptcy of Baring Brothers, a firm with a two-hundred-year history. Poor service of clients by derivative sales specialists destroyed the reputation of Bankers Trust, one of the greatest American banks. In other words, at every point of the function chain derivatives require professional treatment.

CONCLUSION

In the last decade, options, like other derivatives, became an essential part of the financial markets. This book is about options, their interaction with other derivatives and their place in the financial market in general. It provides the reader with a complete picture of the market and will help the reader to obtain skills to use options in a variety of fields.

PART One

Basic Knowledge

CHAPTER 1

Basic Terms

Options are financial contracts similar to insurance contracts. Option sellers charge buyers a premium, just as insurance companies do. Similarly, the option premium is calculated using standard mathematical models. An option contract, like any contract, specifies the transaction amount, the contract price, the final date, and the rights and obligations of the parties. So what makes them unique?

KEY TERMS

Most of us feel comfortable discussing price moves of stocks, currencies, bonds, and other assets. Let's suppose that you are jewelry producer and that on November 10 you should buy a large amount of gold. You choose to buy an insurance that will compensate you for losses if the price of gold on November 10 is higher than $300 per ounce. In the financial markets, such an insurance contract is called an *option*.

It's obvious that the closer the gold price is to the contract level, the more expensive is the insurance (option), since the probability of the insurance claim being filed increases. An option is a financial instrument whose price depends on the price of some other asset (in this example, gold). In other words, option prices are derivatives of other asset prices. That is why options are called *derivative financial instruments*. Naturally, you may possess options on stocks, bonds, oil, and even weather. The asset from which options derive their value is called an *underlying asset* or simply *the underlying*.

Each option transaction is a legally binding contract that doesn't differ greatly from any other contract. The price paid to the seller by the buyer is called the *premium* (similar to an insurance premium) or the *option price*. An option contract stipulates the price and is valid within some agreed period of time (*tenure*). The *option life* is limited by an *expiration date* defined in the contract. On this expiration date, the option comes to an end, and a buyer has to either *exercise* the rights given by the contract or let it *expire*.

Under the terms of an option contract, on that date an option buyer has a right to make a transaction (buy or sell) with the underlying asset. The option's seller (also called the *writer* of the option) is obliged to satisfy the buyer's demand. The price at which the transaction may take place on the option's expiration is called the *strike* price.

DEFINITIONS OF CALL AND PUT OPTIONS: CALLS

Options are divided in two types: ones that give buyers a right to buy (*call*) the underlying asset and those that enable them to sell the asset (*put*). If you are a buyer,

a *call* gives you the right (but not the obligation) to *buy* the underlying asset on a specific date, at a predetermined price;

a *put* gives you the right (but not the obligation) to *sell* the underlying asset on a specific date, at a predetermined price.

It is important to remember once again that the option's buyer has a right but not an obligation to exercise the contract. The seller, however, must satisfy the buyer's request.

Suppose that IBM trades at $120 per share and you own an IBM $100 call. The option owner has the right to buy the stock at $100 on the day of expiration (at expiration). If you (buyer) choose to exercise this right, you will exercise the option by informing the option's seller that you are buying the stock at $100. After that, you can immediately sell the stock at $120 in the market, collecting a $20 profit.

Once the option is exercised, it stops existing (similar to insurance, once the contract is settled). In this example, if you paid a $10 premium for the option, your net gain will be $120 (current stock price) – $100 (strike) – $10 (option's premium) = $10.

Let's consider another outcome. On the expiration date, the IBM stock trades at $90 per share. In this case, if you exercise your option and buy the shares at $100, you would sell them in the market only at $90. Therefore, you will lose $10. Since the option is a right but not an obligation, why should you make a losing trade? That is why you will let the option expire. No notice to the option's seller is required.

To summarize, the option buyer will never exercise a call, if the price of stock (an underlying asset) is lower than the option's strike (the price at which you can buy the stock through the option). Consequently, the option will expire worthless, and the buyer will lose the money invested in the premium.

PUTS

Understanding put options, or puts, seems to be universally more difficult than understanding call options, or calls. Take your time. Imagine you bought a right to sell your AIG stock at $80 on the expiration date. At that time, you would be able to buy the stock at any price below $80, and simultaneously exercise the option. For example, if on the expiration date the stock trades at $60, you would purchase it and exercise the option. You would end up selling the stock you've just bought at $60 to the option's seller at $80.

You will never exercise that option (sell the stock at $80), if the stock trades above $80, because you would have to buy it back at a higher price, thus losing money. Since option buyers do not have any obligations, they would not do anything against their own interests. If on the expiration date you choose not to exercise the option (and sell the AIG stock), the option would expire worthless.

One generally *buys options* in the following circumstances:

One buys a *call* if one is *bullish* (expecting the market to go up).

One buys a *put* if one is *bearish* (expecting the market to go down).

SELLING OPTIONS

Initially, the implications of *selling options* are more difficult to understand. To simplify the task, let's just make the opposite assumptions to those we made when we were buying:

One *sells a call* if one is *bearish* (expecting the market to go down).

One *sells a put* if one is *bullish* (expecting the market to go up).

For example, if you expect a particular stock to trade down (a bearish outlook), you do not need a right to buy the stock (a call), so you will sell it.

However, if you expected the market to go up (a bullish outlook), you would not need a right to sell a stock. Therefore, you would sell a put.

Remember, the crucial difference between the option buyers and sellers is that option *sellers* (ones who write options) are *obliged* to do what the buyers ask them to do, while the *buyers* can *choose* whether or not to exercise their options.

In other words, if you sold somebody the right to *sell you* the AIG stock at $80 and the stock is trading at $60 per share, you have no choice but to buy the stock from the option's buyer at $80! If after that you go back to the market and sell it at $60, you end up losing $20 per share.

Of course, if the stock trades above $80 per share, the buyer will not exercise the option. The option will expire worthless and your profit will be equal to the premium you collected by selling the option in the first place.

A point of importance: If it costs $10 in option premium to own a stock at $100 per share, you can either buy 1 share (for $100) or 10 options ($10 × 10) to achieve exposure to market price. If the stock price goes sharply up, the options' position will make many times more money than one share of the stock. This is one of the core advantages of options: they provide substantial leverage, offering you greater exposure to the trade with the same size investment. However, this extra opportunity does not come free. Since the option's life is limited, if the price does not increase sharply, the entire investment in the premium is lost, as the option stops existing on expiration. Meanwhile, the stock is most likely to still have some value at that time, even if its market price is below $100.

QUESTIONS

Please remember that many concepts will be repeated in the coming chapters. Therefore, do not get discouraged, if something seemingly easy does not settle in your mind on the first try, it will sink in later.

1. Which option is equivalent to the bet that the price of silver will trade higher?
2. Which option is equivalent to the bet that the price of silver will trade lower?
3. If you bet against the view that silver will trade higher, what would you do in terms of options?
4. If you bet against the view that silver will trade lower, what would you do in terms of options?
5. If you believe that the stock price will rise, what would you buy and/or sell?
6. If you believe that the stock price will go down, what would you buy and/or sell?

7. Summing up Questions 1–6, which options will you buy or sell, if you believe that the stock price will
   a. increase
   b. not increase
   c. decrease
   d. not decrease

8. What will you do at expiration, if you own a call on Nokia with $200 strike and the stock is trading at
   a. $220?
   b. $180?

9. What happens if you own the put option on Nokia with $200 strike and the stock is trading at
   a. $220?
   b. $180?

10. What should happen in the market for you to make money, if you bought an option that entitles you
    a. to buy the IBM stock at (strike) $100
    b. to sell the IBM stock at $95

11. You have $100 to invest and the IBM stock trades today at $100. How much money will you make when it appreciates to $110
    a. if you invest $100 and buy 1 share?
    b. if you invest $100 and buy 10 calls with a strike of $100 (i.e., you pay $10 per 1 call)?

    If at the end of the investment term the stock trades at $100, what is the worth of your

    c. stock position?
    d. options' position?

    If at the end of the investment term the stock trades $150, what is the value of your

    e. stock position?
    f. options' position?

    If at the end of the investment term the stock trades at $50, what is the value of your

    g. stock position?
    h. options' position?

12. What inference can you make from the previous exercise about advantages and disadvantages of using options vis-à-vis outright purchase of a given underlying?

ANSWERS

1. If you are ready to bet that silver will trade higher, you can buy a call on silver.
2. If you are ready to bet that silver will trade lower, you can buy a put on silver.
3. If you are ready to bet that silver will *not* trade higher, you can *sell* a call on silver.
4. If you are ready to bet that silver will *not* trade lower, you can *sell* a put on silver.
5. If you believe that the stock price will rise, you buy a call or sell a put.
6. If you believe that the stock price will go down, you buy a put or sell a call.
7. To summarize Questions 1–6, if you believe that the stock price
   a. will increase, you buy a call.
   b. will not increase, you sell a call.
   c. will decrease, you buy a put.
   d. will not decrease, you sell a put.
8. If you own the call option on Nokia with a $200 strike price and the stock is trading at
   a. $220, you can exercise the option buying the stock at $200, sell it in the market for $220 and make $20.
   b. $180, you will let the option expire because you can buy it in the market at a better price.
9. If you own the put option on Nokia with a $200 strike and the stock is trading at
   a. $220, you will let the option expire because if you sell it at $200 a share, you will have to buy it back in the market at $220!
   b. $180, you can exercise the option selling the stock at $200, buy it back in the market at $180 and make $20.

10. a. Since you have a right to buy the IBM stock at (strike) $100 (you bought a $100 call), you expect that the market will trade up above $100.
    b. Since you have a right to sell the IBM stock at $95 (you bought a $95 put), you expect that the market will trade down below $95.

11. If the IBM stock appreciates to $110 and you own
    a. one share, you will make $10 ($110 – $100)
    b. 10 calls with a strike $100, you will make $0 (($110 – $100) × 10 – $100 (options' premium)

    If the IBM stock trades at $100,

    c. one share of stock is still worth $100
    d. You lose $100: the options expire and you lose all the money that you spent on the premium.

    If the IBM stock trades at $150,

    e. one share of stock is still worth $100, and your profit is $50 ($150 – $100).
    f. 10 calls will be worth $400 (($150 – $100) × 10 – $100).

    If at the end of the investment term the stock trades at $50,

    g. one share of stock is still worth $50, and your loss is $50 ($50 – $100).
    h. You lose $100: the options expire, and you lose all the money spent on the premium.

12. The previous exercise demonstrates that options offer more leverage (opportunity to benefit from a large move) than investments in stocks. However, if the market is stable, the options expire worthless (thus you lose all the money invested) while the stock holds some of the initial value.

    In other words, if the market lacks direction or volatility and a small move is expected, a long stock position is better than long options. On a significant move, options provide an opportunity to make more money than stock positions.

    The moral of this story: if you are not expecting a significant market momentum, you should not buy options. Odds are you will not be compensated for the option premium you have paid.

FURTHER INFORMATION FOR THE READER

Terms Used in Trading

Traders have their own professional language. Some of the terms are used universally across the trading world. Others are instrument- or market-specific. This means that every time you call a new broker, you should make sure that the terms you use are commonly used for a given instrument. For example, when you trade currency options, terms used for the same options combinations are different on exchange floors and from those used in the interbank (OTC) market. Moreover, if an OTC foreign exchange options trader starts working with OTC interest rate options, he has to verify the language used for the same options combinations. OTC foreign exchange options traders on other continents also use different terms. Be cautious with the terminology of new markets. For example, a combination of a long call and a short put is called a risk reversal in the FX OTC market, combo on an exchange, and collar in the fixed income market.

Below we will list some relatively universal terms used across the markets and in this book.

P/L, P&L a profit and loss statement, that is, results of a trading activity.
Strategy a combination of financial instruments aimed at benefiting from the market views.
Breakeven a price level of a given commodity or financial instrument at which P/L of a strategy is equal to 0.
FX Foreign exchange.
Long position a position in which you purchased a given underlying or financial instrument.
Short position a position in which you sold a given commodity or financial instrument.
Go long something to purchase something.
Go short something to sell something.
Notional amount, Face value a size of the contract.
Leg one portion of a strategy. For instance, to buy a straddle $5 million a leg (both call and put has face value of $5 million).
Mio million.
JPY Japanese yen.
USD U.S. dollar.
EUR euro.
AUD Australian dollar.
EUR/USD (USD/JPY, etc.) foreign exchange rate of euro against U.S. dollar (yen against dollar, etc.).
Long $1 million USD/JPY long $1 million against yen equivalent of $1 million.

CHAPTER 2

Drawing Option Charts

Charts help to visualize the risks and rewards of options. They show the profit and loss profiles of options (and options strategies) with respect to the price changes of an underlying asset.

PRINCIPLES OF DRAFTING CHARTS

In drawing a chart, we will answer the question of how the price of the underlying asset (in this case, stock) influences the price of a stock option. The horizontal axis shows the stock (or any other underlying asset) price changes. The vertical axis reflects changes in the prices of options position. If the *premium* of an option is 0, it becomes profitable as soon as the price of the underlying asset *exceeds* the strike price (*calls*) or *falls below* the strike price (*puts*).

Let's say you bought an IBM 110 call. It gives you the right to buy the stock at $110. As you see in Figure 2.1, as long as the stock stays below

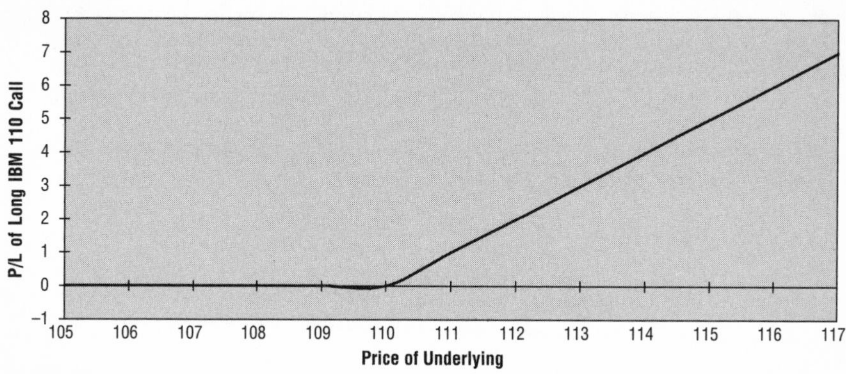

FIGURE 2.1 P/L of the Long IBM 110 Call (0 Premium Paid)

$110, the option's value is 0. If the stock trades below $110 per share, one would not exercise the call. That would mean that one has to buy the stock at $100—higher than the market price. *But the higher the stock is above $110, the greater is the call option's value.*

In other words, while the stock price is going up, every dollar above $110 per share increases the option's value by $1. That is, on exercise, one would buy the stock at $110 and sell in the market at $111 or above!

If you sold that call, you would be losing $1 for each $1 stock price change (Figure 2.2). That is because the option owner will buy from you the stock at $110, and you will have to buy it back in the market at the current higher market rate!

If you buy the $110 put (Figure 2.3) you will receive the right to sell the stock at $110. That is, it is a substitute for a bearish position in the stock (for selling the stock at $110). Therefore, the put will not make money as long as the stock is above $110: it does not make sense to sell the stock at $110, if the market trades at $120. Hence, you would not exercise the put, if the price is *higher* than the exercise price. However, if the stock trades at $100, you will exercise the put (sell the stock at $110 to the option's seller) and buy the shares back in the market at $100.

When you draw the chart you will leave the area above 110 equal to 0. The area below 110 will be profitable because your option will gain $1 for each $1 drop in the stock price. *Therefore, the lower the stock price, the more money you make as the put buyer (i.e., "long the put").*

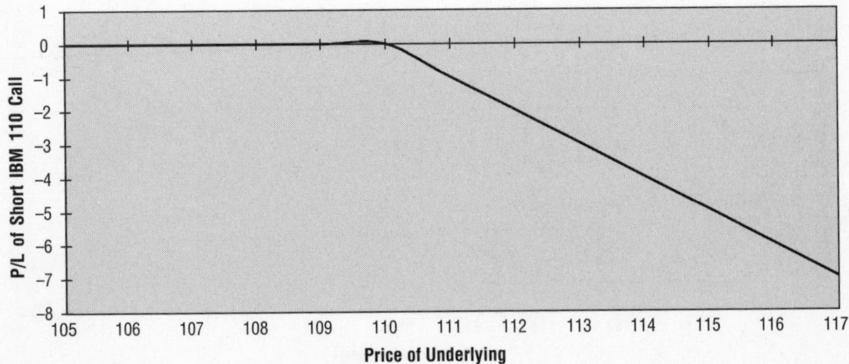

FIGURE 2.2 P/L of the Short IBM 110 Call (0 Premium Received)

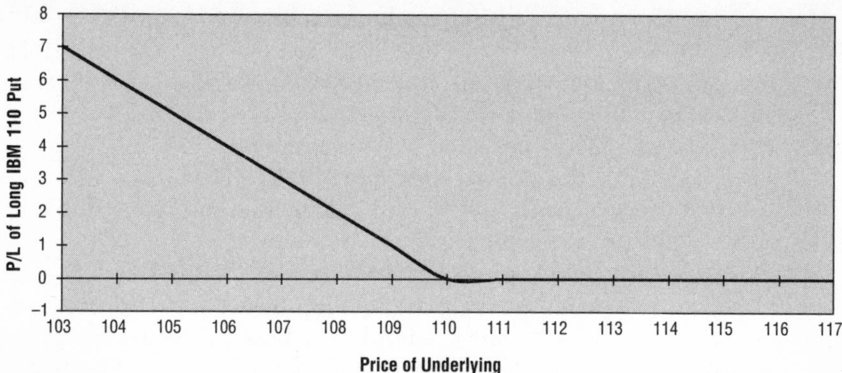

FIGURE 2.3 P/L of the Long IBM 110 Put (0 Premium Paid)

ACCOUNTING IN CHARTS FOR OPTIONS PREMIUMS

Let's now introduce the premium in our calculation. The *premium* is the money one pays for the right to own the option (when one buys it) or as a payment for taking risk (when one sells it).

In general, the higher the probability that the option will make money, the higher the premium. For a call option to be profitable on expiration, the underlying should trade above the strike level plus premium. In our example, if you paid $10 for the right to buy the IBM stock at $110, it should trade at $120 for the option to break even (Figure 2.4). At $130, you will realize a $10 profit ($130 – ($110 + $10)).

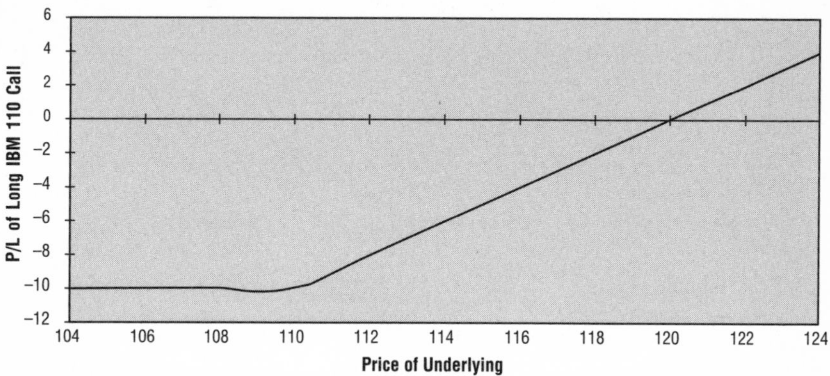

FIGURE 2.4 P/L of the Long IBM 110 Call ($10 Premium Paid)

If the premium is \$23, then the option will start making money when the stock trades above the \$133 level (\$110 + \$23). That is, the higher the premium, the higher the *breakeven* of the trade.

One can generalize the case by saying that, if at the end of the option's life (on *expiration*)

- IBM trades below the strike, the entire premium is lost (e.g., at \$100, you lose the premium you paid for the option).
- If it trades above the strike, you get back at least a part of the premium (e.g., if you paid a \$10 premium for an option with a \$110 strike, and it trades at \$115, you will lose only \$5 (\$115 – (\$110 + \$10)).
- If it trades higher than the strike + the premium paid, your strategy (buying the call) is profitable.

RISK PROFILE[1] OF PURCHASED OPTIONS

Figures 2.5 and 2.6 clearly demonstrate that at any price your loss is limited to the premium you paid!

Rule 1. If you buy an option, you *cannot* lose more than the premium paid for the option. The profit is unlimited for the call. For the put, profit is limited by the option's strike minus 0.

In some way there is an analogy between options and insurance. If you buy insurance, you pay a little bit, but have a chance to collect a lot. If you sell the insurance, you collect a little and may lose a lot.

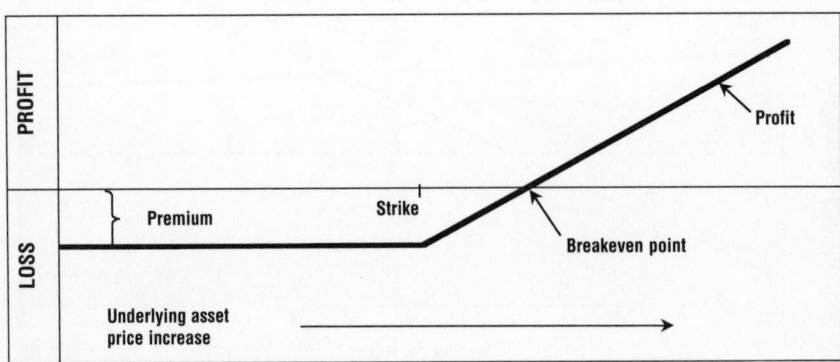

FIGURE 2.5 P/L of a Long Call

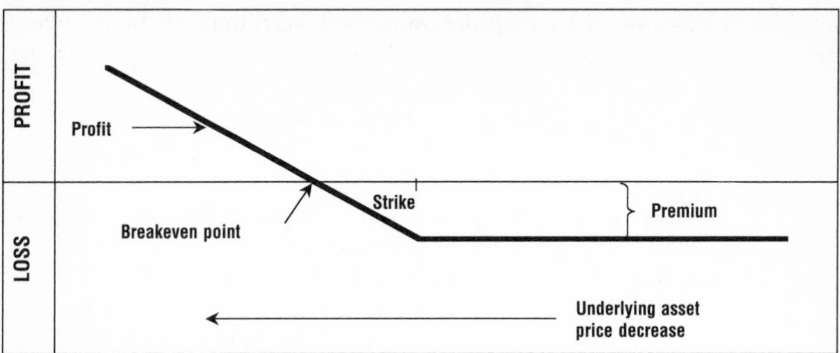

FIGURE 2.6 P/L of a Long Put

RISK PROFILE OF SOLD OPTIONS

Let's discuss put options. Let's say you *sold* an IBM 100 put and *received* a $5 premium. As you can see in Figure 2.7, the put that you sold as the put writer starts losing money when the stock is below $95. Notice that your risk area is between $95 and $0. That is, your maximum loss on this trade is $95.

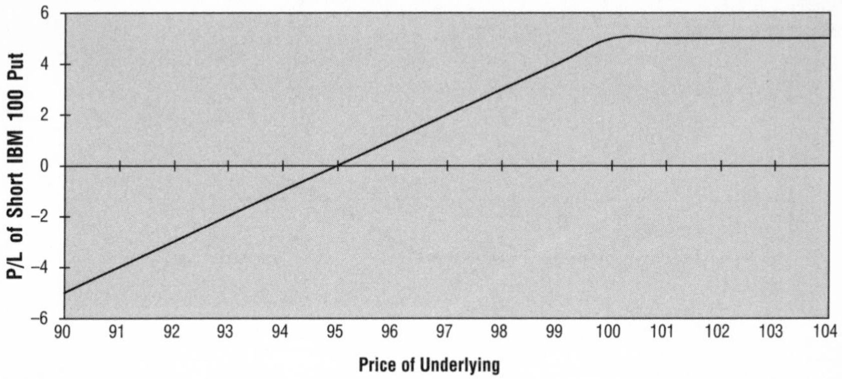

FIGURE 2.7 P/L of the Short IBM 100 Put ($5 Premium Received)

Rule 2. If you sold an option, your risk is unlimited for calls and limited to (Strike-0) for puts. Your profit is limited to the amount of premium collected.

Let's summarize:

If you *buy a call*, you have a *right to buy* the underlying at the *price beneficial to you.*

If you *sell a put*, you have an *obligation to buy* the underlying at the *price not beneficial to you.*

If you *buy a put*, you have a *right to sell* the underlying at the *price beneficial to you.*

If you *sell a call*, you have an *obligation to sell* the underlying at the *price not beneficial to you.*

Breakeven of the call on expiration is equal to strike + premium.

Breakeven of the put on expiration is equal to strike – premium.

HEURISTIC RULES OF CONSTRUCTING CHARTS

Although the charts seem easy to understand, every time the question comes up most people have to recall the principles and somehow reconstruct the charts in their minds. We can suggest some visual associations that may speed up any such recollections and provide memory reinforcement.

The idea is simple: if you draw simultaneously long and short calls on one chart, the picture will look like letter "c" (the abbreviation for "call"), as shown in Figure 2.8.

If you draw simultaneously long and short put on one chart, the picture after a small alteration will look like letter "p" (the abbreviation for "put"), as shown in Figure 2.9.

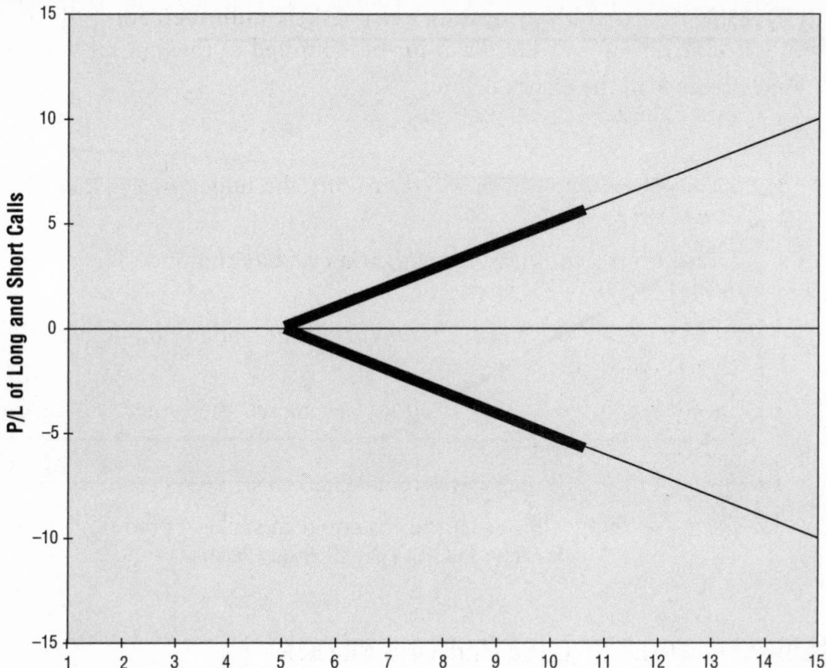

FIGURE 2.8 The P/L Profile of Long and Short Calls Resembles the Letter C

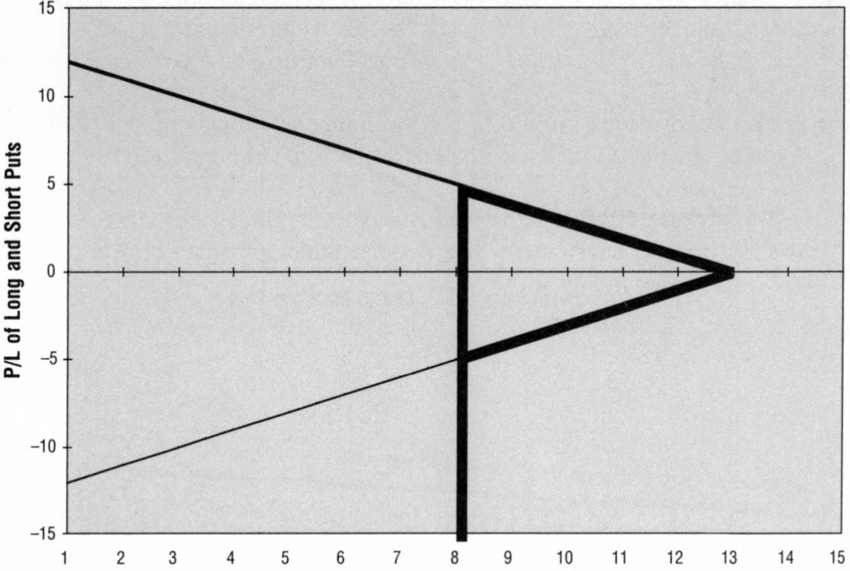

FIGURE 2.9 The P/L Profile of Long and Short Puts Resembles the Letter P

QUESTIONS

1. Find mistakes in the charts below:

a.

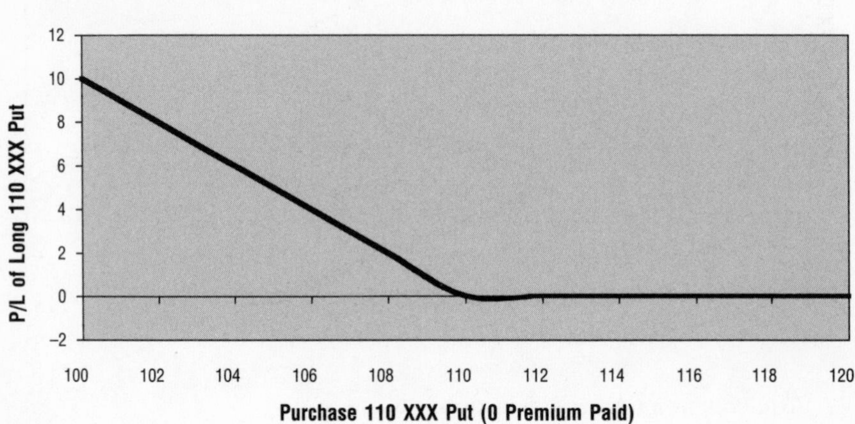

b.

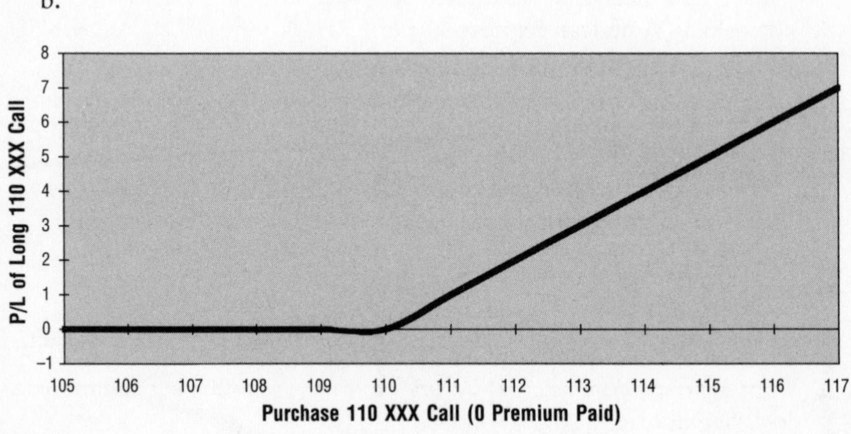

c.

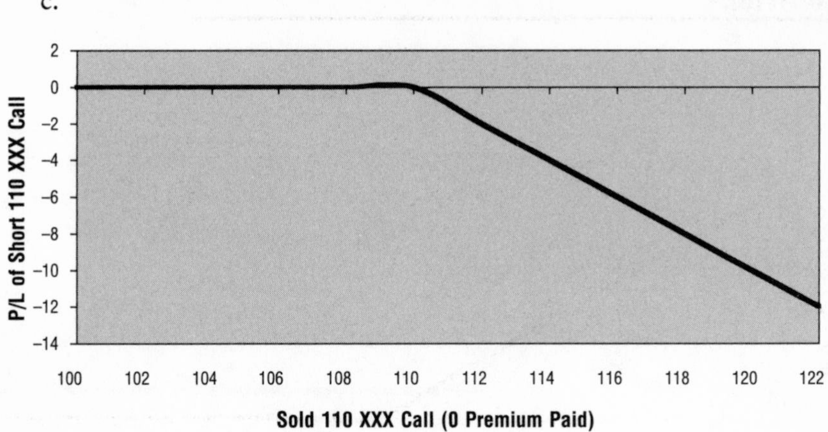

2. You bought an American Express 45 call:
   a. draw a chart of your profits and losses
   b. draw a chart of your profits and losses if you paid $5 premium
3. You sold an American Express 45 put:
   a. draw a chart of your profits and losses
   b. draw a chart of your profits and losses if you collected a $2 premium
4. You bought an IBM 90 put:
   a. draw a chart of your profits and losses
   b. draw a chart of your profits and losses if you paid $6 premium
5. You sold an IBM 85 call:
   a. draw a chart of your profits and losses
   b. draw a chart of your profits and losses if you collected $8 premium
6. What is your maximum risk in question for the following situations as described above:
   a. 2b
   b. 3b
   c. 4b
   d. 5b

ANSWERS

1. a.

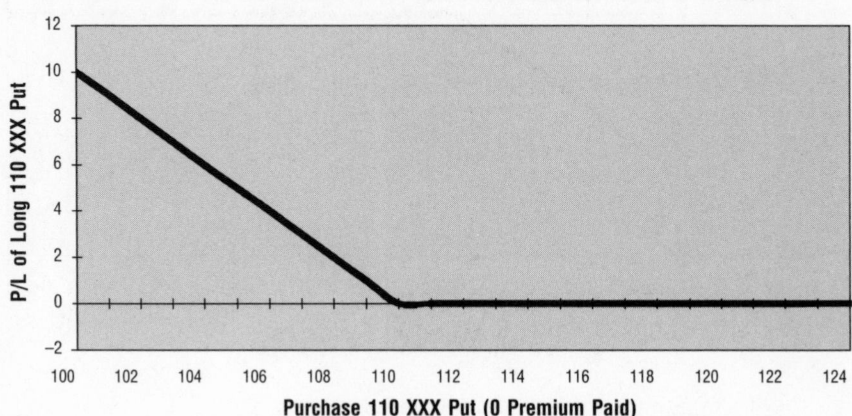
P/L of Long 110 XXX Put
12
10
8
6
4
2
0
−2
100 102 104 106 108 110 112 114 116 118 120 122 124
Purchase 110 XXX Put (0 Premium Paid)

b.

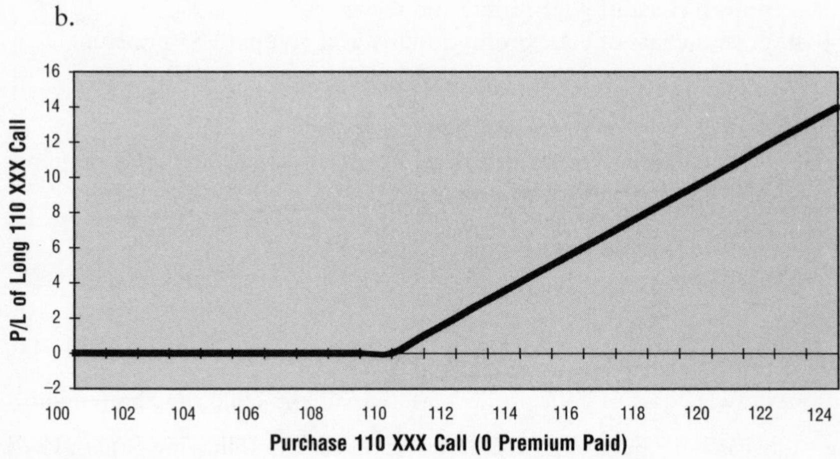
P/L of Long 110 XXX Call
16
14
12
10
8
6
4
2
0
−2
100 102 104 106 108 110 112 114 116 118 120 122 124
Purchase 110 XXX Call (0 Premium Paid)

c.

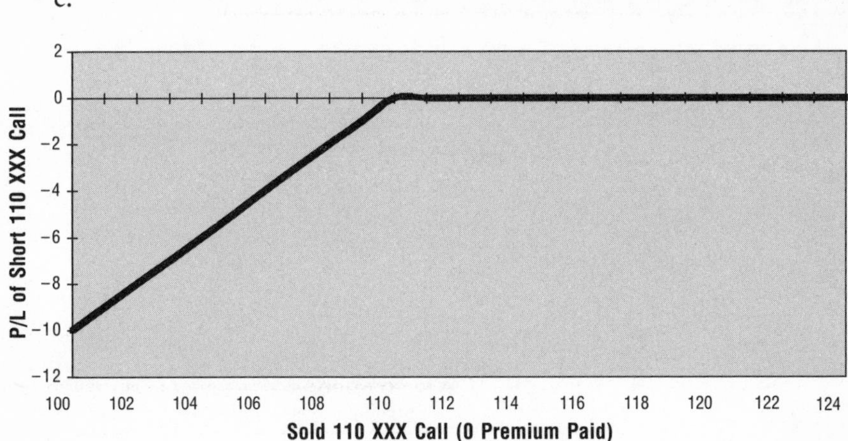

2. a. You bought an Amex 45 call, 0 premium paid.

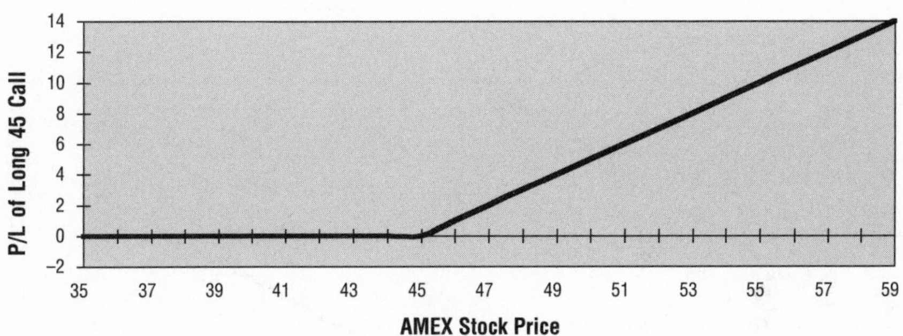

b. You bought an Amex 45 call, $5 premium paid.

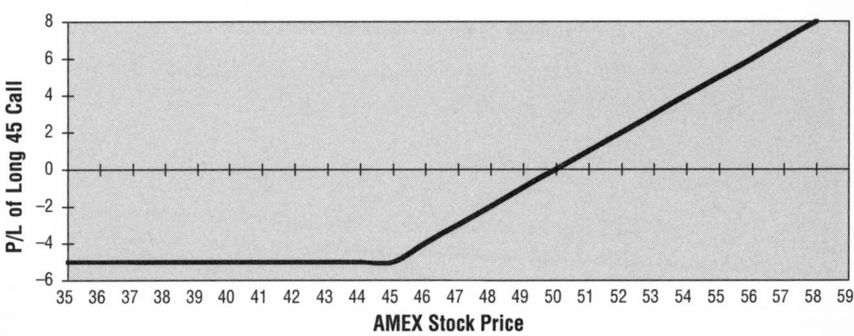

3. a. You sold an Amex 45 put, 0 premium paid.

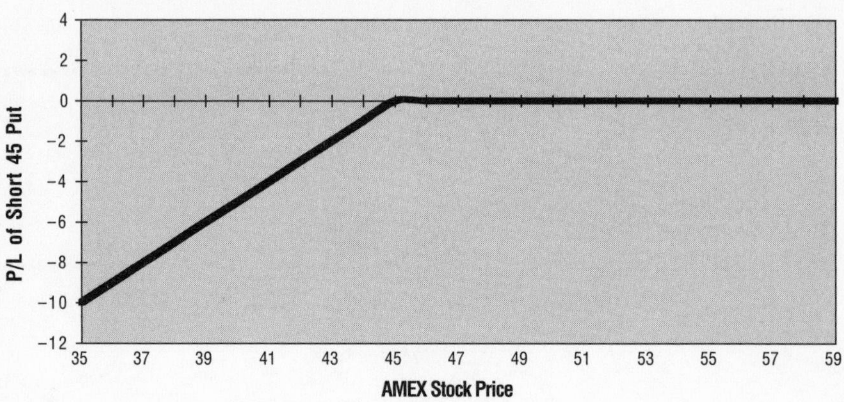

b. You sold an Amex 45 put, $2 premium paid.

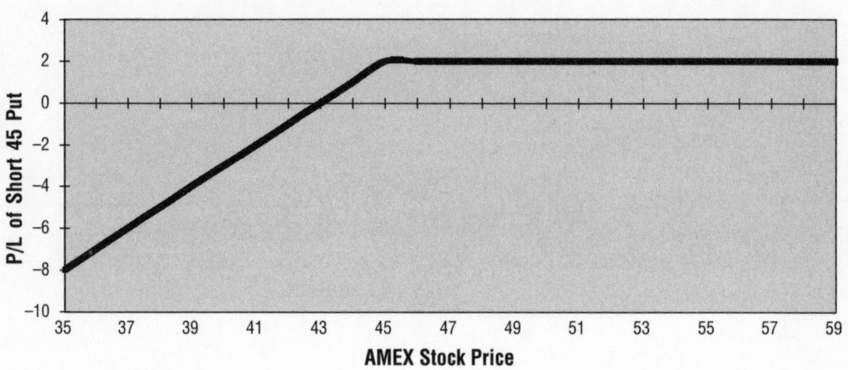

4. a. You bought an IBM 90 put, 0 premium paid.

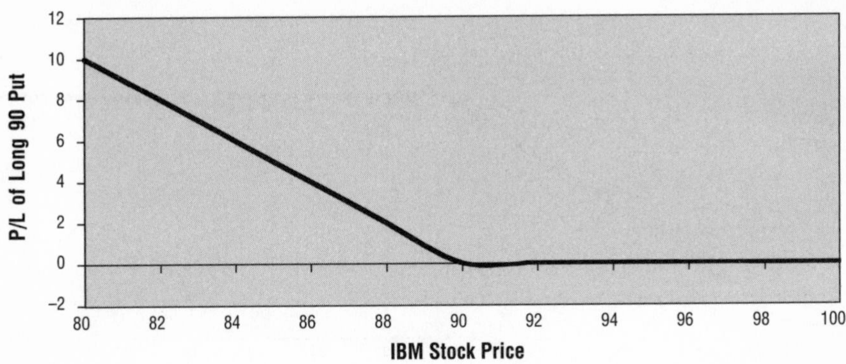

b. You bought an IBM 90 put, $6 premium paid.

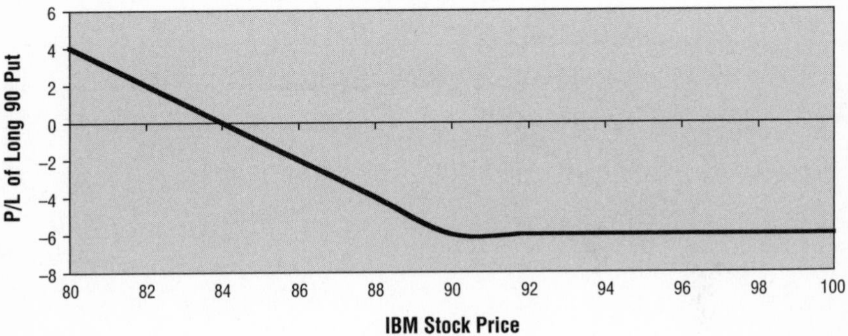

5. a. You sold an IBM 85 call, 0 premium paid.

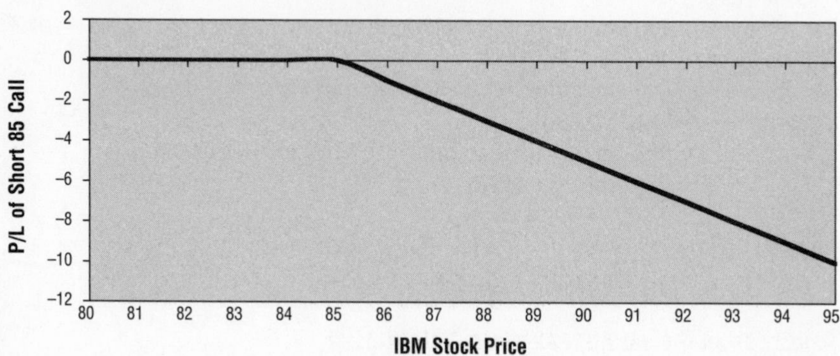

b. You sold an IBM 85 call, $8 premium collected.

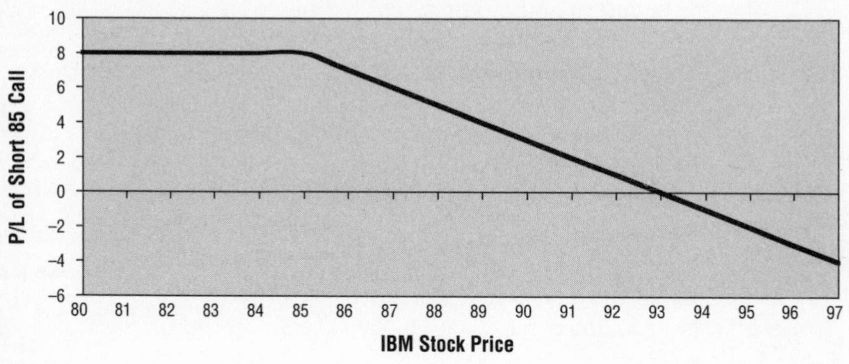

6. a. $5—premium paid;
   b. $43—when you sell a put, your risk equals the difference between (strike – premium) and 0 because the asset price can't fall below 0;
   c. $6—premium paid;
   d. the risk is unlimited—when you sell a call your risk is unlimited.

In other words,

- When you buy an option (pay premium) your risk is *limited* to the premium paid,
- When you sell an option (collect premium) your *risk* is
  - *Unlimited*, if you sold a call;
  - And *limited* by 0, if you sold a put (because a price can go up to infinity but can not go below 0).

FURTHER INFORMATION FOR THE READER

How to Make an Approximate Calculation of an Option's Value

"PRICE OF THE UNDERLYING ASSET": WHAT DOES IT MEAN? For someone who has not dealt with different financial products (stocks, bonds, etc.), it may be interesting to know that although the vast majority of options derive their value from the price of underlying assets, some do not. For example, options on most bonds (fixed income instruments) derive their price from yields rather than from bond prices.

Options on currencies are also peculiar: the price of an underlying (foreign exchange rate) can be expressed in either Currency 1 to Currency 2, or Currency 2 to Currency 1. That can cause confusion because a call on one currency is *at the same time* a put on the other within the currency pair. For example, in EUR/USD, a call on the euro is also a put on the U.S. dollar. This makes sense because if the euro goes up, the U.S. dollar has to go down. Therefore, the terms are interchangeable.

In view of this, the call and put currencies should be clearly defined when entering into option transactions. Although it is perfectly acceptable to ask for a "sterling call against U.S. dollars," it would be better to ask for a "call on sterling, put on USD." This problem does not occur in equities, where there is only one way to express a price: USD per share.

The latter point is very important in general: every product, instrument, exchange, and country has its own generally acceptable terminology. Not that they differ a lot, but since there is a difference, one must always check terms before entering in the first trade.

(Continued)

FURTHER INFORMATION FOR THE READER *(Continued)*

MAKING AN APPROXIMATE CALCULATION OF THE OPTION VALUE The first software capable of calculating options values was introduced in the 1970s. It was based on a formula: the Black-Scholes Model[2] for European options. To make a calculation it's necessary to input a few numbers (described later). In other words, it's not obligatory to know the formula by heart—it is a PC's prerogative. Since its creation, the Black-Scholes formula has enabled thousands of traders, investors, and risk managers—even those without a special mathematical education—to trade options.

As mentioned before, the writings of Aristotle prove options were traded in antiquity. How were the options' prices determined in a pre-formula period? Let's introduce a method used in the past to calculate the approximate value of the premium based on the trader's personal forecast. Suppose a market maker wants to sell a one-month 120 call on a stock currently trading at $100. He begins by determining the probability of the asset price closing within particular price ranges at the end of the one-month period. By summing up the range outcomes weighted by their probability, he calculates the total risk of the option's sale.

TABLE 2.1 Approximate Calculation of the Option Premium (the Underlying Asset Price Is 100)

Price Range	120 Call Result (at the Range's Middle Price)	Probability of the Range within a Month	Call Price
Below 60	0	0.03	0
60–70	0	0.05	0
70–80	0	0.065	0
80–90	0	0.09	0
90–100	0	0.14	0
100–110	0	0.25	0
110–120	0	0.14	0
120–130	5	0.09	5*0.09=0.45
130–140	15	0.065	0.975
140–150	25	0.05	1.25
150 and above	40	0.03	1.2
Total:		100	3.875

FURTHER INFORMATION FOR THE READER *(Continued)*

Thus, the option's approximate value is 3.875 assuming normal distribution of prices.

Interestingly, you can calculate the option price for different periods. You can do this by assigning different probabilities for the price ranges. For instance, if the option is long term, the wide range of outcomes would be considered. The 120 strike will end up closer to the middle of distribution and, thus, become more likely and more expensive.

This price valuation principle was the basis for the Cox-Rubinstein equation (1979) that values American-style options (we'll discuss them later).

Notice an interesting and important detail: options pricing models assume an equal probability of price movement in both directions; that is, they ignore directional forecasts of underlying asset price changes.

CHAPTER 3

Introduction to Option Strategies

The saying that "there are just seven notes, but so many boring melodies!" is directly related to options. Calls, puts, futures, forwards, and their underlying assets can be combined in an unlimited number of strategies. In this chapter, we will consider the most popular combinations.

A *strategy* is a combination of different options and, perhaps, underlying assets in one portfolio, which aims to benefit from a specific market view. For example, buying a call creates a bullish strategy that consists of one option.

A *straddle* is a strategy that consists of a call and a put with *the same strike price* and *the same expiration date.*

For instance, GM's quarterly results announcement may contain unexpected information. One would want to make money on a sharp price move in either direction. Buying a call ensures profit, if the price goes up, while a put will benefit the buyer, if the announcement is negative, and the stock price sharply goes down.

A *strangle* is a strategy similar to a straddle, but a cheaper one because a call and a put have *different strike prices* and *the same expiration date*. One buys a *strangle* when expecting a substantial price move in either direction and not having enough money to buy a *straddle.*

VERTICAL SPREADS

Spreads help to make options positions cheaper or less risky.

A *bull (call) spread* involves buying a call and simultaneously selling a call with a higher (or lower) strike. For instance, let's say one expects the GM share price to exceed $90 but to stay below $100. One could buy a $90 call and sell a $100 call. The premium collected for the sold $100 call partially finances the purchase of the $90 call. However, the short $100 call limits maximum profit.

A *bear (put) spread* involves buying a put and simultaneously selling a put with a lower (or higher) strike. A bear spread is recommended when one expects the GM stock price to:

a. *Fall below $80 but not lower than $70.* One can *buy* an $80 put and *sell* a $70 put. The short put limits a potential gain of this strategy, but it reduces the cost under the most likely scenario. One who buys the more expensive option is considered *to take a long position* in a bear spread.

b. *Increase or not decrease.* In this case one can *sell* an $80 put and buy a $70 put. The $70 put protects the position if the stock drops much farther than expected. By selling an $80 to $70 put spread, one collects a premium (because an $80 put is more expensive than a $70 put) and takes a *short position in a bear spread* (selling a more expensive option).

Example (a) demonstrates a case in which a spread helps to make options positions cheaper, while (b) shows how to make positions less risky.

QUESTIONS

1. Draw the chart of a *long* AIG 80 straddle,
   a. if no premium was paid.
   b. if it cost $12.
2. Draw the chart of a *long* AIG 70–90 strangle,
   a. if no premium was paid.
   b. if it cost $4.
3. Draw the chart of a *short* IBM 100–110 strangle,
   a. if no premium was received.
   b. if it cost $6.
4. Draw the chart of a *short* IBM 105 straddle,
   a. if no premium was received.
   b. you received $4.

5. Draw the chart of a *long* AIG 70–90 call spread,
   a. if no premium was paid.
   b. if it cost $5.
6. Draw the chart of a *short* IBM 110–100 put spread,
   a. if no premium was received.
   b. you received $2.
7. Draw the chart of a *short* Chrysler 50–40 put spread,
   a. if no premium was received.
   b. you received $4.
8. Draw the chart of a *short* Apple 20–25 call spread,
   a. if no premium was received.
   b. you received $1.

ANSWERS

1. a. You bought an AIG 80 straddle, 0 premium paid.

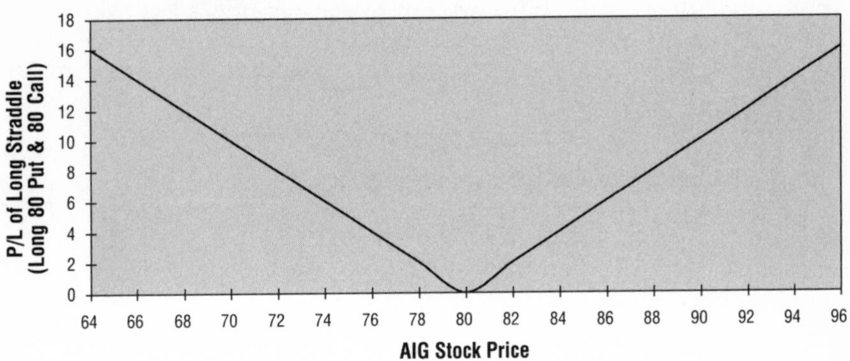

b. You bought an AIG 80 straddle, $12 premium paid.

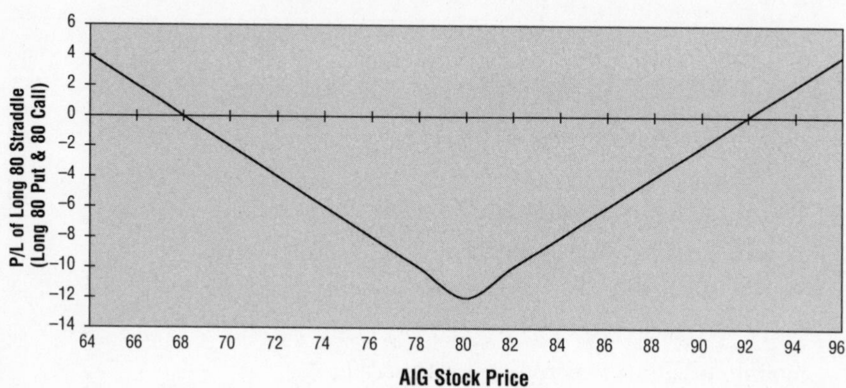

2. a. You bought an AIG 70–90 strangle, 0 premium paid.

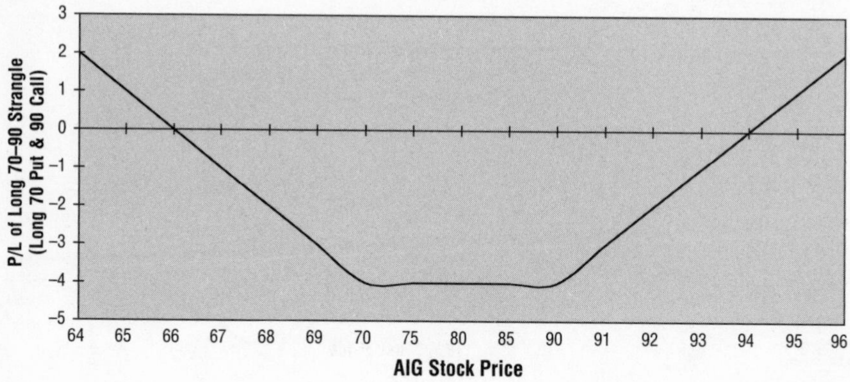

b. You bought an AIG 70–90 strangle, $4 premium paid.

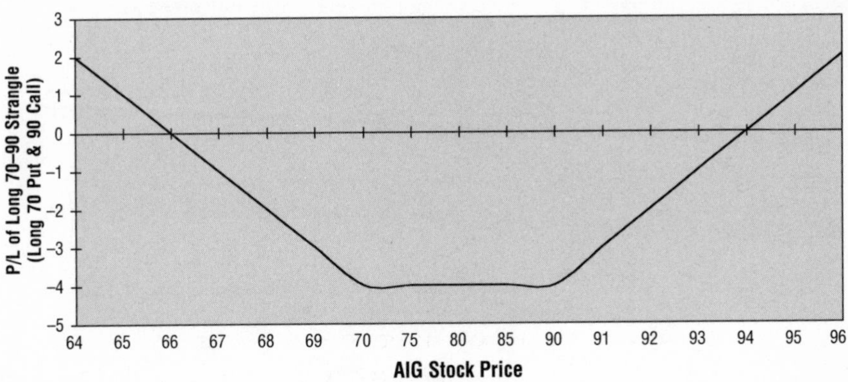

3. a. You sold an IBM 100–110 strangle, no premium received.

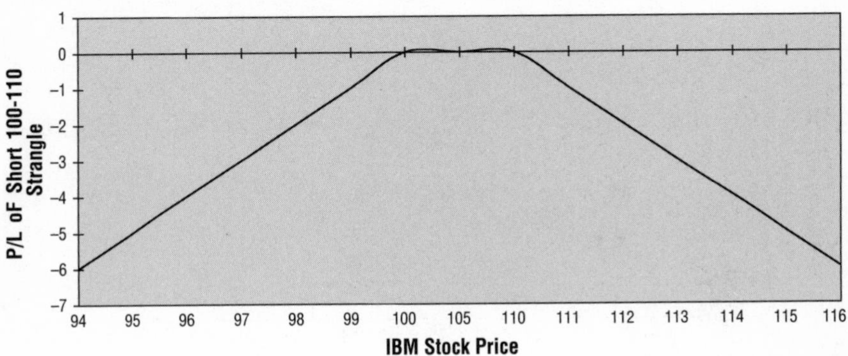

b. You sold an IBM 100–110 strangle, $6 premium received.

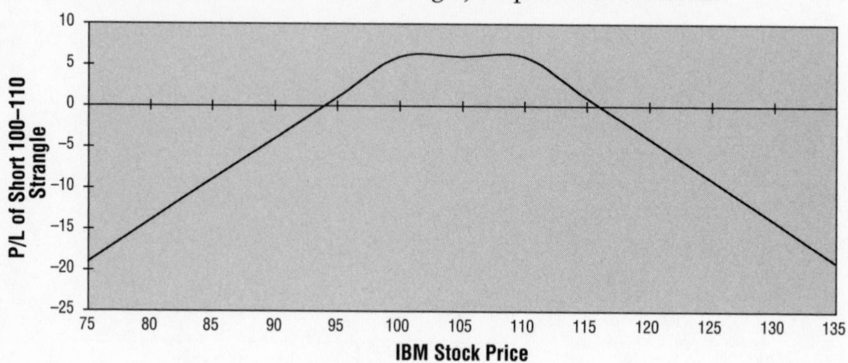

4. a. You sold an IBM 105 straddle, no premium received.

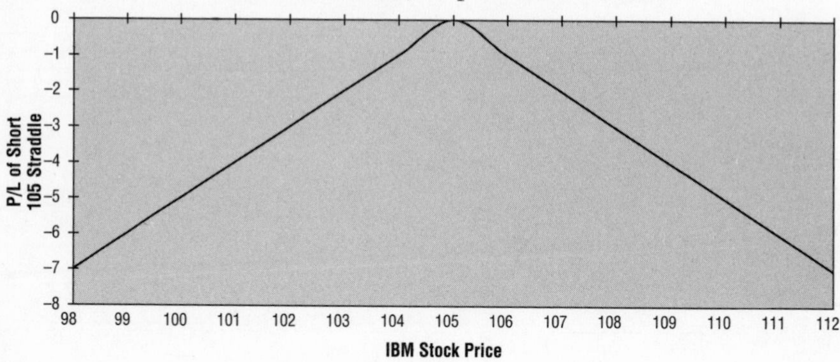

b. You sold the IBM 105 straddle, $4 premium received.

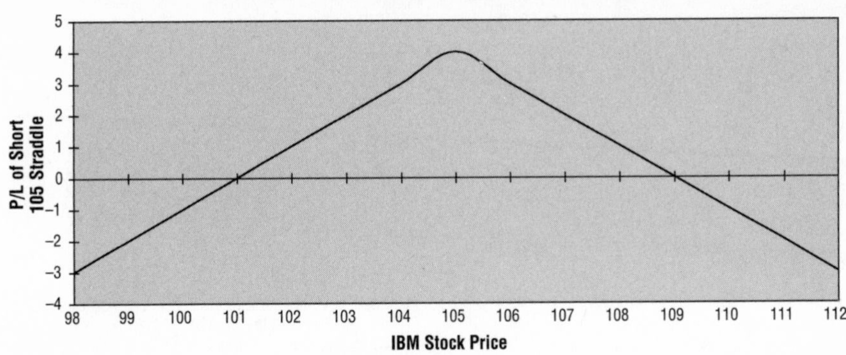

5. a. You bought an AIG 70–90 call spread (bull spread), no premium paid.

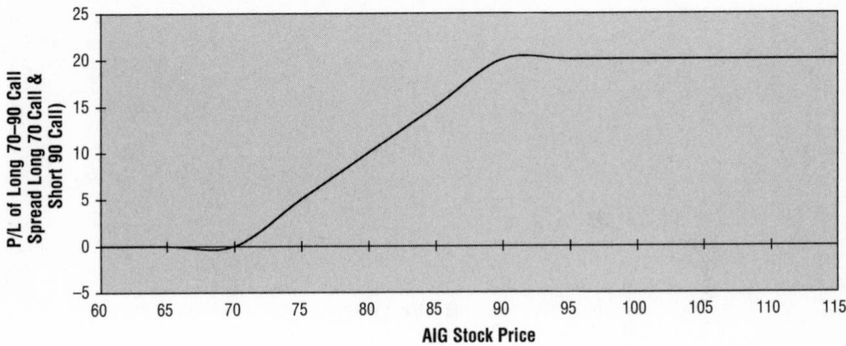

b. You bought an AIG 70–90 call spread (bull spread), $5 premium paid.

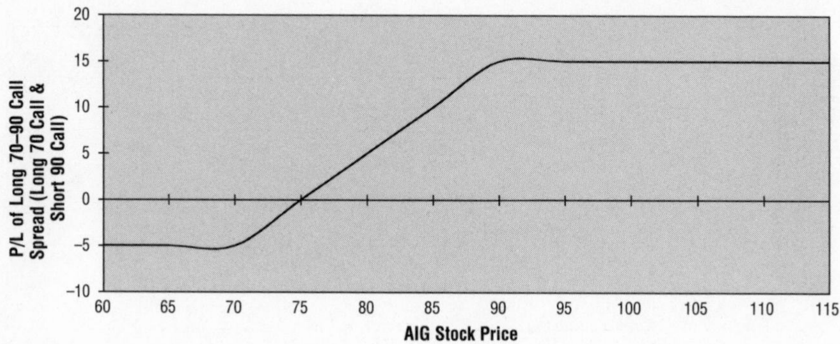

6. a. You sold an IBM 110–100 put spread, no premium received.

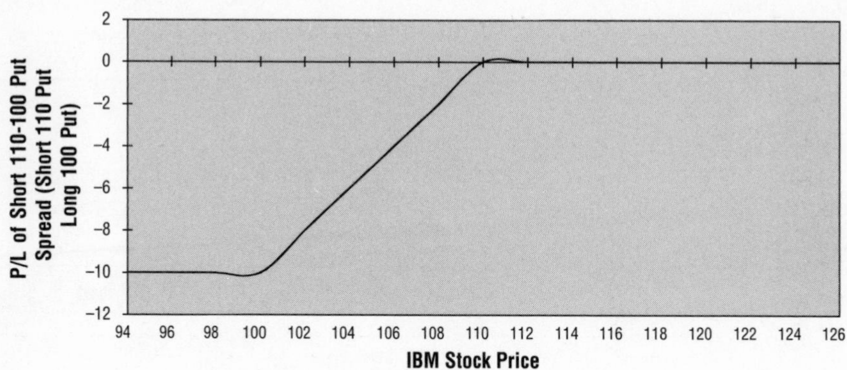

b. You sold an IBM 110–100 put spread for $2.

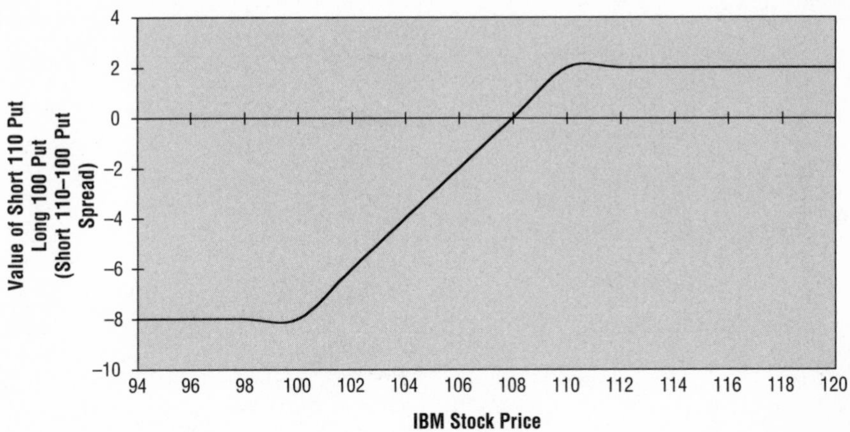

7. a. You bought a Chrysler 50–40 put spread, no premium paid.

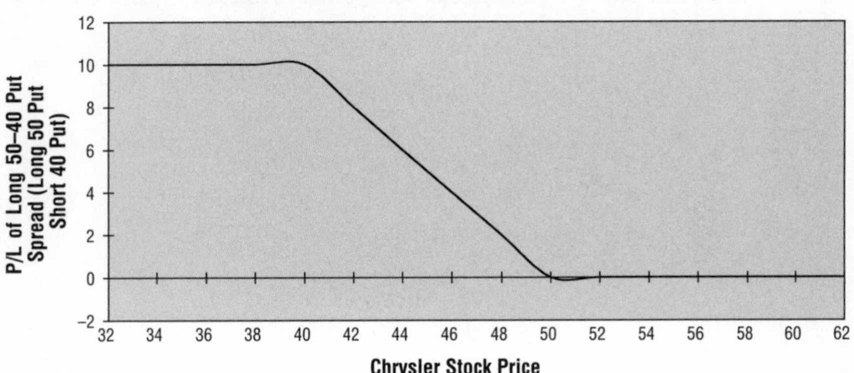

b. You bought a Chrysler 50–40 put spread, $4 premium paid.

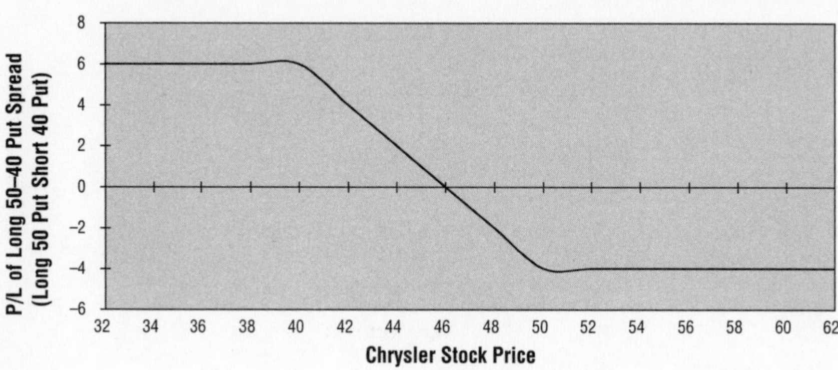

8. a. You sold an Apple 20–25 call spread, no premium received.

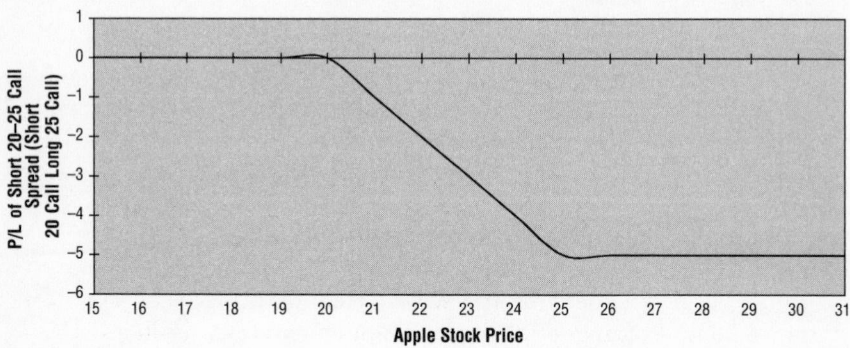

b. You sold an Apple 20–25 call spread, $1 premium paid.

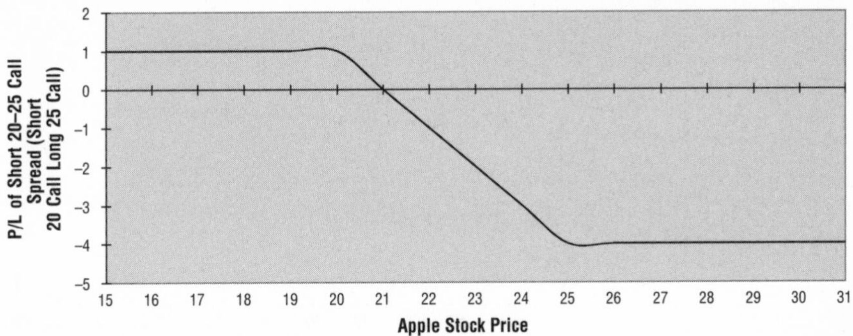

FURTHER INFORMATION FOR THE READER

Contract Face Value

As we mentioned, there are discrepancies in terminology and rules in each option market. One such difference is the wording of the amount traded. On exchanges, traders talk in terms of contract sizes, while in the OTC wording differs on each underlying market. Forex dealers trading OTC options would express the amounts in face values rather than in contracts. For example, one would say, "I buy $1 million against the Japanese yen" rather than "I buy 20 contracts." However, the same trader calling an exchange would say the latter.

The size of underlying in each contract differs as well. For instance, one exchange-traded stock option contract includes 100 stocks. It means that when you buy one IBM option contract for $7, you have to pay $700 ($7 × 100).

In addition to confusion caused by differences in lingo, standard conditions for a contract in an underlying stipulate the amount of money (*margin*) the investor has to deposit with a broker to start trading.

Finally, each market has a different "step"—risk per a minimal unit ("1 tick") move in price: a one-point move in dollar terms. Value of a tick can fluctuate between $10–20 and $300–400, depending on an underlying contract.

CHAPTER 4

Put/Call Parity

The energy conservation principle states that energy does not come from nowhere and does not go anywhere. It transforms from one form into another. The principle applies to finance as well. This chapter is devoted to a formula that balances all market components and does not allow arbitraging.[1]

PUT/CALL PARITY

The put/call parity formula is the basis of the option theory. According to the formula, there should be no opportunity for arbitrage combinations of options and underlying asset (cash/spot/futures/forwards). The formula should contain such parameters as dividends and forward rates. The simplified version looks as follows:

Long (bought) Call + Short (sold) Put = Long (bought) Spot[2]

where both call and put are on the same underlying asset, with the same expiration date and the same strike price; and the stock is bought at the price equal to the strike. For example,

Long IBM 90 Jan Call + Short IBM 90 Jan Put =
Bought IBM Shares (at $90)[3]

Transforming this equation, we can see the risk-return profile of various option/underlying combinations. For example, a purchase of a June 100 call on the IBM stock will earn/lose the same money as the portfolio comprised of a long June IBM 100 put and long IBM shares at $100. (For the OTC-quoted options, one mentions both the day and the month as an expiration date. For the exchange-traded options, one mentions only a month since normally exchange-traded options expire on only one set day during a month.)

A graph of profits/losses (P/L) profile of the portfolio (Long Put and Long Cash/Spot[4]) looks like the one of the long call positions. The similarity is easy to explain: as IBM goes up, you gain $1 for each dollar increase above the strike. However, if it goes down, you lose nothing as the long put protects your downside. For each dollar lost on the stock position, the put gains $1 as well. In other words, one can exactly substitute the long IBM June 100 call for a combination of long IBM June 100 put and long position on IBM stock bought at $100.

To summarize, the P/L of the position composed of long put and long spot:

- equals 0, if the stock trades below $100
- and makes money, if the stock trades above $100.

But the behavior of the long call is the same! Thus, there is no opportunity for arbitrage on these two positions. Therefore, the positions are equal.

AT-THE-MONEY, IN-THE-MONEY, AND OUT-OF-THE-MONEY OPTIONS

In this chapter we will define the following terms: *at-the-money* (ATM) options, *in-the-money* (ITM) options, *out-of-the money* (OTM) options. These terms reflect the relationship between the current price of the underlying asset and the strike of the option.

If the option's strike is equal to the current price we call it "at-the-money." For instance, IBM is at $100—both the IBM June 100 call and the IBM June 100 put are at-the-money because the strike prices of these options and the current stock price are the same. In-the-money (ITM) options should be profitable in case of their immediate exercise. That means that the underlying *asset price is higher* than the *strike of a call* or *lower* than the *strike of a put*.

For example, if the current price of IBM is $110, then the June IBM 100 call is in-the-money.

"Out-of-the-money" (OTM) options in case of their immediate exercise are worth nothing. That means that the price of the underlying asset is *lower* than the *strike of the call* or *higher* than the *strike of the put*. If the current price of ATT is $65, the ATT June 60 put is out-of-the-money. Another example: if the current price of IBM is $90, the

IBM June 100 call is out-of-the-money, while the IBM June 100 put is in-the-money.

INTRINSIC VALUE AND TIME VALUE OF OPTIONS

The price of any option can be divided into two components: intrinsic value and time value.

Intrinsic Value If you exercise an in-the-money option, you will gain the difference between the current price of the asset and the option's strike. This difference is an intrinsic value. For example, you own an IBM 100 call and the current price of the stock is $120. It means that the intrinsic value of the option is $20 ($120 – $100). Only in-the-money options have intrinsic value.

Another example: you own an AIG 80 put. The current AIG stock price is $65. Therefore, the intrinsic value of the option is $15 ($80 – $65).

Time value is the difference between the option's premium and its intrinsic value. It is a portion of price paid for the right to own the option. In other words, if you obtain a right to make money, you pay time value. Time value amortizes with a passage of time and is similar to insurance. The latter gives a right to limit a certain risk during its validity. For example, IBM trades at $100 per share and you buy an IBM 120 call at $5. Its time value is $5 and intrinsic value is 0, because if you exercise the option you will lose money.

Out-of-the-money and at-the-money options are not exercised since they do not have intrinsic value.

To understand how to divide the premium into parts, let's consider another example. The current stock price of IBM is $110, and the price of an IBM June 100 call is $18. This means that the intrinsic value of the option is $110 – $100 = $10 (in-the-money part). The balance of the premium is time value: $8 = $18 – $10.

Take another example: the current price of IBM is $92 and the price of an IBM June 100 put is $15. That means its intrinsic value is $100 – $92 = $8, and the time value is $7 ($15 – $8).

Conclusions

- Only in-the-money options have intrinsic value;
- At-the-money, in-the-money, and out-of-the-money options have time value;
- The price of at-the-money and out-of-the-money options is comprised of only time value.

SOME PROPERTIES OF TIME VALUE

It is interesting that time values of call and put options on the same underlying asset with the same strike price and expiration date are the same, if calculated for the same price level of the underlying asset. We will consider the reasons of this phenomenon after getting acquainted with principles of hedging and financing options.

Returning to the two previous examples, if the current price of IBM is \$110, and the price of an IBM June 100 call is \$18, the intrinsic value is \$110 – \$100 = \$10, while the time value is \$8 = \$18 – \$10. Therefore, the time value of a \$100 put is also \$8 (since the put is an out-of-the-money option, its intrinsic value equals 0).

If the current price of IBM is \$92, and the price of an IBM June 100 put is \$15, the intrinsic value is \$100 – \$92 = \$8, while the time value is \$7 = \$15 – \$8. Therefore, the time value of a \$100 call is also \$7. Since the call is an out-of-the-money option, its intrinsic value equals 0.

QUESTIONS

1. XXX stock is trading at \$100. Which of the options below are out-of-the-money, at-the-money, and in-the-money?
   a. 120 call
   b. 120 put
   c. 90 call
   d. 80 put
   e. 100 put

The next few questions are subject to put/call parity (let's assume the options' premiums are 0). Assuming that the long call is equal to the long put + long spot, which positions can substitute for the following positions?

2. The client bought 100 AIG shares at \$80 and one AIG January 80 put (each equity option is on a lot of 100 shares). To which position is this one equivalent?
3. The client sold 5,000 shares of IBM at \$110. Which combination is equivalent to this position?
4. The client bought 10 ATT February 60 calls. To which position is this one equivalent?
5. The client sold 50 AIG February 70 puts. To which position is this one equivalent?

6. A dealer buys an IBM June 100 call at $20 and an IBM June 100 put at $10. What is intrinsic value of the call?

7. A dealer buys an IBM June 80 call at $30. The stock trades at $100. What is premium of an IBM June 80 put?

ANSWERS

1. a. OTM: by exercising the 120 call, you will buy the shares at $120. If you sell on the market at the current price of $100, you will lose money—therefore, the call is out-of-the-money.
   b. ITM: by exercising the 120 put, you will sell the stock at $120. If you buy it on the market at the current price of $100, you will make money. Therefore, the put is in-the-money.
   c. ITM
   d. OTM
   e. ATM

2. It is equivalent to a purchase of one AIG January 80 call; long cash + long put = long call.

3. The client can buy 50 IBM 110 puts and sell 50 IBM 110 calls – the total premium equals 0; short spot = long put + short call.

4. The client can buy 1,000 shares of ATT at $60 and 10 ATT February 60 puts; long call = long spot + long put.

5. The investor can buy 5,000 shares of AIG at $70 and sell 50 AIG February 70 calls; short put = long spot + short call.

6. $10 = $20 – $10. The time values of calls and puts with the same strike price and expiration date are the same. Since the call's premium is higher than that of the put, the put is out-of-the-money. The premium of the out-of-the-money option consists of time value only. Therefore, the premium of the put consists of time value only. Thus, the time value is equal premium ($10).

7. $10: The call is in-the-money by $20 ($100 – $80). The total premium of the call is $30; it consists of $20 of intrinsic value and $10 of time value. Since the 80 call is in-the-money, the 80 put is out-of-the-money. As is known, time values of calls and puts with the same strike price and expiration date are the same; therefore, the premium of put equals $10.

PART Two

Option Strategies

CHAPTER 5

Basic Option Strategies

In this chapter, as in previous ones, we assume that the options are held till expiration. At this point, most authors start discussing more theoretical concepts. However, we will discuss them later to avoid going deeply into theory before the basic terms are properly understood.

NEW STRATEGIES AND THEIR BREAKEVEN POINTS' CALCULATION

Recap of the Studied Material

Option users have their market forecasts. To execute them, they combine different options and, perhaps, an underlying asset in one portfolio. Such a combination is called a *strategy*. For instance, buying a call is a bullish strategy, composed of one option.

The breakeven point is a price level at which the P/L of the strategy (including investments) at expiration equals 0. In other words, if your investment is $100 and your gain is $100, that is, the investment is paid, your strategy is at the breakeven point.

The breakeven point of a long call is a strike price plus premium paid. Long calls become profitable when the underlying asset's price exceeds this breakeven point. The breakeven point of a long put is a strike price minus premium paid. Short call strategies are profitable if the underlying asset price does not exceed the breakeven point.

Covered Calls (Puts)

Covered calls (puts) are one of the most popular strategies. Such a strategy implies a sale of a call against a long stock position or of a put against a short stock position.

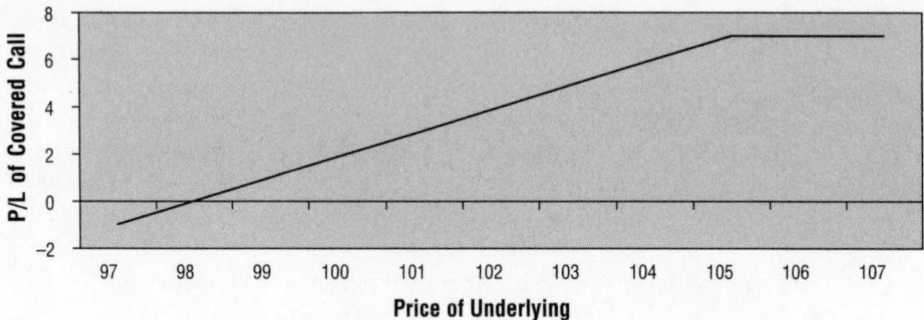

FIGURE 5.1 P/L of the IBM 105 Covered Call

Let's assume that you hold 100 IBM shares bought at $100. You do not expect the stock price to rise substantially. To increase your stock position yield, you can sell a call with the strike higher than the current market price. For example, with IBM trading at $100 per share, you will sell an IBM 105 call at $2 (Figure 5.1).

If on expiration the stock trades below $107 ($105 strike + $2 premium), your strategy is profitable. If the stock trades above $105, on expiration date you will have to sell the stock to the option's buyer at $105.

Not only does the strategy increase your stock position yield, it also reduces the position's risk in case the price falls. Your losses will be reduced by the $2 premium collected. That means that *a covered call strategy's breakeven is on the downside*. You start losing when the stock price falls below $98 (stock price minus premium collected[1]).

A covered put would be sold against a short stock position. *The strategy's breakeven is also on downside.*

Straddle

This strategy is composed of a call and a put with the same strike. An investor would buy a straddle (buy a call and a put) if he expects a price move to surpass the premium *in either* direction.

Suppose that IBM has been trading for three weeks in the 100–120 range. You expect the market to break out of this range. You buy a one-month 110 straddle; that is, you buy an IBM June 110 call and an IBM June 110 put at $5 for each.

To calculate the breakeven points, you should add the sum of the prices you paid for both options to the strike. The breakeven points are $10 away from the strike (110) in either direction. Thus, you will profit if the spot goes beyond the range of $100–$120.

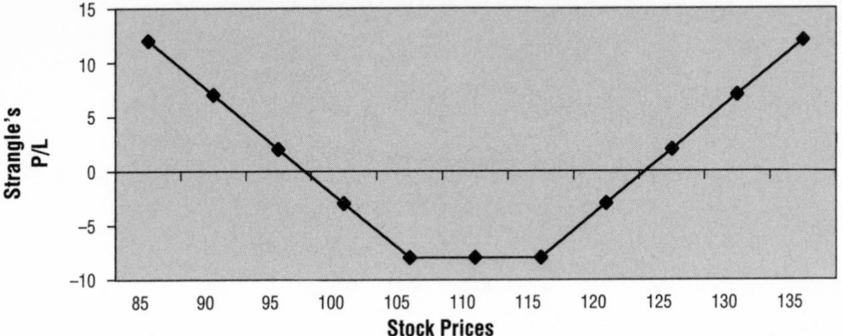

FIGURE 5.2 P/L of the IBM June 105–115 Strangle

Strangle

This strategy is composed of a call and a put with different strikes. An investor would buy a strangle if she expects a price move exceeding the *breakeven points in either direction.* The major difference between straddles and strangles is the amount of premium. If the investor does not have enough money to buy a straddle or wants to buy a larger face value of investment (to have greater leverage), she would purchase a strangle instead of a straddle. For example, if she buys a 105–115 strangle (see Figure 5.2), this means that she buys a 105 put and a 115 call. If the put costs $3 and the call costs $5 ($8 total premium), the strategy becomes profitable below $97 ($105 – $8) and above $123 ($115 + $8).

To calculate a strangle's breakeven points, one adds the sum of premiums to the strike price of the call and subtracts it from the put's strike price.

Bullish/Bearish (Vertical) Spread

A spread is achieved by a purchase of a call (a put) and a simultaneous sale of a call with a higher strike (sale of a put with a lower strike). An example of a call spread is an IBM June 105–115 spread (see Figure 5.3). If you bought an IBM 105 call at $8 and sold an IBM 115 call at $3 ($5 net premium paid), the strategy's breakeven point is $110 ($105 + $5).

Another example: if USD/CHF is at 1.4000 and you believe that the U.S. dollar will appreciate to 1.4100 but not over 1.4200, you can buy a 1.4100 USD call and sell a 1.4200 USD call (in market terms *buy 1.4100–1.4200 call spread*).

To calculate the breakeven point, you should add the premium you

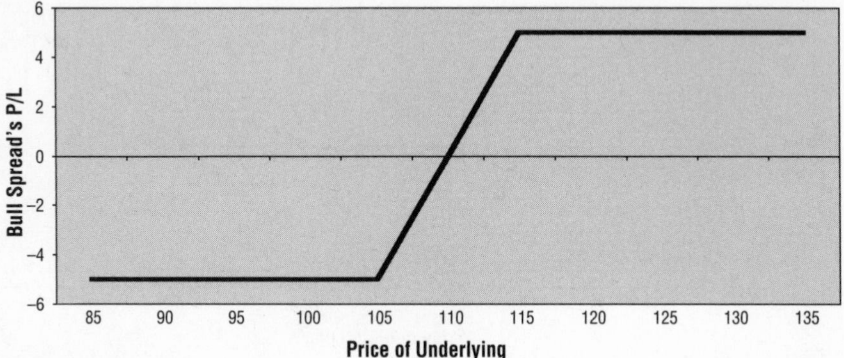

FIGURE 5.3 P/L of the IBM June 105–115 Bull Spread

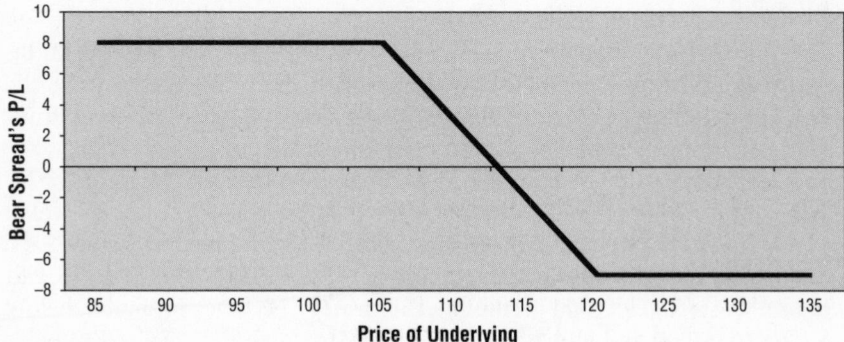

FIGURE 5.4 P/L of the IBM June 120–105 Bear Spread

paid (expressed in the second currency terms) to the strike price. Your position will become profitable over the level (strike + premium).

An example of a put spread is an IBM June 120–105 put spread (see Figure 5.4). If you bought an IBM 120 put at $10 and sold an IBM 105 put at $3 ($7 net premium paid), the strategy's breakeven point is $113 ($120 – $7).

Range Forward (also Known as Risk Reversal, Combo, Cap and Floor, Tunnel, Collar)

A range forward is the purchase of a call (a put) and a sale of a put (a call) with different strikes, but for the same expiration date.

This strategy is often used by corporations and investors for hedging.

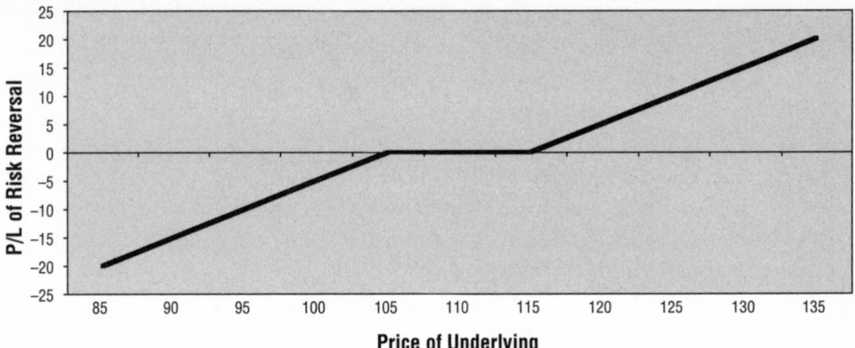

FIGURE 5.5 P/L of the IBM June 105–115 Risk Reversal (You Buy a Call)

Suppose in one month you are to receive EUR 10 million, which you will have to convert into dollars. That means you face a EUR/USD risk and have to secure your position against the euro falling in U.S. dollar terms. To hedge the dollar value, you will buy a EUR put[2] with EUR 10 million face value expiring in one month. You can reduce the price of hedging by selling a EUR call/USD put.

You can also do risk reversals (RR) for speculative purposes. It is a very popular directional strategy. It costs little or nothing because the purchase of options in the direction you prefer is financed by selling options in the direction you do not view as risky. For example, you sell an IBM 105 put and buy an IBM 115 call. As a result you get the P/L chart shown in Figure 5.5.

If you buy a call and sell a put, the breakeven point is the sum of the call's strike and net premium paid. If the premium is received, then there is no breakeven on the call side (see Figure 5.6).

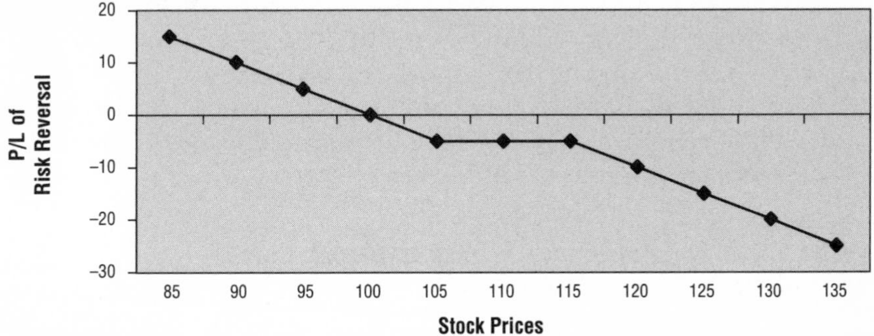

FIGURE 5.6 P/L of the IBM June 105–115 Risk Reversal (You Buy a Put and Pay a $5 Premium)

On the short put side the breakeven point exists, if the net-premium was received. It is calculated by subtracting the amount of premium received from the put's strike price. Effectively the received premium pushes the breakeven lower than the put's strike.

To summarize, if you paid option premium, the underlying should trade above the strike you are long plus premium. The received premium buffers your losses on the downside. *In other words, if you paid option premium, your breakeven is on the call's side. If you received, your breakeven is on the put's side.*

The opposite logic works for the situation when you buy a put and sell a call.

QUESTIONS

1. How many straddles can be composed of the following options?
    1. 50 Dec 75 calls
    2. 50 Jan 75 puts
    3. 60 Dec 75 puts
    4. 50 Dec 75 puts
    5. 60 Jan 75 calls
    6. 60 Mar 75 calls
        a. 1
        b. 2
        c. 3
        d. none

2. Which positions lose when the price increases?
    a. short bearish put spread
    b. short bullish call spread
    c. short straddle
    d. short naked[3] call

3. Which position is profitable when the price increases?
    a. long bearish put spread
    b. long bullish call spread
    c. covered put (short put + short stock)
    d. short naked put

4. **TABLE 5.1** The Premium of USD/CHF Options* Expiring on March 1, Priced at 1.4100 Spot Level

Strike price	Call	Put
1.3800	454	235
1.3850	426	256
1.3900	398	277
1.3950	371	300
1.4000	346	325
1.4050	322	350
1.4100	299	376
1.4150	277	404
1.4200	256	433

*Prices in CHF points per USD (CHF pips[4])

Using the data in Table 5.1, please calculate the breakeven point of:

a. 1.3800 USD call
b. 1.3800 USD put
c. 1.4000 USD call
d. 1.4200 USD put

5. a. 1.3800 straddle
b. 1.4000 straddle
c. 1.4200 straddle

6. a. 1.3800 – 1.4000 strangle (1.3800 put and 1.4000 call)
b. 1.3950 – 1.4200 strangle?

7. a. 1.3850 – 1.4050 call spread,
b. 1.3800 – 1.4200 call spread?

A client buys 10 AIG March 70 calls at $4 and 10 AIG March 70 puts at $3.

8. What are the breakeven points of the strategy?

9. The price increased to $80, and the client exercised the call prematurely. What is the client's position?

(Starting independently from Question 10)

On the expiration date the stock is trading at $60. The put is exercised. The call expires worthless. The client does not close the stock position (which has emerged for him as the direct result of the option's exercise) in the market.

10. To close the position, what does the client have to do with the shares that appeared as a result of the option's exercise?
11. What is the client's gain?
12. What is the maximum potential loss?
13. On expiration, the stock is trading at $68. What is the client's P/L?

A client sells 5 AIG January 80 calls at $6 and buys 5 AIG January 80 puts at $5.

14. What are the breakeven points of the strategy?
15. The price in the market went up to $90, and the client exercised the call prematurely. What is the client's position?

(Starting independently from Question 16)

On the expiration date the stock is trading at $60. The put is exercised. The call expires worthless.

16. What should the client do with the stock position which has appeared for him as a direct result of the option's exercise?
17. What is the strategy's financial result?
18. What is the maximum potential loss (if the stock position, appearing as a result of option's exercise, would not be closed)?
19. On the expiration date, the stock is trading at $74. What is the client's P/L?
20. What is the maximum potential gain?

ANSWERS

1. a, 1 and 4 compose a straddle.
2. b, c, d.
3. b, d.
4. a. 1.4254 (1.3800 + 0.0454)
   b. 1.3565 (1.3800 – 0.0235)
   c. 1.4346 (1.4000 + 0.0346)
   d. 1.3767 (1.4200 – 0.0433)

5. a. 1.3111 – 1.4489 (1.3800 + (0.0454 + 0.0235))
   b. 1.3329 – 1.4671 (1.4000 + (0.0346 + 0.0325))
   c. 1.3511 – 1.4889 (1.4200 + (0.0256 + 0.0433))
6. a. 1.3219 – 1.4581 (1.3800 – (0.0235 + 0.0346)) and (1.4000 + (0.0235 + 0.0346))
   b. 1.3394 – 1.4756 (1.3950 – (0.0300 + 0.0256)) and (1.4200 + (0.0300 + 0.0256))
7. a. 1.3954 (1.3850 + (0.0426 – 0.0322))
   b. 1.3998 (1.3800 + (0.0454 – 0.0256))
8. 63 and 77: (70 ± (4 + 3))
9. Client is still long the put and also long 1,000 AIG shares bought at $70.
10. The client has to buy shares at $60 to deliver them to the put buyer.
11. $3,000: $3 per share = 1,000 × $3 = $3,000
12. Unlimited, because after the options' exercise the client is in effect short the stock at $60. Above this level the client has unlimited risk.
13. The call expires as worthless, and the put is exercised. The client's loss is $5 per share = 1,000 × $5 = $5,000
14. $81: $80 + $6 (premium collected for the call) – $5 (premium paid for the put)
15. $9 loss per share = 500 × $9 = $4,500. The client is long on 5 AIG January 80 puts and short on 500 shares of AIG stock sold at $80.
16. He has to buy the shares in the market to deliver them to the put buyer.
17. 10,500 gain: 500 × $21 = $10,500
18. Unlimited, since the client sold the uncovered call.
19. $3,500 gain: gain of $7 per share = 5 × 100 × $7 = $3,500 gain
20. $81 per share = 5 × 100 × $81 = $40,500

FURTHER INFORMATION FOR THE READER

Currency Options' Price Formats

Since the users of options are domiciled all over the world, they would like to pay premiums and collect results in the currency of their preference.[5] For example, for U.S. companies it is convenient to pay the premium and to book results in dollars. To satisfy these needs, options are quoted in different formats. The two main ones are percentage points of the first currency or the second currency points (also known as "pips").

To get the monetary expression of the option price, one should multiply the prices by an option's face value. The U.S. investors and corporations prefer to get quotes *on the nominal amounts (face values) denominated in U.S. dollars.*

Example

a. You buy $3 million of a 1.4000 USD call (CHF put) at USD 0.2%. In this case, the first currency is USD. You pay $3,000,000 × 0.002 = $6,000.
b. You sell $5 million of a 1.5000 call at 25 CHF points, or pips. You collect $5,000,000 × 0.0025 = CHF 12,500.

To convert the dollar premium into the CHF one, you have to use the spot rate at the moment of the deal.

In our second example, if the spot for the moment of the deal is 1.4100, you collect CHF 12.500:1.4100 = $8,865.

European clients and the "Merc"—the Chicago Mercantile Exchange (CME)—prefer quotes on the *nominal amounts (face values) denominated in a currencies rather than dollars.* The quotes are given in the same format: in percentage points of the first currency or second currency points (pips).

Example

a. A European corporation buys EUR 3 million of a 1.000 put for EUR 0.3%. In this case, the first currency is EUR. The corporation pays EUR 3,000,000 × 0.003 = EUR 9,000.

FURTHER INFORMATION FOR THE READER *(Continued)*

b. A U.S. investor trades on the Chicago Mercantile Exchange (CME) and buys 10 contracts[6] on a 100 USD call against Japanese yen at 40 pips. In this case, the amount is expressed in JPY, but the premium is expressed in USD pips. The investor will pay JPY 12,500,000 × 10 × 0.00004 = USD 2,500.

Now that the premium is converted in the other currency, we should convert the contract face value from dollar pips into the second currency as well. For that, we multiply the face value *by the strike price and not by the spot.*

For example, if you buy $1 million of a 120.00 USD call against JPY at 0.4% USD ($1,000,000 × 0.004 = $4,000) at 110.00 USD/JPY spot and you have to convert it in the other currency, you will follow these steps:

Step 1. Convert the face value

$1,000,000 × 120.00 = JPY 120,000,000

Step 2. Convert the premium amount

$4,000 × 110.00 = JPY 440,000

Step 3. Convert the premium amount in pips

JPY 440,000/ JPY 120,000,000 = 0.00367

Step 4. Convert the strike from USD/JPY format in JPY/USD

1/120.00 = 0.8333

Thus, you can say either: "the 120.00 USD call against JPY with the $1 million face value, worth 0.4% USD of the face value" or "0.8333 JPY put against USD with the JPY 120,000,000 face value, worth 36.7 JPY pips of the face value."

CHAPTER 6

Complex Option Strategies

We have already covered some basic option strategies. Some of them, such as a purchase (sale) of calls or puts and risk reversals are "directional." These strategies become profitable when we guess correctly the market's trend. Other strategies are "range-bound." They are oriented to the price corridor, that is, the market without trends. Strangles and straddles are examples of such strategies. Finally, spreads and "butterflies" (to be covered in this chapter) have characteristics of both types. While studying a strategy, you should be aware of the strategy's purpose, that is, whether it is a directional or range-bound one. This will help you to understand each strategy more completely.

REVIEW OF STRATEGIES

Covered call (put) A sale of an option in the direction of the long underlying position aimed to increase its yield (for instance, a sale of a call against a long stock position *or* a sale of a put against a short stock position).

Straddle A purchase (sale) of a call and a put with the same strike. The price of the straddle is equal to the sum of the call and the put prices.

Strangle A purchase (sale) of an out-of-the-money call and put with different strikes. The price of the strangle is equal to the sum of the call and the put prices.

Risk reversal (also known as **Combo/Collar/Range Forward**) A purchase of a call (put) and a sale of a put (call). To calculate the price, you should subtract the price of the option you sold from the price of the option you purchased.

Bull (bear) spread (also called **Vertical spread**) A purchase of a call (or of a put) and a sale of a call with a higher strike (or of a put with a lower strike). To calculate the price you should subtract the price at which you sold the option from the price at which you bought the option.

NEW STRATEGIES

Calendar (Horizontal) Spreads

A vertical (bull/bear) spread consists of two options with the same *expiration date* but with different *strikes*. On the contrary, a calendar (horizontal) spread consists of two options that have the same *strike* but different *expiration dates*. For example, you can sell a Nokia June 50 call at $3 and buy a Nokia November 50 call at $5. Traders use this strategy to benefit from an upward trend, when they believe that a given asset may appreciate slowly. In the case of a slow trend, the June call will expire out-of-the-money, while the November call may end up in-the-money.

Here are some specific points to keep in mind when calculating the maximum loss in such strategies:

- If you buy an option with a long maturity and sell an option with a short one, your maximum loss will be net of the premium paid and collected, as you always pay for such strategy.
- If you buy an option with a short maturity and sell an option with a long one, your maximum loss is unlimited, since the short-term option may expire out-of-the-money; and as a result you will end up with a short longer-term option position.

Diagonal Spread

A diagonal spread consists of two options with different expiration dates and different strikes. For example, you can sell a Nokia June 50 call at $3 and buy a Nokia November 60 call at $5. This cheap strategy is also a play on a slow upward price trend.

Maximum loss calculations for such strategies are similar to calculations for calendar spreads though they take into account the distance between the strikes;

- If you buy a *long-term* option and sell a short-term one, your maximum loss is net of the premiums paid and collected. According to this strategy, you may be not only a net-payer, but also a net-receiver[1] of a premium, as in this case when you sell a deep-in-the-money short-term option and buy an OTM long-term option.
- If you buy an option with a *short maturity* and sell an option with a long one, your maximum loss is unlimited, since the short-term option can expire out-of-the-money; and as a result you will end up with a short position on the unsettled call option with an unlimited potential loss.

Ratio Spread

In this case you buy a call (or put) and simultaneously sell a call with a higher strike (or put with a lower strike) and with a *greater face value*. This strategy is very popular among investors and speculators since it is cheap. As in the case of range forwards, an investor compensates the long position by the short one. However, in the case of the range forward, the investor ends up with a short position in the direction opposite to the one he favors, while in case of the ratio spread he ends up with a short position in the direction favorable to him (see Figure 6.1).

To calculate the breakeven point of a debit call spread (that is, you are a net-payer of premium), you should add the paid premium to the strike of the option you bought. Your position will become profitable above that threshold level (strike + premium). (A debit strategy is a strategy for which you pay premium, in this case, the long call spread. A credit strategy is a strategy for which you receive premium.)

If you buy a put spread, the same logic is applied: you buy a put with a higher strike and sell a put with a lower strike with a different face value. Your position will become profitable below that threshold level (strike – premium).

Backspread

At the heart of the backspread, there is a combination of ratio and horizontal spreads. *The backspreads are the options with different strikes, face values, and expiration dates.* An example of a backspread is a purchase of $1 million of a March 1.4100 call and a sale of $2 million of a June 1.4200 call.

An investor would sell a short-term ATM put/call and buy a long-term

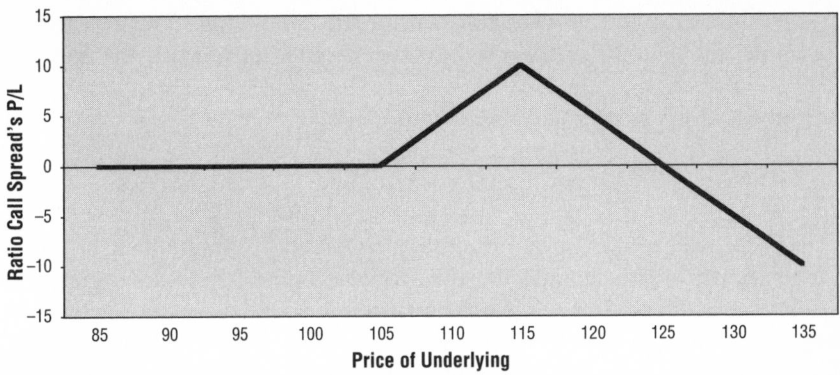

FIGURE 6.1 P/L of the IBM June 105–115 Ratio (1 by 2) Call Spread

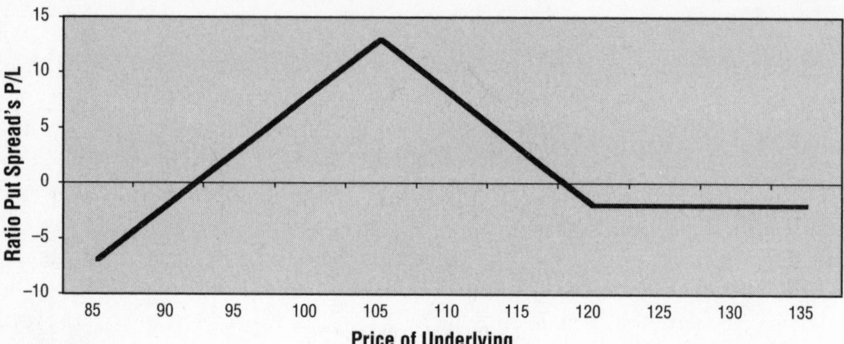

FIGURE 6.2 P/L of the IBM June 120–105 Ratio (1 by 2) Put Spread with a $2 Premium Paid

OTM put/call with a face value two to three times larger. Traders like backspreads since they provide both leverage and time necessary to justify their expectations. (We will discuss them in detail after studying implied volatility and its impact on the pricing of options.)

The calculation of backspreads' breakeven points is similar to that of ratio spreads, but the risk calculation is like that for horizontal spreads. To explain this, consider the worst outcomes of scenarios:

- A backspread, where you *buy* a short-term ATM option, will behave like a ratio spread (imagine you do a call backspread; if the underlying asset's price appreciates sharply, both bought and sold calls will be exercised);
- A backspread, where you *sell* a short-term ATM option, will behave like a diagonal spread: if it is a call backspread and the underlying's price appreciates slowly, the call you sold is exercised, and you will end up short the underlying asset. If at expiration of the option that you bought the underlying's price doesn't reach the strike, the option expires worthless and you retain short in the appreciating underlying asset.

Butterfly

The butterfly is a speculative strategy oriented toward the price fluctuation in the range. If you believe that the spot remains in a range, you will sell a straddle. To secure yourself from the forecast failure, you should buy a strangle around the straddle. For instance, you sell a IBM 100 straddle and buy a IBM 90–110 strangle (see Figure 6.3).

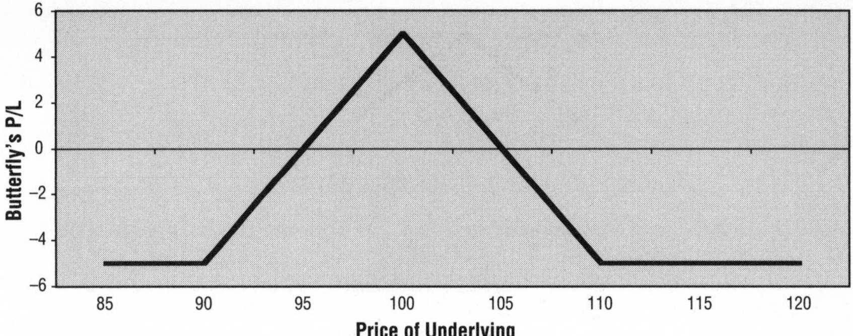

FIGURE 6.3 P/L of Short IBM 100 Straddle and Long IBM 90–110 Strangle ($5 Premium Received)

Albatross, Iron butterfly

This strategy is very similar to the butterfly in respect to the P/L profile, but consists of options with a single direction (only calls or only puts). For example, you buy one IBM 90 call, sell two IBM 100 calls and buy one IBM 110 call. This strategy may be divided into two call spreads: a long 90–100 call spread and a short 100–110 call spread.

RARE STRATEGIES

There are other strategies, but they are used rather seldom. We will just mention names of two of them: *Christmas trees* and *horizontal butterflies*. A Christmas tree looks like a multilayer pie consisting of long and short options. You buy one ATM call, sell two OTM calls, buy three calls far-out-of-the-money and so forth. One would use such a strategy if one believes that the market would trade down (or up) to some level. If the level is broken, the market would go to another level. The strikes are placed accordingly.

A horizontal butterfly is composed, for instance, of one short June call, two long July calls and one short August call. A horizontal butterfly would help if you expect the prices of short-term options to drop considerably more than medium-term ones. *Some speculators like these strategies, but in fact the more complex the strategy, the more difficult it becomes to manage it. In other words, these strategies are often not effective.*

QUESTIONS

A dealer buys 200 IBM shares at $120 and sells two IBM March 130 calls at $5 (each call is on 100 shares).

1. What is the maximum loss of the total position?
2. If the IBM stock price falls to $104, what is the dealer's gain or loss?
3. On the expiration date, the stock price fell to $116. What is the dealer's gain or loss?
4. The stock price increased to $128. What is the dealer's gain or loss?
5. The stock price rose to $140 and the dealer exercised the call by the stock delivery. What is his gain/loss?

To answer the questions[2] concerning the ratio spreads it is necessary to do the following calculations.

Consider an example: you entered a 2:5 spread by buying 2 IBM 100 calls and selling 5 IBM 115 calls.

a. Start by determining the exceeding notional amount of the short position over the notional amount of the long position. To do so, subtract the value of the long position from the value of the short one: 5 – 2 = 3.
b. Calculate your maximum gain. Start by finding a difference between the strikes of long and short positions and multiply the result by the notional value of the long position. In our case, the maximum gain equals $30 = ($115 – $100) × 2 (notional of the long position).

If you paid the premium, you should take it into account in your calculations. For example, if you paid $9 to open the position, your maximum gain is $21.

c. Calculate the stock price change necessary for the net short position (3 calls) calculated in a) to eat up the gain calculated in b) plus/minus the premium you collected or paid. In our example, a $10 increase above $115 will eat up the maximum profit of the strategy (see b)). You will get the result by dividing the maximum gain by the excess amount of the short position above (see a)): $30/3 = $10.
d. Add the received result to the strike of the short call (subtract from the strike of the short put). It is the breakeven point in case you didn't pay or collect premium. If you paid the premium, you would have two breakeven points (the second one around the long strike)!

A dealer bought ABC Jan 80 (90, 1 to 2 call spread) and paid \$0. What is his profit/loss, if the stock trades at:

6. 76
7. 84
8. 96
9. 110

For Questions 10–19, refer to Table 6.1.

10. a. How much do you have to pay for the 1.3900 USD call?
    b. How much can you receive for the 1.3900 USD put?
11. a. How much do you have to pay for the 1.3900 straddle?
    b. How much can you receive for the 1.3900 straddle?
    c. How will you quote the market price to the client?
12. a. How much do you have to pay for the 1.4100–1.3800 strangle?
    b. How much can you receive for it?
    c. How will you quote the market price to the client?
13. a. How much do you have to pay for the 1.3900–1.4150 range forward (a purchase of the 1.4150 call and a sale of the 1.3900 put)?
    b. How much can you receive for it?
    c. How will you quote the market price to the client?

TABLE 6.1 Premium of Options

USD/CHF* Strike	Expiration on March 1 Call bid/offer	1.4100 spot Put bid/offer
1.3800	454/461	229/235
1.3850	426/432	249/256
1.3900	398/405	271/277
1.3950	371/378	294/300
1.4000	346/353	318/325
1.4050	322/328	343/350
1.4100	299/305	369/376
1.4150	277/283	397/404
1.4200	256/263	426/433

*Prices in CHF points per USD (CHF pips).

14. a. How much does the 1.4000 – 1.4150 USD call spread (you buy a 1.4000 call) cost?
    b. What is the breakeven point?
    c. How much can you receive for it (you sell a 1.4000 call)?
    d. What is the market price?
    e. Explain the price.

15. a. How much can you receive for the 1.4000 – 1.4150 USD call spread 1 by 2 (you buy one 1.4000 call and sell two 1.4150 calls)?
    b. What is the breakeven point?
    c. How much does it cost you to sell one 1.4000 call and buy two 1.4150 calls?
    d. What is the two-way price (i.e., bid/offer)?
    e. Explain the price.

16. How many USD will you receive for
    a. 1.4000 $ put?
    b. 1.4200 $ call?

17. What is the breakeven point of
    a. 1.3850 – 1.4050 call spread 1 by 2?
    b. 1.3800 – 1.4200 call spread 1 by 3?
    c. 1.3850 – 1.4050 call spread 1 by 3?
    d. 1.3800 – 1.4200 call spread 1 by 4?

ANSWERS

1. $23,000: $115 per share if the price falls to zero = 200 × $115 = $23,000.
2. $2,200 loss: $104 – ($120 – $5) = loss of $11 per share = 200 × $11 = $2,200 loss.
3. $200 gain: ($120 – $5) – $116 = gain of $1 per share = 200 × $1 = $200 gain.
4. $2,600 gain: gain of $13 per share = 200 × $13 = $2,600 gain.
5. $3,000 gain: gain of $15 per share = 200 × $15 = $3,000 gain.
6. Zero. Both calls expire worthless.
7. Long position gain of $4 per share = 100 × $4 = $400.
8. $400 gain: $4 × 100 = $400.

9. Loss of $1,000 (max profit of $1,000 – $2,000 loss on the second short call).

10. a. 0.0405
    b. 0.0271

11. a. 0.0682 (0.0405 + 0.0277)
    b. 0.0669 (0.0398 + 0.0271)
    c. 0.0669 to 0.0682 in market terms like 669/682 since zeros are not taken into account

12. a. 0.0540 (0.0235 + 0.0305)
    b. 0.0528 (0.0229 + 0.0299)
    c. 0.0528 to 0.0540

13. a. 0.0012 (0.0283 – 0.0271)
    b. 0 (0.0277 – 0.0277)
    c. 0 to 0.0012

14. a. 0.0076 (0.0353 – 0.0277)
    b. 1.4076
    c. 0.0063 (0.0346 – 0.0283)
    d. 0.0063 –.0076
    e. You are ready to pay 63 for the spread and sell it at 76.

15. a. 0.0201 (2 × 0.0277 – 0.0353)
    b. 1.4501 (1.4150 + ((1.4150 – 1.4100) + (2 × 0.0277 – 0.0353)))
    c. 0.0220 (2 × 0.0283 – 0.0346)
    d. 201/220
    e. 201 bid for 1.4150

16. a. 2.255% (0.0318/1.4100)
    b. 1.815% (0.0256/1.4100)

    Pay special attention to the following:

    a. The breakeven point of a ratio call spread is calculated as follows: strike of sold option + [maximum gain: difference between the face values of sold and bought options]

    The breakeven point of a ratio put spread is calculated as strike of sold option – [maximum gain: difference between the face values of sold and bought options], where the maximum gain equals the face value of the bought option multiplied by the distance between the strikes of bought and sold options.

b. In case the premium of the bought options differs from the premium of the sold options, the premium difference is divided by the difference between face values of sold and bought options. In the case of a credit, the received result is added up with the breakeven point calculated in point a). If it were a debit, you would subtract the result from the breakeven point.

17. a. 1.4462 (1.4050 + (1.4050 – 1.3850) + (2 × 0.0322 – 0.0432));
    b. 1.4535 {1.4200 + [(1.4200 – 1.3800) + (3 × 0.0256 – 0.0461)]/(3 – 1)}.
    c. 1.4417 {1.4050 + [(1.4050 – 1.3850) + (3 × 0.0322 – 0.0432)]/(3 – 1)};
    d. 1.4521 {1.4200 + [(1.4200 – 1.3800) + (4 × 0.0256 – 0.0461)]/(4 – 1)}.

FURTHER INFORMATION FOR THE READER

Terminology Used in Trading Spreads and Risk Reversals

This subject causes certain difficulties for those who trade on exchanges. We would like to point to *the larger premium concept*. It is *key* for understanding quotes brokers give investors trading in spreads and range forwards.

The market is quoted in terms of the more expensive option in respect to absolute premiums.

Example

Suppose that USD/CHF trades at 1.4100.

The price of $1 million of a 1.4100 USD call is 298/299.

The price of $1 million of a 1.4200 USD call is 259/260.

It's obvious that the 1.4100 call's premium is higher. But if you buy $2 million of a 1.4200 call and sell $1 million of a 1.4100 call, the premium of the 1.4200 call is higher.

Which of the "higher premiums" should be taken into account?

You will receive the quotes in terms of the more expensive option in respect to the total premium—that is, when the broker says the

FURTHER INFORMATION FOR THE READER *(Continued)*

price is 10 to 20, he means 10 to buy a more expensive option, 20 to sell it. In this case, the quote is based on the call with the 1.4200 strike, because 2 × 260 is more than 1 × 299. In other words, without a preliminary valuation of each option composing the strategy or by asking the broker, you won't know what you are being quoted!

The confusion worsens, if you change the face value (buy 1:1, rather than 1:2). The broker will quote in terms of another option, as its premium is greater!

Example

If you ask for a price on:

a. 1.4100 – 1.4200 USD call spread $1 million to $1 million, the broker's quotation for you will be approximately 38 to 40:
   - that is, you will sell the 1.4100 call to the broker at 298 and buy the 1.4200 call at 260 (receiving 38) or
   - You will buy the 1.4100 call from the broker at 299 and sell the 1.4200 call at 259 (paying 40).

   In this case all quotes are given in terms of the 1.4100 call.

b. *1.4100 – 1.4200 USD call spread $1 million to $2 million*, your quote will be 219 to 222:
   - In other words, you will sell $2 million of the 1.4200 call to the broker at 2 × 259 and buy $1 million of the 1.4100 call at 299 (receiving 219), or
   - You will buy $2 million of the 1.4200 call from the broker at 2 × 260 and sell $1 million of the 1.4100 call at 298 (paying 222).

   In this case all quotations are in terms of the 1.4200 call.

This is an extra demonstration of how important it is to know the terminology of a specific market!

In the beginning you should be careful and ask for an explanation of the terms of which option the broker gives the quotes.

In the OTC market a broker would identify an option, in terms of which the quotes are given, in the following way: "219 bid for the 1.4200 call," which makes the life of those who trade in the OTC market a whole lot easier.

CHAPTER 7

Practical Steps in Creating and Designing Strategies

The objective of this exercise is to demonstrate practical application of the principles covered in the previous chapters.

STRATEGY DESIGN

Take the following situation. USD/CHF appreciated from 1.3900 to 1.4400 in three days. You think the market has reached the top and consider four likely scenarios for the future:

1. The spot stays at the current level for a while;
2. The spot retraces and stabilizes at a lower level;
3. The spot retraces and, if the support level[1] at 1.4200 is penetrated, it may continue to fall further;
4. The spot is about to fall sharply.

Which option strategies will help you take advantage of these scenarios?

Since you expect the spot to fluctuate around the current level, you should sell a strangle. The stronger your conviction, the more expensive options you can sell for the same expiration date. Options will have a higher premium, if the strikes are closer to the current spot level.[2]

1. You can sell a call or a call spread. You can also buy a 1:2 ratio put spread 1.4400–1.4300 (buy $1 million of the 1.4400 USD put and sell $2 million of the 1.4300 USD put). The total paid premium approximately equals 0. If your forecast is right, the spot will not go down by much, and at expiration you will exercise the 1.4400 put while the 1.4300 put will expire worthless.
2. You can sell ATM calls, or a call spread, or buy a 1:1 put spread. Since you do not exclude the possibility of the downside breakout, you

should avoid taking excessive risk and selling a ratio spread position. To save money, you can sell an option with a higher (than in the previous example) strike or buy an option with a lower strike.

3. If you believe the spot will go down sharply, you should buy a USD put or sell the USD spot position. In general, the more you are sure of your forecast, the higher delta options you should buy. In fact, you should buy/sell spot as it is always easier to manage than options.

QUESTIONS

When answering the following questions, you should imagine how traders think in practice rather than in theory. Traders search for strategies to act. That's why the phrase "a trader doesn't expect" a movement over a certain level, means that he disregards "what if I am wrong." If he takes into account all possible "ifs," the number of outcomes becomes unlimited. In such situations, any action becomes impossible. Try to keep in mind only the prevalent view when deciding between spreads and nonhedged strategies.

Please offer a strategy to your client in the following situations:

1. Suppose that the spot has been fluctuating in a narrow range for three weeks. You think that it is about to move beyond the range but are not sure in which direction,
   a. your client has a substantial amount to invest;
   b. your client's capital is limited (two alternative strategies should apply);
   c. your client is well capitalized and wants a position with high leverage.
2. The spot has reached a significant support level. You are not sure whether it will move further down, but if that happens,
   a. it will not go much lower;
   b. it may really collapse, and your client wants to limit his risk;
   c. it will bounce back up.
3. The spot price has been at this level too long. You think it will significantly appreciate from here and
   a. your client is well capitalized;
   b. your client doesn't want to pay the premium for an option strategy;

c. your client wants a high leverage position and is well capitalized;
d. your client is not sure about the extent of the spot appreciation.

ANSWERS

1. a. The client should buy a straddle to make money when the spot moves in either direction.
   b. The client should buy a strangle or a "butterfly." The strangle will become profitable only with a substantial spot move, while the butterfly will make money, if the spot reaches either the top or bottom of the range (beyond the strikes you are short).
   c. The client should buy a strangle; it is cheaper than a straddle and increases the client's leverage (a larger notional amount of the contract).

2. a. The client should sell a put or buy a longer-term call (you don't have a view for how long the spot will stay on the bottom of the range).
   b. The client should buy a put spread (to pay less premium) or buy a low-delta put. He can also buy low-delta calls in case the spot bounces back. That is at extremes of a trading range one expects a sharp move in either direction and should buy a strangle.
   c. The same as in point b), but the client should sell a call to finance his purchase.

3. a. The client should buy an ATM call.
   b. The client should buy an ATM call and sell:

      an ATM put
      OTM puts with larger face value;

   He should not sell OTM calls since he expects the spot to appreciate sharply.

   c. The client should buy a large notional amount of OTM calls.
   d. The client should buy a short-term ATM call to benefit from appreciation; or

      The client can sell short-term puts; or
      The client should buy a call spread, since she is not sure that the spot will go to a higher level. Lack of fluctuations will prevent her from making a lot on the purchased call.

FURTHER INFORMATION FOR THE READER

Styles of Options

There are three major styles of options: American, European, and Asian.[3]

The buyer may exercise an *American option* at any time before the contract expiration, at her choice.

A buyer of a *European option* has a right to exercise it only at a stipulated time (the market standard for each market) on the expiration date.

The ability to take profit by exercising an American-style option appeals to many. However, let's point out *something very important*. Although a buyer of a European option cannot exercise it before the expiration date, nothing prevents him from changing his position (he can buy some more options or sell his position at any time). In other words, *both American and European options may be removed from the position before the expiration date.*

In practice, American options are rarely exercised before the expiration date due to the cost of position financing (explained later in the book). There is another reason why the market makers don't like them: *the forward hedge of American options may significantly exceed the option face amount*; that is, it may exceed 100%. You can buy an option with $1 million face value, and you will have to hedge it by $1.3 million of underlying asset. That makes hedging more difficult.

CHAPTER 8

Delta

To develop a better feeling for options, one has to touch on the so-called Greeks (the options' risk parameters as designated by the letters of the Greek alphabet). Most traders do not have a mathematical education so that if Greeks were very difficult, traders would not be able to use them! We recommend that you visualize their practical value or just learn them by heart. They will surely click in later!

BASIC CHARACTERISTICS OF DELTA

The most important risk parameter of options is delta. It is the sensitivity of an option's premium to changes of the underlying asset price.[1] Delta shows the extent the option's premium changes, if the underlying asset price moves by one point. For instance, the price of a 20-delta call will increase 0.2 points with a 1-point increase of the underlying asset price.

Example

If the EUR/USD went up from 1.000 to 1.200 (by 2 cents), and the price of a EUR/USD call option changed from \$.03 to \$.04, what's the delta of the call?

The option's price increased by 1 cent while the underlying asset has changed by 2 cents. Therefore, delta of this option is 0.5 (1 cent of premium change divided by the underlying asset change of 2 cents). It means that every point of movement in the underlying asset price will cause the option price to change by 50%.

In layman's terms, delta is the probability that the given option will be in-the-money on expiration date. Although this definition is not quite correct, it helps to visualize the term's meaning. Options with a very low risk to be exercised (out-of-the-money options) have a delta close to 0%. The delta of options likely to be exercised (in-the-money options) is close to 100%.

UTILIZING DELTA IN HEDGING STRATEGIES

Delta is also called the hedge ratio because it determines the size of the options' hedge.[2] One hedges an option to secure its value against a move in an unfavorable direction of the underlying asset. Hedging equalizes results profit (for long options) (loss for short options) money on an equal movement in either direction. For instance, a 20-delta option will need a hedge equal to 20% of the face value. To hedge $10 million of a long 20-delta call, you will have to sell $2 million spot. To calculate the amount of hedge, one should multiply the option's face value by delta.

$$\text{Face Value} \times \text{Hedge Ratio} = \text{Hedge Amount}$$

The hedge direction is opposite to the option's strategy. In other words, you hedge a "bullish" strategy with a "bearish" strategy and a "bearish" one with a "bullish" one.

Call to hedge a long call (bullish strategy), you should sell the underlying asset (bearish strategy). If the spot goes up you will make money on the option, if it goes down, you earn on the short spot/cash position. For instance, to hedge $1 million of a long 1.3800 call, you should sell $0.58 million (see Table 8.1). However, if you sold a bullish strategy (sold a call) you would hedge your position by buying spot.

Put to hedge a long put (bearish strategy) you should buy the underlying asset (bullish strategy). If the spot goes up, you make money on the spot position, if it goes down you earn on the option. For instance, to hedge $1 million of a long 1.3800 put you should buy $0.42 million in the spot market.

To hedge strategies, one should start by calculating a hedge for each option, comprising a strategy, and then add hedges together.

Straddle The strategy consists of a call and a put with the same strike. You should separately calculate the amount of the spot to hedge the call and to hedge the put. Then, you subtract the smaller amount from the greater amount. For instance, if you bought the 1.4200 straddle (see Table 8.1), initiate the following steps:

a. Calculate how much you should sell to hedge the 1.4200 call (0.41 of the face value);
b. Calculate how much you should buy to hedge the 1.4200 put (0.59 of the face value);
c. Subtract the smaller amount from the larger one: 0.18 (0.59 – 0.41);
d. Determine the direction of the hedge (to sell or to buy); since the put has a higher delta, you have to make a net purchase.

Therefore, to hedge the 1.4200 straddle you should buy 18% of the put's face value (not of the entire face value of the straddle).

Strangle The strategy is comprised of an out-of-the money (OTM) call and an OTM put with different strikes. To calculate a strangle's delta, you should initiate the same steps as for a straddle.

Range Forward[3] The strategy includes a *purchase*/sale of a call (or put) and a *sale*/purchase of a put (or call). To get the total delta you should add up deltas of options you have purchased and sold. For instance, to calculate the hedge of the 1.3800–1.4200 range forward (see Table 8.1), where you buy a 1.4200 call and sell a 1.3800 put, you should take the following steps:

a. Calculate how much to sell to hedge the long 1.4200 call (0.41);
b. Calculate how much to sell to hedge the short 1.3800 put (0.42);

TABLE 8.1 Delta* of Options

Currency USD/CHF	Current Spot 1.4100	
Strike	Call	Put
1.3800	58%	–42%
1.3850	56%	–44%
1.3900	54%	–46%
1.3950	51%	–49%
1.4000	49%	–51%
1.4050	47%	–53%
1.4100	45%	–55%
1.4150	43%	–57%
1.4200	41%	–59%

*Delta is calculated using FOCUS software.

c. Add up both hedges: 0.83 (0.41 + 0.42)
d. Determine the hedge's direction (to sell or to buy); since you have to sell on both legs you will sell the overall hedge.

Therefore, to hedge the 1.3800–1.4200 range forward, you should sell 83% of the face value of one of the legs (not of the entire range forward).

Vertical and **Horizontal Spreads (Bull/Bear** and **Calendar)** Vertical spreads assume a purchase/sale of a call (or put) and a sale/purchase of a call with a higher strike (or of a put with a lower strike), for example, consider the 1.4100–1.4200 call spread. In case of the vertical (bull/bear) spread both options have the same expiration date. In case of the horizontal (calendar) spread, both options have different maturities.

To calculate the delta, you subtract the delta of the sold option from the delta of the purchased one. For instance, if you buy a 1.4100–1.4200 call spread (see Table 8.1), you should take the following steps:

a. Calculate how much you should sell to hedge the long 1.4100 call (0.45);
b. Calculate how much you should buy to hedge the short 1.4200 call (0.41);
c. Subtract the smaller amount from the larger one: 0.04 (0.45 – 0.41);
d. Determine the hedge's direction (to sell or to buy); since the delta of the call you bought is higher, you should sell the hedge.

Therefore, to hedge the 1.4100–1.4200 call spread you will have to sell 4% of the face value of one option (not of the sum of the face values).

Ratio Spreads, Backspreads Similar to vertical and horizontal spreads, *ratio* spreads normally consist of options with *different* strikes and face values but with the *same* maturity, while the *backspreads* consist of options with *different* strikes, face values, and *different* maturities.

An example of a ratio spread is a purchase of $1 million of the 1.4100 call and a sale of $2 million of the 1.4200 call. An example of a backspread is a purchase of $1 million of the March 1.4100 call and a sale of $2 million of the June 1.4200 call.

To calculate delta you should make almost the same steps as in the previous case:

a. Calculate how much you should sell to hedge \$1 million of the long 1.4100 call (\$0.45 million);
b. Calculate how much you should buy to hedge \$2 million of the short 1.4200 call (\$0.82 million = 2 × \$0.41 million);
c. Subtract the smaller amount from the larger one: \$0.37 (\$0.82 – \$0.45);
d. Determine the hedge's direction (to sell or to buy); since the hedge of the call you bought is lower than that of the two calls you sold, to hedge this strategy you should buy.

Therefore, to hedge the 1.4100–1.4200 1:2 million ratio spread you have to buy \$0.37 million.

The hedges calculated above are used for so-called delta-neutral hedging. Due to them, at the current underlying asset price your P/L is *indifferent* to insignificant *spot fluctuations* in either direction. If substantial fluctuation occurs, you will have to recalculate the hedge amount to get the delta-neutral position. We will discuss this subject in detail after studying *gamma*.

QUESTIONS

Based on Table 8.1:

1. a. What is delta of a 1.3900 call? If you buy \$10 million of this option, how will you hedge it?
   b. What is delta of a 1.3900 put? If you buy \$10 million of this option, how will you hedge it?
   c. What is the net delta of a 1.3900 straddle? If you buy *\$10 million face value* (\$10 million of call options and \$10 million of put options) of this strategy, what do you have to do to hedge it?
2. You bought \$10 million of a 1.3800–1.4200 strangle (\$10 million of call options and \$10 million of put options). What is its delta? How will you hedge it?
3. You bought \$10 million of a 1.4000 straddle. What is its delta? What do you have to do to hedge it?

4. What is delta of a 1.3800–1.4200 risk reversal? If you buy $10 million of a 1.3800 put and sell $10 million of a 1.4200 call, how will you hedge the strategy?
5. You sold $10 million of a 1.3850–1.4150 strangle. What will you do to hedge this strategy?
6. What is delta of a 1.3950–1.4200 call ratio spread with the face values of $10 by 20 (10:20) million? What do you have to do to hedge this strategy?
7. What is delta of a 1.3850–1.4150 risk reversal? If you buy $10 million of a 1.3850 put and sell a call, what is the hedge?
8. What is delta of a 1.3800–1.4150 call ratio spread $10:20 million? What do you have to do to hedge, if you buy the 1.3800 call?
9. The current spot is 1.4100, how much will a 1.4100 call and a 1.3800 put cost at 1.4200?
   a. Current premium of the 1.4100 USD call (45 delta) is 300 CHF pips;
   b. Current premium of the 1.3800 USD put (42 delta) is 150 CHF pips.
10. Based on Table 8.1, what will be delta of a 1.4000 USD call, if the spot moves from 1.4100
    a. to 1.3900?
    b. to 1.4200?
11. How much will the 1.4000 USD call cost under scenarios described in Question 10, if it costs 250 CHF pips at 1.4100? Please make an assumption for the delta to be used in calculations.

ANSWERS

1. a. 54, sell $5.4 million ($10 million × 0.54);
   b. 46, buy $4.6 million ($10 million × 0.46);
   c. 8, sell $0.8 million (sell $5.4 million – buy $4.6 million)

      Step 1. Calculate the call's delta: sell $5.4 million;
      Step 2. Calculate the put's delta: buy $4.6 million;
      Step 3. Calculate the total delta: $0.8 million ($5.4 million – $4.6 million);

Step 4. Determine the direction of the hedge; since the call has a larger delta, you will sell on the hedge $0.8 million.

2. 1% delta (0.42 – 0.41); buy $100,000 (buy $4.2 million; sell $4.1 million)

3. 2% (0.51 – 0.49); buy $200,000 (buy $5.1 million; sell $4.9 million)

4. 83%; buy $8.3 million (buy $4.2 million to hedge the 1.3800 put, buy $4.1 million to hedge the 1.4200 call)

5. 1%; sell $100,000 (sell $4.4 million to hedge the short 1.3850 put, buy $4.3 million to hedge the short 1.4150 call)

6. 31%; sell $3.1 million (buy 1 × $5.1 million; sell 2 × $4.1 million)

7. 87%; buy $8.7 million (buy $4.4 million to hedge the 1.3850 put, buy $4.3 million to hedge the 1.4150 call)

8. 28%; buy $2.8 million (sell 1 × $5.8 million to hedge the long 1.3800 call; buy 2 × $4.3 million to hedge short 1.4150 call)

9. To answer this question you must recall the delta's definition: delta shows to what extent the option's premium will change, if the underlying asset's price moves by 1 point. To answer this question we have to calculate the premium change in respect to the price alteration not by 1 point, but by 100 points. Thus, our answer will not be exact.

   a. 345 (300 + 0.45 × (1.4200 – 1.4100));
   b. 108 (150 – 0.42 × (1.4200 – 1.4100));

10. a. 41%; with the price at 1.3900, the 1.4000 call will be 100 points out-of-the-money (OTM). To answer this question, find the option that is currently 100 points OTM at 1.4100 and calculate its delta—that is, a 1.4200 call whose delta is currently equal to 41.

    b. 54%; 1.4200, 1.4000 call will be 200 points in-the-money (ITM). To answer this question calculate delta of an option, which is currently 200 points ITM at 1.4100; that is, a 1.3900 call whose delta equals 54.

11. This question summarizes Questions 9 and 10. The delta of the 1.4000 call will be lower at 1.3900, than at 1.4100. Therefore, the option will lose its value at a different rate because the delta is lower. It means that in calculating the results you should use different deltas at different spot levels. The better you estimate them, the more exact your result will be. As a simple approximation, one can take the average of the initial and final deltas.

To determine the option's deltas at 1.3900 and 1.4200 levels, you should follow the procedure described in Question 10.

a. 160 pips; (0.0250 + ((1.3900 – 1.4100) × (0.49 + 0.41)/2) × 100: because the spot is moving down, the option is losing its value;
b. 301.5 pips; (0.0250 + ((1.4200 –1.4100) × ((0.54 + 0.49)/2) × 100: because the spot is moving up, the option value is increasing.

FURTHER INFORMATION FOR THE READER

Some Other Derivatives: Forwards, Futures, and Swaps

Derivatives tend to scare first-time readers. To make the topic less threatening, we advise focusing on practical aspects of their utilization rather than on pricing techniques. Imagine you are tasting an exotic fruit for the first time. It was tasted by millions of people before you. You don't think about its chemical composition, growing process, and how much a supplier has earned on it. You evaluate its taste and price. The same is true for derivatives: users don't give much thought about the complexity of their terminology. Rather, they utilize them in trading and hedging, and price them with readily available standard software.

FUTURES The first exchange for derivatives (futures) was founded in the middle of the nineteenth century. At that time, farmers started using it to protect their profits against price fluctuations in the agricultural production markets.

Futures contracts can be cash-settled or physically settled instruments (nondeliverable and deliverable, respectively). The difference is in the closing procedure of a standard exchange contract. In the first case, the buyer collects (or pays) the difference between the price set in the contract on the trade date and the price at which the exchange closed on the contract expiration date.

In the second case the buyer can chose either cash payment or a physical commodity delivery (underlying product). If he prefers to receive the product, the exchange gives him warehouse certificates for the quantity stipulated in the contract.

FURTHER INFORMATION FOR THE READER *(Continued)*

Examples

1. A month ago, you made a contract for the sale of gold on June 15 at $295 per ounce. Today is June 15 and the exchange fixed the closing price at $290 per troy ounce. Your contract is cash-settled, and the exchange will pay $5 (295 – 290) into your account.
2. A month ago, you made a contract for the purchase of oil on January 15 at $42 per barrel. Unlike the gold, the oil contracts are subject to cash and/or physical settlement. Today is January 15, and the exchange fixed the closing price at $44 per barrel. Your contract may be cash-settled and the exchange will pay $2 (44 – 42) into your account. Or you can require warehouse certificates. After your payment of $42 (purchase price) is made, you can take oil from the exchange warehouses.

Futures on most financial products (currencies, equity indices) are cash-settled. Futures on commodities can be both cash settled and physically settled. Futures are often used for hedging: protecting from market fluctuations. For instance, an exporter selling abroad and paid in foreign currency, can fix the exchange rate of the foreign currency to the local one by selling futures on the foreign currency for the export contract maturity date and amount.

An importer will do the opposite: he will buy futures on the foreign currency. In other markets, it works the same way: buyers can buy futures to be protected from an asset appreciation, while sellers will sell futures to be secured from asset devaluation.

FUTURES MARKETS The futures are traded only on the exchanges because they are standardized contracts. Every exchange has its own specifics, including different standard contracts for products. Notwithstanding their differences, contracts everywhere in general have the same components: contract size, expiration dates, procedure of their settlement, minimal price step (*tick*), etc. Commodity contracts specify product quality and warehousing requirements.

A futures contract on an underlying asset is set for a few expiration dates.[4] For example, heating oil contracts may expire in January, February, March, June, and September. All contracts trade simultaneously. One could say that the futures have a "given name" and a

(Continued)

FURTHER INFORMATION FOR THE READER *(Continued)*

"family name." The contract expiration date is the given name, and the underlying asset is the family name. For instance, "March Fuel oil" stands for a contract on fuel oil expiring on the fourth Tuesday of March. In another example, "January EUR/JPY" means a January contract on EUR against JPY.

Exchanges strictly control their clients' financial standings. To secure mutual trust, clients are required to pledge deposits (*initial and variation margins*). Due to control procedures, the exchanges have high credit ratings.

An important characteristic of futures contracts is leverage. As a rule, to purchase a contract it is necessary to pay initially less than 10% of the contract value. However, buyers have to add to the initial deposit (*make a marginal payment*) when prices fall. Sellers face similar requirements, if the prices increase.

If the marginal payments are not made, the exchange has a right to close the client's position at a current market price. The client receives the balance of cash on the account after deduction of the losses. For example, when you sold gold on January 15 at $295 per ounce, you had to deposit $29 to the exchange. If the price rose by 10% (i.e., moved against you), you would have to increase your deposit by $3 to cover the increased exchange risk. If the price returns to $295, the additional $30 would be returned to you.

PRICING OF FUTURES CONTRACTS

Theoretical Prices of Futures and the Theoretical Price Curve Basic elements of futures contracts prices are the following: underlying price on the day of transaction; financing cost of the underlying between the day of the purchase and the day of contract closing; cost of warehousing (for commodities). For example, if the oil price today (April 1) is $40 per barrel, its monthly storage costs $0.15 per barrel, and monthly financing costs $0.13 per barrel, then futures price for June 1 should be $40.56 (40 + 0.15 × 2 + 0.13 × 2). In this case, you are indifferent whether to buy oil today and keep it till June 1 in storage or with future delivery of oil on June 1.

This kind of calculation works for any date in the future. Hence, on May 1 this price will be 40.28 (40 + 0.15 × 1 + 0.13 × 1), on July 1 the price will equal 40.94 (40 + 0.15 × 3 + 0.13 × 3). The results of

FURTHER INFORMATION FOR THE READER *(Continued)*

these calculations may be plotted on graph of *theoretical* prices for each period, which will look like a curve.

Market Future Price Curves in the Commodity Markets: Contango and Backwardation Commodities futures price curves do not concur with the theoretical ones. Just as production cost differs from price, theoretical and market curves differ due to market expectations. The market curves depend on demand and supply as well as the theoretical considerations discussed previously. Thus, if the market forecasts demand growth for gasoline in July (due to summer auto tourism), the price on oil with July delivery will be higher than the theoretical one. At the same time, if by the end of September the gasoline storage is full, the prices on October delivery may fall below the theoretical prices.

That is why commodities prices curves (market prices for different periods) depend on demand and supply for a given commodity. Today's price is the basis of such calculations.

In the commodity markets, the curve configuration is considered to be *flat* when it concurs with the theoretical one. It is said to be *contango* when the current prices are lower than theoretical ones (supply exceeds demand), and in *backwardation* when the current prices are higher than theoretical ones (demand exceeds supply)—see Figure 8.1.

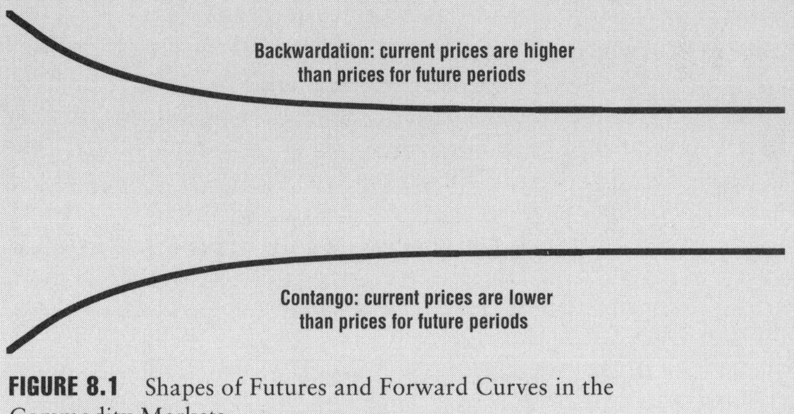

FIGURE 8.1 Shapes of Futures and Forward Curves in the Commodity Markets

(Continued)

FURTHER INFORMATION FOR THE READER *(Continued)*

Backwardation appears when insufficient oil deliveries force refineries to pay a higher price for the commodity, since even temporary shut-ups are very expensive. On the other hand, contango is a result of high production volume, weak demand, and filled-up oil storage facilities.

Let's consider another situation. In 1997 it was announced that Iraq and the UN were about to sign the oil-for-food program. That meant that in three months additional oil would appear on the markets. Such an announcement would have caused the oil price to fall along the entire curve, but the prices beyond three months would fall disproportionately lower. In such a case, oil for longer delivery periods should have become cheaper than for the closer ones. As a result, the curve would become backwardated.

Later, in 1998–1999, there was an excess of oil in the market caused by lack of coordination of OPEC members, the UN program for Iraqi oil sales, and the economic crisis in Southeast Asia. The oil storage facilities were so full that tankers were used for storing oil. The forward price curve became contangoed.

And when OPEC solidified in 2000–2001, oil prices sharply increased, especially current prices. Five-year forwards went up as well but to a smaller extent. That caused backwardation of the curve.

Financial manipulations are an example of how demand and supply influence the curve shape. For example, the amount of oil in warehouses of an exchange may be less than the volume of futures contracts sold. That is normal since some of the exchange participants are financial speculators who do not take physical delivery.

Sometimes strikes, catastrophes, and other unexpected events delay scheduled deliveries to warehouses. Since the volume of real consumption doesn't decrease, the financial speculators who sold oil futures, but do not have oil to deliver have to buy back their contracts or deliver oil to a warehouse. And what if the futures' holders don't sell them back? The financial speculators cannot deliver oil on time and face a default. They scramble to buy back futures contracts close to expiration and the short-term prices increase by 10% to 15%.

In the 1990s, Hamonako, a Japanese copper trader, cornered speculators several times over by demanding delivery. The speculators had to buy back short contracts at sky-high prices. Another textbook example is the history of silver speculation by the Hunt Brothers. In 1979–1980, they managed to increase the silver price from $10 to $50

FURTHER INFORMATION FOR THE READER *(Continued)*

per troy ounce. Only interference of the US Antimonopoly Committee made them stop their market manipulations.

Price Curves in the Currency Markets The foreign exchange (FX) curve depends on the spot price and on the ratio of interest rates between two currencies (see Currency Forward, page 90). As a result, price curves in FX markets are theoretical ones unlike those in commodity markets.

Price Curves in Equity and Fixed Income Markets Price curves in equity and fixed income markets in general are closer to foreign exchange markets. They depend on current interest rates (like currencies) and are rarely affected by demand for and supply of the instrument (like commodities). The exceptions are the short-term curve segments. From time to time, the market pays up for a certain security (for example, one needs to borrow a stock to sell it short). In this case, the curve's shape depends on demand for and supply of a given security.

Such situations are more frequent for illiquid stocks and bonds than for liquid ones. Even for them, in the longer term the market curve concurs with the theoretical one.

FORWARDS The *forward* is a contract that guarantees an exchange of a certain amount of one currency into the other one at a set rate on a set date.

Forwards and futures are twin brothers serving the same purpose: to fix today a price of future payments. The main difference between them is markets: futures are traded on exchanges and forwards are traded over-the-counter (OTC). Due to the absence of standardization, forwards are more flexible. With their help it is easy to create contracts with different expiration dates (for futures normally only one date per month exists) as well as flexible size, price expression, points of delivery, and the like.

The maximum expiration for futures doesn't exceed 18 months. Forward contracts may be made for any term. Five-year deals are common practice. Besides, the OTC market is often more liquid due to participation of major financial institutions.

(Continued)

FURTHER INFORMATION FOR THE READER *(Continued)*

The pricing principles of forwards and futures are similar. Curves may differ a bit due to the market makers' bid-offer spreads and trading counterparty credit adjustment. Spreads on the OTC market depend on clients' credit standings and relationships, while on exchanges credit procedures are standard and spreads are not credit adjusted. That means that the price on the same contracts and curve will be the same for all exchange clients.

Another important distinction is that in the commodity markets a forward is a deliverable instrument, while a future, as a rule, is nondeliverable (even if a futures contract can be settled in cash or physically).

Currency Forward FX forwards are calculated using spot price and ratio of interest rates between two currencies. When someone buys a foreign currency in exchange he sells another currency. When a United States investor buys yen for US dollars, he loses an opportunity to keep dollars on an interest bearing deposit and to collect interest. Instead, he can collect interest on a yen deposit.

Suppose interest rates on dollar deposits are higher than the rates on yen deposits. Then, one can borrow yen, convert the sum into dollars and deposit dollars in an American bank. Such a combination secures profit equal to the difference of deposit rates on yen and on dollars.

There is one problem: On the deposit's expiration day, yen may appreciate against dollars. In such a case, an investor converting dollars back into yen will receive less than what he borrowed initially. That is, he will lose capital. The profit from the difference in interest rates may be insufficient to compensate for the loss. To secure his capital at the time of the initial conversion, he can use an *FX forward*—an instrument that guarantees the future FX rate. He would gain an immediate *arbitrage* profit: no risk on exchange rate and guaranteed profit on the interest rate differential.

But the financial markets know this trick, and the forward price will reflect the rates' difference. That prevents everybody from engaging in operations of this kind: borrow low interest-rate currencies, buy with them higher-yielding currencies and hedge the latter by a forward.

If the dollar rate is 6% and the yen rate is 1%, the one-year interest rate differential is 5%. If you were to borrow the $1 million equivalent of yen, you would make 500 pips (5 yen = 5%). A bank from which you buy the forward knows the market itself. To stop you from

FURTHER INFORMATION FOR THE READER *(Continued)*

arbitraging it, the forward will be priced 500 pips below the spot price! For instance, if spot trades at 105.00, the one-year forward is at 100.00.

Suppose a trader plans to open a yen deposit for three months. As dollar and yen deposit rates are known beforehand, he can calculate the amount of yen he will get at the end of period. A party, who bought dollars from him, knows beforehand how many dollars he will have at the end of the period. Knowing the two amounts, both parties can calculate the three-month FX rate at which they are indifferent between the currencies. Such a rate is called *a forward rate.*

Since the rates on deposits in two currencies differ, the spot is different from the forward rate to the extent of the *forward differential* (also called *swap points*).

Thus, the forward pricing concept adheres to the principle of an arbitrage-free market.

Most companies use proceeds from their foreign operations to buy their national currency on a certain date in the future. Using forward contracts (forwards), they are able to fix the exchange rate for the future exchange today. When the date arrives, they exchange the *future* proceeds into national currency *at an exchange rate they fix today.*

Calculation of FX Forward Rates To meet the condition of indifference between investments in both currencies,

- The forward on the higher yielding currency *is quoted at discount* (lower); thus, the forward rate *is lower* than the spot, so the *swap points are negative.*
- The forward on the lower yielding currency *is quoted with the premium*, thus, the forward rate *is higher* than the spot; *so the swap points are positive.*

The forward rate is calculated according the following formula:

$$\text{Forward}(C_1/C_2) = \text{Spot}(C_1/C_2) \times (1 + R_2 \times T/360)/(1 + R_1 \times T/360)$$ [5]

(Continued)

FURTHER INFORMATION FOR THE READER *(Continued)*

where

Spot(C_1/C_2)	= current spot (e.g., USD/JPY)
Forward(C_1/C_2)	= forward rate
R_1	= compound interest rate on Currency 1 (also called *foreign* currency) (Currency 1 in our example is USD)
R_2	= the compound interest rate on Currency 2 (also called *domestic* currency) (Currency 2 in our example is JPY)

In other words, *if*:

the USD/JPY spot is 110.00 (you can buy 110 yen for $1),
the three-month (90-day) USD deposit yields 6% per annum,
the three-month (90-day) JPY deposit yields 3% per annum;

then:

the three-month USD/JPY forward rate is: $110.00 \times (1 + 0.03 \times 90/360)/(1 + 0.06 \times 90/360) = 109.18$,
the swap (forward differential): $109.18 - 110.00 = -0.82$.

Thus, the P/L of a deal settled in three months at 109.18 is the same as if it is settled on the spot date at 110.00.

SWAPS Unlike futures, swap contracts are cash-settled only. They don't fix the prices completely but fix the differentials of initially set prices. Metaphorically, a nonhedged position is a tumbleweed moving at the market's will, a position that is hedged by futures/forwards behaves like a metal rod remaining at the same place whatever happens. The swap is a flexible wooden rod fixed at one point but changing its shape as the market moves.

An oil producer uses futures for hedging. If he expects a price increase, he would be better off selling production in the future at higher prices of future periods. However, if he expects a price decrease, he would be better served by fixing the future prices

FURTHER INFORMATION FOR THE READER *(Continued)*

today. Today, he will sell futures for the production amounts and corresponding to production dates. If today were January 1 and the production cycle takes two months, an expected two months of production should be sold for March delivery at a March price.

Swaps function differently from futures. As the name says a buyer and seller swap something.[6]

Moreover, the term "swap" *implies different calculations for different underlyings.* For example, the currency swaps are calculated differently from commodity and interest rates swaps. The latter are calculated differently from each other.

Interest Rate Swaps Initially, the swaps constituted an exchange of a fixed obligation for floating ones. One gets a fixed interest rate by lending for a term at a fixed rate. Therefore, a *seller of the fixed leg* (a lender in banking terms or "the receiver" in swaps language) receives fixed payment and the buyer of fixed leg (debtor) pays a fixed rate[7] ("the payer" in swaps language).

Suppose the current six-year rate is 5% and three-month LIBOR[8] is 2%. (LIBOR, the London Interbank Offered Rate, is the bid/ask rate for U.S. dollars of the largest London-based banks. The rate is used as the basis of interest calculations.) A trader expects interest rates to increase. Therefore, he will buy the fixed leg of a swap and will sell the floating one. In other words, he will fix the interest he receives for six years and will pay a three-month LIBOR rate, which will be reset every three months. If LIBOR goes down he pays less, while collecting the same six-month rate. Since he receives the fixed rate, he is called a *buyer* of the swap.

The trader will have to pay 3% for the first three-month period. If in three months LIBOR goes

- Down to 1.75%, he will receive 5% and pay 1.75%, making an extra 0.25%;[9]
- Up to 2.3%, he will receive 5% and pay 2.3%, losing 0.3%.

Imagine issuing a fixed rate bond as borrowing, and reinvesting the proceeds in a floating rate bond as lending.

(Continued)

FURTHER INFORMATION FOR THE READER *(Continued)*

This example demonstrates that

- The swap is settled on reset dates in cash;
- The settlement amount is the difference between the price differential on the trade date and on the reset date;
- If the trader expected a parallel shift down along the entire interest rate curve (directional, rather than a relative value expectation), he would be better off trading interest rate futures, because the relative value of fixed and floating payments will not change.

Commodity Swaps Swaps came to commodity markets from the fixed income markets, but they differ a bit, because in interest rates you exchange the floating index for a fixed index.

As we saw, LIBOR is fixed for three months at the beginning of each three-month period. The floating leg of commodity swaps is calculated as an average price for a period. If there is no major seasonality, fixed prices in swaps are kept the same during the lifetime of the swap. For example a one-month rate is calculated as an average price for all trading sessions of the month. Traditionally, the calculation of the floating index is an average of daily prices, sometimes paid with a two- or three-month lag.

Producers of raw materials prefer *not* to fix their price beforehand, if they expect their price to increase. They prefer selling at higher *floating* prices in the future. That means buying the swap (i.e., making fixed payments and receiving floating ones). For instance, if there is a three-month swap and prices are reset in January and February, prices for January and February deliveries will rise greater than the price on March delivery, the producer will make money on the swap.

Airlines (consumers) would prefer to sell fixed (receive higher prices) and buy floating (pay lower prices) when they expect a price decrease.

Currency Swap One can view a currency swap as a simultaneous FX spot buy (sell) and FX forward sell (buy). Both prices are fixed in one transaction. They differ by the swap points, in other words, by the interest rate differential between the two currencies.

One buys $1 million against yen at 116.00 for delivery on January 31, 2001, and simultaneously sells $1 million against yen at

FURTHER INFORMATION FOR THE READER *(Continued)*

113.00 for delivery on January 31, 2002. He receives Y300,000 up-front (300 *swap points*).

Notice that while the amount of the first currency is the same for both FX and forward transactions ($1 million), the amount of the second one differs. The amount of the second currency for the first (spot) date is JPY116,000,000 ($1 million × 116.00), and for the second date it is JPY113,000,000 ($1 million × 113.00). The second currency amounts for both dates are different unless the interest rates of both currencies are the same.[10]

TRANSACTING IN CURRENCY FORWARDS AND SWAPS IN PRACTICE

Calculation of Time Periods in Forward Market In forward and option markets the terms "week" or "month" differ in meaning from when they are used in everyday life. The time periods are estimated *from the spot/premium delivery (settlement) date to the forward delivery date*, not as 7 or 30 days from the *trade date*. For example, on Thursday, June 30 (trade date), a trader buys a one-week USD/CHF option.[11] In an ordinary situation, the premium settlement date is July 4 (the second business day), but since July 4 is a bank holiday in the United States, the second business day is July 5. Now, we add a week to July 5—as a result the delivery for an expiration date is July 12 (Tuesday). Count back two business days. The result is July 8—Friday. In other words, if the one-week option exercise date is Friday, July 8, then the delivery date is July 12. Thus, "one week" in this case consists of eight *calendar* days from Thursday, June 30, till Friday, July 8, although there are just seven business days between the dates of deliveries.

Making Forward and Swap Deals on FOREX To calculate the forward rate, one fixes the spot at a current level by making the spot transaction. To reduce the transaction costs, most traders prefer to choose a rate on their own rather than entrust this to a counterparty. Having sold/bought the spot at the best price, they make a swap deal like buy/sell or sell/buy with a forward dealer who offers the best forward price. For example, if one needs to buy a forward, she would buy the spot, then buy a swap. In the swap transaction she would simultaneously sell the spot she purchased earlier and buy the forward. That transforms the original spot position into the forward one.

(Continued)

FURTHER INFORMATION FOR THE READER *(Continued)*

Example

To reiterate:

Step 1. You buy dollars and sell yen in the spot market at 110.00.

Step 2. You phone a forward dealer and do a swap. You *simultaneously* sell *spot* USD at 110.00 (buying JPY, thus reversing the spot position from Step 1) and buy dollars forward (selling yen) for the *settlement in three months*. As a result, the spot position is closed, and you become long the USD forward position.

Thus, an FX forward deal is completed either by doing two transactions, spot and swap, or by buying just a forward contract.

The spot transaction in Step 1 reduces your transaction costs because you choose the best spot rate yourself. Otherwise, the forward dealer could buy it cheaper and resell it to you at a worse level, earning spread on both the forward and the spot.

CHAPTER 9

Spreads

In this chapter, we will discuss ratio spreads and some other complex strategies in more detail. Most readers face difficulties in mastering these strategies. Since spreads are one of the cornerstones in options trading, let's consider them through the prism of simple geometry.

ALTERNATIVE METHOD FOR CALCULATING THE BREAKEVEN POINT OF RATIO SPREADS

It may be difficult to comprehend ratio spreads from a purely arithmetic standpoint. Let's consider them from the geometric one. Imagine an area calculation problem. Let's suppose that rectangle A has the same area as rectangle B. The length of A is 4 centimeters, and its width is 3 centimeters. The length of B is 6 centimeters. What is the width of B?

a. As you know, the area of a rectangle is calculated by multiplying the length by its width. Therefore, the area of A = $4 \times 3 = 12$ cm^2.
b. Since we know that the area of A = the area of B, we can say that the area of B = 12 cm. We know the length of B = 6 cm, and now we can calculate its width by dividing the area by its length: 12 cm^2/6 = 2 cm.

In other words, the two rectangles, notwithstanding a visual difference, have the same area. This principle is sufficient to calculate the breakeven point of a ratio spread. Imagine you bought one 100 call and sold three 110 calls (1:3 spread.) What is the breakeven point of this strategy (point after which it starts losing)?

To answer this question, let's imagine the area where the profitable strategy is to be equal to the unprofitable one. The area is determined as the position's size multiplied by the distance traversed by the underlying asset. In other words, in carrying out this task you know the "*length*," (*face values* of the purchased and sold *positions*). You also know the "*width*" of the profitable position (*distance* between the strikes on which you are long and on which you are short). At last, we should find the "*width*": the distance the underlying asset will have to travel from the strike of sold options to the breakeven point.

To answer this question, do the following:

1. Calculate the difference between the long and short positions' sizes. The long position is the actual amount you bought; the net short position is the *difference* between the amounts you bought and you sold! Therefore, your long position equals 1 (below 110), and short position (above 110) is – 2 (3 – 1).
2. Determine the maximum profit, "the area where the strategy is profitable": 1 × (110 – 100) = $10. Now, we know that the breakeven point is at a level where the position loses the $10.
3. Calculate the "width"—price distance needed for the short position to absorb the $10 profit: 10:2 = 5.

Therefore, the breakeven point is $5 above the *strike of the short option's position*, or 110 + 5 = 115.

Notice: the *short* strike is the borderline separating the area where the position gains in value from the losing area. It serves as a pivot for breakeven points calculation. Thus, *this strategy is profitable in the range of 100–115.*

CALCULATIONS OF OPTIONS BREAKEVEN POINTS IF PREMIUM IS NOT EQUAL TO ZERO

To raise the level of challenge, let's introduce the premium factor. If you collect the premium, the breakeven point moves further in your favor. So the collected premium is a form of protection from some losses.

For example, if you *collected* the $4 premium, the breakeven of the above-mentioned strategy 1:3 will move away to 117! This happens because now you can add this premium to the profit and calculation (3) will be the following: 115 + 4/2 = 117, *that is, this strategy is profitable in the range of 0–117.*

However, if this spread *costs* you $2, the breakeven point will move closer! In this case, calculation (3) will have the following view: 115 – 2/2 = 114.

Besides, a lower breakeven point appears! You should remember that the option you are long should appreciate enough to cover the $2 investment! In our case, the lower breakeven is 100 + (2:1) = 102. *That is, this strategy is profitable in the range of 102–114.*

QUESTIONS

A dealer bought a January XYZ 100 120, 1:3 call[1] spread and collected $4. What is his P/L if the stock trades at:

1. 112
2. 120
3. 133
4. 141
5. What is the maximum profit of the strategy?
6. What is the maximum loss of the strategy?

A dealer bought a January XYZ $60 $45, 3:9 put spread and paid $6. What is his P/L if the stock trades at:

7. 80
8. 45
9. 35
10. What are the breakevens of the strategy?
11. What is the maximum profit of the strategy?

Continuation: A week before the option expiration date the stock trades at $50, and the dealer exercises two $60 puts:

12. He immediately buys 200 shares. What are the new breakeven points?
13. He does not buy 200 shares. What are the new breakeven points of the remaining position?

ANSWERS

1. $1,600 profit: gain of $16 per stock = $16 × 1 × 100 = 1,600
2. $2,400 profit: gain $24 per share = $24 × 1 × 100 = $2,400
3. $200 loss: 2 × (133 – 120) – ((120 – 100) + 4)
4. $1,800 loss: 2 × (141 – 120) – ((120 – 100) + 4))

5. \$2,400
6. Unlimited
7. \$600 loss: $\$6 \times 100 = \$600$ loss of the paid premium if the contracts expire worthless
8. \$3,900 gain: $\$13 \times 3 \times 100 = \$3,900$
9. \$2,100 loss: $\$3.5 \times 6 \times 100 = \$2,100$
10. \$58 and \$38.5: $\$60 - (\$6{:}3)$ and $\$45 - (3 \times (60 - 45) - (6{:}2))/(9 - 3)$
11. \$3,900: $(3 \times (60 - 45) - (6{:}2)) \times 100$
12. There will be one breakeven point = \$41.375: Since the investor closed his open positions, he is left with the 1:9 put spread for which he paid \$600 (\$6 premium × 100). He also has a \$2,000 realized gain $((\$60 - \$50) \times 2 \times 100 = \$2,000)$. Selling one \$60 put will realize a \$1,500 gain at the price of \$45. Therefore, his total position is the 1:9 put spread and \$2,900 in cash (\$2,000 + \$1,500 – \$600). The breakeven point is $[\$45 - \$2,900/(100 \times (9 - 1))] = \$41.375$
13. 38.5 and 58, the same as in Question 10): The investor has the 1:9 put spread and is short 200 shares. With the downward move, the total position behaves like a 3:9 spread because the short 200 shares behave similarly to long 2 puts. But when the stock trades above \$60, it has a different profile.

FURTHER INFORMATION FOR THE READER

Designing an Option Strategy

You buy a put, when

- You are LONG an underlying asset and want to hedge it;
- You are SHORT a put and want to close or hedge the position;
- You need to sell an underlying asset;
- You expect the price to go down;
- You think the market will be unstable;
- You are ready to pay a premium; or
- You don't want to take a risk.

FURTHER INFORMATION FOR THE READER *(Continued)*

You buy a call, when

- You are SHORT an underlying asset and want to hedge it;
- You are SHORT a call and want to close or hedge the position;
- You need to buy an underlying asset;
- You expect the price to go up;
- You think the market will be unstable;
- You are ready to pay a premium; or
- You don't want to take a risk.

You sell a put, when

- You are SHORT an underlying position and want to hedge it;
- You are LONG a put and want to close the position;
- You need to buy an underlying;
- You expect the price to go up;
- You think the market will be stable;
- You want to collect a premium; or
- You are ready to take high risks.

You sell a call, when

- You are LONG an underlying position and want to hedge it;
- You are LONG a call and want to close the position;
- You need to sell the underlying;
- You expect the price to go down;
- You think the market will be stable;
- You want to collect a premium; or
- You are ready to take high risks.

CHAPTER 10

Utilization of Options for Spot/Cash Trading

Let's continue improving our option trading skills in real market situations.

ANALYZING THE REAL WORLD

Consider the following situation: the USD/CHF spot is at 1.4800. Your client is long $3 million at 1.4700. He needs you to suggest an option strategy that would provide him either an extra yield or some insurance.

Scenario 1

You believe the market will continue going up, but at a slower pace.

You can suggest a covered call sale: while keeping his spot position, he sells a 1.4900 USD call for one day at 30 CHF pips.

If the option is exercised (i.e., spot is above 1.4900 tomorrow at 10 A.M. NY time) he will sell the $3 million at 1.4930 (1.4900 + 0.0030). Otherwise, your client will collect 30 pips and will have an opportunity to take some other action tomorrow.

Scenario 2

You believe that the spot will fluctuate in the range, and the client would like to increase the position at 1.4600 and to sell some at 1.4900.

He can sell a one week 1.4700–1.4900 strangle at 70 CHF pips: a 1.4700 USD put and a 1.4900 USD call.

He would not mind if any of these options is exercised. Otherwise, he will collect the premium.

Scenario 3

You believe the spot is close to the top, and you would recommend that he cut his position at 1.4750. You can suggest doing a range forward: to sell a

1.4850 USD call and use the collected premium to buy a 1.4650 USD put. If the spot goes up, he will sell the dollars at 1.4850. However, the position stop-out at the 1.4650 level is guaranteed to him.

Scenario 4

Your client is very bullish and ready to double his position, if the spot falls back to 1.4700. But 1.4700 is far from the stop-out level of 1.4500 he initially had in mind in calculating a maximum loss. If he doubles the position now, the stop-out has to be moved closer to prevent maximum losses from exceeding the planned ones. How can we circumvent the limit?

You can suggest that he buy a 1.4700 USD put for one week. If the spot falls to 1.4700, he will be able to buy additional "three dollars" (three million dollars) using the option as a cheap insurance. And expected maximum losses will increase to the amount of premium paid.

Notice the difference between Scenarios 2 and 4. The first one represents a neutral view on the market, while the second one is very bullish. The first one helps increase profit on the existing position, while the second one increases the position itself.

> This point brings us to a very critical philosophical conclusion: a **spot/cash dealer makes money when the spot moves in his direction. An option dealer makes money when his spot forecast turns out to be correct** ***or at least the spot doesn't move against him.*** (The italic part of the previous sentence is the philosophical base for traders and investors specializing in options selling.)

The sellers hope that the premium collected for selling an option will exceed the losses if the sold option is exercised. This wish is fulfilled when the spot moves in an opposite direction, *but also* when the spot remains stable or doesn't cross the sold strike against the seller.

Scenario 5

You believe that tomorrow the spot will jump up.

You can suggest the client to buy a low-delta USD call for one week. Its price is relatively low, but it will explode in value, if your expectations come true.

QUESTIONS

1. Your client is short a 1.5400 straddle at 174 points. She would like to buy a strangle to limit his risk.

   A 1.5300–1.5500 strangle costs 32 points; a 1.5325–1.5475 costs 51 points; a 1.5350–1.5450 costs 72 points. Which of these strangles provides the best risk/reward?

2. The current spot is at 1.4750. Your client sold $10 million against CHF at 1.4225. To hedge a "catastrophic scenario" she bought a 1.4500 USD call at 35 CHF points. The client does not think that the spot will go below 1.4500 till the option's expiration. How can she close the position (think about another position equivalent to the current one)?

3. The client bought $10 million of a 1.4600 USD put and bought $5 million on hedge (in this hypothetical example she pays no option premium). If instead of that strategy she:
   a. bought $5 million of a 1.4600 call and $5 million of a 1.4600 put (a 1.4600 straddle), will the behavior of her position change?
   b. bought $10 million on the spot hedge, what will the position behavior be like?

4. Your client sold $1 million of a 1.4400 USD put at:
   a. 37 CHF pips and on expiration date the spot was at the 1.4350 level. From which spot level does she become long USD?
   b. 0.40% of the USD amount ($1 million × 0.004 = $4,000) and on an expiration date the spot was at the 1.4350 level. From which spot level does she become long USD?

5. Your client is long $10 million against CHF. The spot is at the 1.4750 level, and she feels safe. An overnight 1.4680 put costs 20 CHF pips. What is the best outcome for her, if to hedge the spot she buys a 1.4680 put? What is the maximum loss?

ANSWERS

1. A 1.5325–1.5475 strangle widens the security area by 25 pips, but it costs 19 pips (51 – 32) more than a 1.5300–1.5500 strangle. Therefore, it does not make sense to use it: she prepays for almost all the increase of the security area. The same situation is true with a 1.5350–1.5450 strangle. One has to remember that in buying a strangle to reduce risk she pays a double for each pip as he pays for both the call and the put.

2. She can sell a 1.4500 put or buy dollars and sell a 1.4500 call. In both cases, she will collect 35 pips. In this way, she fixes the losses between 1.4225 and 1.4500.
3. To answer this question, one should draw a chart of the position at the levels of 1.4500 and 1.4700 on expiration.
   a. No change. At both extremes, you will have the same P/L for the both positions.
   b. The new position will behave like the 1.4600 USD call.
4. a. from 1.4363 (1.4400 – 0.0037)
   b. from 1.43426 (1.4400 – 0.00574) ($4,000 × 1.4350)/1,000,000 = 0.00574
5. The best outcome is when the market continues appreciating and the money spent on hedging is lost. The maximum loss equals the premium of 10,000,000 × (1.4750 – 1.4680 + 0.0020) CHF.

FURTHER INFORMATION FOR THE READER

Advice to Beginning Traders

- The face value of a conservative position should equal half of a position with which a trader feels safe. That is, think of the minimal position with which you feel safe and take a half of it.
- Don't sell cheap options (usually OTM); even if their sale does not look dangerous, the risk is not compensated by the collected premium.
- Make sure that the position's term corresponds to the time period of your forecast.
- Make a risk/reward analysis of your position, prepare exit strategies before the market turns against you.
- As soon as your gain is equal to the premium (i.e., premium doubles), you should close half of your position.
- If you do not know what to do with your position, reduce it by half.

Advice and Observations for Beginning Marketing Specialists

- Neither you nor your client are gods. That's why it is impossible to know in advance that your ideas are correct and his are not.

FURTHER INFORMATION FOR THE READER *(Continued)*

Don't criticize the views and strategies of your client. Rather try to find the strategy that fits his views the best.

- "The best strategy" does not exist in abstract—there are strategies that fit the client's views the best.
- You should ask your client many questions to understand what he *really* wants: the first requests of clients are seldom the real ones.
- Clients always want it all without paying anything; but explanations why this is impossible irritate them.
- Clients do not hedge risk while everything is all right, and demand low prices for hedging when it is too late.
- Phone your client more often to remain in tune with what he thinks about his current option position: the majority of investors and even hedgers like to change it before expiration. A phone call in the middle of a term is an opportunity to make one more deal.
- Don't waste clients' time explaining to them the riskiness of their ideas: they will listen to you, but will still make this deal with somebody who appeases them. Even if you are right 10 times in a row, a client will keep dealing with optimists, although "respecting your experience and advice."
- Don't scare clients, but mention the unlimited risk of selling options—in case a client loses, you won't have to make excuses for yourself.
- Contact clients when their positions are losing money: the worst is to hide from them in such moments.
- Don't panic with your client—suggest alternatives.

PART Three

Risk Parameters of Options[1]

The previous 10 chapters prepared you to quote options and design strategies. The only thing you are missing is practice in option pricing with software. Therefore, if you plan to work in options marketing, you can scan through the chapter *Volatility*, skip the rest, or proceed directly to *Credit Risk* or *Hedging*.

Part III is for those who plan to do relative value trading in options or build market neutral strategies. It is obligatory for those who plan to *manage* their option positions rather than keep them until expiration. This part is also important for risk managers.

Up until now, we have considered options to be held until expiration. We have drawn charts, calculated breakeven points, and done delta hedging without considering factors that influence *options' prices during their lives*. In other words, we have not studied the resale value of options during their lives.

However, an option can be sold just like any other asset. At any moment of an option's life, one can determine its market value. In other words, an option can be marked-to-market the same way as a stock or a bond. Therefore, you should study factors influencing its price. These factors are not limited to a market direction as in the case of stocks or other underlying assets. They include time left till expiration, market volatility (standard deviation) of an underlying asset movement, and also a number of less important factors (e.g., changes in interest rates/in dividends of an underlying asset, etc.).

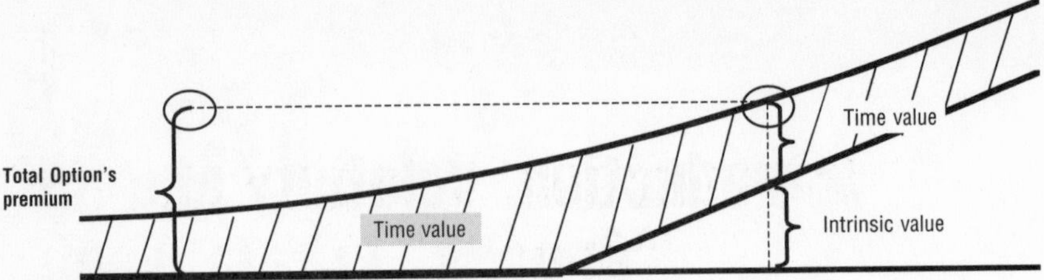

FIGURE III.1 Option Value during Lifetime Split into Time and Intrinsic Value

As you see in Figure III.1, the previously studied charts were the *graphs of intrinsic value* as they assumed just an option value at the moment of expiration. An option price before expiration should be *higher than its intrinsic value by the amount of its time value.*

A variety of factors influencing the time value will lead us to a simple conclusion: *options trading is mostly based on relative values rather than on absolute ones.* Cars are a good comparison. One can generalize by saying that a Mercedes is more expensive than a Fiat, just as two assets have different implied volatilities (i.e., chances to make money).

That general understanding, however, does not help in comparing different Mercedes. We know that new cars have longer lifespans and smaller maintenance costs. In other words, it may seem to be an expensive car based on a sticker price, but overall, after taking into account low maintenance, it is not as expensive, *especially if you plan to sell it shortly*! The same is true with options: since they trade at different premiums, have different strikes and expiration dates, one can not say which of them is relatively cheap or expensive based only on the *absolute* prices (e.g., an option that costs $1 is not necessarily more expensive than a $0.50 option). To compare option prices, one has to consider their current *theoretical* prices—prices expressed in points of *implied volatilities rather than dollars.* Implied volatility, not money, is the measure of an option's price.

The following chapters will discuss options risk and pricing parameters essential for a complete options analysis. Remember, by the end of Part III you will have to explain why *options trading is mostly based on relative values rather than on absolute ones.*

CHAPTER 11

Introduction: Volatility and the "Greeks" (Theta, Vega, and Gamma)

Most option market participants limit their knowledge to the material covered in the first 10 chapters. This is sufficient to start trading. That's why further chapters go beyond the average market knowledge of most professionals dealing with options.

An engagement ring price depends on the prices of the precious metal and of the gem. The same is true for options: their prices mostly depend on the underlying asset price changes and changes of its volatility. That said, one will analyze other factors influencing resale value: for examples, interest payments (if you bought the ring with borrowed money), and depreciation (value wearing off) are all factors to consider. These factors are measured with help of risk parameters called Greeks. This chapter gives an overview of these parameters. Each of them will be considered in depth separately in the forthcoming chapters.

VOLATILITY[1]

When the market fluctuates, we say it is volatile. Statisticians can actually calculate volatility by finding the annualized standard deviation of the logarithm of the daily relative changes in the underlying asset (closing) price.[2] *Volatility does not change if the movements are upward or downward, only the absolute values of the price fluctuations matter!* This seemingly insignificant fact has a critical importance, because market participants, other than options market makers, operate based on their forecasts of market direction.

Option players start with an assumption about future market volatility rather than its direction. Once the assumption is made, they use a very simple formula to calculate the parameter. We will discuss the formula in the next chapter. For now, think of the market volatility just as "market fluctuations from closing to closing."

There are three types of volatility:

1. *Historical volatility:* the actual volatility of the underlying's price over a certain historical period;
2. *Implied volatility:* the market forecast of the future volatility;
3. *Historical implied volatility:* the historical record of implied volatilities.

When we talk about the *volatility used for options pricing*, we have in mind *the implied volatility*.

INTRINSIC VALUE AND TIME VALUE: DEFINITION OF THETA

As we discussed earlier in the book, option premium is comprised of two parts: time value and intrinsic value.

1. *Intrinsic value* is equal to the value the owner can receive if she exercises her option immediately. That is, only an in-the-money option has an intrinsic value. For instance, if she is long an IBM 100 call and the stock currently trades at $110, the intrinsic value of option is $10, because, if she exercises the option she immediately receives $10 ($110 – $100).
2. *Time value* is a difference between an option's premium and its intrinsic portion. Actually, *time value is the reason to buy options*—it is the cost of opportunity to make money with risk lower than on the underlying asset. Everything being equal, the longer time remaining till an option's expiration, and/or the greater the likelihood that it will end up in-the-money, the more expensive it is. Therefore, time value depends on the time left till the option's expiration. It also depends on volatility. The higher the volatility in the future, the greater the chance that an option will be in-the-money, and the more expensive the option will be.

Theta measures sensitivity of the *time value portion of an option's premium* to time remaining till expiration. It is the portion of time value, which is amortized daily.[3] For instance, if the price of the OTM option is 10 and theta is 2, overnight it will lose two ticks[4] and will be worth 8 tomorrow.

DEFINITION OF VEGA

Vega measures sensitivity of an option's price *to changes in volatility*. Vega and delta are a sister and a brother. One measures sensitivity of the premium to the spot price while the other does the same with regard to volatility. The higher the vega of an option, the greater its price changes when *implied* volatility changes.

DEFINITION OF GAMMA

Imagine that you are driving at 30 miles (delta) an hour, and then speed up to 35 miles an hour. If, *in option terms*, your *speed* (change of distance in time) at any moment of time is *delta*, the five-mile-an-hour *acceleration* (30 to 35 miles an hour) is *gamma*. *Gamma* is an *acceleration of delta* (acceleration of the premium's change) as an underlying asset price changes.

Delta shows the change in an option price with respect to the price change of an underlying asset. In other words, it measures a speed of the option price changes per one-point move of an underlying asset price.

The same option has different deltas at different underlying asset price levels. Gamma measures the speed at which delta changes as the price of the underlying asset changes. In other words, gamma shows the extent of delta change with a one-point change in the spot/cash price.

We will go over the parameters in depth in the following chapters. For now these definitions will help you better visualize the entire spectrum of finer aspects of options trading that is essential to market participants.

QUESTIONS

1. The spot USD/CHF is at 1.4500. What are the time and intrinsic values of:

   a. a 1.4500 USD call that costs 100 CHF pips;
   b. a 1.4600 USD put that costs 150 CHF pips?

2. Delta hedging makes an option position delta-neutral, that is, the *value* of a delta-neutral position (option + hedge) changes the same when price moves in either direction. *Since time value is a payment for an opportunity to make money and in both cases we make the same profit, the time value of a hedged call and put (with the same strike and expiration date) should be the same.*[5] Therefore, you should be indifferent

between buying a delta-hedged 1.4600 call or a delta-hedged 1.4600 put, *if you plan to run hedged positions.*

a. What is the time value of the 1.4600 USD call in Question 1.b.?
b. If the market prices it at 140 pips, what would you do?

3. If you want a position that gains value quickly when the spot changes, to which of the Greeks should you pay the most attention?
4. If you want a position that gains value quickly when volatility changes, to which Greek should you pay the most attention?
5. If you want to sell an option that loses time value quickly, to which Greek should you pay the most attention?
6. Unexpected news has just hit the market. It can sharply change market dynamics. Increase of which parameter should it lead to?
7. Which component of an option premium (time value or intrinsic value) changes, when the implied volatility moves (without a change in the price of an underlying asset)?
8. Today, the time value of an option increased. What will happen to its theta?
9. Let's suppose that you agree that the same chance to make money should cost the same premium. In respect to a simplified definition of delta—the chance of an option to be in-the-money at expiration:
   a. what can you say about the time value of a 30-delta call and a 30-delta put (the same underlying asset and expiration date)?
   b. if a 1.4700 call has 70 delta and a 1.4300 put has 30 delta, what can you say about their thetas (use the same logic as in Question 2).
10. A difficult question: If implied volatility increased and the initial vega of the option A was higher than that of the option B, and both options expire on the same date,
    a. the premium of which option would increase faster?
    b. how do the thetas of the options behave?

ANSWERS

1. a. The time value of the 1.4500 call is 100, since it is an ATM option. ATM options do not have intrinsic value;
   b. The intrinsic value of the 1.4600 put is 100 pips since it is 100 pips in-the-money. Therefore, its time value is 50 (premium – intrinsic value = 150 – 100).

2. a. 50 pips; the time value of the 1.4600 put is 50 pips, the time value of a call and a put with the same strike and expiration date should be the same;
   b. You would buy the hedged 1.4600 put and sell the hedged 1.4600 call, collecting an arbitrage profit.
3. You would buy a position with higher gamma.
4. You would buy a position with higher vega.
5. Theta measures an option's time value.
6. It should lead to an increase of implied volatility because the market expects an increase of volatility.
7. Time value. For example, if spot is at 1.5000, the *intrinsic value* of the 1.4500 USD call is 500 pips regardless of the volatility level the market expects. The increase of implied volatility means that the market expects that a (hedged) option position will have a better chance to make money. A better chance of profitability is more expensive in terms of premium. Yet, because the spot did not change, the intrinsic value remains unchanged. Therefore, the increase in volatility causes a rise of the time value portion of the option's premium.
8. Theta will increase. When an option's time value increases (as in the previous example), a greater amount of premium is to be amortized during the same remaining time period. Therefore, its time decay (theta) increases.
9. a. The same. As you remember, delta gives a rough indication of the chances that an option will end up in-the-money on expiration. They are the same for a 30-delta call and a 30-delta put. The options' time value should be the same.
   b. The question reiterates the concept that equal chances to make money should have a similar price. In Question 2 we stated that the chances of making money on a delta-hedged call and a delta-hedged put (with the same strike and volatility) are the same. This means that a delta-hedged 70-delta call should be as profitable as a delta-hedged 30-delta put. Similarly, in Question 9a we decided that a 30-delta call and a 30-delta put should cost the same as they have the same chance to end up in-the-money. Since both the 1.4700 call and the 1.4300 put expire on the same day, their premiums and time decay (theta)[6] should be the same.
10. a. The premium of option A, as it is more sensitive to the implied volatility, because its vega is higher.
    b. Theta of option A will increase more. Therefore, its amortization (theta) should increase more as well.

FURTHER INFORMATION FOR THE READER

Options History

Aristotle mentioned options in *The Politics* as a "universally applicable" financial instrument. Options were actively used during the tulip mania in Holland in 1630s. Already at that time, both calls and puts were in use. In the United States, trading in options on New York Stock Exchange was launched in the 1790s. Louis Bachelier was the first to try to find a mathematical approach to the valuation of options in 1900.

The formula to price options was found in 1970 by Myron Scholes and Fischer Black with assistance of Robert Merton. The method worked out by them made it possible to calculate a "fair" premium for a European call option on any stock. Although by that time options had already been in use for centuries, academic journals took three years to publish their article on the option valuation formula. When finally published, the article coincided with the creation of the Chicago Board Options Exchange (CBOE) in 1973, where the idea for an exchange-traded option market found supporters. In 1978, a daily options turnover at CBOE was about 100,000 contracts.[7]

At the heart of the Black-Scholes model is the principle of put and call parity, which we discussed earlier. According to that principle, when the stock price goes up, the same happens with the call option price, but not necessarily by the same amount. The same is true when the stock price goes down. Thus, it is necessary to hold or sell some shares (in alignment with an option's delta) that balance the option position to equalize the losses and gains on the option. By continuously adjusting the amount of shares (the process of hedging) held throughout the option's life, a riskless position should be maintained. In this case, profit from the long call will be fully covered by the underlying losses from hedging or vice versa.

Despite its elegance, the Black-Scholes model is based on a few unrealistic assumptions. For example, the model assumes that *the market moves in random fashion*—often referred to as random walk—and that the probabilities of a rise and of a fall are equal. Furthermore, the model assumes that *the prices move continuously without gaps*. For example, after 100 it can be 99 or 101 rather than 80 or 104. It is also assumes that a chart of frequency function of market closing prices for a period should look like a bell-shaped curve with a wider right side, also known as a lognormal distribution.

FURTHER INFORMATION FOR THE READER *(Continued)*

Another no less important assumption is that not only the underlying asset prices are normally distributed but that the market *volatility is fixed* as well.

In 1976 and 1979 Cox, Ross and Rubenstein published their own option pricing model that could be applied to American-style options, accounting for the early exercise possibility.

In 1982, Garman and Kolhagen transformed the Black-Scholes model making it useful for currency options. The new model took into account the fact that two interest rates instead of one influence the currency option price.

Later on, other additions made the old models more exact. Some of them dealt with the unrealistic assumptions of early versions, such as the assumption that market volatility is fixed.

In 1994, Derman and Kani combined the binominal tree and the model for long-term American-style equity options to work out a barrier options model. It used a volatility curve (a volatility level corresponding to a time period).

Gradually, the binomial models evolved into trinominal ones, giving an opportunity for more exact valuation of the options.

It is worth mentioning again that most of the assumptions on which the Black-Scholes model and other models are based do not hold in real life:

- Volatility and interest rates do change and often rather chaotically; that is, they are neither static nor normally distributed.
- Frequently price movements are not explained by a lognormal distribution. An unforeseen event causes a break in a market trend and price gaps.
- Transaction costs such as bid/ask spreads and commissions, which are not taken into account in models, are also very significant factors. Sale and purchase of options turn out to be more expensive than sale and purchase in spot/cash markets. There is only one spread in price of a spot/cash market. An option price includes three spreads: a spread quoted by an option dealer in terms of implied volatilities, a spread quoted by a dealer in the spot/cash market, and a spread quoted by a dealer in the forward/repo market.

(Continued)

FURTHER INFORMATION FOR THE READER *(Continued)*

- Furthermore, OTM currency options tend to be underpriced due to assumption of lognormal distribution of prices. In the early days, banks lost money by religiously sticking to the theoretical prices formulated by their models. As a result, they often sold OTM options at a lower price than was perhaps justified.

The market makers learned to circumvent these limitations by adjusting implied volatility.

CHAPTER 12
Volatility

Volatility is the key concept to understanding options. Its importance is easy to demonstrate by comparing an option and an engagement ring. The price of the ring depends on two components: the price of the precious metal and the price of the diamond. The option's price also largely depends on two components: the price of an underlying asset and its volatility.

THREE TYPES OF VOLATILITY

Let's reiterate some of the previously discussed issues.

There are three types of volatility:

Historical the actual volatility of an underlying over a given period of time;

Implied the market estimate of the underlying's volatility in the future;

Historical implied the historical record of implied volatility.

The S&P 500 futures historical volatility chart shows that a 10-day volatility has recently been much higher than a 100-day one. But in March, we see it was lower. (See Figure 12.1.)

The implied volatility is used to compare options values. For example, in comparing two bags of potatoes, one should start with their weight rather than sizes of individual potatoes. The options are compared based on their individual implied volatilities (like weight). There is no other way to compare: like potatoes can have the same weight but different sizes and shapes, the options with the same premium may have different strike prices and expiration dates. Volatility for options traders is a universal measure as weight is for potato traders.

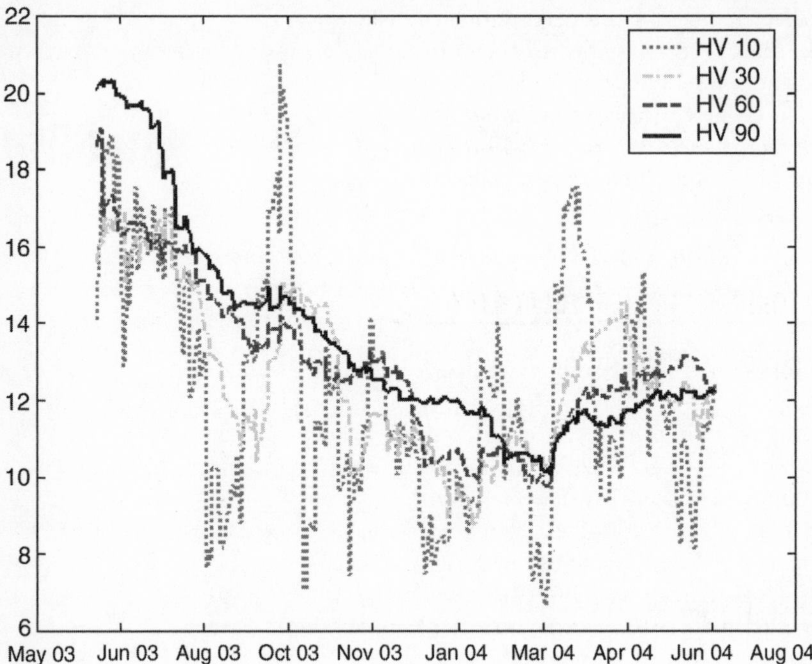

FIGURE 12.1 Historical Volatility for S&P 500
Source: Ivolatility.com.

At the same time, implied volatility is the market makers' estimate of the future underlying volatility rather than an exact calculation. It is easy to find it by calling a broker or checking Internet sites of exchanges, the same way as you would do with a price of coffee or aluminum. Therefore, you have to think of *implied volatility as a standard measure for option pricing denominated in percentage points. When we talk about* the volatility used as a unit of option's price, *we are talking about implied volatility.* Nobody would be surprised if a trader said, "I buy oil at 50," meaning he buys oil at $50 per barrel. Similarly, you should not be surprised if someone says that he buys a 30-delta call at "50 volatilities."

Thus, volatility is a commodity on its own. Admittedly, implied volatility is a bit more abstract than potatoes. Yet some exchanges have discussed a possibility of introducing contracts on volatility, just as there are contracts for commodities. Don't lose too much sleep over this difficult concept. Take it for granted: you can buy and sell volatilities. If one can predict changes in the perceptions of risk, one can make money trading risk, that is, volatilities. Profits can be collected simply by buying volatility low and selling volatility high.

In other words, *implied volatility is simultaneously an estimate of future risk, a measure for comparative valuation of the options, and a commodity.* It is measured in percents or basis points.

HISTORICAL IMPLIED VOLATILITY

Historical implied volatility is a history of implied volatility, that is, prices of market makers. On the graph shown in Figure 12.1, dotted lines are historical volatilities of S&P for different periods.

Notice in Figure 12.2 that the charts of historical volatility and historical implied volatility differ. This happens for many reasons. Some of them are related to the way these two volatilities are derived. To calculate a historical volatility, one can use historical data. The implied volatility is a prediction of the future market behavior made by participants, rather than a calculation. In other words, historical implied is the history of predictions of implied volatility. Among the reasons for the differences is the fact that implied volatility takes into account *intraday* market fluctuations, while historical volatility is calculated based on *daily closing prices*. To understand other reasons for differences, one has to learn how the market estimates implied volatility.

IMPLIED VOLATILITY

Implied volatility depends on a number of factors:

- *Historical volatility:* significant recent market fluctuations are likely to keep expected future volatilities—or "vols"—high;
- *Political and economic calendars* (elections, economic releases, etc.): volatility (price) of options expiring after the dates of economic releases ("*figures*") is normally higher than on the dates preceding the releases. That happens because the new information may cause a substantial market move. That is why implied volatility (price) of days prior to G8 meetings is lower than that of the days following these meetings. The same holds true for elections. A new parliament or prime minister can

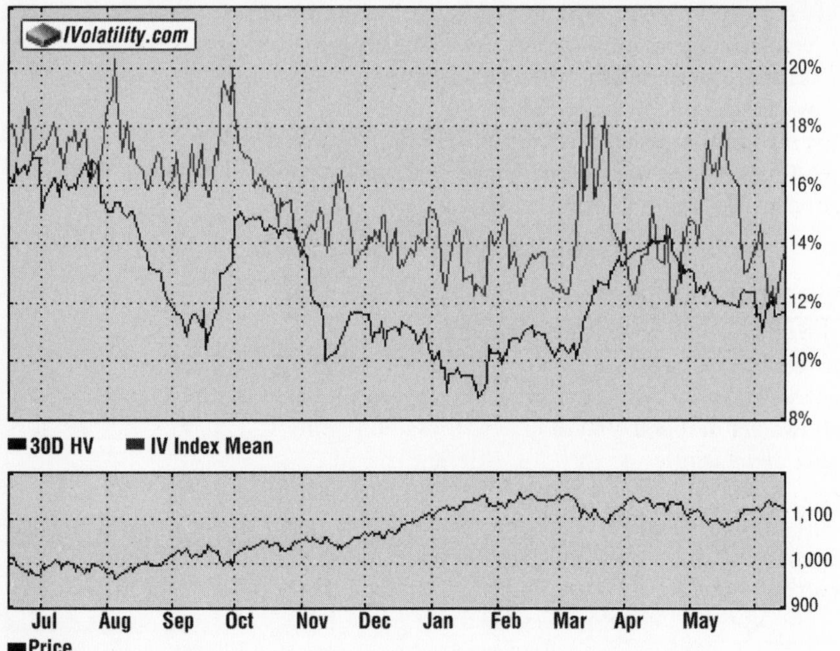

FIGURE 12.2 Historical Volatility and IVIndex vs Price for S&P 500
Data source: Ivolatility.com.

redefine a country's economic policy. Uncertainty over the election results causes options prices (implied volatility) to increase;

- *Market (demand/supply) liquidity:* volatility prices are determined by demand and supply as with other assets. If supply exceeds demand the prices go down and vice versa. In other words, if market takers (clients) sell volatility (options), the implied volatility goes down, even if market makers expect an increase in volatility;
- *Change in technical levels:* if an important price level on a historical chart of the underlying asset prices[1] is broken, the market expects a volatile follow through. The technical levels are the underlying asset price levels. They can be defined by any method of technical analysis: trendlines, support/resistances, previous historical highs/lows, that is, anything the market considers to be significant;
- *On which day of the week the expiration falls:* an option loses value each day of the week (because of the premium amortization, *theta*, see Chapter 14). Those expiring on Monday lose a three-day amortization (weekend and Monday). Therefore, options expiring on Friday or Tuesday should be more expensive in volatility terms than those expir-

ing on Monday, since you pay for less wasted time (weekend). The volatility premium for options expiring on days other than Monday reflects a better chance of making money.

Average *historical implied volatility* differs depending on an underlying asset. One to three month implied volatilities of USD/CHF is around 11%, of copper—25%, on DJ Index—18%.

VOLATILITY CURVE

If we draw a line connecting implied volatilities of ATM options of different periods, we will get the *volatility curve*. The example in Figure 12.3 shows the implied volatility curve of ATM options on S&P 500 futures

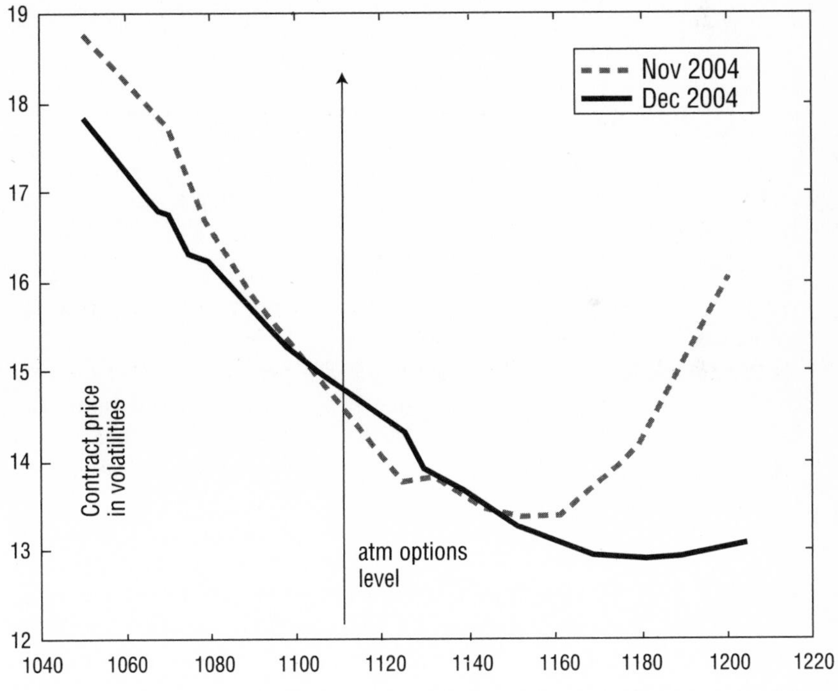

FIGURE 12.3 Implied Volatility Curve
Data source: Ivolatility.com.

TABLE 12.1 Volatility of S&P Options Expiring in November, December and June

27 Oct 04	Nov 2004		Dec 2004		Jul 2005	
Strike	Put	Call	Put	Call	Put	Call
1050	18.8	14.89	17.86	16.92	17.37	17.09
1060	18.22	15.23	17.25	16.49		
1070	17.68	15.58	16.7	16		
1075	17	15.42	16.34	15.83	16.67	16.39
1080	16.48	15.26	16.16	15.58		
1100	15.16	14.31	15.15	14.62	15.99	15.74
1125	13.76	13.6	14.29	13.59	15.35	15.11
1130	13.82	13.22	13.9	13.49		
1135	13.71	12.91	13.74	13.29		
1140	13.5	12.85	13.6	13.07		
1150	13.35	12.43	13.3	12.59	14.75	14.5
1155	13.35	12.39	13.21	12.66		
1160	13.37	12.36	13.08	12.52		
1165	13.58	12.2	12.98	12.37		
1170			12.91	12.25		
1175	13.96	12.59	12.9	12.13	14.18	13.95
1180	14.18	12.63	12.88	12.12		
1190			12.91	11.96		
1200	16.06	13.6	13.03	12.02	13.7	13.43
1205			13.09	12.02		

when futures with the September expiry were trading at 1,125.00. (See Table 12.1.)

APPROXIMATE FORMULA FOR VOLATILITY CALCULATION

Daily implied volatility may be estimated based on the following formula:

$$\sigma = D \times 16, \text{ where}$$

σ is an annualized volatility;

D is a ratio between an expected daily[2] high/low range and a price of an underlying;

16 is the square root of the average number of working days per year.[3]

For example, you expect EUR/USD to move 20 pips a day, and the current spot is 0.2000. What is the daily implied volatility? $(0.0020/0.2000) \times 16 = 0.16$. In this case, you expect implied volatility to be around 16%.

Conversely, if your broker tells you that the implied volatility of the USD/JPY is 8% while the spot is 110.00, that means that the market assumes a daily range of 55 pips $(0.08^{*} \times 110.00)/16$.[4]

The formula was devised to calculate historical volatility, based on daily *closing prices*.[5] However, traders apply this formula using intraday high/low prices to determine the correctness of the short-term options'[6] prices (implied volatility). Based on their individual forecasts of intraday price behavior, they calculate implied volatility and compare the result with the current implied volatility prices.

SIMPLIFIED FORMULA FOR ATM OPTION PREMIUM CALCULATION

An approximate price of a European at-the-money option (using a flat forward curve) may be calculated with the following formula:

$$0.4 \times \text{strike price} \times \sqrt{365/N} \times \text{volatility}$$

For example, if the strike price is 50; volatility is 14%, and time to expiration is 65 days; the option premium equals $0.4 \times 50 \times \sqrt{65/365}$[7] $\times 0.14 = 1.18$.

QUESTIONS

1. Today is October 1; you expect that on October 15 the Fed might cut short-term rates.
   a. For which period is the volatility higher 10 days, or 20 days?
   b. If they are the same, what kind of spread would you do?
2. On the average, would you expect implied volatilities of December to be higher than those of January?
3. If spot is at 1.4000 and the average high/low range of previous days is around 140 pips, what implied volatility would you pay for an ATM option?
4. If implied volatility is 26%, and cash is trading around 12,000, which intraday range is assumed?

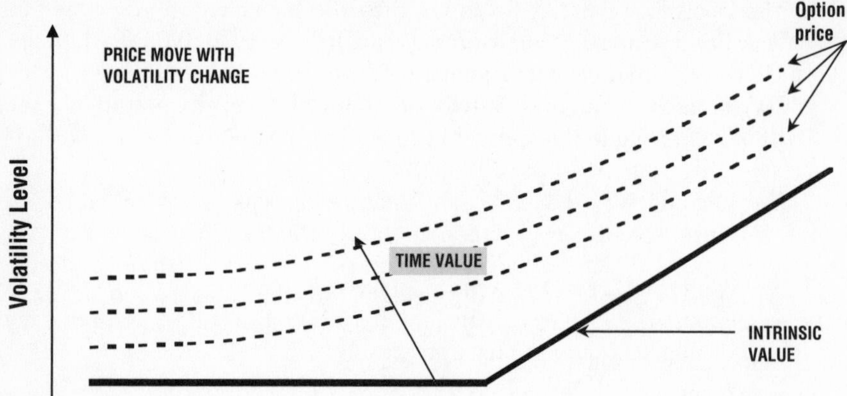

FIGURE 12.4 Dependence of Time Value and Option Price on Volatility Changes

5. On December 1, you expected spot to remain in a narrow range for two weeks (until December 15) and then to go sharply up. What kind of spread would you do, if
   a. Two-week volatility[8] was cheap (7%), one-month more expensive (8%) (expiration date December 30), and two-month the most expensive (10%) (after the New Year holiday markets are more volatile)?
   b. Two-week volatility was trading at 12%, one-month was trading at 11%?
6. If historical volatility is very low and implied is very high,
   a. What might it mean?
   b. Is there a trading opportunity?
7. Try to explain the correlation between the option price (and its components) and the volatility level shown in Figure 12.4.

ANSWERS

1. a. 20 days
   b. buy the 20-day option, sell the 10-day one

2. The December volatility is lower than the January one. After the New Year holiday markets are more volatile: in December, there are holidays. Moreover, market participants tend to have fiscal year-end, which makes them very conservative. As a result, they do not trade much while expecting the new fiscal year.

3. 16%: $(0.014/1.4000) \times 16 = 16\%$

4. 195 pips: $(12{,}000 \times 0.26)/16$

5. We would buy a January option, since we do not expect high volatility in December, but expect it in January. Short December options would help to finance long January options.
   a. We should sell a one-month and buy a two-month option because one-month volatility is more expensive than the two-week one;
   b. We should do a two-week–two-month spread, buying two-month and selling two-week. In the second case the market gives us an opportunity to sell more profitably the two-week option. Although premium of a one-month option is more expensive than of the two-week one, but we'd rather sell the second two-week option on expiration of the first one since the total premium of two sequential two-week options is likely to be higher than the one-month option's premium.

6. a. The market might be:
      - expecting important news (e.g., a political event or economic release).
      - illiquid: there is high demand for options and no supply.
   b. Remember our example with the ring? If implied volatility is higher than historical volatility, it means that one portion of the ring is overpriced. In some situations, you can sell it:
      - If the market trades in a range, you can sell a strangle, and have a high chance of collecting the entire premium upon expiration.
      - If the market is trending, you will take a spot position in the direction of the trend and sell overvalued options.
      - You can enter a proportional credit spread. Credit is the amount that the seller receives. If the premium of the options you sell is larger than that of options you buy, the difference between the prices (the credit) will be your profit.

7. The chart shows that the greater is volatility, the higher is time value and an option's price. When volatility falls to zero, the option price is theoretically equal to its intrinsic value.

An increase in volatility causes premium appreciation because it increases probability that the option will end up in-the-money. Therefore, the higher the volatility, the greater the chance that the option will make money. In Chapter 17 on dynamic hedging of delta-neutral option positions, you will learn another explanation of the fact that a volatility increase causes a premium increase: the higher the volatility, the more the option's owner can make by rehedging the option.

CHAPTER 13
Vega

Vega is crucial to options because it helps to manage exposure to implied volatility. This Greek will once again demonstrate that there is no free lunch in options. Two positions with the same value would have some parameters better and others worse. In other words, for the same value you cannot get the absolutely optimal position because by improving one Greek you will increase exposure to another one.

BASIC CHARACTERISTICS OF VEGA

Vega measures *sensitivity of* option *prices to changes* in volatility. That is, as mentioned before, vega and delta are like sister and brother. One measures sensitivity of the premium to spot, while the other to volatility.

Vega is expressed in percents or basis points. An option with 0.04% vega will gain 0.04% of its price, if the volatility increases by one full percentage point. For instance, if you have bought an option with $1 million notional amount for $1,000, and its vega is 0.0025%, then, if the volatility increases by 1%, it will cost $1,025.

SHORT AND LONG VEGA POSITIONS

If a position makes money when volatility increases, it is referred to in market slang as a *long vega position.* If its value falls with an increase in volatility, it is called *short vega.*

BEHAVIOR OF VEGA

Long-term options are not that sensitive to price changes of an underlying asset, and the time decay of their premium is very small. However, they are very dependent on volatility changes. Their vega is higher in absolute terms than vega of short-term options (e.g., ATM options with the same face value but with different expiration).

The reverse is true for short-term options. Prices of short-term options are less sensitive to changes in volatility than those of long-term options; in other words, they have smaller vega. Therefore, volatility changes have a relatively minor impact on their value.

Buyers of options benefit when volatility rises. Sellers of options (vega sellers) benefit when volatility falls.

ATM options have higher vega than ITM and OTM ones. The questions will discuss in depth the relative vegas of options with different maturities and deltas.

QUESTIONS

1. Based on Table 13.1, how will the price of the one-week 20% option change when the volatility increases by 1%?
2. Based on Tables 13.1 and 13.2, what is going to be the price of three-week 50-delta option, if the volatility goes down by 0.5%?

TABLE 13.1 Premium of EUR/USD Options Priced at 20% Volatilities

Delta	1 Week	3 Weeks	3 Months	1 Year
10%	0.13%	0.23%	0.48%	0.99%
20%	0.31%	0.54%	1.15%	2.39%
30%	0.53%	0.93%	1.98%	4.19%
40%	0.80%	1.40%	3.02%	6.50%
50%	1.12%	1.97%	4.33%	9.70%

TABLE 13.2 Vega of EUR/USD Options Priced at 20% Volatilities

Delta	1 Week	3 Weeks	3 Months	1 Year
10%	+0.025%	+0.043%	+0.091%	+0.18%
20%	+0.039%	+0.068%	+0.14%	+0.26%
30%	+0.048%	+0.084%	+0.18%	+0.35%
40%	+0.054%	+0.093%	+0.19%	+0.38%
50%	+0.055%	+0.095%	+0.20%	+0.39%

3. What is the relationship between vegas of 50-delta and 20-delta options expiring in:
   - one week,
   - three weeks,
   - one year.
4. What is the quantitative relationship between premiums of 50-delta and 20-delta options expiring in:
   - one week,
   - three weeks,
   - one year.
5. What conclusion can you make about the relationship of premiums and vegas based on Questions 3 and 4?
6. What is the relationship between vegas of 50-delta options expiring in:
   - one week and three weeks,
   - three weeks and three months,
   - three months and one year.
7. What is the relationship between premiums of 50-delta options expiring in:
   - one week and three weeks,
   - three weeks and three months,
   - three months and one year.
8. What conclusion can you make about the relationship of premium and vega in the Questions 6 and 7?
9. Is it cheaper to buy a one-year ATM option or to buy a three-month ATM option and roll it four times?
10. The volatility is very high, and you expect it to fall sharply. Your client wants to buy and is choosing between two-month and four-month options. Which alternative is cheaper?
11. You are prepared to pay $2 for a 50-delta three-week option. Which two options with different expirations but with the same delta can you buy with $2?
12. Please find three maturity/delta combinations where premium doubles. (For instance, one can buy two one-week 50-delta options for the price of one 3-week option.)

ANSWERS

1. 0.349 = 0.31 + 0.039
2. 1.9225 = 1.97 – (0.095/2)
3. around 1.4 throughout the example
4. around 3.6–4.0
5. Vega:
   - the relationship of vegas of 50- and 20-delta options is stable throughout all maturities;
   - vega of long-term options is higher. While deltas are related 50/20 (2.5), vegas are related around 1.4, that is, interdelta and intervega relationships are different.

   Premium of 50-delta options is approximately double that of 20-delta for all maturities.
6. 57, 47, 51
7. 56, 45, 44
8. The ratio fluctuates around 2:1; long-term options have higher premium and vega, that is, are more susceptible to fluctuations in volatility prices.
9. Remember the relationship of vegas and premiums of the same delta options with different maturities? The premium of one one-year option is roughly equal to that of two rolls of three-month options. Therefore, one one-year option is cheaper than four three-month rolls.
10. Buy the two-month option, because it is less sensitive to volatility decreases.
11. Two one-week options.
12. One-week: 10–30 deltas, 30-delta: three-week–three-month maturity, 10-delta: three-month–one-year maturity.

CHAPTER 14

Theta

"Nothing is certain but death and taxes" and an option's time decay. The extent to which an option's premium decreases when the expiration date approaches is reflected by theta. Although the concept sounds simple, there are significant misconceptions one has to keep in mind.

BASIC CHARACTERISTICS OF THETA

The option premium is comprised of *time value* and *intrinsic value.* Only in-the-money options have intrinsic value. Should the ITM option's owner exercise it immediately, *intrinsic value* is what he will collect.

Time value is the option's premium in excess of its intrinsic portion. As the time to expiration decreases, time value amortizes.[1] A portion of the time value amortized daily is *Theta.*[2] In other words, theta measures the sensitivity of the *time value portion of option premium* to time. For instance, if an OTM option price is 10 and theta is 2, overnight it will lose two ticks and will be worth 8 tomorrow.

Premiums of **at-the-money** *options with different maturities correlate with each other through the square root of annualized time left to expiration,*[3] assuming flat volatility and forward curves (similar interest rates of both currencies). For instance, a 10-day option premium relates to a 1-year option premium as $\sqrt{10/365}$.

Based on these characteristics, let's make some simple calculations. Knowing the 365-day option premium, we can find out premiums of other options with different expiration dates (assuming flat volatility and swap curves). Moreover, theta levels of these options will be inversely correlated to the premiums' ratio. For instance, if the one-year (365 days) option's premium equals 215 (see Table 14.1), the one-month (33 days[4]) option premium should be $215 \times \sqrt{33/365} = 64.64$. The reverse is true for the theta calculation, the one-month (33 days) option theta should be 0.3 $\sqrt{365/33} = 0.998$.

TABLE 14.1 Premium and Theta of ATM Options with Different Expiration Dates Calculated for CHF/USD Spot –0.5405; Forward = Spot = 0.5405; Volatility = 10%

Maturity Left	Days to Expiration	Premium (CHF to USD Face Value)	Theta
1 week	7	30	–2.1
2 weeks	14	42	1.5
3 weeks	21	51	–1.2
1 month	33	65	–1
2 months	63	89	–0.7
3 months	92	108	–0.6
4 months	125	126	–0.5
5 months	153	139	–0.5
6 months	182	152	–0.4
7 months	214	165	–0.4
8 months	245	176	–0.4
9 months	273	186	–0.3
10 months	306	197	–0.3
11 months	336	207	–0.3
1 year	365	215	–0.3

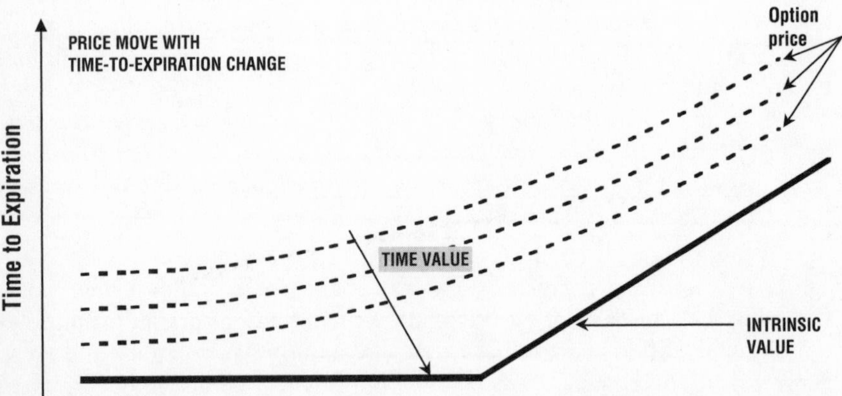

FIGURE 14.1 Time Value and Option Price Changes as Time Remaining until the Expiration Elapses

Some observations regarding Figure 14.2:

1. The curve is shaped in the form of the square root function.
2. One can conclude, as in case with vega, that:
   - a one-week *ATM* option on the average loses its time value twice as rapidly as a one-month ATM option (if both are calculated using the same volatility); the similar trend is observed in other pairs' behavior: one-month–three-month and three-month–one-year.
   - a one-year option will lose only half of its value during the first nine months of its existence.

   Now that we are aware of the annualized square root time function, we can explain the observation for at-the-money options priced on flat volatility and forward curves: *the premium is half of the period four times shorter because* $\sqrt{1/4} = 1/2$. Since 365/4 = 91, a one-year option premium is equal to premium of the double-face-value option expiring in 91 days.
3. *Even if an option is expensive it doesn't mean that it will lose its time value rapidly.* The correlation between theta and maturity is more important. *The shorter the option's maturity, the higher is the premium's decay.* For instance, if you spend $10,000 on a $1 one-week ATM option and $1 one-month ATM option. The one-week option has higher theta, and therefore it will lose its value faster. At the end of the week, the value of the one-week option will be 0, while the one-month option will preserve its value. *The option's maturity is as important a factor for theta determination as the amount of premium.*

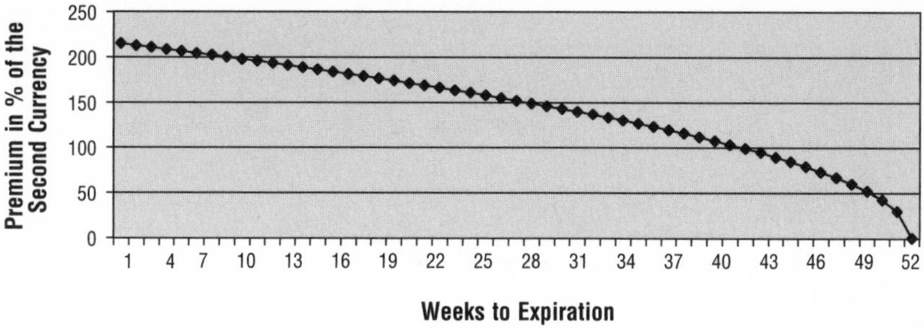

FIGURE 14.2 ATM Options Premium Calculated by Multiplying One-Year Option Premium by $\sqrt{(maturity)/365}$

THETA BEHAVIOR OF OPTIONS WITH DIFFERENT DELTAS

The decreasing time value curves on Figure 14.3 depict the behavior of at-the-money options. Options with deltas other than 50% lose value in their own particular ways. For instance, amortization of short-term 25-delta options looks more like a straight line. Time value decay of deep in-the-money (more than 80% delta) or far-out-of-the-money (less than 20% delta) options may well decelerate with expiration approaching.

The following tables and figures show the impact of time to expiration changes on the deltas and premiums of options. To make the demonstration more effective, the options' strike prices are fixed till expiration. Spot is also fixed.

Table 14.2 is very useful for experts since none of the other option books known to the author focus on nuances of behavior of out-of-the-money options.

Notice the following in Table 14.3 and Figure 14.4:

1. A 20-delta option loses more than half of its value in the beginning of its life. Behavior of theta of a 30-delta option is closer to that of an ATM option, that is, loss of its value accelerates as the expiration date approaches! In other words, *the dynamics of time value loss of different delta options are different.* Moreover, *the options that are cheapest and most recommended by salespeople, in fact, lose their value the fastest.*
2. In absolute terms, time decay of low delta (or high delta) options is lower than that of ATM options. For instance, theta of a one-week 25%-delta put option is 3.1 while theta of a one-week 50%-delta put option is 3.9.

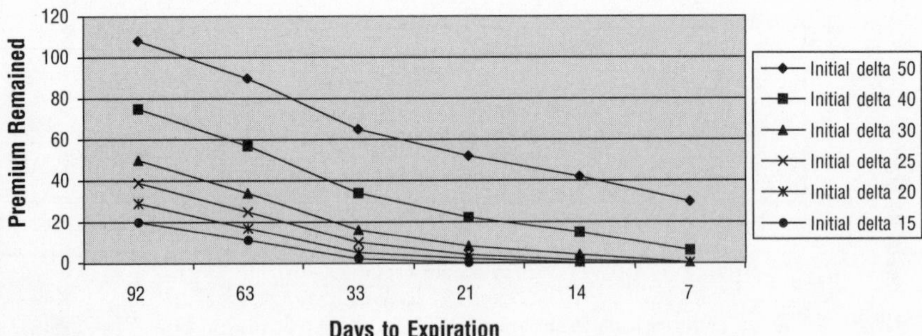

FIGURE 14.3 Premium Behavior of Options with Initially Fixed Delta as Option Approaches Expiration

TABLE 14.2 Premium Behavior of Options with Different Deltas as Option Approaches Expiration

Spot CHF/USD –0.5405; Forward = Spot = 0.5405; Volatility = 10%							
Initial Delta (%)	Initial Strike Price	Initial Premium	Premium Left on Last:				
		92 Days	63 Days	33 Days	21 Days	14 Days	7 Days
51	5405	108	90	65	52	42	30
40	5482	75	57	34	22	15	6
30	5557	50	34	16	8	4	0
25	5599	39	25	10	4	1	0
20	5646	29	17	5	2	0	0
15	5701	20	11	2	0	0	0

TABLE 14.3 Delta Behavior of Options with Different Initial Deltas on Expiration Spot CHF/USD –0.5405; Forward = Spot = 0.5405; Volatility = 10%

Initial Strike Price	Initial Delta (%)	Delta Days Remaining Until Expiration				
	92 Days	63 Days	33 Days	21 Days	14 Days	7 Days
5405	51	51	51	51	51	50
5482	40	38	33	28	24	16
5557	30	26	18	13	8	2
5599	25	20	12	7	4	1
5646	20	15	8	4	1	0
5701	15	10	4	1	0	

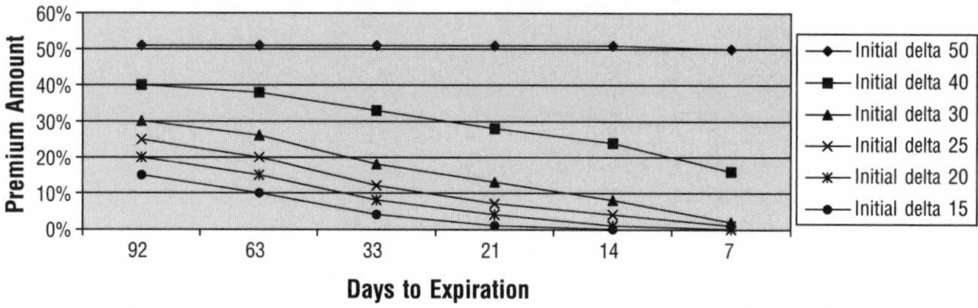

FIGURE 14.4 Delta Behavior of Options Priced at Constant Spot as Option Gets Closer to Expiration

Thus, if you buy an ATM option with $1 million *face value*, its theta will be higher (greater time decay) in absolute terms than that of an out-of-the-money (or in-the-money) option with the same ($1 million) face value.

However, if *you* invest *equally in a low-delta and an ATM option, the first ones lose value faster!* For instance, if you spent $1 million on premium (rather than buy a $1 million face value option) to purchase an ATM option, you will lose *less* time value than if you buy $1 million worth of OTM options. *Notice, in the first case you buy equal face value of options, while in the second one you have equal investment (different face value) of options.*[5]

In the above mentioned example, you buy $2 million face of a 25-delta option for $1 million, and lose overnight 3.1 × 2. At the same time, if you buy $1 million of 50-delta option for $1 million, it loses 3.9% overnight. Therefore, the value of your investment in lower-delta options falls faster, although the size of investments is the same.

Intuitively, it makes sense because one can buy a greater face value of OTM options than of ATM options! For greater leverage (chance to make money), you pay higher decay. Therefore, if you (a) have to chose between investing in $1 million in an ATM option or in $2 million face of a 25-delta option and (b) you are concerned with value preservation, you will buy $1 million of the ATM, giving up the leverage of a $2 million position in order to preserve value.

Another observation: since low-delta options lose their delta quickly, it's more difficult to make money with them[6] on position rehedging.[7]

THETA BEHAVIOR OF IN- AND OUT-OF-THE-MONEY OPTIONS

Time decay of ITM and OTM options with the same expiration date and the same strike should be the same.[8] Let's review once again the logic behind this statement.

1. A delta-hedged 1.4000 call has the same risk/reward profile as delta hedged 1.4000 put.
2. If the risk/reward of both positions is the same, you would pay the same amount of *time value* for both options (although the premiums will be different, because the premium of ITM includes intrinsic value).
3. Since theta shows amortization of time value (not of intrinsic value), thetas of both options will be the same.

FORWARD RATE IMPACT ON THETA

Most option-pricing software programs show time decay rather than theta. That is, they add up theta and premium/discount of the forward differential (swap).[9] For instance, if the USD interest rates are higher than those of JPY, to hedge a long put, one purchases USD (selling JPY). Since the dollar rate is higher, the hedge earns financing. Thus, the put's price should be higher (as well as theta) to compensate for the gain on financing. The reverse is true for the long hedged call position.

QUESTIONS

1. a. Is it cheaper to buy \$1 of a one-month ATM option or twice in a row \$1 of a one-week option (one after expiration of the other)?
   b. What part of its value will a one-month ATM option lose in the last week of its life?
2. You bought a \$1 million face value of a three-month ATM option. Assuming that the volatility and interest rate swap curves are flat,
   a. What face value of a one-month ATM option do you need to sell to receive equal premium?
   b. What will be the theta of this position? (Use the theta of the three-month option as an initial unit of price.)
   c. What is the vega of this position?
3. Your client bought \$10 million of a 1.4600 USD put (CHF call) and bought \$5 million on a hedge.
   a. If instead he bought \$10 million of USD call and sold \$5 million on a hedge, would the behavior of his position change?
   b. Considering the risk/reward profile of both positions, what would you expect the P&L and theta to be?
   c. Since the USD interest rates are higher than that of the CHF, he will gain on financing of the first position. Considering the risk/reward profile, do you think that the thetas should be different?
4. The client is buying an option that will cost him \$1 million. What maturity and delta should he choose if he wants to end up with a position that will:
   a. hold value well and
   b. have high leverage.

5. If the premium of an ATM option expiring in 306 days equals 197, what is the premium of an ATM option expiring in 182 days?

6. If the theta of the option expiring in 63 days equals –0.7, what is the theta of the option expiring in 153 days?

ANSWERS

1. a. Should be approximately the same;
   b. It should lose about 50% in the last week!

2. a. 2 million;
   b. Twice as much;
   c. The same.

3. a. The same.
   b. The same, because the same risk/reward should carry the same costs.
   c. Yes. The theta of the position that gains on financing should be greater. Otherwise, there is an arbitrage, where two positions providing the same risk/reward differ in the hedge's financing costs (also called cost-of-carry).

4. a. Longer maturity, closer to ATM;
   b. Shorter maturity, lower delta (OTM)

5. 151.92: $197 \times \sqrt{182/306}$

6. 0.45: $(-0.7)/\sqrt{153/63}$

CHAPTER 15

Gamma

Gamma is an acceleration of premium change. Options with the highest acceleration are short-term ones. They have the highest time decay. The nature of options seems to say: "Since short-term options have such a short time to live, they should have their chance to make money on an accelerated pace."

BASIC CHARACTERISTICS OF GAMMA

We would like to bring back the example discussed before. Imagine that you are driving at 30 miles (delta) an hour. Then you speed up to 35 miles an hour. If, *in option terms*, your *speed* (change of distance in time) is delta, then the five-mile-an-hour acceleration (from 30 to 35 miles an hour) *is gamma*. Gamma is an *acceleration of delta* (acceleration of the premium's change) as an underlying asset price changes. In other words, it is the second derivative of an option premium in respect to an underlying asset price.

Let's once again go over these concepts. Delta shows the change in an option price in respect to the price change of an underlying asset: it measures a speed of the option price changes per one-point move of an underlying asset price. The same option has different delta at different underlying asset price levels. Gamma measures the speed at which delta changes as the price of the underlying asset changes. In other words, gamma shows the extent of delta change with a one-point change in the spot/cash price.

In the absence of gamma, on a two-point underlying asset move an option's premium would gain twice as much as on a one-point move. But with gamma, an option that appreciated 10% on the *first* one-point spot move, will appreciate 25% on the *second* one-point move. In this example the appreciation accelerates. Gamma on the second portion of the move is (25 – 10)/10 = 1.5.

Gamma is measured in percentage points or in basis points. If a 50-delta option has 10%-gamma, it will have 49/51 delta if the spot changes by 10 pips (see Table 15.1).

PRACTICAL ASPECTS OF GAMMA

1. Short-term options have higher gamma than long-term ones.
2. At-the-money options have the highest gamma. The further the delta from 50% (ATM), the lower the gamma of an option. For instance, a 75-delta and a 25-delta option have similar gammas.
3. Price changes of the underlying asset have greater effect on the premium of higher-gamma options.
4. That is why, when an underlying asset price moves, the premiums of long-term options change like the delta-equivalent (or spot), because they have very low gamma.
5. Two options with equal deltas but different gammas will behave differently: the premium of an option with higher gamma will increase or decrease faster than that of a lower gamma option (if compared within one day and priced at similar volatility).
6. *The higher the gamma*, that is, the higher the probability of the option's price increase, if the market moves in your direction, *the more you have to pay for it* in time decay (higher theta). Therefore, *theta of an option rises with an increase of its gamma.* In other words, if your position gains value quickly, it also loses value quickly due to time decay, if the market move favorable to you does not occur immediately.

The points 2–6 are demonstrated in Table 15.2.

SHORT AND LONG GAMMA POSITIONS

A hedged position is called *long gamma* if it makes money with the spot move, or *short gamma* if it loses money with the spot move. The phrase "it

TABLE 15.1 Gamma of USD/CHF Options with Different Maturities and Deltas (%)

Delta/Maturity	1 Week	1 Month	3 Months	1 Year
20	+28.15	+8.81	+5.16	+2.58
30	+34.92	+10.91	+6.38	+3.15
50	+39.96	+12.37	+7.14	+3.37

TABLE 15.2 Gamma and Theta of USD/CHF Options with Different Maturities and Deltas

Delta/Maturity		1 Week	1 Month	3 Months	1 Year
20%	gamma	+28.15%	+8.81%	+5.16%	+2.58%
	theta	−6.80	−2.09	−1.21	−0.58
30%	gamma	+34.92%	+10.91%	+6.38%	+3.15%
	theta	−8.85	−2.59	−1.49	−0.70
50%	gamma	+39.96%	+12.37%	+7.14%	+3.37%
	theta	−10.4	−2.93	−1.65	−0.69

makes money with the spot move" implies movement in any direction. **That assumes a hedged position.**

QUESTIONS

Let's compare the behavior of delta and gamma of a one-week ATM call and a one-year ATM call. The face value of both is $1,000,000. Note the following points with regard to Table 15.3:

a. Delta's sign means that a hedge against a long call is to be sold to make a position "delta-neutral." If spot falls, the call becomes more OTM. In this case, you should buy back a portion of the hedge sold beforehand, as the option delta falls.

b. The plus sign in gamma's position means that you have bought an option.

TABLE 15.3 USD/CHF Delta Position

Spot	Delta	Gamma	P&L	Delta	Gamma	P&L
	One-Week ATM Option			One-Year ATM Option		
1.4130	$−942,015	$+103,826	$+14,756	$−575,209	$+34,156	$+10,786
1.4202	$−870,090	$+162,134	$+10,132	$−554,931	$+34,324	$ +7,914
1.4274	$−768,433	$+221,993	$ +5,972	$−534,792	$+34,419	$ +5,159
1.4346	$−640,730	$+267,032	$ +2,413	$−514,825	$+34,440	$ +2,518
1.4418	$−495,000	$+282,740	*$ −446*	$−495,000	$+34,390	*$ −10*
1.4491	$−358,802	$+264,020	$ −2,580	$−475,275	$+34,268	$ −2,460
1.4563	$−236,897	$+217,833	$ −4,048	$−456,027	$+34,078	$ −4,768
1.4635	$−142,715	$+159,090	$ −4,974	$−437,078	$+33,822	$ −6,970
1.4707	$ −78,131	$+103,034	$ −5,505	$−418,457	$+33,501	$ −9,069

c. Gamma doesn't completely explain changes in delta! (–495,000 –282,740) is not equal to –640,730, and (–495,000 + 282,740) is not equal to –358,802! The discrepancy comes from *gamma/theta effect*. This causes an option to lose part of its value overnight, and its gamma rises or falls as well.

d. Pricing software can evaluate delta for today or for tomorrow! How can we find out what kind of report is presented: today's or tomorrow's? Let's turn to the central line of the table:

1.4418	$–495,000	$+282,740	$–446

It shows that the calculation includes time decay: if spot remains at the same level, the position loses $446 (time decay). That means that we deal with a report for the future. If the decay was equal to zero, it would mean that the calculation was done for today. Then, the gamma/theta effect would equal 0, and therefore delta + gamma at any spot would constitute the new delta.[1]

1. Which of the two options gains delta faster (has higher gamma) when the spot goes up—the one-week one or the one-year one?
2. Considering 1.4418 is the strike the one-week option,
   a. what is theta of this option?
   b. what happens with gamma as the spot moves away from the center of the range?
   c. what could you say about gamma at 1.4707 and 1.4130? Which of the points in the previous discussion does this example illustrate?
3. If the spot remains at 1.4418 during one day the one-week option will lose $446 while the one-year option will lose only $10. These are time decays of the options. Which of the points above does this example illustrate?
4. For which of the two positions does the P&L behave more like the spot?
5. If the spot remains at 1.4418 during one day, what will happen to the one-week option's gamma? What will happen to its theta (time decay)?
6. Taking into account that the premium of the one-year option is much higher than that of the one-week option, how does a change of the time left to expiration influence the gammas of the options?
7. Taking into account the theta discussion in Chapter 14,
   a. how will gamma of the one-year option change in nine months?
   b. what will happen to its vega?
   c. what will happen to its theta?

8. If you have a long hedged option position,
   a. is the one-year option better described as a long gamma position or a long vega one?
   b. is the one-week option better described as a long gamma position or long vega one?

9. If your position is called "long gamma/short vega,"
   a. options of which maturities are you long and short?
   b. when will you take such a position?

10. If your position is called "long vega/short gamma,"
   a. options of which maturities are you long and short?
   b. when will you take such a position?

ANSWERS

1. one-week

2. a. It loses $446, if the spot remains at the same level for one day;
   b. It falls;
   c. Gamma falls almost symmetrically as the option goes father from the at-the-money level and moves toward out-of-/in-the-money.

3. Higher-gamma options lose time decay faster.

4. The one-year option's gamma is very low; therefore, the delta doesn't change much and the P/L of the slowly changing delta looks like the P/L of the spot.

5. Will increase; will increase correspondingly.

6. The longer the maturity, the smaller the gamma. Delta changes of the one-year option are very small, while the one-week's delta changes are very fast.

7. a. It will double, if the option is still ATM;
   b. It will become twice smaller, if the option is still ATM;
   c. It will double, if the option is still ATM.

8. a. Long vega;
   b. Long gamma.

9. a. Long position in short-term options, short position in long-term options;
   b. This position is useful when you expect significant volatility in the short term (e.g., before elections) or within a price range.
10. a. Long position in long-term options, short position in short-term options.
    b. You enter such a position when the market is in a narrow range. The short-term options will lose time decay in your favor, while the long-term ones will make money after the market breaks the range at a later date.

CHAPTER 16

Impact of Interest Rates on Options Pricing and Strategies

Theory is often difficult to comprehend on the first try. Let's go over some key concepts again before moving into specifics of day-to-day trading.

ADDITIONAL ASPECTS OF THE OPTION ARBITRAGE FORMULA

In the previous discussion of the put/call parity we used a simplified version of the formula. Let's now substitute spot prices for forward ones to obtain the complete formula:

$$\text{Call}(K) - \text{Put}(K) = \text{Forward}^1 - K(^2)$$

Call is the value of a call,

Put is the value of a put,

Forward is the value of a forward on an underlying asset which for

- equities are equal to a *current price of the asset ± financing cost ± dividends*;
- currencies (FX) are equal to a *current price of the asset ± forward differential*;

K is the strike price for a call and a put.

Let's test the formula on the 1.0000 EUR/USD call and put on expiration day.

At expiration, the EUR/USD spot may be higher than 1.0000 (K), lower than 1.0000 or at 1.0000:

- *EUR/USD is higher (at 1.0250):*
  the value of the 1.0000 call is equal to its intrinsic value of 2.5 cents, while the 1.0000 put option expires. Thus, 2.5 cents (the call value)

minus zero (the put value) should be equal to *F* minus *K* (1.0250 – 1.0000) and it is.

- *EUR/USD is lower (at 0.9850):*
  the value of the call is zero, while the put's value is equal to its intrinsic value of 1.5 cents.

  Thus, *C* (zero) minus *P* (1.5 cents) should be equal to 0.9850 minus 1.0000. The arbitrage formula is confirmed once again.
- *EUR/USD is at 1.0000:*
  both options expire. The left side of the equation (zero minus zero) equals the right side of 1.0000 minus 1.0000.

Two Important Remarks

1. In all these calculations, we buy and sell the forward contract in the amount equal to the option's face value[3] and not to the hedge ratio (delta)!
2. The put/call parity works not only at expiration, but at any time prior to it as well.

SYNTHETIC POSITIONS[4]

As we saw in Chapter 4, the relationship of call and put prices established by the put/call parity permits traders to combine options and forwards in creating *synthetic positions.*

Parity also was the basis for the argument that the time value part of premium of call and put with the same strike must be equal. If they are not, there is an opportunity for arbitrage. Let's return to the USD/CHF example: with spot at 1.4500, the price of a two-month 1.4600 USD put is 150 CHF pips. Since the intrinsic value of the option is 100 pips, the time value of the option should be 50 pips.

If the forward differential between currencies is equal to 0, the time values of an OTM call and an ITM put with the same strike and maturity should be equal. Thus, if the call's price is less than 50 pips, there is an arbitrage opportunity. One can

- sell the 1.4600 put and USD/CHF forward and
- simultaneously buy the 1.4600 call.

The combination of the long 1.4600 call and short forward USD/CHF is equivalent to the synthetic long 1.4600 put. Since the call was underpriced, you would buy it. A difference between the correctly estimated time value of the put (fair) you sold and the call you bought would be an arbitrage (riskless) profit.

A great number of other combinations can be used to create synthetic positions.

short forward + short put = synthetic short call

short forward + long call = synthetic long put

long forward + short call = synthetic short put

It is important to remember that:

- The formula is intended for ATM options (50-delta) and
- The strikes of options are at the forward level.

Synthetic Positions with a Forward Differential[5] Not Equal to 0

Let's consider how interest rates influence options pricing.

In the FX market, the forward rate determines the strike level of the at-the-money option.[6] When we used the put/call parity without taking into account the interest rates we said that:

long call (strike = spot) = long put (strike = spot) + *long spot*

In other words,

long spot = long call (strike = spot) + short put (strike = spot)

The following formula reflects different interest rates:

long forward = long call (*k* = forward) + short put (*k* = forward),

where

forward – strike price = spot ± forward differential[7]

Forward differential doesn't influence the ATM options premium, but it changes the level of the ATM strike.[8]

Example

If the two-month USD/CHF forward is (–30 pips), it means that the interest rates in the U.S. are higher than in Switzerland. Therefore, to keep the parity and prevent arbitrage, the strike of an ATM call CHF (put USD) should be 30 pips lower.[9]

IMPACT OF FORWARD RATE CHANGES ON OPTION DELTA

The forward differential initially determines the price at which the ATM option has its strike. During any option's life, changes in forward differential move options in- or out-of-the-money. The forward differential changes because of time and forward curve alteration.

Example

Let's consider a one-year USD/JPY option. The USD interest rates are higher than those of the JPY; that is, the dollar is quoted at discount. Thus, forward differential is negative. That, in its turn, means that the *forward* USD/JPY rate will be lower than the *spot*.

A forward dealer will quote you a one-year forward –500/–499 (since –500 is "cheaper" than –499—this is a bid of a market maker). Therefore, if the spot trades at 110.00, a one-year at-the-money (forward) option will have a strike at 105.00.

Let's suppose the spot stays at 100.00 for six months. What will the forward differential be by that time? –500/2 = –250. It means that after the six months the forward rate increased by 250 pips. Now a six-month ATM option would have a strike of 107.50. Hence, the 105.00 call is 250 pips in-the-money!

This phenomenon has a number of applications. For instance, if you buy a 40-delta USD call, your strike is at the current *spot* level, while the strike of 40-delta put is almost 10 figures lower! That is, a 40-delta USD call has a strike at 110.00, while the strike of a 40-delta USD put is at 100.00.

Why? *Because you should calculate strikes in respect to forward, not spot!* In other words, the strikes of a call and a put should be equidistant from 105.00 rather than from 110.00! In time, the 110.00 USD call will become deeper ATM and the 100.00 USD put will become farther OTM. Therefore, even if the spot remains at the current level for six months, the 110.00 USD call will still have a great chance to be in-the-money!

OPTION PRICE BEHAVIOR WITH RESPECT TO THE FORWARD PRICE LEVEL

The previous observation leads us to a peculiar fact: straddles are the cheapest when their strikes are at the level of price of the *current* forward. This happens because the premium of ATM straddle consists of only time value, without intrinsic value.

For example, you buy a one-year 105.00 ATM USD/JPY straddle. For six months, the spot fluctuates in the range of 107.50 to 115.00. After that period, you decide to sell it. Spot is at 107.50, and you think that it will trade at 108.50 at the end of the day. You want to know when it is better to close your position: now or at the end of the day.

Since after six months the forward is approximately equal to a half of a one-year forward, it should be 250 yen pips lower. This means that a 105.00 strike is at-the-money when the spot trades at 107.50! Therefore, at 107.50, your straddle's value is at a minimum, and you are better off waiting until the spot moves as far as possible above/below 107.50!

The strangle is similar: the closer the arithmetical center of a strangle [(strike of call + strike of put)/2] is to the current forward level, the lower its price. For instance, you buy a one-year 102.00–110.00 strangle. The forward is at 105.00. The average of the options' strikes is 106.00 [(102.00 + 110.00)/2]. Thus, deltas of the 102.00 USD put and the 110.00 USD call should be different. They would have been the same, if the forward rate and the arithmetical average of the options' strikes had been equal.

Let's continue. After the spot kept staying in the 107.50 to 115.00 range for six months, you decide to sell the strangle. The spot is at 108.50, and you expect it will trade at 106.50 by the end of the day. Should you wait to close your position?

The current six-month forward contract rate should be equal to almost a half of a one-year forward, that is, 250 yen pips. This means that when the spot trades at 108.50 the forward rate is 106.00; that is, it coincides with the center of your strangle. Since at this spot the price of the strategy is minimal, you are better off waiting until the spot moves as far as possible above or below 108.50!

IMPACT OF INTEREST RATE CHANGES ON OPTION PRICE

Let's consider the influence of interest rates on FX options' premium. This time, we'll buy a 105.00 ATM USD call. On the same day, the USD/JPY swap increases to –600 yen pips. This means that if you were to buy an ATM USD call now, its strike would be 104.00 (110.00 – 6.00). Since the current ATM option's strike is 104.00 and you are long the 105.00 USD call, your option becomes out-of-the-money and its price drops![10]

Let's summarize:

1. Assuming that the spot remains constant, the USD call option premium decreases, and the USD put option premium increases when:
   - the U.S. dollar ("foreign currency") interest rate goes *up*, compared with the interest rate on another currency; or
   - another currency's ("domestic currency") interest rate falls comparing with the interest rate on the U.S. dollar.
2. Assuming that the spot remains at the same level, the USD put option premium decreases, and the USD call option premium increases when:
   - the U.S. dollar interest rate ("foreign currency") goes *down*, comparing with the interest rate on another currency; or
   - another currency's interest rate ("domestic currency") goes *up*, comparing with the interest rate on the U.S. dollar.
3. Finally, theta of "deep-in-the-money" USD call will be lower than that of the put with the same strike since it assumes that on the hedge you have to sell USD. Since the U.S. interest rates are higher than the Japanese ones, you will incur additional interest expense. Thus, the theta of the call should be lower to compensate for the extra interest expense.

INACCURACY OF THE TERM "RISKLESS RATE"

Let's discuss another rarely mentioned detail. The riskless rate used for pricing options is assumed to be an interest rate independent of any credit events (Black and Scholes use the term "a zero-beta rate"). In practice, no rate is absolutely independent of such events, although it is assumed that in every country the interest rates on government bonds or on short-term deposits serve as such a rate.

In practice, the rates on short-term deposits (for example, LIBOR) are the average rates for deposits in the first-class banks of a country. But banks rarely have equal credit ratings. For example, the average rating of Japanese banks is not comparable with those of European banks. Thus, a riskless rate in Japan embeds a much higher credit risk than in Europe. Hence, option models ignore these points.

Moreover, deals done by counterparties with different credit ratings theoretically should be priced at different riskless interest rates. For example, a lower-rated counterparty sells you a two-month 100-delta put for 10 dollars. You pay the premium today, and in two months you exercise the option and collect 9.99 dollars (having deducted some commission upfront). This transaction is essentially a loan to your counterparty since you effectively have loaned money at LIBOR or, at your refinancing rate. Yet, you would charge your counterpart a higher rate if you were to give him a loan.

RHO

Rho measures sensitivity of option prices to changes in interest rates. For options on low-yielding currencies, it is fair to say that the impact is minimal. However, in the case of the currencies of emerging economies, rho is extremely important.

One can see that in volatility terms puts on emerging economies' currencies are more expensive than calls with the same strikes. This statement contradicts the proposition we proved in the beginning of the chapter! If it is true, shouldn't there be an opportunity for an arbitrage? That is, one would buy a call on the currency of an emerging economy (let's say the Russian ruble). To hedge it, one should sell it in the cash market for a lower-yielding currency. As we know, in order to sell it, one has to borrow it. Since the one-year ruble rate is around 10% p.a., the financing costs would be huge. Such a substantial daily interest expense is annoying. That is why in such cases the put/call parity may not work in practice: traders are ready to overpay for the ruble puts to avoid annoyance.

QUESTIONS

1. A one-month USD/CHF forward is quoted –30 pips (U.S. rates are higher than in Switzerland), the spot is 1.4730. If you buy an ATM forward option,
    a. What will its strike be?
    b. You bought that option. The overnight forward loses one pip a day (0.003:30 days). At which spot will the option be ATM (and the cheapest) in one week?

2. A one-month USD/JPY forward is quoted –120 points (–1.2 figures); you are going to buy a 105.00–108.00 strangle. At which spot will this strangle be the cheapest today?
3. The USD/CHF spot is at 1.4700. A three-month forward is –90 pips (USD rates are higher).
   a. Which is more expensive: an ATM *forward*[11] USD call or an ATM *forward* USD put?
   b. Which is more expensive: an ATM *spot* USD call or an ATM *spot* USD put?
   c. You buy a three-month 1.4800 USD call and want to sell a put to finance the purchase. What strike should the option you sell have to get the same delta?
   d. Which of the options in the previous question is more expensive: the USD call or the put?

ANSWERS

1. a. 1.4700;
   b. 1.4723 (30 – 7).
2. 107.70, the middle of the strangle is 106.50 ([105.00 + 108.00]/2), at this forward price the strangle is the cheapest. To find the cheapest spot to buy the option, you have to take into account the forward price. Since it is –120 points, you have to add it to the middle of the strangle to get the spot (106.50 + 1.2 = 107.70).
3. a. Their price will be the same. The forward differential influences the strike change, not the premium.
   b. The USD put is more expensive. With the strike fixed at the level of the current spot (1.4700) and the forward at 1.4610, the put is in-the-money.
   c. 1.4420;
   The three-month forward rate is 1.4700 – 0.0090 = 1.4610. To calculate the strike of the equidistant put, you should calculate the difference between the strike of the call and the forward rate, and then subtract it from the forward rate: 1.4610 – (1.4800 – 1.4610) = 1.4420.
   d. They will have the same price, since they are equidistant from the forward rate.

FURTHER INFORMATION FOR THE READER

Why Do Options Dealers Use Volatility as a Unit of Price?

To answer this question, we have to discuss factors used in option pricing. They are time remaining until an option's expiration, its strike, the current price level of an underlying asset, the strike level, market volatility, the interest rate on riskless assets, and the dividend rate (for stocks).

Factors Determining the Option Price

Time remaining till expiration The classical explanation of this factor is that the longer the option's life, the higher the probability that the option will be profitable at expiration. But one can make an argument that it can lose money as well. This argument fails when you consider that the option can be resold before expiration, when it is in-the-money, rather than just at the time of exercise. Therefore, the longer the option's life, the higher the chances that it will be profitable at some moment.

Relationship of the asset price to the strike This reflects the probability that the option will be in-the-money at expiration. One can see that if the option is in-the-money, it has a better chance to be exercised than an out-of-the-money option.

Volatility The explanation is similar to the one for time.

Interest rate on riskless assets and risky rate (dividends) The explanations of the influence of riskless and risky rates in options on different underlying assets are varied across asset classes. In the case of FX options, to understand the riskless interest rate one has to understand the forward curve's influence.

Let's consider a USD call/JPY put. The U.S. dollar is a foreign currency and the yen is the domestic one (USD/JPY). A forward rate, which is a ratio of forward yen to forward dollar rates, will increase (increase of the numerator) as domestic riskless interest rate rises (domestic rate—JPY) and will decrease (increase of denominator) as the foreign (dollar) interest rate rises. The changes of the forward rate

(Continued)

FURTHER INFORMATION FOR THE READER *(Continued)*

will cause changes in the price of our call: the rate appreciation will result in the premium rise; that is, a premium will increase when the domestic rate goes up and will fall when the foreign rate increases.

Logically, it can be easily demonstrated: let's suggest that the spot of some asset is at 100 today and the one-year yen deposit rate is 5%. If you buy a one-year ATM JPY call, its strike will be 105 (since the strike is a forward price). Tomorrow, the yen's rate will increase to 6%. It is clear that if you would buy an ATM call tomorrow, its strike would be 106. Therefore, the call you bought yesterday is already 100 pips in-the-money.

The premium behavior of the put is precisely opposite to that of the call. With an increase in "domestic" currency rate a premium of put will decline, and with an increase in the foreign currency rate, it will rise.

The Answer to Why Do Option Dealers Use Volatility as a Unit of Price?
Now that we know all factors used in the pricing models, we can answer the question of why option dealers use volatility to measure option prices. Let's review the way dealers trade in options with each other.

First, when two dealers do a trade, it is assumed that the option will be *exchanged together with the hedge at the current price of the underlying asset*, that is, after exchanging the buyer and the seller will end up having a delta-neutral positions.

Second, all dealers use the same pricing models, which calculate the same prices for the same options given similar input.

Third, in liquid markets the underlying asset price and interest rates are known at any moment of time.

Fourth and most important, since they know beforehand that the strike, the underlying asset price, and the interest rates will be fixed at a current market price, then the only price parameter they will negotiate will be volatility. As soon as they agree on it, the standard option model will calculate an option price denominated in money terms. In other words, assuming that all other components are fixed, they adjust only volatility, and that is why it is easier to trade in terms of volatility.

Unfortunately, the tradition to quote in terms of volatility exists only on several liquid markets such as the foreign exchange OTC option market. Here, all dealers talk in terms of volatility (not

FURTHER INFORMATION FOR THE READER *(Continued)*

premium!) as a unit of price because after hedging the option by the underlying asset, the only component to fix is volatility. In less liquid markets, the options are quoted in money terms. However, even there, when estimating an option price, a dealer still establishes a bid and offer that are acceptable for him in volatility terms and then quotes in money terms equivalent to volatility. If a deal takes place, he hedges an option by an underlying asset, transforming the portfolio into delta-neutral just like an option dealer on a liquid asset.

CHAPTER 17

Dynamic Option Hedging

Dynamic hedging serves to make a portfolio risk neutral. The market, like a pendulum, moves an option price; and delta-hedging, like a holder of the pendulum's string, makes the clock stand still, notwithstanding the pendulum's swings.

BASIC PRINCIPLES OF HEDGING

A delta-neutral option's portfolio has equal chances to make (lose) money when an underlying asset moves by one point. To keep the portfolio delta-neutral, it should be rehedged as the underlying asset's price moves. For example, when you are long a hedged (synonymous to delta-neutral) position and spot changes slightly, you earn on the option as much as you lose on the hedge, or vise versa. That is, your entire position's (option plus hedge) value does not change with an insignificant underlying price change.

However, if the spot moves significantly, the delta of the portfolio will change as well, and you will have to adjust the hedge amount to make your position delta-neutral. For instance, if the stock trades between 20.00 and 20.10 an option's delta is 40%. If the stock moves to 20.80, the delta becomes 42%.

The process of adjusting hedge amounts is called *dynamic hedging*. Its purpose is to equalize chances of making (losing) money in either direction.

Let's study this topic through the following example.

Example

You believe that USD/CHF will fluctuate in the 1.4500–1.4700 range. You buy $1 million of 1.4600 USD call.

a. The spot is at 1.4700, the option's delta is 60%.
   What can you do in the spot market to hedge your option position?
   You can sell $0.6 million ($1 million × 0.6)

b. The spot falls to 1.4500, and the option's delta becomes 20%.
What can you do with your total (spot + option) position?
To hedge a 20-delta call option, you should have a short position on \$0.2 million. Since you are short \$0.6 million, you can buy back 40% (60% – 20%) or \$0.4 million.

c. Now, the spot appreciates to 1.4800, and the option's delta becomes 75%.
What can you do with your total (spot + option) position?
You can sell 55% more (\$0.55 million).

You hope that the results of the dynamic hedging will pay off the premium you paid to buy the options. To achieve that, you have to take into account theta. That is, every day you must check the theta of your position and the theta breakeven points.[1] You want the spot to go beyond them to rehedge and make sure that the theta is paid. If you are long options, you have to be especially careful on weekends: on Monday, the value of an option position is reduced by a three-day time decay.

SIMILAR BEHAVIOR OF HEDGED PUT AND CALL OPTIONS AT EXPIRATION DATE

The concept of similar behavior of hedged put and call options doesn't seem obvious to many people. That's why we'll repeat it once again.

Example

Step 1. When you buy a 1.2300 call on the hedge you should *sell* a delta-equivalent of spot. If you buy a 1.2300 put, on the hedge you should *buy* a delta-equivalent of spot. That is, at the initial stage hedging directions for calls and puts are different.

Step 2. If the spot goes up, the call's delta increases; and to keep the portfolio delta-neutral, you should sell more spot. When the spot goes up, the delta of the put falls; and to keep the portfolio delta-neutral you should . . . sell a portion of the hedge. That is, hedging is the same for both the long call and the long put.

Step 3. When exercising calls and puts, your actions differ.

To conclude, when option positions are initiated or exercised/expire, the option type is very important. During the option's life, the hedging process is the same. *That's why an 80-delta call* and *a 20-delta put* (for example, 1.2500 call and 1.2500 put) with the same strike and expiration date *will be sold at the same volatility.*

MORE COMPLEX CONCEPTS

Example 1

To begin let's compare the behavior of a 1.2200 ATM straddle. It is comprised of a call and a put with equal face values of EUR 1 million (in trading slang *straddle EUR 1 million a leg*), which costs 40 pips (the call and the put cost the same). The breakeven points of such strategy are 1.2200 ± 0.0040. In other words, the strategy is profitable if the euro is below 1.2160 or above 1.2240 at expiration. Pay attention: this is the position's profitability *at expiration*!

During its life, the strategy can become profitable if the implied volatility sharply increases, even if the spot remains stable. Besides, it can be sold at premium if the spot moved to the breakeven points. Or you can pay for the premium through dynamic hedging. In other words, profit is possible before expiration, even if the spot doesn't go beyond the breakeven points.

Example 2

Suppose we buy EUR 2 million of 1.2200 ATM EUR call for 20 pips. To hedge it, we sold EUR 1 million at 1.2200. To calculate the low breakeven point let's resolve the simple equation:

$$2{,}000{,}000 \times 0.0002 = 1{,}000{,}000 \times X$$

This equation can be rephrased: how far should the euro move down for the hedge to compensate the loss in premium? The answer is 40 pips.

Now let's calculate the high breakeven point by means of the following equation:

$$2{,}000{,}000 \times 0.0002 + 1{,}000{,}000 \times X = 2{,}000{,}000 \times X$$

This equation can be rephrased: how far up should the euro move for the option position of $2 million (face value of option) to compensate the loss in premium and loss on the 1 million of hedge? The answer is 40 pips.

Check the breakevens in Example 1. Interesting, isn't it? At expiration, the breakevens in both examples are the same, although face values of the options are different! Now, consider the breakeven points of both strategies during the option's lifetime. If volatility is constant, the breakeven points will deviate from the center of the delta-neutral position by the amount of time decay.[2] That is, if you pay 40 cents for the strategy and overnight it loses 2 pips due to the time decay, a spot's movement beyond 2 pips in either direction will compensate one-day time decay losses (not the entire 40 pips!). Behavior of the hedged long EUR 2 million of 1.2200 ATM EUR put at 20 pips will be the same.

This example demonstrates once again that the behavior of the 1.2200 ATM straddle EUR 1 million a leg, of the hedged EUR 2 million of 1.2200 EUR put and of the hedged EUR 2 million of 1.2200 EUR call are *absolutely the same*. That's why the prices of these positions are the same. In all examples, we assume that the forward curve is flat; in other words, interest rate swaps = 0. In these examples we assume that the spot is equal to the forward (1.2200). If the forward curve is not flat, the logic holds as long as the ATM strikes are at the forward price level.

Example 3

Let's consider the position composed of the *OTM* hedged option. Let's suppose that we bought EUR 1 million of a 1.2300 call (30-delta) for 15 pips and on the hedge we sold EUR 300,000 at 1.2200. We need to calculate the breakeven points.

For the calculation of the low point we will use the formula known to us:

$$1{,}000{,}000 \times 0.0015 = 300{,}000 \times X$$

Thus, the spot has to fall by 50 pips to compensate for the premium spent on the call's purchase. The low breakeven point is 1.2150 (1.2200 – 0.0050).

Let's calculate the high breakeven point.

$$1{,}000{,}000 \times 0.0015 + 300{,}000 \times (1.2300 - 1.2200 + X) = 1{,}000{,}000 \times X$$

This equation can be rephrased: how far up should the euro move for EUR 1 million (the option's face value) to compensate for the premium loss and the loss on EUR 300.000 of the hedge? Notice: the hedge loses money within the entire interval from the spot/option trade level until the option's strike (from 1.2200 till 1.2300). The answer is 64 pips.

This example demonstrates that *the strategies composed of hedged OTM options can lose more than the premium paid due to possible losses on hedges*. In the example given, the maximum loss will take place, if at expiration the spot closes at the strike (1.2300). The loss will be equal to \$4,500 (1,000,000 × 0.0015 + 300,000 × (1.2300 – 1.2200)).

Another important observation: the breakeven points of the strategy are not symmetrical as in the cases of ATM options. The high point is 64 pips above the strike. The low point is 50 pips below where the spot was sold on the hedge and 150 pips below the strike.

QUESTIONS

1. The purchase of a call against short position on the spot market hedges (protects) the position's value when the market is:
   a. rising
   b. stable
   c. falling

2. Purchase of a put in addition to a long spot position hedges (protects) the position's value when the market is:
   a. rising
   b. stable
   c. falling

3. A client buys 1,000 IBM shares at $120. How would you hedge this position by means of options (each option is written on 100 shares)?

For Questions 4–8: A dealer buys 500 Intel shares at $100 and 5 Intel March 95 puts at $5.

4. What is the maximum total position loss?

5. What is the dealer's gain or loss when the Intel stock falls to $97?

6. When the stock falls to $93, the dealer exercises the put delivering the shares. What is his gain or loss?

7. If the stock price falls to $80 and the dealer exercises the put delivering the shares, what is his gain or loss?

8. The stock price rises to $120 and the put expires worthless. If a dealer sells the shares, what will be his gain or loss from the total position?

On November 30, you bought $1 million of a 1.4400 USD call with expiration on March 15. In the following questions, we show the deltas of this option for tomorrow.

Spot	Delta
1.4000	+30%
1.4100	+34%
1.4200	+38%
1.4300	+41%
1.4400	+45%
1.4500	+48%
1.4600	+52%
1.4700	+55%
1.4800	+59%

Delta is estimated by means of Focus software.

9. If the transaction was done at 1.4200 spot level, what hedge do you have to make?
10. The spot went up to 1.4700. What kind of delta adjustment do you have to make for your position?
11. The spot fell from 1.4700 to 1.4300. What should you do to make the position delta-neutral?

> When you trade one-day options, delta becomes almost irrelevant, and you can consider an option as equivalent to a spot position. For example, you can use it as a stop-loss order (to limit the risk) or as a substitute for an additional spot position (to increase the risk).

Let's suppose that the spot is at 1.4200 and you buy $1 million of a one-day 1.4200 USD call at 20 pips. In the following questions, you should pay attention to both realized and unrealized profits and losses.

12. What is the breakeven point of the position?
13. The spot falls to 1.4190. You have just learned that the European Central Bank (ECB) sells dollars. What will you do if the market dynamics confirm these rumors? What is your maximum net loss?
14. You decide to sell only $0.5 million at 1.4190. What is the breakeven point of your total position after the sale?

15. The spot goes up to 1.4430. You sell the remaining $0.5 million. What is your position now? What is your maximum gain? What is your risk?
16. How will your P/L change in Question 15 if the spot goes up to 1.4600?
17. How will your P/L change in Question 15 if the spot falls to 1.4150?
18. The spot falls from 1.4430 to 1.4390. What is the position's P/L now?
19. Summarizing the answers to Questions 16, 17, and 18, to what synthetic position is the total position (composed of option + spot) equivalent?
20. You think the spot will not decrease much. What can you do with your position?
21. The spot rises to 1.4450. What can you do?

ANSWERS

1. a
2. c
3. Buy 10 IBM 120 puts: the long spot is hedged by the long put.
4. $5,000: $10 per share, or 500 × $10 = $5,000
5. $4,000 loss: loss of $8 per share, or 500 × $8 = $4,000 loss
6. $5,000 loss: loss of $10 per share or 500 × $10 = $5,000 loss
7. $5,000 loss: loss of $10 per share or 500 × $10 = $5,000 loss
8. $7,500 gain: the put expires worthless, gain of $15 per share, 500 × $15 = $7,500 gain
9. Sell $380,000
10. Sell $170,000 (new delta is 55, but you have already sold $380,000)

11. Buy back $140,000 (new delta is 41, but you are short $550,000)

12. 1.4420 (1.4400 + 0.0020)

13. You should sell $1 million at 1.4190. In this situation, you use an option as hedge (stop-loss order), that is, the spot position will be closed if the market drifts above the option's strike. In this case, the maximum loss is 30 pips: if the spot rate goes up, you will exercise the option and cover the short position at 1.4200 (losing 10 pips) plus you will lose 20 pips of premium.

14. 1.4250; a) you will lose 10 pips between 1.4190 and 1.4200 due to the short spot position; b) in other words, your position costs 25 pips (20 pips of premium plus 0.5 × 10 pips of spot losses); c) since with upward movement your delta-equivalent position is USD 0.5 million (1 million of USD option and 0.5 million of short USD spot position) the 50-pips price change is necessary to compensate the loss of 25 pips.

15. Long 1.4200 USD call and short $1 million ($0.5 million were sold at 1.4190 and $0.5 million were sold at 1.4430; that is, the average price of the $1 million sale is 1.4310). The maximum gain is reached if the spot falls to 0. Since you have fixed the gain of 90 pips ((1.4190 + 1.4430)/2 – (1.4200 + 0.0020)) there is no risk.

16. The gain will not change; the option price appreciation will be nullified by losses on the short $1 million.

17. Long the 1.4200 USD call and short USD 1 million ($0.5 million were sold at 1.4190 and $0.5 million at 1.4430; that is, the average sale price of the $1 million sale is 1.4310). At the 1.4150 level the profit will be 140 pips ((1.4090 + 1.4430)/2 – 1.4150 – 0.0020).[3]

18. A profit of 90 pips is the same as in Question 15: ((1.4190 + 1.4430)/2 – (1.4200 + 0.0020)).

19. Long 1.4200 call + short spot = long 1.4200 put (plus P/L = 90 pips).

20. a. Close both sides of the position and collect a part of the remaining time value of the option (if the premium is higher than the intrinsic value);

    b. Sell 1.4200 put.

21. The same as in Question 20.

FURTHER INFORMATION FOR THE READER

Influence of Historical Volatility on Implied Volatility of Short-Term Options

An understanding of dynamic hedging mechanisms will develop your skills in calculating implied volatility. Let's remember that implied volatility is calculated on the basis of **intraday highs and lows.**

It is obvious from a price chart of any asset that the difference between daily closing prices quite rarely exceeds intraday price fluctuations. Therefore, most of the time the historical intraday volatility exceeds the historical volatility measured in respect to daily closing prices. Can we conclude that implied volatility is always higher than the historical one, especially in cases of short-term options (up to two weeks till expiration)? Unfortunately, in reality this guess doesn't always come true.

The first reason for this is liquidity: at certain time periods, a supply of options (thus of implied volatility) can be very high. Just as the case with any other product, implied volatilities may be sold below their cost price (historical volatilities).

The second reason is less obvious. A trader who has bought an option and is delta-hedging it, will **not** be able to sell a portion of the hedge at the highest and to buy it at the lowest intraday price. If he is lucky, he will catch 80% of the range, since without knowing beforehand the highs and lows of the trading day, a trader will miss at least one of them. That's why traders seldom evaluate the implied short-term volatility based on the maximum daily ranges. Nevertheless, if the intraday volatility is very high and during the day you can rehedge several times, it is possible that the wider range will be used to calculate the implied volatility.

The individual trader's rehedging style and estimates determine his view on short-term volatility. At the moments of high intraday volatility, the prices of interbank (OTC) traders may be arbitraged as their views differ. Thus, bids of one group may exceed offers of the other.

Additional Thoughts about the Characteristics of Implied Volatility In most cases the volatility decreases, when

- after a significant break the spot turns back (false breakout) or bounces back from the support (resistance) level in the previous

(Continued)

FURTHER INFORMATION FOR THE READER *(Continued)*

price range. At such moments the ambiguity regarding future price action goes away. Besides, hedging of the sold options in the known range is easier.

- The news expected by the market is confirmed, and that decreases vagueness.
- The spot moves towards the established trend, since it is easy to hedge risk and the funds hedge their directional positions with risk reversals: they buy a hedge against the market direction and sell the options toward the direction. It is especially true for the S&P index options, since mutual funds sell calls against their long stock positions (covered sales of calls).

CHAPTER 18

Summing Up

This chapter sums up most of the covered material and attaches practical direction to it. This material is not described in any other option book known to the author. In order to understand how to use options, one has to be familiar with the Greeks—risk management parameters discussed earlier. They measure sensitivity of option prices to changes in prices of an underlying or forecasts of volatility or time. Liquid markets do not offer anything for free. For example, we have two almost identical ATM options at the same price. If one of them has a higher gamma than the other, another parameter of that option must be lower. That is, if two options trade at the same premium, one of them cannot have both higher gamma and higher vega than the other. Don't spend money on searching for a covert error in a model, and don't bother looking for the riskless profits. (See Appendix B for a mathematical explanation of this thought.)

To start with, one has to keep in mind that buying and selling options costs more than buying and selling the underlying, because there are three spreads implied in the option's price and only one spread in the spot's price.[1] That is why every investor's mistake in options is potentially more expensive than mistakes in other instruments.

FACTORS INFLUENCING SHORT-TERM POSITIONS

Let's assume that one can get to a 2 basis point (b.p.) dealing spread (i.e., two pips) (see Table 18.1). It will constitute 16% of the price of the 1.5020 USD call ((14 – 12)/12) = 0.16). This means that closing the position immediately after the deal is done will cost 16% of the investment (see Table 18.2).

TABLE 18.1 Breakeven Point of Options with Different Deltas if Immediate Positions Closed Immediately

Currency	Delta	Strike	Call/ Put	Maturity	Bid/ Offer	Premium as a % of Spread	Move to Cover (CHF bp) Premium
USD/CHF	10	1.5020	USD	1 week	12/14	16%	20 bp
(1.4630)	30	1.4810	Call		52/54	3.8%	7 bp
	60	1.4590			150/152	1.4%	1.3 bp

Observation 1. The lower the delta of an option, the more expensive is the exit.

Now, let's calculate how far the spot should move during the same day for the trader to cover the price spread and exit at the same price at which she entered. To do that, one has to recall the definition of delta: change of premium caused by change of spot. So, a 10-delta option gains CHF 1 b.p. in premium if the spot moves by CHF 10 b.p. By the same token, a 30-delta option will gain 1 CHF b.p. in value every CHF 3.3 b.p. spot move. To cover a CHF 2 b.p. with a 30-delta option, the spot has to move 6.6 b.p. (2/30). From observing the results, one can infer:

Observation 2. The lower the delta of the option, the longer it takes to start making money.

Let's repeat the definition of theta: theta says how much value an option loses overnight. The lower the delta of an option, the greater portion of its value it loses overnight. Intuitively, this means that with every passing

TABLE 18.2 Breakeven Point of Options with Different Deltas at Position Closing (Accounted for Theta)

Currency	Delta	Strike	Call/ Put	Maturity	Offer Paid	Theta (CHFbp)	Theta % of Premium	Move to Cover Theta
USD/CHF	10	1.5020	USD	1 week	14	3.6	25.7	36 bp
(1.4630)	30	1.4810	Call		54	7.1	13.1	24 bp
	60	1.4590			151	7.9	5.2	10 bp

day there is much less chance that the owner can make money on that option. Therefore:

Observation 3. The lower the delta of an option, the faster it loses value (i.e., the more sensitive it is to time).

Let's repeat the definition of vega: vega is a change of premium with a 1% change in volatilities (see Table 18.3). Thus, a 10-delta option will gain CHF 4.6 b.p. if volatility goes from 11 to 12. Therefore:

Observation 4. The lower the delta of an option, the more sensitive it is to change in volatilities (see Table 18.3).

Note: From Rules 3 and 4 one can notice that influence of time on option premium is almost identical to influence of volatility! A longer time period and higher volatility have equal influence on option premium—or, to be more specific—on time value of option premium.

Let's now find practical implications for our observations.

Implications for Trading

If you want to increase your odds of making money:

1. Buy low-delta short-term options only if you expect
   - the market to go your way soon;
   - volatility to increase.
2. An investment is better preserved when one buys $1 worth of higher-delta options than $1 worth of lower-delta options.

Conversely,

3. It is safer to sell lower-delta options: it takes a substantial spot move against you for this option to lose money.

TABLE 18.3 Sensitivity of Options with Different Deltas to Volatility Changes

Currency	Delta	Strike	Call/ Put	Maturity	Offer	Vega	Vega % of Premium
USD/CHF	10	1.5020	USD	1 week	14	4.6	32.8
(1.8630)	30	1.4810	Call		54	9.1	16.9
	60	1.4590			152	9.9	6.5

FACTORS INFLUENCING LONG-TERM POSITIONS

Let's analyze the price relationship of long- and short-term options, options with different deltas and some other parameters.

As you can see:

Observation 5. As seen in Table 18.4, the premium of at-the-money options almost doubles with maturity going from one week to one month, one month to three months, and two months to nine months (for more exact calculations, see Chapter 14, Theta).

Conversely:

Observation 6. A one-month at-the-money option will lose almost half of its value during the last week. A nine-month option will lose almost halt of its value during the last two months ("almost" because the strikes may be different).

Observation 7. Within one maturity, the price of a 50-delta option is approximately twice that of a 30-delta option. The price of a 30-delta option is twice that of a 17-delta option (see Table 18.5).

Observation 8. While the prices are doubling with the change of deltas, thetas and vegas are not.

TABLE 18.4 Relationship of Prices on ATM USD/CHF (Forward) $ Call Options

	1 week	1 month	3 months	2 months	9 months
Strike	1.4790	1.4760	1.4635	1.4720	1.4465
Premium (CHF pips)	112	228	456	320	666

*At-the-money option's strike is calculated as current spot (1.4800) +/– forward.

TABLE 18.5 Relationship of Prices of $ Pull Options with Different Deltas ($/CHF Option Expiring in Two Months)

Strike	1.4720	1.5310	1.5670
Delta (%)	50	30	17
Premium (CHFbp)	320	155	75
Vega (CHFbp)	30	26	19
Theta (CHFbp)	2.7	2.4	1.8

Observation 9. Initially, time decay of long-term options (theta) is minuscule compared to the initial price.

Observation 10. Very important! If you look at the $1.5670 $ call, a one-figure move in spot will make as much money as a one-figure move in volatilities. The option's delta is 17, which means that its premium will gain 17 b.p. if the spot moves from 1.5700 to 1.5600 (100 b.p.). It also will gain 19 b.p. if the volatility goes up from 11.7 to 12.7. However, if the spot goes the trader's way and volatility goes against him, the result will be 0, even if the trader is right on the direction and timing.

Tables 18.1 and 18.2 are the keys to taking medium- and long-term positions. Table 18.2 reveals the phenomenal speed at which the option loses value at the end of its life. It emphasizes the importance of understanding that the values of at-the-money options with different maturities are related through the square root rather than linearly (see Chapter 15).

Table 18.3 shows that direction is as important as volatility. The lower the delta of an option, the more important it is to look at both in choosing the strategy (see Observation 4). However, longer-term options do not lose as much time value. Remember Observation 6? It takes a nine-month ATM option seven months to lose half of its value.

Important Warnings

1. When considering a certain option, you must model time decay: the aforesaid is true for ATM options. For options with delta higher than 60 and lower than 40 delta, the abovementioned dynamic changes considerably.
2. Delta (and respectively the dynamics of theta) changes as the forward curve moves. It is true especially for long-term options.

Implications for Trading

In conclusion, do not short long-term options based only on the directional view only: since an option's premium amortizes very slowly, its premium changes almost proportionally to the changes of the option's delta equivalent spot position. However, such options are subject to volatility and forward risk. Therefore, if you do not intend to take a volatility position, it is safer to take a spot position, since its P/L will be more predictable. In addition, when you buy options, treat them like an investment: you invested $1 and would like to preserve its value.

QUESTIONS

1. Your client is concerned with risk of volatility change. Should he sell (buy) long- or short-term options to cover it?

2. Your client is concerned with his exposure to gamma risk. Should he sell (buy) long- or short-term options to reduce it?

3. Your client is upset about the fact that his position loses value too fast. If the spot and volatility remain stable, what is the most effective way to reduce his position?

4. You have just sold a one-month ATM straddle and bought a six-month ATM straddle of an equal face value.
   a. How would you describe this position in gamma/vega terms?
   b. Is your position's theta positive or negative (do you make or lose money on time decay)?
   c. Do you expect to make or to lose money on this position, if, while the spot changes, the volatility remains constant and time decay isn't taken into account?
   d. Volatility level rises in parallel along the volatility curve, while the spot remains stable (time decay isn't taken into account). Do you expect to make or to lose money on this position?

5. You expect the spot to remain in a slow upward trend, and you want to finance a purchase of a call by a sale of a put. If your expectation comes true, how will changes in the spot and volatility affect your P/L?

6. The spot has been moving upwards for a long period of time. What is the better bid (what is in demand) in volatility terms: calls or puts?

ANSWERS

1. He should sell long-term options, since they are more sensitive to volatility.

2. He should buy short-term options, since they are more sensitive to gamma.

3. He has a long option position, and the position's theta is negative. To reduce the theta risk, he should sell short-term options.

4. a. You have long vega (the six-month option is more sensitive to vega) and short gamma.

b. You have a short position in short-term options (gamma). Therefore, you earn on time decay since short-term options lose value faster than long-term ones.
c. You will suffer losses since you are short gamma. Thus, the value of the options you sold will increase faster than the value of the options you bought.
d. You will earn since your position is long vega. Thus, the options you bought are more sensitive to volatility changes. You will make more money on your long position than you will lose on your short position.

5. You will make money on spot move and suffer losses when volatility falls. Since the spot is rising, the put you sold will lose gamma, while the call you bought will gain gamma. The same will happen to vega. However, the lower market uncertainty regarding the direction will reduce the implied volatility. Thus, although your position becomes more positive in terms of vega, since volatility is falling, you start losing money on vega and theta, while earning on gamma. This explanation is true for hedged positions, because you use terms "gamma" and "vega" to describe a hedged position. If the position is not hedged, the factor of gamma will be less significant than the delta-equivalent of the calls you are long: the higher it is, the more money you will make. Vega will remain important, since the volatility will influence the unhedged position, just as it does a hedged one.
6. The demand for puts should increase. Since everybody takes long positions in the underlying in the direction of the move, the demand for hedging a downward correction will increase. Similarly, as the spot appreciation is decelerating, people will start selling calls to increase profitability of their underlying positions.

FURTHER INFORMATION FOR THE READER

Instructions for Directional Option Trading

To develop a suitable directional (unhedged by an underlying asset) option strategy, you should have a scenario comprised of the following: direction of spot move, time period in which the move will happen, and behavior of implied volatility during the move.

(Continued)

FURTHER INFORMATION FOR THE READER *(Continued)*

From experience, we can say that most people start option trading based on an assumptions about spot behavior. Then, they realize that in developing an option strategy they should think of a position holding period. And even later, they start understanding the role the volatility scenario plays in strategy development.

How to Start Developing a Strategy

1. Let's say that you expect the USD/CHF to be in a 1.4000–1.4500 range for a while. On the basis of this forecast, you would like to develop an options strategy.
2. You should begin by determining the time period during which you expect the market to be range bound. In most cases, the shorter the period of the forecast, the more chances of your assumption being correct.
3. After you have made a forecast regarding the underlying asset's behavior and have determined its maturity, you should ask a market maker for the relative level of implied volatility. If *implied volatility is high* in respect to its historical record, you may want to *sell* an OTM *option. The same premium provides you with a farther strike and a better protection when volatility is high. If volatility is low you try to buy an ATM option.*

The preceding steps point out at two key moments in strategy development:

1. It is simple to develop a basic options strategy;
2. At least two factors must be taken into consideration: direction and holding period.

Key Aspects of Directional Option Trading When opening long positions ("debit" trades, where you are a premium net-payer), it is necessary to make:

A forecast of an underlying asset's behavior with respect to

- direction
- expected extremes
- catastrophic extremes

FURTHER INFORMATION FOR THE READER *(Continued)*

A forecast of the holding period (a position's life period) with respect to

- when a move will happen
- how long spot will remain at the expected level

  (A rule of thumb for experts: maturity of a long option position should be 2.5 times longer than the period during which you expect the move.)

A forecast of volatility in which you take into account of the following issues:

- Is the implied volatility high or low in respect to the last two weeks?
- Will volatility increase or decrease if the spot moves in the expected direction?
- If volatility is high or you expect it to go down, sell options or buy spreads.
- If volatility is low or you expect it to go up, buy options.

When opening short positions ("credit" trades, in which you are a premium net-recipient), it is necessary to make:

A forecast of an underlying asset's behavior with respect to:

- direction in which the spot will not move
- expected extremes in case the range changes
- the worst maximum spot's extension

A forecast of maturity (a position's life period) with respect to:

- when a move in the unfavorable direction may happen
- how long spot can remain at the present level and how much a short position will gain through time decay (the shorter the maturity of an option, the faster it gains time decay)

A forecast of volatility with respect to:

- Is the implied volatility high or low comparing to the previous two weeks?

(Continued)

FURTHER INFORMATION FOR THE READER *(Continued)*

- Will volatility increase or decrease if the spot moves against the expect direction?

If you expect volatility to decrease, sell options.

If you expect volatility to increase, you'd better sell spreads.[2]

CHAPTER 19

Introduction to Exotic Options

At the beginning of the 1990s, options few could price were called exotic. *To separate exotic types from the ones that were predominant then (European-style options), the latter were given a new nickname "vanilla." If you hear the term "vanilla option," recognize an old friend. Nowadays, the pricing of most exotics is a standard feature of any financial software.*

CLASSIFICATION

Exotic options are divided into barrier, binary, optimal, and average options. We will consider the first two types.

The simplest of the *barrier options* are knock-ins and knock-outs, double knock-ins and double knock-outs. They resemble vanilla options, but in addition to strikes, they have "barriers," also known as "triggers." The *trigger*[1] is a price level of an underlying set in an option contract. If the market trades at this price during the option's life, the option is either validated (*gets knocked in*) or invalidated (*gets knocked out*). For instance,

- a 100 call with 95 knock-in trigger (or simply **knock-in**) is a right to buy the shares at $100 only if the stock trades at $95 during the option's life. Trading at $95 validates (*inspires*) the option.
- an 100 IBM call with 120 knock-out trigger (or simply **knock-out**) may be exercised as long as the stock *does not trade* at 120 during the option's life. The moment it trades at $120 your option is invalidated (*expires*).

BINARY OPTIONS

Binary options, like betting, follow the win/lose principle. Some types of binary options are not defined in terms of strikes and face values. Instead, they have the previously mentioned triggers (barriers) and *payouts*. For instance, for the premium of $10,000, one receives a right for a payout of $25,000, if the USD/CHF rate *does not touch* the 1.5000 level during the next five months. Such an option is called "no touch."

The opposite is true for "one touch" options. Their owners receive a payout, if a trigger is touched. For example, for the premium of $10,000, you receive a right for the payout of $25,000 if the USD/CHF "touches" 1.5000 during next five months.

Digital options are another type of binary. They look like a symbiosis of vanilla and touch options. Like vanilla, they have face value and strike. They are exercised if they are in-the-money on the expiration date. However, as in touch options, the payout is fixed. If you own a 1.5200 digital USD call/CHF put, you will collect $10,000 if the option is exercised. The payout ($10,000) is fixed, no matter whether the spot trades on expiration at 1.5205 or at 1.5700.

Keep in mind:

- Payouts for "touch" options may be validated/invalidated at any moment of option's life[2] while for digital options—only at option expiration (similar to European-American options),
- however odd the options' names may appear, the ideas behind them are very simple.

BARRIER OPTIONS

Let's consider barrier options in detail. Out of a few synonymous options' names, we prefer reverse knock-in, reverse knock-out, knock-in and knock-out. The first category consists of **reverse knock-ins**, also known as *up-and-in call*, or *down-and-in put*.

Reverse knock-in call the option is *validated*[3] (gets knocked in, *in*spired) being in-the-money. For instance, 1.5000 USD call with 1.6000 knock-in trigger, becomes a right to buy USD at 1.5000 only if the market trades at 1.6000 during the option's life. Therefore, the option will be deep in-the-money when inspired.

Reverse knock-in put the option is *validated* being *in-the-money*. For instance, 1.5000 USD put with 1.4000 knock-in trigger becomes a right to sell USD at a 1.5000 only if the market trades at 1.4000 during the option's life. The option will be deep in-the-money when inspired.

The second category consists of **reverse knock-outs**, also known as *up-and-out calls* or *down-and-out puts*.

Reverse knock-out call the option is *invalidated* (gets knocked out, *expired*) when *in-the-money*. For instance, a 1.5000 USD call with a 1.5500 knock-out is a right to buy USD at 1.5000 as long as the market does not touch 1.5500 during the option's life.

Reverse knock-out put the option is *invalidated* being *in-the-money*. For instance, a 1.5000 USD put with a 1.4400 knock-out is a right to sell USD at 1.5000 as long as the market does not trade 1.4400 during the option's life.

Thus, as soon as the word *reverse* appears in the option's name you know that it is triggered when "in-the-money."

The third category consists of **knock-ins**, also known as *down-and-in calls* or *up-and-in puts*.

Knock-in call the option is *validated* being out-of-the-money. For instance, a 1.5000 USD call with a 1.4000 knock-in trigger gives a right to buy USD at 1.5000 only if the market trades at 1.4000 during the option's life. Should it not be *triggered in*, the option will expire worthless, even if the USD the market is trading above 1.5000. However, even if the option is validated (triggered in), it does not mean that it will be in-the-money on the expiration date.

Knock-in put the option is *validated* being *out-of-the-money*. For instance, a 1.5000 USD put with a 1.6000 knock-in trigger is a right to sell USD at 1.5000 only if the market trades at 1.6000 during the option's life. In other words, the option will be out of the money when inspired.

The fourth category consists of **knock-outs** (*down-and-out calls* or *Up-and-out puts*).

Knock-out call the option is invalidated being *out of the money*. For instance, a 1.5000 USD call with a 1.4000 knock-out trigger is a right to buy USD at 1.5000, as long as the market does not trade at 1.4000 during the option's life. The option is knocked out when out-of-the-money.

Knock-out put the option gets knocked out being *out-of-the-money*. For instance, a 1.5000 USD put with 1.5500 knock-out trigger is a right to sell USD at 1.5000, as long as the market does not trade at 1.5500 during the option's life. The option is knocked out when out-of-the-money.

More Complex Types

Double-Barrier Options *Double reverse knock-in, double knock-out, double no touch, etc.* Instead of one barrier (trigger), there are two barriers! Note: the spot is always inside the two triggers, while the strike may be outside (see below). "Double" (double-barrier) options *are very risky* strategies since it is very difficult to guess the market range in the future. As a rule, investors *buy* double knock-*out* strategies because they are cheap. Hedgers sometimes *sell* double knock-*ins*, which often cost almost as much as vanilla options, to secure an extra chance not to be exercised selling options for the purpose of funding a hedging strategy.

An interesting type of double barriers is in-the-money double knock-outs; for example, a 110.00 USD call/JPY put with 115.00–120.00 knock-outs. The spot should stay between the 115.00–120.00 triggers throughout the option's life. Due to a relatively narrow range between the triggers, the option is very likely to be triggered out at some point. That's why in spite of the fact that option is in-the-money, it should be cheap.

Similarly, double no touch options (also known as *range binaries*) give a chance of high payout for a small premium. However, their chances of surviving till expiration are not high.

Rebate Options These have several rows of triggers. If you invest $1,000 and USD/JPY fluctuates in the 115.00–120.00 range for three months, you collect $2,000. However, if the market touches either trigger, the payout amount drops to the initial premium paid. But if the market touches 113.00 or 122.00 (the second-level triggers), you lose the entire premium. In other words, rebate options keep you longer in the game by protecting your investment (or a part of it) at the expense of a lower payout within the first internal range.

Passport Options These allow trading of a certain volume of an underlying asset. The number of transactions in the underlying is also limited. An option seller receives the premium and assumes responsibility for all buyer's trading losses. For example, for the premium of $1 million, one receives a right to trade in lots no larger than euro 1 million, not more than two times a day for one month. At the end, the buyer keeps net profit, the seller assumes net loss.

Window Options These are a variation of barrier or binary options. They become valid not from the moment of trade, but after some period set in the contract. For instance, the contract terms of a three-month 110.00–120.00 double knock-out purchased today will be in place in a month. It doesn't matter whether the spot trades at or beyond 110.00 or 120.00 in the first month. The most important issue is that these triggers are not touched during the last two months of the option's life.

Choice Option At the moment of trading, the type of an option (call or put) is not stipulated. A contract sets a date when a buyer chooses the option's type.

Compounded Option This is an option on another option, which plays the role of an underlying asset. When a compounded option is exercised, its buyer receives a right to buy or sell the initial (internal) option.

QUESTIONS

1. You are long a 1.4500 USD put with a 1.4000 knock-in trigger. During the option's life, the spot traded at 1.4005 and now trades at 1.4200. If the option expires today, how much will you earn?

2. You are short a 1.4350 USD call with a 1.4100 knock-out trigger. During the option's life, the spot stayed above 1.4217 and now is at 1.4360. If the option expires today, how much will you earn?

3. Compare the values of two positions:

   X—Long a 1.4800 USD call;
   Y—Long a 1.4800 USD call with a 1.5000 knock-in trigger and long a 1.4800 USD call with a 1.5000 knock-out trigger.

   The spot is at:

   a. 1.4700;
   b. 1.4900;
   c. 1.5500;
   d. which of the two positions (X or Y) should be more expensive?

4. What is a vanilla-option-equivalent position of the two positions below:

   X—Long 1.4700 USD call with a 1.4600 knock-in trigger;
   Y—Short 1.4700 USD call with a 1.4600 knock-out trigger, and long 1.4700 USD call.

   A week before expiration the spot is at:

   a. 1.4550;
   b. 1.4900;
   c. which of the two positions (X or Y) should be more expensive?

5. The spot trades at 1.4400. You expect it to move down and want to buy a 1.4000 USD put with a 1.4420 knock-out trigger (the closer is knock-out level, the cheaper is an option). This option is cheaper when:
   a. implied volatility is high or low?
   b. time until expiration is one week or one month?
   c. Why?

6. The spot is at 1.4230. You are long a 1.4400 USD call with a 1.4200 knock-out. The probability of the option being triggered out is high. What is a better hedge in this situation: to buy or to sell USD?

7. The spot is at 1.4230. You are long a 1.4400 USD put with a 1.4200 knock-out. The probability of the option being triggered out is high. What is a better hedge in this situation: to buy or to sell USD?

ANSWERS

1. 0. The spot has never reached 1.4000; therefore the option wasn't validated (knocked in).

2. 10 pips. Since the spot has never reached 1.4100, the option is still valid and is 10 pips in-the-money.

3. a. Both positions expired worthless;
   b. Both positions are 100 pips in-the-money. At 1.4900 the reverse knock-in expires worthless, while the reverse knock-out will be in-the-money;
   c. Both positions are 700 points in-the-money. At 1.5500, the reverse knock-in is in-the-money, while the reverse knock-out expires worthless;
   d. Theoretically, they should cost the same since they yield the same P/L along the entire spot range. However, usually the market makers quote exotic options much wider than theoretical prices. As a result, you'll have to pay twice the spread when buying two options than when buying one. Therefore, a vanilla option will be cheaper.

4. a. Both positions are long a 1.4700 USD call; X: the USD call was knocked in at 1.4600, Y: the short USD call was knocked out at 1.4600;
   b. Both positions expired worthless; Y: both the short and long options are in-the-money compensating each other, while the position X was not knocked in;
   c. The answer is similar to 3d.

5. a. The higher the implied volatility, the cheaper the option, because the chance of it being knocked out is greater;
   b. While the spot is close to the trigger, if the knock-out option is deep in-the-money, its premium behaves like that of the vanilla option, the more time is left until expiration the cheaper is the option;
   c. The higher the volatility and the lower the probability that the option will survive, the cheaper the option should be. The same logic is true for maturity: the higher the probability of being knocked out, the cheaper the option. That is, as in other cases, volatility and time influence the option's premium similarly.
6. You will sell USD. You will hedge the same way as in the case of the vanilla option.
7. You will sell USD. This decision contradicts common sense since you hedge the opposite way to vanilla option hedging. Questions 6 and 7 emphasize the difference between reverse knock-out and ordinary knock-out.

FURTHER INFORMATION FOR THE READER

Strategies Used with Exotic Options

Strategies, Reverse Knock-in

1. You believe that the spot USD/CHF will not fall below 1.3700, but if it happens you expect it not to rebound above 1.4100 during the next two weeks.

   Your position is as follows:

Value of USD/CHF Options	Expiration Date	Tools	Strike	Knock-in	Amount	Delta
+ [4]7,000$	25.07.2004	Knock-in USD Call	1.3950	1.3710	+1 million$	+29%
– 8,700$		Knock-in USD Call	1.4200	1.3650	+2 million$	–19%

This is an example of knock-in spreads. Such a strategy is interesting when 1.3700 is a strong level of technical support; that is,

(Continued)

FURTHER INFORMATION FOR THE READER *(Continued)*

you believe that the spot will not go lower than 1.3700. Accordingly, you place your knock-in trigger above 1.3700, and the trigger of the sold option below. In doing so, you hope that the long option will get inspired and the sold one will not.

a. If the spot reaches 1.3710 and rebounds upward, you will become long a vanilla 1.3950 USD call. But if 1.3650 is touched, you will become short a 1.4200 USD call. As a result, you will be short $2 million of a 1.4200 USD call and long $1 million of a 1.3950 USD call.

   - If both sides are triggered tomorrow, the position value at 1.3650 will be 0 (if volatility stays the same). If you decide to close the position, the costs will be minimal.
   - If this happens in a week, the position will have a positive value, because the time decay of the short 1.4200 calls is higher than of the long 1.3900 call.

   Should you decide to keep the call spread in your position, you become synthetically short $1 million of a 1.4150 USD call and, therefore, have an unlimited risk on USD $1 million above 1.4150.

b. The best outcome of the strategy is if you end up long $1 million of a 1.3950 USD call and the spot rebounds from 1.3710 and closes above 1.3950 (i.e., your prediction of the technical support proves to be correct). Then your call will be free.

2. The next strategy is based on the forecast that USD/CHF will remain in the 1.4660–1.6000 range for six months and will most likely stay around 1.5200.
   - It is based on a 1:2 spread.
   - It uses barrier options: short $2 million of a 1.5300 USD call is validated only if the USD/CHF reaches 1.6100 during the life of the strategy. For instance, if at expiration the spot is at 1.6000 (and has not traded at 1.6100), you will exercise the 1.4660 USD call while the 1.5300 call will expire worthless.

Investments:	$8,000
Maximum risk:	unlimited above 1.5940, if the spot goes above 1.6100

FURTHER INFORMATION FOR THE READER *(Continued)*

Maximum profit: $80,000 at 1.6095, if the spot stays below 1.6100
Profit range: 1.4790–1.6095

	Expiration Date	Strike	Knock-in	Amount
USD/CHF	23.07.2004	1.4660 call		+USD 1 million
		1.5300 call	1.6100	–USD 2 million reverse knock-in

Strategy Utilizing "No Touch" Option This strategy consists of a purchase of an out-of-the-money USD call combined with a sale of a no-touch option with the trigger in the opposite direction. This combination may be called a *contingent (pay-later)* call because the buyer of the call will have to pay the premium only if the trigger is "touched." In essence, it is a risk reversal (combo) with limited risk on the downside. That is, if the investor finances a USD call by selling a vanilla USD put, he faces an unlimited risk by shorting the put. The one-touch option limits the risk beforehand by the amount of payout if the barrier is touched.

Current spot: 112.00
Investment: $1,000 ($8,000 premium of 112.00 call minus $7,000 of the premium of "one-touch" option)
Maximum risk: $13,000 (if 103.90 is touched, you will have to pay the owner of the "no touch" option $12,000 while the long call's value on expiration date will equal 0)
Maximum profit: unlimited above 113.10 (112.00 + premium)
Profit range: above 113.10

Notice: if you buy a call now, it will cost $8,000, and that will be your maximum loss. Using a contingent option, you reduce your initial investments to $1,000, but in the worst case you may lose the total of $13,000. However hard you try, there is no free lunch!

(Continued)

FURTHER INFORMATION FOR THE READER *(Continued)*

Strategy Utilizing Reverse Knock-out A reverse knock-out option can capture a wide range of USD/JPY. As long as the spot does not touch 112.00 during the life of the option, this option is profitable.

Investments and maximum risk:	$5,000 (yen 550,000)
Maximum profit:	$27,000 at 111.99, if the spot has not broken 112.00 before the expiration date
Profit range:	108.55–111.99

Currencies	Expiration date	Strike	Knock-out	Amount
USD/CHF	24.04.2004	108.00C	112.00	+USD 1 million

CHAPTER 20

Advanced Exotic Options Strategies

Initially, having studied calls and puts, we rushed into spreads and other strategies. Now, we are about embarking on the same route to study strategies, utilizing not only vanilla, but also exotic options.

CONTINGENT OPTIONS

Contingent options constitute a group of option strategies including such well-known strategies as "buy now pay later." An example of such a binary strategy is a purchase of a 1.5000 USD call with no premium, but with an obligation to pay off X dollars, if spot touches 1.4500. In this case, you would pay a greater amount than if you paid the premium while buying the option.

This strategy is comprised of a long 1.5000 USD call and a short 1.4500 no-touch. It looks like a kind of a range forward. In the latter, a short put would finance a call's purchase. When you sell a put, the amount of maximum losses is not known. Your maximum loss on a short no-touch is limited to the amount of payout in case the market touches 1.4500. For inexperienced investors, this strategy seems like a dream—a purchase of something for nothing, but, as we have proved before, there is no free lunch.

Contingent options can also be comprised of other option combinations. For example, to buy a 30-delta put on copper, you should pay 4% of its face value. If you choose a contingent option, the price will decrease: a 30-delta copper put costs 2% of face value, but if the price on gold reaches $300 per ounce for the same period you will pay out 3.5% more.

It's easy to guess that the price of the copper put decreased due to the sale of a gold no-touch.

RESETTING FORWARD

Resetting forward is a strategy of two or three call/put options with different strikes but with knock-outs and knock-ins at the same level. They are arranged in such a way that at the moment when the trigger "kill" one component of the strategy it simultaneously knocks out/validates another one.

For example, at this moment a two-month USD/CHF forward is at *1.5500*. Instead of buying a regular forward, you buy a resetting forward. According to the contract, you will buy USD (sell CHF) at *1.5000* USD/CHF, if USD/CHF does not trade at 1.4500 or at 1.6500 during the two months. If the market touches one of these barriers, you will buy USD (sell CHF) at *1.5900* USD/CHF on expiration day! In other words, you receive an opportunity to improve the rate, if you agree to a possibility to get a much worse rate.

This strategy consists of a synthetic forward with the strike at 1.5000, the knock-outs at 1.4500 and 1.6500, and a synthetic forward with the strike at 1.5900, with the knock-ins at the same levels. Thus, whatever happens you buy USD and sell CHF:

- In both synthetic forwards you buy a USD call and sell a USD put;
- All four synthetic calls and puts have double triggers at *the same* levels;
- When the market touches the barriers/triggers, knock-out options expire and knock-in options get inspired (become a real liability). That is, you become obliged to buy USD at 1.5900.

BARRIER FORWARD (BARRIER RISK REVERSAL)

The *barrier forward* is a variation of standard synthetic forward or a range forward (risk reversal). The sold option is not a vanilla but a knock-in. The trigger is placed far away from the strike. This strategy allows a trader to reduce a probability of an exercise of the options you are short.

For example, if a two-month USD/CHF forward is at 1.5530, you can create a barrier forward, which will consist of a long 1.5530 USD call and a short 1.5530 USD put with a 1.5290 knock-in. If the spot is below 1.5530, you can choose the rate as long as during the option's life spot has not touched 1.5290. If it has, you would have to buy dollars at 1.5530. The advantage of this strategy is that if on expiration the spot is below 1.5530 and hasn't reached 1.5290, you have a chance to buy USD at a better price than if you have sold a 1.5530 put.

QUESTIONS

1. You bought $1 million of a 1.4500 USD call for $10,000 and sold $1.5 million of a 1.4500 call with the 1.4300 knock-in for $10,000. If the spot falls to 1.4300, this position will make you short $0.5 million of the 1.4500 call. What is an equivalent to this position?
2. You bought $1 million of a 0.3000 EUR call for $10,000 dollars and sold 0.3500 no-touch at $10,000. What should be a payout on the no-touch to avoid arbitrage between the two options?
3. You bought $1 million forward USD/JPY at 107.00. The spot is at 108.25. To hedge the forward, you bought $1 million of a 107.00 JPY call/USD put with the 112.00 knock-out and have financed it by a sale of $1.3 million of a 107.00 JPY put/USD call with the 112.50 knock-in:
   a. What is the P/L profile of this strategy?
   b. And what if you financed the strategy by the sale of $0.5 million of a 107.00 USD put/JPY call with the 105.50 knock-out instead of by using a 107.00 JPY put/USD call?

ANSWERS

1. The answer is based on the calculation of the value of $0.5 million of a 1.4500 call at 1.4300. Suppose the spot falls to 1.4300 right after the position's purchase. Let's assume that at that moment $0.5 million of a 1.4500 call at the 1.4300 level costs $3,000. It means that the given position is equivalent to a 1.4300 no-touch with payment 1:1.9 plus $1 million of a 1.4500 call. In other words, instead of financing the purchase of the 1.4500 call with the sale of the 1.4500 call with the 1.4300 knock-out trigger, you can finance it with the sale of the 1.4300 no-touch.

   Let's analyze the answer: if the spot goes upward, the 1.4500 call makes money in both cases.

   If the spot falls to 1.4300, the value of your original position is $–3,000. That happens because you become short $0.5 million of the 1.4500 call. At that moment, its value is $3,000, and you have an alternative whether to buy it back or not. In the case of the no-touch, you incur an immediate debt of $3,000. That is, the positions are equal only at the moment of purchase of the touch! However, while the payout of the no-touch stays constant throughout the option's life, the value of the 1.4500 call will fall. That is why the original strategy is better.

2. To avoid an arbitrage, the value of the 0.3000 EUR call at 0.3500 must be equal to a payout on the 0.3500 no-touch. The value of the 0.3000 EUR call at 0.3500 equals $50,000. Since the premium of the 0.3500 no-touch was $10,000, to reach a nonarbitrage deal the 0.3500 no-touch must provide the payout of 1:5.

3. a. A maximum profit is reached when the dollar is up to 112.49. If it falls below 107.00, the result of the strategy is a loss of debit (the premium's surplus) paid for the strategy. If dollar touches 112.00, you end up without the hedge while the dollar is falling below 107.00. If the dollar touches 112.50, you end up being short $0.3 million at 107.00.

   b. If the dollar appreciates, your spot position equals $0.5 million. But if initially the spot falls to 105.50 and then rises above 107.00, the position will make money on $1 million, since the sold option will expire (i.e., get knock-out). In this case, the maximum gain is unlimited. If at expiration the dollar is below 107.00 (and has never traded at 112.00), the result of the strategy is a loss of debit (the premium's surplus) paid for the strategy.

PART Four

Market Support (Market Making)

The transformation of stand-alone deals (singular transactions) into the market occurs with the appearance of market makers. They are traders (dealers) in banks or on exchanges[1] who quote (*make prices*) on certain instruments, to each other and to clients. Access to prices enables users to buy or to sell their positions. This creates *market liquidity*: an opportunity to purchase a certain instrument or to transform portfolio of instruments back into money.

The more liquid the market, the cheaper the opportunity to change portfolios, since the difference between purchase and sale prices (*trading spread*) is smaller. Examples of superliquid markets are the currencies and treasury notes traded in the United States.

The liquid markets are more predictable since thousands of participants forecast the market dynamics differently, and at every price level there are sellers and buyers. That is, the process of "fair price discovery" in liquid markets is relatively protected from sharp alterations of prices.

In nonliquid markets, there is no guarantee that participants can satisfy their needs. Additionally, the difference between purchase and sale prices (the spread) is greater since both buyers and sellers try to be compensated for their own risk of exiting a new position.

That is why illiquid markets attract few participants. In turn, because of poor liquidity such markets become jumpy—prices change in gaps. This is a normal occurrence on equity and bond markets of emerging economies.

Thus, market liquidity greatly depends on the quantity of market makers and their financial standing. In next two chapters, we will study the process of market making on option markets.

CHAPTER 21

Market Making: Price Support of the Market

Everyone knows how to make money: to buy low and to sell high. In the case of options, this is done a bit differently. This chapter covers some of the specifics of profitable market making.

BASIC TERMS

Buying low and selling high (not necessarily in this order) is the purpose of a market maker's work. This implies buying a bit below the average current price and selling a bit above it. For example, with the price at 10–11, a market maker hopes to buy at 10 (or to sell at 11) and to sell at 11 (or to buy at 10), earning 1 tick on the deal.

Such a definition of market making is more correct for spot/cash trading. In options, the benchmark price (i.e., "the market price") is not the average of purchase and sale (bid and offer) prices, but the volatility curve of 50-delta options. A trader makes money if he buys an option below the volatility curve and sells one above it. Unlike in the case of the spot, the purchased and sold options may have different maturities or strikes. As a result, he earns *theoretical profit*. For example, if the price of a one-month 50-delta option is 10% and the price of a two-month 50-delta option is 12%, the trader will receive a theoretical gain if he buys a one-month option at 9.9% and sells the two-month one at 12.1%.

Gain is called "theoretical" (or "paper") because it is not realized and a price ratio between the two options may change until their expiration, thus changing theoretical profit. In other words, a spot trader realizes profit/loss when buying and selling equal face values. Options dealers run a *book* (position) portfolio comprised of many options, and a substantial portion of the result is unrealized (theoretical).

Open spot positions run mostly directional risks. Options' books are hedged, that is, less dependent on direction, but they run the risk of losses due to time decay, gamma, interest/dividend rates, and volatility changes. As we discussed, these and other risks are measured by Greeks. For instance, risk of a spot move is measured by delta and gamma. When hedging volatility, one uses vega.

Delta and gamma may be hedged by means of spot/forward or another option (combination of options) with analogous delta/gamma. Volatility may be hedged only by another option (combination of options).

Therefore, *options market makers make money by purchasing cheap option combinations and selling more expensive ones with analogous risk parameters.*

READING MARKET MAKERS' PRICING SHEETS

Table 21.1 shows a pricing sheet used by dealers to quote prices on exchanges.

Parameters Used in Pricing

Horizontal Line The options' prices on five months options series currently traded on an exchange are set in rows: May, June, July, September, December.[1]

The prices and parameters are revaluated each two pips. For instance, the first section of the page is priced at 72.14,[2] and the second one would be at 72.16 or 72.12.

Vertical Line under Each Month The first line:

64 69[3]—currency swap

May—option contract's expiration[4] month

12.00%—(implied) volatility price

The second line:

D = 3—days till expiration,

Rd = 6.15%—domestic (dollar) interest rate

The third line:

72.14—current futures price (equivalent to spot). It is different for June, September, and December futures[5] because of the different interest rates implied in the futures for different months.

TABLE 21.1 Market Makers' Pricing Sheet

<table>
<tr><th colspan="5">S: 83 + 64-69 MAY 12.00%
D = 3 sd = .19 rd = 6.15% 64
= > 72.14–1.3825–72.33</th><th colspan="5">S: 222-217 220 JUN 11.70% D = 38 sd =
.19 rd = 5.93% 217
= > 72.14 - 1.3825 –72.33</th><th colspan="5">S: 283-282 287 JUL 11.60% D = 66-sd =
.19 rd = 5.93% 282
= > 71.86-1.3878-72.06</th><th colspan="5">S: 384 380 + 39SEP 11.30% D = 129 sd =
.19 rd = 5.98% 380 +
= > 71.86 - 1.3878 –72.06</th><th colspan="6">S: 483 + 482 + 494 + DEC 11.10% D = 220-sd =
.19 rd = 6.17% 482 +
= > 71.76 - 1.3898 –71.96</th></tr>
<tr><td>< 0/0.0></td><td>66.0</td><td>614
200</td><td>(100)</td><td>0
0</td><td>(0) |<1/ 0.0></td><td>66.0</td><td>614
195</td><td>(100)</td><td>1-
6-</td><td>(1) |<3/ 2.6></td><td>66.0</td><td>589
183</td><td>(98)</td><td>8
17</td><td>(4) |<0/ 0.0></td><td>62.0</td><td>986
198</td><td>(100)</td><td>2
6-</td><td>(1) |<2/ 4.7></td><td>62.0</td><td>977-
189-</td><td>(98)</td><td>10
14-</td><td>(4) |</td></tr>
<tr><td>< 0/0.0></td><td>67.0</td><td>514
150</td><td>(100)</td><td>0
0</td><td>(0) |<2/ 1.3></td><td>67.0</td><td>515
142+</td><td>(98)</td><td>2
8</td><td>(2) |<4/ 4.3></td><td>67.0</td><td>496
131</td><td>(92)</td><td>12-
19-</td><td>(7) |<1/ 0.0></td><td>63.0</td><td>886
193</td><td>(99)</td><td>4
9</td><td>(2) |<2/ 6.4></td><td>63.0</td><td>881-
181</td><td>(96)</td><td>15+
20</td><td>(6) |</td></tr>
<tr><td>< 0/0.0></td><td>68.0</td><td>414
100</td><td>(100)</td><td>0
0</td><td>(0) |<4/ 2.6></td><td>68.0</td><td>419
91-</td><td>(95)</td><td>6+
9</td><td>(5) |<6/ 6.3></td><td>68.0</td><td>406
82</td><td>(87)</td><td>22+
18-</td><td>(12) |<2/ 3.6></td><td>64.0</td><td>788
186</td><td>(97)</td><td>7+
15-</td><td>(4) |<3/ 8.4></td><td>64.0</td><td>788
172+</td><td>(92)</td><td>24-
27</td><td>(8) |</td></tr>
<tr><td>< 0/ 0.0></td><td>68.5</td><td>364
100</td><td>(100)</td><td>0
0</td><td>(0) |<6/ 3.5></td><td>68.5</td><td>373
87</td><td>(92)</td><td>10
13-</td><td>(8) |<7/ 7.4></td><td>68.5</td><td>364
78+</td><td>(84)</td><td>30
21</td><td>(16) |<3/ 5.2></td><td>65.0</td><td>693
178-</td><td>(94)</td><td>13
22</td><td>(6) |<4/ 10.5></td><td>65.0</td><td>700
163</td><td>(88)</td><td>35+
35+</td><td>(11) |</td></tr>
<tr><td>< 0/ 0.0></td><td>69.0</td><td>314
100</td><td>(100)</td><td>0</td><td>(0) |<7/ 4.5></td><td>69.0</td><td>328+
83</td><td>(88)</td><td>16-
17</td><td>(11) |<8/ 8.4></td><td>69.0</td><td>324
74-</td><td>(80)</td><td>40
26-</td><td>(20) |<4/ 7.2></td><td>66.0</td><td>602
167+</td><td>(90)</td><td>22
32-</td><td>(9) |<4/ 12.8></td><td>66.0</td><td>616-
153</td><td>(84)</td><td>51-
44</td><td>(15) |</td></tr>
<tr><td>< 0/ 0.0></td><td>69.5</td><td>264
100-</td><td>(100)</td><td>0
+</td><td>(0) |<9/ 5.6></td><td>69.5</td><td>286-
78-</td><td>(84)</td><td>23-
22</td><td>(15) |<9/ 9.4></td><td>69.5</td><td>286-
68+</td><td>(76)</td><td>51+
31</td><td>(24) |<5/ 9.4></td><td>67.0</td><td>515+
155</td><td>(86)</td><td>35
43</td><td>(14) |<5/ 15.1></td><td>67.0</td><td>537
142+</td><td>(79)</td><td>71-
54</td><td>(19) |</td></tr>
<tr><td>< 1/ 0.1></td><td>70.0</td><td>214
98-</td><td>(100)</td><td>
2+</td><td>(0) |<11/ 6.6></td><td>70.0</td><td>246-
72</td><td>(79)</td><td>33-
28-</td><td>(21) |<10/ 10.3></td><td>70.0</td><td>250+
64</td><td>(71)</td><td>66-
35+</td><td>(29) |<6/ 11.6></td><td>68.0</td><td>435
141+</td><td>(80)</td><td>54-
56+</td><td>(19) |<5/ 17.2></td><td>68.0</td><td>463-
129-</td><td>(74)</td><td>95
67</td><td>(24) |</td></tr>
<tr><td>< 5/ 0.3></td><td>70.5</td><td>164+
91-</td><td>(98)</td><td>
9-</td><td>+ (2) |<12/ 7.6></td><td>70.5</td><td>208
65+</td><td>(73)</td><td>45-
34</td><td>(26) |<11/ 11.1></td><td>70.5</td><td>217+
60</td><td>(66)</td><td>82+
41</td><td>(34) |<7/ 13.6></td><td>69.0</td><td>360+
126</td><td>(73)</td><td>78
71+</td><td>(26) |<6/ 18.9></td><td>69.0</td><td>394+
116-</td><td>(68)</td><td>125-
80</td><td>(30) |</td></tr>
<tr><td>< 17 /0.9></td><td>71.0</td><td>116
77+</td><td>(93)</td><td>2+
22+</td><td>(7) |<14/ 8.4></td><td>71.0</td><td>174-
58</td><td>(67)</td><td>60
42-</td><td>(33) |<11/ 11.6></td><td>71.0</td><td>187-
53-</td><td>(60)</td><td>101
47-</td><td>(39) |<8/ 15.3></td><td>70.0</td><td>294-
110+</td><td>(66)</td><td>110
87</td><td>(33) |<6/ 20.3></td><td>70.0</td><td>334
105-</td><td>(62)</td><td>162
91</td><td>(36) |</td></tr>
<tr><td>< 37/ 1.9></td><td>71.5</td><td>73
57-</td><td>(69)</td><td>9
43+</td><td>(20) |<14/ 8.9></td><td>71.5</td><td>143-
51-</td><td>(60)</td><td>79
49</td><td>(40) |<11/12.0></td><td>71.5</td><td>159+
47+</td><td>(55)</td><td>124-
52</td><td>(45) |<8/ 16.3></td><td>71.0</td><td>234+
91</td><td>(58)</td><td>150-
108</td><td>(41) |<6/ 21.1></td><td>71.0</td><td>279
92</td><td>(55)</td><td>205-
103</td><td>(42) |</td></tr>
</table>

(Continued)

TABLE 21.1 *(Continued)*

< 51/ 2.6>	**72.0**	39 33+	(57)	25 67-	(43)	|<15/ 9.2>	**72.0**	116- 44-	(53)	102- 56	(47)	|<11/ 12.1>	**72.0**	134 41+	(49)	148 58	(50)	|<8/ 16.7>	**72.0**	183 78+	(50)	197 119	(49)	|<7/ 21.4>	**72.0**	229+ 78+	(49)	253 117	(49)	|
< 47/ 2.4>	**72.5**	17- 15+	(32)	53- 85-	(68)	|<15/ 9.2>	**72.5**	92 37	(45)	128 62+	(54)	|<11/ 11.9>	**72.5**	112 37	(43)	175+ 63-	(56)	|<8/ 16.4>	**73.0**	140+ 63+	(41)	253- 134	(57)	|<6/ 21.2>	**73.0**	187- 67	(43)	308- 129-	(55)	|
< 28/ 1.4>	**73.0**	5+ 5	(14)	91+ 95	(86)	|<14/ 8.8>	**73.0**	72 31	(38)	158- 69-	(61)	|<11/ 11.6>	**73.0**	93- 32-	(38)	206 68-	(61)	|<8/ 15.4>	**74.0**	105 49+	(34)	316 148+	(65)	|<6/ 20.4>	**74.0**	151 58	(37)	370 138+	(61)	|
< 11/ 0.6>	**73.5**	1+ 1+	(4)	137+ 99-	(96)	|<13/ 8.2>	**73.5**	55 25-	(31)	190 75	(68)	|<10/ 11.0>	**73.5**	75 26	(33)	238 73	(67)	|<7/ 13.9>	**75.0**	77 38+	(27)	387 160	(72)	|<6/ 19.2>	**75.0**	120- 47-	(31)	436+ 150-	(67)	|
< 3/ 0.2>	**74.0**		(1)	186 100	(99)	|<12/ 7.4>	**74.0**	41 19	(25)	226 80+	(74)	|<10/ 10.3>	**74.0**	61 23-	(28)	273+ 77-	(71)	|<6/ 12.1>	**76.0**	56- 29	(21)	464+ 170	(78)	|<5/ 17.7>	**76.0**	93 38	(26)	508 159	(73)	|
< 0/ 0.0>	**74.5**		(0)	236 100	(100)	|<10/ 6.5>	**74.5**	30 15	(20)	265+ 85	(80)	|<9/ 9.4>	**74.5**	49 19	(24)	311 81-	(76)	|<5/ 10.2>	**77.0**	39- 21	(16)	547- 178	(84)	|<5/ 15.9>	**77.0**	73 31+	(21)	586 167-	(78)	|
< 0/ 0.0>	**75.0**	0 0	(0)	286 100	(100)	|<9/ 5.5>	**75.0**	22- 11+	(15)	307- 88+	(84)	|<8/ 8.5>	**75.0**	38 15	(20)	350 84+	(80)	|<4/ 8.3>	**78.0**	27- 15+	(11)	634 185	(88)	|<4/ 14.0>	**78.0**	55+ 24	(17)	667+ 175-	(82)	|
< 0/ 0.0>	**75.5**	0 0	(0)	336 100	(100)	|<7/ 4.6>	**75.5**	15+ 8+	(12)	350 91+	(88)	|<7/ 7.5>	**75.5**	30 12+	(16)	392- 87+	(84)	|<3/ 6.5>	**79.0**	17+ 10+	(8)	725 191-	(92)	|<4/ 12.1>	**79.0**	41+ 19	(14)	753- 181	(86)	|
< 0/ 0.0>	**76.0**	0 0	(0)	386 100	(100)	|<6/ 3.7>	**76.0**	10+ 6	(8)	395 94	(92)	|<6/ 6.5>	**76.0**	23 10	(13)	434+ 90	(87)	|<2/ 4.9>	**80.0**	11+ 7	(6)	819 195	(95)	|<3/ 10.2>	**80.0**	31+ 15	(11)	842 186+	(90)	|
< 0/ 0.0>	**76.5**	0 0	(0)	436 100	(100)	|<4/ 2.8>	**76.5**	7 4	(6)	442- 96	(94)	|<5/ 5.6>	**76.5**	18- 6	(10)	479 92	(89)	|<2/ 3.6>	**81.0**	7 4+	(4)	915+ 198+	(98)	|<2/ 8.5>	**81.0**	23- 11-	(8)	934- 191+	(93)	|
< 0/ 0.0>	**77.0**	0 0	(0)	486 386	(100)	|<3/ 2.1>	**77.0**	5- 5-	(4)	489+ 489+	(96)	|<4/ 4.7>	**77.0**	13 13	(8)	524+ 524+	(92)	|<1/ 2.6>	**82.0**	4 4	(2)	014 014	(99)	|<2/ 6.9>	**82.0**	16 16	(6)	028 028	(96)	|
< 0/ 0.0>	**77.5**	0 0		536 536	(100)	|<2/ 1.6>	**77.5**	3 3	(3)	538- 538-	(98)	|<3/ 3.9>	**77.5**	9+ 9+	(6)	571 571	(94)	|<1/ 1.8>	**83.0**	3- 3-	(2)	114 114	(100)	|<2/ 5.5>	**83.0**	12 5	(5)	125 125	(98)	|

Parameters for Market Makers

66.0–77.5—strikes

and 72.0—the strike the closest to 50-delta's one.

To the left of the strike

<51/2.6>—are gamma (51)[6] and vega (2.6)

To the right of the strike

39 (57) 25 (43) —price and delta of call and put

DETERMINATION OF A STRATEGY PRICE

Let's assume you are making markets in options. Suppose a broker yells out: "May 72–73 call spread!" and you are to determine the price with the help of the market maker's pricing sheet.

Looking at a monitor where the current quotation of June futures (72.14) appears and at corresponding options prices on your pricing sheet, you yell back to the broker in no time: "33–35!"

What does this price mean? The price of a May 72 call is 39 ticks and of a 73 call it is 5 ticks (39 – 5 = 34). You want to buy below 34 and sell above 34; therefore, the price is 33–35. To look at it another way, you buy or sell the May 72 call at 39, and buy or sell the May 73 call at 4 or at 6[7] respectively.

But a market maker can say 32–34 as well. Why? We discussed the concept of a volatility *smile*:[8] a premium of OTM over ATM options *with the same expiration* expressed in volatilities. Such a premium is paid for options in the price direction, in which a greater volatility is expected. For example, in the S&P market volatility rises when the market falls. That's why prices in volatility terms on OTM S&P puts (for example, on 20-delta put is 14.5 volatilities) are higher than on ATM puts (for example, 14 volatilities).

What does the existence of a smile imply? Why, for example, is *implied* volatility of OTM calls higher than of ATM calls? It means that traders expect that market volatility of an underlying asset will increase when spot goes in that direction. In our example, implied volatility and, therefore, the dollar price of the May 73 call will be higher than currently estimated by ATM options. For example, it will not be 12%, but 13%. The dollar equivalent of 13% is not 5 cents, but 6 cents.

That is why the price of the "May 72–73 call spread" is 32–34, if you buy or sell May 72 call at 39, and buy or sell May 73 call at 5 or 6 respectively.

DETERMINATION OF DELTA FOR HEDGING

A client bought 5 contracts at 34.

Since an exchange market maker's position must be delta-neutral, once a new option enters the book, one should immediately hedge it with futures.

To begin, one should understand what "call spread sold at 34" means. It implies that one sold a May 72 call at 39 and bought a May 73 call at 5. Delta of the May 72 call is 57, and delta of the May 73 call is 15. Therefore, total delta of the spread on one contract is 42 (57 – 15). Since you *sold the call* with higher delta, to hedge the position you should buy 0.42% × 5 option contracts = 2 futures contracts.

If you are an OTC trader and prefer hedging with spot rather than futures, you should recalculate the futures contracts into spot-equivalent.

2 futures contracts × 62.500 = 125.000 Swiss francs

That is, you should buy 125.000 Swiss francs on the OTC.

QUESTIONS

Based on May futures at 72.14 (see the pricing sheet on pages 197–198):

1. What is the price of a June–July 73.0–74.5 call spread (without a smile). In terms of which option is the price made?
2. What is the price of a July 72.0–73.0 combo, "puts are 2 (volatility) ticks over calls" (smile). In terms of which option is the price made?
3. What is the price of a December 71.0–76.0 call, 1:2 (ratio spread), where low-delta calls are 3 (volatility) ticks over the ATM curve? In terms of which option is the price made?
4. September volatility increased by 2 ticks. How much does 74.0 call cost?
5. Futures moved to 72.12 (not in the table), what is the price of December 72.0 put?

ANSWERS

1. Price is 22/24. A 73 call costs 72 ticks (U.S. cents), a 74.5 call costs 49. 72 – 49 = 23 (price is 22/24).

   On exchanges the price is established based on the more expensive option (in this case the 73 call). That's why 22 is your bid on the 73 call and 24 is your offer on the 73 call.

2. The price is 56.5/58.5. The 73 call costs 93 cents;

   the 72 put costs 148 + smile (0.2% vol × vega 12.1) = 148 + 2.4 = 150.510. 150.5 – 93 = 57.5 (price is 56.5/58.5).

   The more expensive option in this case is the 72 put. That's why 56.5 is your bid on the 72 put, and 58.5 is your offer on the 72 put.

3. The price is 81/83. The 71 call costs 279;

   2 × [the 76 call costs 96 + smile (0.3% vol × vega 17.7)] = 98.5.

   279 – 197 = 82 (price is 81/83).

   The more expensive option in this case is the 71 call (but if the value of the 76 call were 136, the quote would be based on the 76 call since there are two of them). That's why 81 is your bid on the 71 call and 83 is your offer on the 71 call.

4. The price is 107/109. The 74 call costs 105 + 0.2% vol move × vega 15.4 = 108.

5. The price is 253/255. The 72 put at 253 – [delta (–0.5) × (72.14 – 72.12)] = 254.

CHAPTER 22

Introduction to Options Portfolio Management

You have done many deals today, and your book is filled with option, spot and forward positions, which are not matched. How should you manage this portfolio? This is the question faced by both traders and risk managers. Both use almost the same methods to understand and manage risks. The difference is that traders use them to adapt the positions to their market views and to be sure that the limits are not broken. Risk managers use the same instruments to control the limits.

MAIN TERMS

Portfolio risks are measured with the help of the Greeks (delta, gamma, theta, vega, rho). Once a trader sees the Greeks of his position, he can make a decision about what he needs to buy or sell to end up with a desirable risk profile.

Risks of options portfolios are reflected by reports similar to Table 22.1. Let's consider the report in details.

Date. This the date when the report was calculated.

Time. This is the time when the report was calculated. It differs for different underlying markets. In general, it makes sense to run reports at least twice a day, at the market opening and closing. Additionally, one can run reports right after option exercises.[1] The end-of-day reports show the portfolio's gamma, vega, and theta for the *next* trading day. This enables traders at the end of a trading day to make the portfolio delta-neutral for the next session.

Spot mark-to-market. This is the spot at the moment of revaluation. When the market changes sharply, one needs an updated report to show the

TABLE 22.1 Position's Sensitivity to Spot Changes

Currency: **Euro/Dollar**

Date: 08.08.03 **Spot on revaluation:** 0.8725
Time: after New-York **Step:** 0.0075

Spot	0.8500	0.8575	0.8650	0.8725	0.8800	0.8875	0.895
Delta	−2,000,000	−1,500,000	−1,000,000	0	500,000	2,000,000	1,000,000
Gamma	−500,000	−500,000	−1,000,000		500,000	1,500,000	−1,000,000
Result[1]			−3950	−200	1675	5850	

put −3.5M @[2] 0.8900
call 1M @ 0.8850

VEGA	
August	−3,000.00
September	2,000.00
October	1,000.00
November	−2,500.00
December	−500
January	−4,000.00
February	3,500.00
March	0
April	200
May	0
June	0
July	0
Total:	−3,300.00

Forward's	EURO	Dollar
August	−1,000,000	−872,500
September	200,000	174,500
October	100,000	87,250
November	475,000	414,438
December	−2,000,000	−1,745,000
January	3,200,000	2,792,000
February	75,000	65,438
March	125,000	109,063
April	0	0
May	0	0
June	0	0
July	0	0
Total:	1,175,000	1,025,188

[1]The results are calculated for a part of ranges. The others are in Questions.
[2]@ is an abbreviation of the preposition "at." In this context it stands for "at some price."

Greeks at the new spot level. However, most of the time reports cover an entire possible daily spot range.

Step (of the underlying). This is a minimal interval between spot levels for which columns are calculated. Steps are adjusted for volatility: the higher the volatility the wider the intervals.

Delta. This shows the amount of an underlying asset to be sold/purchased to make the option delta-neutral at the given spot level.

Gamma. This shows delta's change between spot values in neighboring columns. There are two types of gamma: *direct* and *pin*. The portfolio generates the direct one. The pin gamma depends on overnight options' expirations. This type of gamma is called pin because it changes by the full amount of an expiring option's face value once the spot crosses its strike. In such moments, its delta changes from 0 to 100% or vice versa. For example, "long 1M @ 0.8850" stands for purchased EUR 1 million of a 0.8850 call or put.[2] When spot crosses the level of 0.8850, the delta will change by EUR 1 million, that is, by the entire option's face value. In this example, EUR 1 million is pin gamma.

Suppose an option with EUR 1 million 0.8850 "face" is to expire today, but we don't know whether it is a call or a put. If it is a call, then at any point below 0.8850, its delta is 0, and above 0.8850 it is +100%. If currently spot is below 0.8850, the option is fully hedged; then above 0.8850 you will be able to sell EUR 1 million and below 0.8850 the option's delta is 0 and doesn't require any action.

In the case of a put, below 0.8850 its delta is –100% and above 0.8850 it is 0. That is, under 0.8850 you can buy EUR 1 million, but above 0.8850 the option's delta is 0, and you have to sell EUR 1 million. Since currently spot is below 0.8850 and rehedging is done throughout the option's life, the ITM long put will be 100-delta. In other words, the entire hedge is in place. However, if five minutes before the expiration time spot goes above the 0.8850 strike, you won't need the hedge anymore, and you will sell 100% of it.

The example confirms that if you are long at 0.8850 **either** a call or a put, you will sell the entire hedge above the strike and buy it below the strike. That is why pin gamma changes delta discretely.

How do we separate direct gamma from pin gamma? We see that in the 0.8800–0.8875 range gamma changes by EUR 1.5 million. We know that at 0.8850, there is a EUR 1 million-face expiration. Therefore, "direct gamma" (gamma generated by portfolio, rather than options expiring today) is EUR 500,000 (1,500,000 – 1,000,000).

Thus, gamma's separation into "direct" and "pin" risk allows the trader to manage hedging better: direct gamma can be managed before expiring strikes are crossed.

Gamma describes our portfolio risk profile (see Table 22.1). We see that as the spot falls the portfolio loses money, but above the current spot level (*revaluation level*) it gains. An options dealer would say: "Short gamma below and long one above [the revaluation level]." Such a profile reflects the position in a risk reversal—short puts and long calls. Hopefully, you noticed that the previous phrase has to be corrected to "the portfolio is long *options with the strikes* above the reval (revaluation) level and short options with the strikes below it."

Theta is located under the price of spot at the moment of revaluation (*reval level*). It is obvious that our report is the end-of-day report: intraday reports would show theta equal 0! The end-of-day report shows the amount to be lost or gained overnight on theta. If the spot doesn't move overnight, the position will lose $200.

If we consider theta together with gamma, we notice that the absolute value of negative gamma (for lower spot levels) is greater than that of the positive one for the higher ones. That means that in the portfolio there are more sold than bought options. But a net short portfolio losing theta does not look reasonable, because the net seller of options should earn theta.

Such a situation occurs when the reval level is close to the strike of a long option expiring the next day. Its long pin theta is much higher than the short position's theta. But an expiring option does not generate a direct gamma to hedge that of sold options. It generates only pin gamma.

P/L's calculation. Let's consider two ranges: 0.8725–0.8800 and 0.8800–0.8875. In the first range, gamma increases from 0 to EUR 500,000. Let's suppose that the average delta in the range is EUR 250,000.[3] If tomorrow the spot closes at 0.8800, you will expect the following result:

$$250{,}000 \times 0.0075 - 200 = \$1{,}675$$

Notice: it is necessary to subtract theta from the spot-move result.

In the 0.8800–0.8875 range, the situation is more complex. There is a direct and a pin gamma. Due to the pin gamma, the portfolio earns

$$\text{EUR } 1{,}000{,}000 \times (0.8875 - 0.8850) = \$2{,}500$$

Direct gamma contributes

$$(1{,}500{,}000 - 1{,}000{,}000) \times (0.8875 - 0.8800)/2 = \$1{,}875.$$

Total gain due to gamma is $4,375 ($2,500 + $1,875). And the entire result of the spot move to 0.8875 with theta taken into account is $4,175 ($4,375 – $200). If the spot moves from 0.8725 to 0.8875 with no interim hedging, the position will earn $5,850 ($1,675 + $4,175).

The explanation above assumes constant volatility and interest rates; therefore the portfolio value depends only on spot changes. But in reality volatility and interest rates change. That's why Table 22.1 contains parameters necessary to control vega and rho.

Vega Report

Vega. This is calculated for each month and for the portfolio as a whole. As a rule, if the volatility curve is relatively smooth, the vega risk may be grouped by three consecutive months (e.g., August, September, October). Only during crises does the curve become steep, and the suggested basketing of vega doesn't reflect the risks precisely. Alternatively, one can consider each month separately, although it is inconvenient in everyday practice.

To understand how vega works, let's study the report. In August, if volatility falls by 1% you earn $3,000 on the position and make $3,000 if volatility increases by 1%. That is, you have a short vega position. Such a position is called *short vega*, since you are "net-short 3,000 vega." Notice: the overall monthly vega position looks like a horizontal butterfly: short-long-short. Such a position structure helps when you expect the spot to remain stable: you will earn on both theta and vega. The long in the middle-curve segment hedges the portfolio against unexpected curve moves.

Vega of 200 in April is also very interesting. Very often position-management software interpolates the portfolio monthly. For instance, an option expiring in one-and-a-half months will assume some split between the first and second months. Sometimes, systems have an incorrect algorithm of vega extrapolation. As a result, a portion of the position appears even in months where there are no options at all, for instance, in the case of a one-and-a-half-month option, the software can show vega in a three-month segment! Perhaps, in our example, 200 is a system's failure of such kind.

On the other hand, if you were to choose managing monthly vega risk, rather than basketing, you will have a very unstable vega. Imagine you have a position where you have been selling lots of OTM options. They are very sensitive to volatility changes, and every time the market moves, a portion of them will gain/lose vega. Thus, while the overall vega position in the segments of one- and two-month is balanced, the portfolio will look unbalanced with every spot/volatility change unless basketed.

Forward Report

Forward. The table's logic is the same as the logic for the vega's table. Forward positions theoretically should be hedged with forwards, but in practice traders use spot/cash. As a result, the option's books may have a significant interest rate exposure.

Our table assumes that there is no difference in interest rates of currencies: for all months the amount of euro is multiplied by the *current* spot. If the interest rates of the euro and the dollar were different, forward exchange rates would differ. In that case, the amount of the euro in each month would be multiplied by the forward rate for a certain month and would be different.[4]

Unlike managing gamma risks, for forwards risk management it does matter whether there is a call or a put in a position, because it really matters whether the spot is bought or sold on hedge. In real life, traders prefer to buy calls on a currency with a lower interest rate. Thus, on a hedge they (borrow and) sell a lower-yielding currency and receive in exchange a higher-yielding currency. As a result, the position earns funding.

Psychologically, of course, it is easier to see a funding gain than a loss. Theoretically, an extra profit on funding should be compensated by a higher price of call options of such currencies. However, traders believe that the options prices do not fully compensate funding advantages. It impels them to compensate their own fear by charging an additional volatility premium for selling calls on a lower-yielding currency.

Having looked through the split by months, you see that to balance the position you should buy EUR 2,000,000 in December and sell EUR 2,000,000 in January.

To determine rho and vega risk, it is important to remember that when the spot moves, vega and forward positions change as well. This happens because some options become in-the-money and others out of the money. That's why on a day of a considerable underlying asset move, traders often break vega limits even without trading their positions. Worst of all is that if forward and vega limits are controlled per month, a move causes rebalancing inside each month, and a trader simultaneously breaks both cumulative and monthly limits of vega. It is a forceful argument for basketing vega and rho in three-month baskets.

HEDGING OF A RISK-FREE PORTFOLIO

How can we maximize the profit of hedging a risk-free portfolio? Theoretically, when delta changes, the hedge should be adjusted. Delta changes with changes in spot, volatility, forwards, and time until expiration. One can imagine thousands of deals necessary to follow theory in practice. Costs of such hedging would be very high. Therefore, a style of rehedging turns out to be a major question. It is an art not a science.

How to Manage Short and Long Gamma?

In answering this question, one has to account for market expectations. To forecast, traders mostly use technical analysis: charts of historical price are analyzed to find, for instance, levels of resistance and support,[5] behavior of averages, and so on. The very process of technical analysis is also an art. Without skillful market forecasting, skillful delta management is not possible.

Let's look at Table 22.2. Suppose a trader believes that the spot will be in a certain range. Then, if a support level (bottom of the range) is close, it will probably move back up.[6] The position will lose money if the support is broken, while with an upward move it will earn.

Thus, the position assumes a bullish view on the underlying market. Besides, vega is negative; that is, a trader will make money when volatility falls. That happens when spot returns to the previous price range. Now, one can guess how the position was built. It is most likely that the spot recently fell to a support level, and the trader sold a great number of puts.[7] Hence, short gamma and short vega on the "bottom" of the range appeared.

Gamma remains steady (500,000 for each basket of a range); this means that middle- and long-term puts were sold: their gamma behaves very smoothly. If short-term OTM puts were sold, on a downward move gamma would change sharply, since gamma of short-term options changes sharply when they approach an ATM level (i.e., gamma of short-term options is localized near their strikes).

Delta/Vega (Delta's Changes Due to Change in Vega)

Understanding the position's "contents" is very important in predicting gamma's behavior when volatilities change. For example, if spot goes up back in the range and implied volatility falls, a negative delta will fall, and you will be able to sell more euros. Let's describe this mechanism: as volatility falls, delta of an OTM option decreases.[8] When delta of the sold options falls, you do not need as much short euro on the hedge. That is, you become "longer" euro. In this case, long-term puts were sold, and a delta's change due to a volatility's change is insignificant. If short-term puts were sold, you would expect a greater delta's change.[9]

TABLE 22.2 Position's Sensitivity to Spot Changes

	Date: 08.08.03				**Spot on revaluation:**	0.8800	
	Time: after New-York				**Step:**	0.0075	
Spot	0.8500	0.8575	0.8650	0.8725	0.8800	0.8875	0.8950
Delta	−2,000,000	−1,500,000	−1,000,000	0	500,000	2,000,000	1,000,000
Gamma	−500,000	−500,000	−1,000,000		500,000	↓ 1,500 000	↓ −1,000,000
							put −3.5M @ 0.8900
						call 1M @ 0.8850	

To summarize, we ascertained that volatility falls when euro appreciates, but that does not change delta significantly. Thus, delta changes due to delta/vega of long-term options (delta's change due to the change of volatilities) can be disregarded.

Hedging "Long Gamma"

We refer a few questions to Table 22.3.

First question: what spot move do we need to "cover" theta (premium's time decay)?

Second question: what portion of delta should we sell to "cover" theta?

To estimate a spot move needed to cover theta ($200), one can assume that on the higher part of the range EUR 100,000 on 20 pips (0.0020). That is, the breakeven point is 0.8725 + 0.0020 = 0.8745.[10] If you sell EUR 200,000 at 0.8733, you are insured against losses on theta. Such a calculation is not precise, but it hardly makes sense to make it more exact, when we talk about art!

And what should we do, if theta is paid off only at an extreme of the interval (e.g., 0.8800)? That happens when you are long short-term options and short one-month ones. You end up being long a lot of gamma locally (in a narrow interval) and paying theta, but the longer-term options make you short gamma on the interval extremes. Because of that, delta increases very slowly, and a substantial move is essential to "cover" theta.

Most of the time, big moves occur seldom, and spot, as a rule, fails to reach the borders of the first interval. Thus, a "long gamma" trader always faces the dilemma: if he sells all current delta to cover theta and the spot moves farther, he will not profit. But if he sells only a part of delta and spot returns to the starting point, he loses on time decay. As a result, he comes to some personal rule of thumb of delta adjustment: 50% to 70% of the

TABLE 22.3 Position's Sensitivity to Spot Changes

Spot	0.8500	0.8575	0.8650	0.8725	0.8800	0.8875	0.8950
Delta	–2,000,000	–1,500,000	–1,000,000	0	500,000	2,000,000	1,000,000
Gamma	–500,000	–500,000	–1,000,000		500,000	1,500,000	–1,000,000
Result			–3950	–200	1675	5850	
					↓ call 1M @ 0.8850		↓ put –3.5M @ 0.8900

delta available. For example, at 0.8733 he will sell not EUR 200,000, but only EUR 140,000.

A "long gamma"-and-"short vega" position makes money, even if spot fluctuates in a narrow range. A trader may not succeed in making up losses on theta by rehedging, but will be compensated by gains when volatilities fall. That is why for the position in Table 22.3, selling 50% of delta on an upward spot move gives a chance to make money if the move continues. In that case, the short vega position will make money as well.

If you expect a sharp spot move and forecast an increase of volatilities, you will build a "long gamma"-and-"long vega" position. You will sell 80% of delta to hedge theta: if spot remains in a narrow range, losses on theta will be amplified by losses on volatilities. Therefore, one should be conservative in delta hedging with greater negative theta.

Hedging of Options' Expiration

Spot may go beyond the first interval and reach expirations (strikes of options expiring *today*[11]). For instance, at that moment spot crosses 0.8850; you can sell EUR 1 million.

This means that under 0.8850 delta was hedged, and there was nothing for you to do on hedging. Above 0.8850, you can sell EUR 1 million more. That is, expirations cause abrupt increase of delta.

What Should We Do with Sold Delta If the Asset Price Starts Falling?

Hedging makes your portfolio locally risk free; that is, if the market keeps going up, there is only gamma (increase in delta) to sell. If the market corrects downward, you can buy back sold above.

In our example, at the beginning spot was at the 0.8725 level, and delta was 0. Then, the spot appreciated to 0.8745, and you sold EUR 100,000. If now it goes back to 0.8725, you will be short EUR 100,000. To make your position risk free, you have to buy the EUR 100,000 back at 0.8725.

By selling EUR 100,000 at 0.8745 and buying it back at 0.8725, you earned $(0.8745 - 0.8725) \times 100{,}000 = \$200$. That was enough to pay for theta.

Hedging of "Short Gamma"

When short options, you are hedging short gamma and do the opposite. When the asset moves up, you should buy it; when down, sell it. This is the opposite to the secret of profitability, "buy low, sell high." The losses on hedging should be covered by a gain on theta.

Suppose the spot fell to 0.8650. Now your position became longer EUR 1 million. You sell EUR 500,000 to avoid losses from a further fall of the euro. If the spot goes back to 0.8725, you will lose $3,750.

To mitigate losses from intraday hedging, many short-gamma traders prefer either hedging once a day (at close) or upon a breakout of a substantial technical support/resistance. In the latter case, the hedging amounts exceed current delta to prehedge. For instance, EUR 1.5 million instead of 1 million is sold, since the downward support breakout should cause a substantial move down.

Therefore, in a long-gamma position hedging helps you to pay for theta, and vice versa a short-gamma position theta compensates your losses on hedging.

QUESTIONS

Refer to Table 22.4 for the following questions:

1. Fill in blank for "Result" assuming direct extrapolation of results.
2. If you do not use direct extrapolation of gamma, where is the average profit in the 0.8725–0.8800 range?
3. How will the result change at 0.8650, if August volatility increases by 0.3 and September volatility by 0.1?

ANSWERS

Calculations in the intervals (see Table 22.5):

1. 0.8650–0.8575: average delta is EUR 1.25 million, EUR 1,250,000 × 0.0075 = $9,375. To calculate the total for the interval, this loss should be added to the result of the previous range of $13.325.

   0.8575–0.8500: average delta is EUR 1.75 million, EUR 1,750,000 × 0.0075 = $13,125. To calculate the total for the interval, this loss should be added to the result of the previous range of $26.450.

   0.8875–0.8900: the calculation is more difficult since there is a pin risk. For tomorrow, the position is short the expiration of EUR 3.5 million of a 0.8900 EUR put. Let's calculate direct gamma: EUR 2.5 million (2 – 3.5 + X = 1). Then average delta is EUR 3.25 (2 + 2.5/2) million. If there

TABLE 22.4 Position's Sensitivity to Spot Changes

Currency : **Euro/Dollar**

Date: 08.08.01 **Spot on revaluation:** 0.8800
Time: after New-York **Step:** 0.0075

Spot	0.85	0.8575	0.865	0.8725	0.88	0.8875	0.895
Delta	−2,000,000	−1,500,000	−1,000,000	0	500,000	2,000,000	1,000,000
Gamma	−500,000	−500,000	−1,000,000		500,000	1,500,000	−1,000,000
Result			−3950	−200	1675	5850	

put −3.5M @ 0.8900
call 1M @ 0.8850

	VEGA		*Forward's* EURO	Dollar
August	−3,000.00	August	−1,000,000	−872,500
September	2,000.00	September	200 000	174,500
October	1,000.00	October	100,000	87,250
November	−2,500.00	November	475,000	414,438
December	−500	December	−2,000,000	−1,745,000
January	−4,000.00	January	3,200,000	2,792,000
February	3,500.00	February	75,000	65,438
March	0	March	125,000	109,063
April	200	April	0	0
May	0	May	0	0
June	0	June	0	0
July	0	July	0	0
Total :	−3,300.00	Total:	1,175,000	1,025,188

TABLE 22.5 Position's Sensitivity to Spot Changes

Currency: **Euro/Dollar**

Date: 08.08.01 **Spot on revaluation:** 0.8800
Time: after New-York **Step:** 0.0075

Spot	0.8500	0.8575	0.8650	0.8725	0.8800	0.8875	0.8950
Delta	−2,000,000	−1,500,000	−1,000,000	0	500,000	2,000,000	1,000,000
Gamma	−500,000	−500,000	−1,000,000		500,000	1,500,000	−1,000,000
Result	**−26450**	**−13325**	−3950	−200	1675	5850	**12725**

were no pin gamma, the result would have been EUR 3,250,000 × 0.0075 = \$24,375. On pin gamma, the position loses EUR 3,500,000 × (0.8950 – 0.8900) = \$17,500. That is, the result of the position is (\$24,375 – \$17,500 + \$5,850).

If there was only a direct gamma, the result would be equal to \$17,100 dollars (try to calculate). Although there is a pin negative gamma in this interval, the position continues making money when spot appreciates, although at a slower rate.

2. Linear delta's extrapolation increases by EUR 100,000 every 15 pips. However, this is not the correct way to forecast delta. Gamma causes nonlinear changes in delta; therefore, profit increases nonlinearly as well. To incorporate gamma in delta forecast we will use another rule of thumb: 50% of the profit will be earned on the last third of the interval. The same is true for the position size. In other words, by 0.8775 the position will increase by EUR 250.000. Such an algorithm is more exact than direct extrapolation, but it is not universal and is subject just to specific origins of direct gamma, which are different for every position.
3. With an August volatility of 3% increase, the portfolio loses \$900 (\$3,000 × 0.3), and with a September volatility increase by 1%, the portfolio increases by \$200 (\$2,000 × 0.1). In other words, change in volatility causes the decrease of \$700, that is, the total loss of the position will be \$–3,950 – 700 = \$–4,650.

PART Five

Hedging Market Risk Reduction for Producers and Consumers

CHAPTER 23

Hedging with Options

Options and other derivatives reduce dependence of financial results of producers and consumers on market prices. They also help investors to protect value of their portfolios. The process of protecting the results is called hedging.

The cost of hedging is an important consideration. Nobody sells cheap life insurance to a 120-year-old person. Similarly, one will not sell a cheap hedge when the market is volatile. To continue with the life insurance example, at age 20 people rarely buy life insurance due to its relative expensiveness and absence of urgency. The hedgers also don't like to pay up in stable markets, since they regard the hedging premium as a cost item. They are partially right: hedges can be expensive. However, they insure business stability. Only firms that experienced severe losses on noncore business components, such as FX exposure, institute hedging as an obligatory program.

FIRST STEPS IN DEVELOPMENT OF A HEDGING PROGRAM

A hedger differs from a speculator in the attitude toward market risk. The hedger's priority is risk reduction. There is no universally correct way to manage market risks. There are those who do not hedge and regard the unexpected profits and losses as God's will. Others regard any market risk as a danger and hedge it mechanically.

For example, many investment funds' managers regard a currency risk from foreign investments as an integral part of decision to invest abroad. Others separate currency risks from risks of movement on local stock markets and hedge their currency exposure.

To start a hedging program development, one must set up its objective. For example, the program should defend budget assumptions (e.g., average

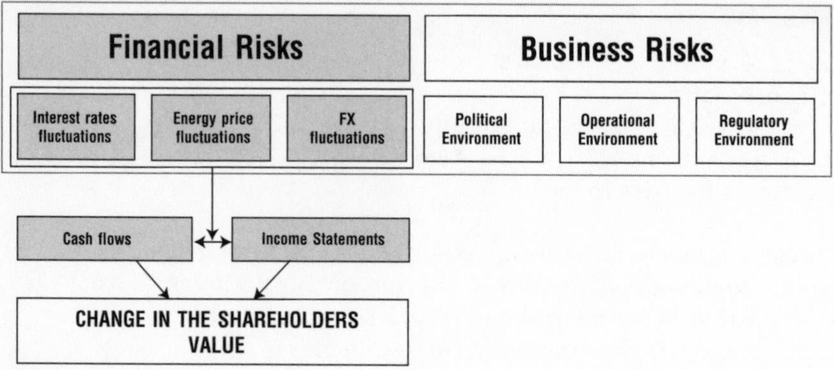

FIGURE 23.1 Associated Risks

annual oil price levels or interest/currency rates, etc.), or insure against catastrophic scenarios, or a primary risk separation from the secondary/noncore ones (for instance, interest rates for international fixed-income investors separate from local currency risk). See Figure 23.1 for associated risks.

Having defined the objective, one chooses hedging strategies[1] and instruments. As a rule, one considers forwards/futures or options, or combinations of the two. When we use forwards/futures, the market risk is completely blocked out together with any opportunity to gain when an underlying asset price move is beneficial. For example, if a corporation is to buy fuel in three months, a treasurer can decide to buy a three-month forward on oil, fixing the price of future delivery today. But he can also choose options.

COMPARISON OF EFFICIENCY OF OPTIONS TO SPOT DEALS AND FORWARD/FUTURES

Options are traded on exchanges and interbank markets. They are contracts that give a buyer a right (but not an obligation) to execute the hedge within (or at the end of) the stipulated period at the specified price. And a seller must honor the option contract at the buyer's request.

In the case of a call, a buyer has a right to buy an underlying asset. A call seller is obliged to sell a certain asset at the optional buyer's request. And a put owner can sell the asset at the strike price of the put. (See Chapter 1.)

Using Calls

You have $2,000 and you want to buy 20 shares of ABC stock trading at $100 per share.

Let's assume that one-month ABC call quotes are available. A right to buy in a month one share of ABC at $100 costs $10. With $2,000, you can buy 200 calls (rights to buy the stock in the future).

Example 1 Suppose in a month ABC's price reaches $200 per share. According to the option contract, you will exercise the option and its seller will have to sell you the stocks at $100.

Let's compare the results of the two strategies:

	A	*B*
Initial capital ($)	2,000	2,000
Bought	20 stocks	200 calls (rights to buy ABC stock at $100 per share)
Price in a month ($)	200 per share	
Position value ($)	4,000 (20 × 200)	20,000 200 × (200 –100)
Gain ($)	2,000 (4,000 – 2,000)	18,000 (20,000 – 2,000)

This example demonstrates one of the main advantages of options' potential great effect in comparison with costs, *if forecasts turn out to be correct.* In other words, this is the *leverage* effect.

Example 2 Suppose that in a month ABC's price falls to $80 per share. In this case, on the expiration day, you will not exercise your option: you have a right but are *not obliged* to buy! Since buying shares at $100 (exercising the options) above the market is against your interests, you will not exercise the option (let it expire).

Let's compare the results of the two strategies:

	A	*B*
Initial capital ($)	2,000	2,000
Bought	20 stocks	200 calls (rights to buy ABC shares at $100 per share)
Price in a month ($)	80 per share	
Position value ($)	1,600 (20 × 80)	0 (reject to exercise)
Loss ($)	400 (2,000 – 1,600)	2,000 (0 – 2,000)

This example demonstrates one of the main disadvantages of the options: they have a finite life time, that is, they stop existing on an expiration day. The position in variant A kept some value, but in variant B all the money was lost, because the option expired.

Example 3 Suppose in a month ABC price reaches $110 per share. On the expiration day, you will exercise the option, since the current market price is higher than the option's strike of $100 per share.

Let's compare the results of the two strategies:

	A	*B*
Initial capital ($)	2,000	2,000
Bought	20 stocks	200 calls
Price in a month ($)	110 per share	
Position value ($)	2,200	2,000
	(20 × 110)	200 × (110 – 100)
Gain ($)	200	0
	(2,200 – 2,000)	(2,000 – 2,000)

This example demonstrates that calls become profitable above the option's strike plus premium paid for the option. If the strike is $100 and the paid premium per option is $10 (200 calls are bought for $2,000), the breakeven point is $110 (100 + 10), and the higher the ABC price the greater the gain.

Using Puts

To study options everyone must overcome four levels of complexity. The simplest concept is a purchase of calls (similar to buying stocks). A more complex one is a purchase of puts (similar to selling stocks). Even more complex is the idea of selling calls (similar to selling stock). And, at last, the most difficult is the idea of selling puts (similar to buying stocks).

Suppose that in a month an oil producer is to sell 100 barrels of oil. Today's price for a barrel with one month delivery is $30. The $30 one-month oil put, the right to sell oil in one month at $30, is quoted at $3.

Example In a month, assume oil costs $20 per barrel.

Let's compare the results of the two strategies:

	A	*B*
Initial steps	Sold 100 barrels at $30 per barrel	Bought for $3 per one put 100 options to sell oil at $30 per barrel
Total received (spent) initially	$3,000	–$300
Gain	$1,000 100 × (30 – 20)	$700 100 × (30 – 20) – 300

In this example, it is assumed that you will use a put—a right to sell oil at $30—while oil's current price is $20. You will do this because you are better off selling oil at $30 to the put's seller by exercising the option than selling it in the market at $20.

Unlike in the examples with calls, your aim is not to receive additional leverage, but to maximize protection against losses. That's why you buy options not with the entire amount available ($3,000), but with a portion of it. In this case, the option hedge is worse than the forward one because of the premium costs. The example demonstrates that when the asset moves in the direction of the hedge, forwards are a better hedge than options with the same face value.

Example Let's assume that unlike in the previous example that the price of oil has risen and in one month oil trades at $40 per barrel.

Let's compare the results of the two strategies:

	A	B
Initial steps	Sold 100 barrels at $30 per barrel	Bought for $3 per one put 100 options to sell oil at $30 per barrel
Total received (spent) initially	$3,000	–$300
Loss/Gain	–$1,000 100 × (30 – 40)	$700 100 × (30 – 40) – 300

Since ownership of the put does not oblige you to sell oil at $30, you sell it at $40, collecting $700 net of premium. The forward hedge loses $1,000. In this case, you will make money because purchase of options does not limit your action.

HEDGING WITH OPTIONS

The Simplest Methods

1. You **buy a call** to hedge an asset price **increase**, that is, your reasons for buying an oil forward or an oil call are the same: not to lose when market rises.
   - A producer will never buy a call! His aim is to hedge against price decline. But a consumer will buy calls in order to reduce risk of a price increase (for example, an airline purchases fuel).
2. You **buy a put** to hedge an asset price **decline**, that is, your reasons for *selling* oil forward and *buying* an oil put are the same: not to lose when the market falls. In this case, a producer is a buyer of puts because a price fall cuts into his profits.
   - A consumer will never buy a put: if oil price goes down, he will start saving money on fuel's costs on his underlying position.

   Selling of options is a weaker form of hedging. Premium from selling increases profit rather than reduces risks.
3. As a rule, if you are a producer and own an underlying asset, you sell a call with a strike above the current forward price of the asset. If the option is exercised, the price at which you sell oil will be higher than the current one. For example, if oil for three-month delivery costs $30, you will sell a $35 call. If the market fails to reach $35, the sold option will not be exercised: the market price will be lower than its strike. In this case, you will collect an additional gain equal to the premium received for the option.
4. As a rule, if you are a consumer and do not own the asset, you sell a put with a strike price lower than the current forward price of the asset. If you are exercised, the price, at which you would buy the asset, would be lower than the current one. For example, if oil for three-month delivery costs $30 you will sell a $27 put. If on expiration date the market is above $27, the option's buyer will not exercise his contract: he will be able to sell oil at a higher market price. In this case, you will collect the premium received for the option.

Hedging by Means of Several Options (Option Strategies) Options are valuable because they provide a flexible toolkit to create strategies to fit the hedger's forecasts.

Example[2] As an oil producer, you may believe that during the next month oil prices will be in the range of $30 to $32 per barrel. At the end of the month, you plan to sell 1,000 barrels of oil. Today, you can fix the sale price at $31 per barrel by selling a one-month forward. However, you expect on expiration the price to be closer to $32 than to $30. Thus, you would like to capitalize on the opportunity for the additional gain, rather than fix the price now.

Based on your expectations, you can design a hedging strategy comprised of a few options. You can sell a $32 call and purchase a $30 put. If the $32 call is exercised, you will be glad to sell at the price higher than the current one. The $30 put prevents uncontrolled losses in case your forecast turns sour.

Now, suppose you collect $1 for the sold call and pay $1 for the bought put. The entire strategy costs nothing! If at the end of the period oil is trading at:

- more than $32 per barrel, a buyer of the option you sold will buy from you oil at $32 (will exercise the option). Again, $32 is better than the price at which you could have sold it initially through a forward sale;
- less than $30, you will sell oil at $30 by exercising the put. You will lose $1 on the incorrect forecast;
- between $30 and $32, both options will expire worthless and you will sell oil at the current price on expiration date with gains or losses within your expected range.

FINAL STEPS

Flexibility of derivative instruments enables corporations or investors to adapt hedging to their risk appetites. One of the main limitations of risk appetite is the company's budgeted profit margin. If a hedger operates on a low profit margin, hedging must be conservative, since even small market fluctuations tip the company's results into losses. This principle is important for wholesale and other highly competitive industries. Their profit is a small premium over costs.

A conservative hedger should use forwards to avoid deviations from budget assumptions. The performance of conservative option strategies is usually a bit behind that of forwards. Yet options are the only choice for an aggressive hedger who would hedge against catastrophic scenarios. For instance, while oil is at $30 per barrel, an oil producer can buy a $30 put. It will hedge the company against a fall of oil below $30. With such a hedge, the producer still risks suffering significant losses if the price of oil declines, while keeping an opportunity to receive high profits if the price of oil increases.

Once the overall hedging program is adopted and preferred instruments are chosen, the hedging procedure should become mechanical: once risk is defined, it must be hedged in accordance to the approved algorithm. For example, 60% of production is hedged, of which half is hedged with forwards. That makes the hedging independent of the company's market forecasts. In practice, it is impossible to avoid the human factor completely since those who execute hedging programs are influenced by their market views.

To summarize, developing a hedging program requires several stages. In the first stage, a company decides whether overall it is going to protect itself against market fluctuations. Once the fundamental decision to hedge is made, a financial department (treasury) has to choose between hedging instruments. If options are chosen, it is necessary to determine risk parameters acceptable for corporations and to budget the cost of hedging (options' premiums). After that, it is necessary to select certain strategies, corresponding to the risk parameters and resources allocated for hedging.

Experience shows that most successful hedging programs are "mechanical"; that is, when execution is independent of market forecasts and the treasury director's personal attitude to risk. Yet, a choice between a mechanical defense of budget and a game of guessing market direction is always very difficult.

QUESTIONS

Let's assume that a Japanese producer is going to export to the United States a $50 million piece of equipment. Dollar depreciation against yen reduces his profit from sale.

1. The USD/JPY spot rate is at 115.00, and a three-month forward is at 113.00. Compare two alternatives: The exporter decides to sell a $50 million forward or he stays unhedged. At what price will the exporter sell his dollars for yen in three months under both scenarios, if the spot falls to 105.00, remains at 115.00, or rises to 125.00?

2. As an alternative to the forward, the corporation's treasury considers hedging with options. One can buy a three-month 113.00 USD put for ¥3.00. It is important to remember that a long put insures against a fall, since a put is an insurance against price decline! How will the results change under the previous scenarios, if the treasury uses options for hedging?

3. Judging from the analysis in Questions 1 and 2, what are the advantages for the treasury in using options instead of forwards?

4. The treasury is probably ready to run the risks of a long dollar position. However, the company's board of directors demands to define the level at which the currency risk is eliminated (stop-loss level). In other words, it wants to secure profit margins in the case of a catastrophic market scenario. The objective is achievable with an OTM[3] option purchase. Its strike should be far from the current price. In this case, a three-month 110.00 JPY call (same as USD put) is bought for ¥1.0. At what rate will the treasury sell the spot on hedge by means of option in previous scenarios?
5. What are the peculiarities of the strategy in Question 4?

ANSWERS

1. Currently, the USD/JPY spot is at 115.00, and a three-month forward is 113.00. Depending on the decision whether to hedge (sell dollars forward today) or not, the exporter will have the following levels at which he will sell his position:

Scenario: Spot USD/JPY in Three Months	105.00	115.00	125.00
Position hedged with the forward/future	113.00	113.00	113.00
Unhedged position	105.00	115.00	125.00

   A forward hedge fixes the rate of the future delivery. It is convenient for the corporation's treasury since it fixes the yen value of the future dollar sale beforehand. Once the forward is sold, the treasury becomes indifferent to the exchange rate fluctuations. In other words, it is insulated from them. But it will be annoyed, if the dollar appreciates during the three months, since the company will not benefit from the appreciation. The hedging program will be even more criticized, if the competitors did not hedge and reported an extra profit from converting their dollar sales into yen at a better rate. Yet the dilemma is that if the future cash flow is left unhedged, the deal will be at a risk of significant losses.

2. Instead of using the forward, the treasury decided to hedge with options. It bought a three-month 115.00 USD put for ¥3.00. Then the spot move will result in the following:

Scenario: Spot USD/JPY in Three Months	105.00	115.00	125.00
Hedged position (after accounting for the option's premium)	112.00	112.00	122.00

3. To obtain a strategy that is more flexible than entering into the forward, the treasury has to pay 1 yen more than the forward would cost. Now, the treasury is flexible in making the decisions in three months: if the dollar is up, it will sell dollars at a more favorable exchange rate. And if the spot goes down, the position is hedged at 112.00. That is, if on the option's expiration the dollar is above 114.00, the option is more profitable than the forward. If it falls below 114.00 the forward would turn out to be cheaper.

   Hence, if the dollar falls or remains stable, the result of hedging with an option will be worse than hedging with a forward. If the dollar appreciates, the company will be able to sell the dollars at a higher rate. *It is for the opportunity to choose a rate at which you will sell your future cash flows that you pay 1 yen more (3 – 2), by buying an option rather than a forward.*

4. If the company's board of directors wants to limit losses (hedge) of a catastrophic scenario, the treasury will buy a cheap OTM option. Since a catastrophic scenario is not likely, it is better to buy a cheap strike. Cheap strikes tend to be far from the current spot price. In this case, it buys a three-month 110.00 JPY call/USD put for JPY 1.0.

   The result in three months will be the following:

Scenario: Spot USD/JPY in Three Months	**105.00**	**115.00**	**125.00**
Hedged position (after accounting for the option's premium)	109.00	114.00	124.00

5. An OTM option is cheaper but provides a smaller degree of protection. The ATM option in the previous example is more expensive but provides a better protection. This is similar to life insurance. If you want to insure against death before the age of 50 (a catastrophic scenario), the insurance is relatively cheap, since the probability is small. If you insure from the death after the age of 100, the insurance will be more expensive, since the probability of such an event is significantly higher.

   If the choice is to hedge with options and the dollar falls/yen rises significantly, the ATM USD put will turn out to be the best investment. In case of the yen fall/dollar rise, an OTM option will be preferable, since it is cheaper. As you see, in hedging against a catastrophic scenario, an option provides greater flexibility while being relatively cheap.

FURTHER INFORMATION FOR THE READER

Instructions for Dealing with Energy Derivatives[4]

Instruments of Hedging

Futures: obligations of parties to buy-sell, trades on exchange, cash-settled

Forward: an obligation of parties to buy-sell, trades on OTC; it is deliverable

Swap: a financial contract: exchange of a price difference between floating and fixed price, stipulated in contract at the beginning of the deal

Option: a financial contract: payment of positive price difference to the option's buyer, premium paid to the seller

Underlying Assets

Brent, WTI, Urals: oil of certain brands

Exchange futures on WTI, Brent, jet fuel, gasoline, heating oil

Spreads (commercial margin, quality, geographical differentials, etc).

Types of Underlying Asset's Price

Averaged spot price (for Asian options and swaps)

Averaged futures price (for Asian options and swaps)

Spot (for European options and forwards)

Sources of Prices

Exchange settlement price: prices of the nearby futures on the exchange's closing or in accordance with the parties' agreement—the prices at some moment of trading

Platt's: oil prices with delivery under the spot terms presented by Platt's.

Petroleum Argus: oil prices with delivery under the spot terms presented by Argus.

(Continued)

FURTHER INFORMATION FOR THE READER *(Continued)*

Parameters of the Option Price

Type of an underlying asset

Term

Source of price

Quantity of dates of the price fixing

Type of averaging (arithmetical, geometrical)

Size of deal (in barrels)

Parameters to Be Used in Calculating the Option Price

Type of an underlying asset

Term

Source of price

The number dates for fixing prices (for example, for European options there is only one expiration date, but for Asian options there are monthly, quarterly, half-yearly and yearly date)

Type of averaging

Strike

Call/put

Size of the deal

Parameters to Be Used in Deals with Exchange Futures

Size of deal

Term

Quantity of contracts

Largest Exchanges

NYMEX

IPE

International Exchange

CHAPTER 24

Advanced Hedging Strategies

In the previous chapter, we discussed general issues related to hedging programs. We also compared hedging with forwards and hedging with basic option strategies. In this chapter, we will consider a few more hedging strategies used in the market. You will see that some "hedging" strategies look more like speculative ones. This is yet another demonstration that once the company staff decides to speculate they can do so while still calling their actions "hedging."

STRATEGIES

Participating Forward

A participating forward is built by a simultaneous purchase (sale) of a call and sale (purchase) of a put *with the same strike and expiration date*. As a result, there is an option strategy absolutely identical to a forward. That's why a "participating" forward is also called a "synthetic" forward" or a "conversion." Like a standard forward, a synthetic forward fixes a rate at which a hedger will buy the asset in the future.

For example, you buy a one-year forward USD/JPY and pay 500 pips for it. If the spot is at 102.00, you will buy dollars forward at 97.00 (102.00 – 5.00). With options, you can synthetically replicate an identical forward, by buying a one-year 97.00 USD call and selling a one-year 97.00 USD put. The strategy will also cost 500 pips. In other words, a participating forward (synthetic forward, conversion) has an absolutely identical risk reward profile to a forward, and the same risk sells at the same price. Yet investors who have small forward and substantial option trading limits prefer this strategy.

Knock-in Forward

A knock-in forward is almost identical to a participating forward. The difference is that instead of selling the 97.00 USD put, you sell a 97.00 USD put with a 93.00 knock-in barrier.[1] In this case, you will have to buy dollars at 97.00 *only* if the spot touches 93.00 during the option's life. That is, if the USD/JPY doesn't touch 93.00 during the option's life, the option does not get *validated* (turned into your unconditional liability). Thus, even if at the option's expiration spot is at 93.50, an option's buyer will not exercise it, as it was not validated! In such a case, you will buy the dollars you need at 93.50 rather than at 97.00, as you would have to if you sold a regular 97.00 USD put.

Such a strategy costs a bit more than a participating forward, but gives an additional opportunity to substantially improve an exchange rate at which the U.S. exporter to Japan can buy dollars.

Risk Reversal

A risk reversal (also known as "range forward," "cap and floor," or "combo") is also similar to a participating forward. The difference this time is that a call and a put have different strikes. As a result, a hedger instead of fixing a certain spot rate, fixes a set price range. For example, see Figure 24.1. You buy a 98.00 USD call and finance it by selling a 96.00 USD put. In this case, instead of fixing the rate at 97.00, as in the initial example, you fix the 96.00–98.00 price range.[2]

In this example, the risk is higher than that of hedging with a forward: if the dollar is at 98.00 or above, you will have to buy it at 98.00 rather than at 97.00. However, if on expiration spot is at 96.00 or lower you earn more, thus reducing the hedging cost by ¥100.

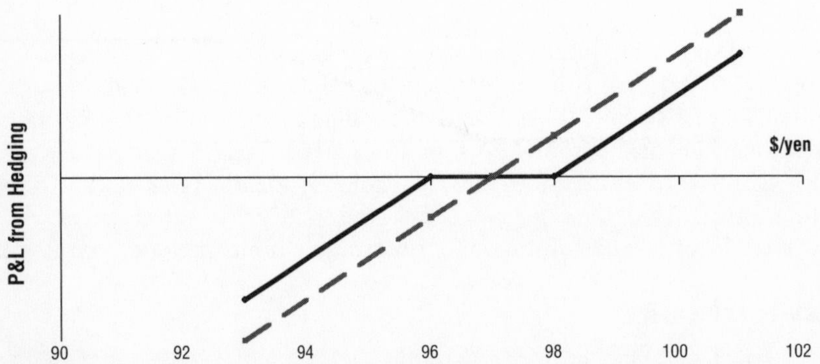

FIGURE 24.1 Comparison of "Participating" Forward and Risk Reversal

If at expiration, spot is between 96.00 and 98.00, both options will expire. For example, if on the expiration date spot is at 96.50, you will not exercise the 98.00 call since you can buy dollars at 96.50. The buyer of the 96.00 put will not want to exercise his put either because that will oblige him to sell dollars to you at 96.00, while he can sell them at 96.50 in the market. Therefore, you will buy dollars in the market at a current spot rate and the options will expire worthless.

Risk reversals are popular with those hedging based on market forecasts rather than mechanically. If a treasurer believes the dollar will depreciate and wants to buy it cheaper, she will use a risk reversal rather than a forward.

Spread

If you do not expect a major dollar appreciation and want to reduce your hedging expenses, you can buy a call spread rather than a risk reversal. For example, see Figure 24.2. You can buy a 97.00 call and sell a 100.00 call. That will hedge you in the 97.00–100.00 range.

You have to pay for such a strategy, since the 97.00 call is always more expensive than the 100.00 call. Moreover, above 100.00, the position becomes unhedged, and you will start losing money. Yet a lighthanded hedge such as this leaves you an opportunity to make money if the dollar falls. For instance, if at expiration spot is at 95.00, you can buy dollars at 95.00.

To hedge from depreciation of underlying assets, treasurers use put spreads.

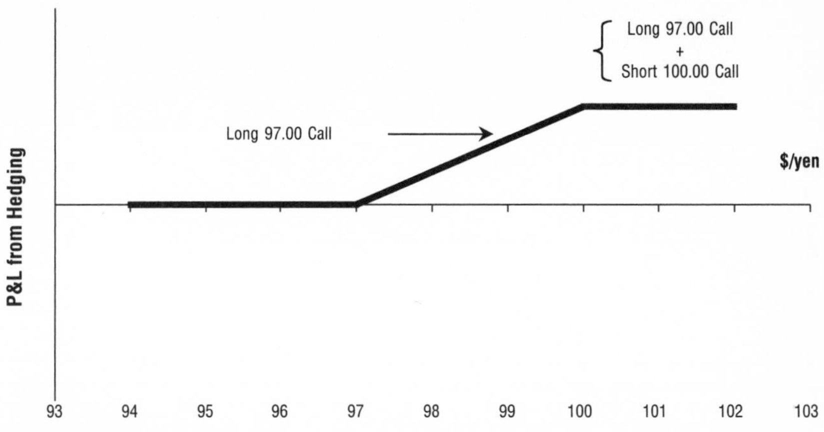

FIGURE 24.2 Spread

Albatross: A Combination of a Spread and a Risk Reversal

You also can do a combination of the previous strategies. For example, you can buy a 98.00 call and sell a 100.00 call and a 96.00 put. This strategy is called an "albatross." It doesn't suit the objective of complete risk avoidance, since it requires correct market forecasts, but it is still pretty popular and not uncommon to see. The strategy assumes that the market will be in a range with a directional drift.

The sale of the 100.00 call helps to finance the purchase of the 98.00 call. You can either keep the savings or use them to lower the strike of the put you sell, for instance, from 96.00 to 94.00. The sum of the premiums of the 100.00 call and the 94.00 put remains equal to the premium of the 98.00 call. As a result you do not pay a premium to hedge with an albatross as you would for a risk reversal[3] (see Figure 24.3).

Sale of Covered Options

The strategy of *selling* a call/put was mentioned in the previous chapter as a "weak" form of hedging. Still, it is actively used in stocks: fund managers sell calls against the shares they owe. A premium collected for an option reduces losses, if the price falls.

Since the options are sold in the direction of positions that the hedgers own, the strategy is called "covered." In fact, covered sales are simultaneously a hedge and a profit enhancement. The collected premium serves as a buffer from losses when prices fall. If the price is stable, it increases a gain on the underlying position.

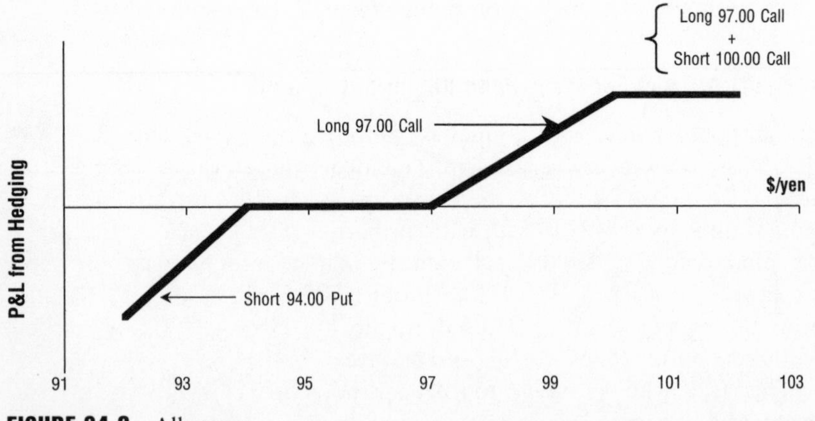

FIGURE 24.3 Albatross

Let's consider three variations of this strategy:

1. *Sale of a deep in-the-money call.* For instance, you sell 1 Apple call against 100 Apple shares[4] you owe while the stock is trading at $120.

   Such a strategy reflects an expectation of a high volatility within a range. You can sacrifice some upward profit potential to provide sufficient safety if the price goes down. Selling an ITM option will allow monetization of a gain from the investment, since the deep ITM option is likely to be exercised. The collected premium will increase profit. The strategy has two risks. First, spot may fall below the call's strike. Secondly, it can go higher than expected and an opportunity loss on the long stock position will be only partially compensated by the option's premium.[5]
2. *Sale of ATM option.* The strategy provides a smaller premium than selling an ITM option and protects less from a fall of an underlying's price. It works better when a stable price range is expected.[6]
3. *Sale of OTM option.* This is a fundamentally different strategy. An investor expects a market growth (or fall in the case of puts). Thus, he needs less protection from the collected premium.

Sale of a Reverse Knock-in Call/Put

The strategy is similar to a covered call/put. A short 97.00 call with a 107.00 knock-in[7] gets validated (turns into an ordinary option and becomes an unconditional liability) only if the spot "touches" 107.00 during its life. If before the expiration spot hasn't reached 107.00, you don't have to deliver USD at 97.00, even if the spot trades at 106.00. Although you collect less for selling such options, the barrier addup provides a chance for greater profitability: if the option is not exercised, you retain the asset.

Purchase of Long-Term Reverse Knock-out Options

Another popular strategy is a purchase of long-term reverse *knock-out* options. These options are very cheap. The longer their term, the farther the barriers are moved away for the current price. For instance, an ordinary (vanilla) three-month 97.00 call without barrier (also known as "trigger") costs more than 2%. A 97.00 call expiring in three months costs 0.34% of its face value if it has a 107.00 knock-out trigger. It behaves like a vanilla option unless spot touches 107.00 during its life. However, if spot touches 107.00, the option stops existing (prematurely expires).

This strategy looks similar to a call spread: it hedges against an adverse move within a range. We do not recommend this strategy for hedging as predicting the maximum of a range is never reliable. As a result, it is too speculative for true hedging. Nevertheless, some investment managers use it when the market is range bound.

Resetting Forward

Resetting forward is another example of an exotic strategy. The strategy gives you a choice of strikes for an exercise. For instance, as long as USD/JPY does not reach either 107.00 or 117.00, you are long a 110.00 USD call (the right to buy dollars at 110.00). However, if during the option's life USD/JPY spot touches either barrier, you will have to buy USD at 113.00.

In other words, you can considerably improve your hedging level if you guess the trend. If you miss it, your hedging would be considerably worse than a current forward price. Such a strategy is built by using a combination of four options: a hedger sells a 113.00 call and put, both with 107.00 and 117.00 knock-*in* barriers. He simultaneously buys a 110.00 call and put with 107.00 and 117.00 knock-*outs*. As you see this strategy is too risky for risk-averse hedgers.

CHOOSING A HEDGING HORIZON

Choosing a hedging horizon (expiration date) is one of the key problems for those who hedge with options. For example, XXX Company expects three payments within a year. When the number of payments is more than one, a hedger faces the problem whether to hedge all payments at once or to hedge them separately.

The premium of the option does not increase proportionally with an increase in time to expiration. Consider a few examples:

- The premium (time value) of a six-month ATM option is more than half of a one-year ATM option's premium.
- The price of a one-week ATM option is approximately half of a three-week option's price.
- The price of a three-month ATM option is approximately half of a one-year ATM option's price.

This observation means that *hedgers are better off buying a longer-term option once rather than a string of short-term options*. For instance, it is more expensive to hedge a six-month risk with a purchase of a three-month option with the intention to buy another three-month option upon the exercise of the first one. The total cost of these two options will exceed the cost of a six-month option.[8]

QUESTIONS

1. Your client is long USD/CHF and expects it not to appreciate much, let's say by no more than 2%. The current spot level is 1.4800. What would you advise him to do to enhance his income?
2. The client doesn't like the increased volatility and is worried about a sudden stock price downward correction. However, he remains bullish overall, although not as much as before. Which hedging strategy suits him better?
3. Your client is long USD/CHF. She would like some protection in case of a local price correction to the previous support level of 1.4670. She doesn't want to pay up for hedging. Which hedging strategy suits her better?
4. The client likes your suggestion, but an advisor from another bank tells her that by selling a USD call with a strike above 1.4670, she gets a free hedge without changing her market outlook. With which strike is she better off selling a call, if the one-month forward is at 1.4780?
5. A company bought equipment in Great Britain and paid in pounds (dealers denote the pound as GBP). The problem is that the company has a multicurrency cash flow. The first installment will come from sales in Germany (EUR), the second from sales in the United States (USD), and the third one from Canada (CAD). Which hedging strategy suits the company better?

ANSWERS

1. You should recommend the client to sell a 1.4800 ATM call for the term of the price forecast. ATM calls have the greatest time value of other options for a given date. Since the client does not expect a major move, selling an option with a strike close to the spot makes sense.

   A more precise answer should account for the current price of a forward for the hedging date. Suppose he chooses a one-month forward. The one-month swap points[9] are –0.0020 ("-" stands for the fact that USD interest rates are higher than CHF rates).

   Maximum time value has an ATM option with the strike at the current forward level of 1.4780. For FX options, the term "at-the-money" implies an option with the strike at the forward's level (in our case 1.4800 – 0.0020 = 1.4780). However, sometimes when users say "at-the-money" they mean that an option's strike is at the current spot level.[10] To avoid confusion, you can ask for an "at-the-money-forward option."

2. The client should sell a call with a deep-in-the-money strike. In this case, he would sell the most dangerous sell-off zone. If the price goes up, the option's premium will compensate some opportunity losses. The more precise statement is: "If the price goes up, the time value portion of the option's premium will compensate some opportunity losses."

3. She should buy a 1.4800 put and sell a 1.4670 put (a put spread.) In this case, she doesn't pay much for the hedge and doesn't limit the profit potential if dollar keeps appreciating.

4. 1.4990 = 1.4780[11] + (1.4780 – 1.4670)

   The description of the strategy implies a risk reversal with 0 premium (for hedging). The strike will be symmetrical around the forward (1.4780). In practice, the strike of the option a client sells is closer to the forward rather than the strike of the option she buys. That accounts for the commission of a market maker.

5. This question implies basketing of hedges. Some underlying assets are correlated. This is true for currencies, equities, fixed income, and so on. For example, GBP/USD and GBP/CAD are strongly correlated. That is why you can reduce the complexity of hedging and suggest two options: the pound against the U.S. dollar (with the face value equal to USD and CAD) and the pound against the euro.

PART Six

Credit Risk Analysis

CHAPTER 25

Forward and Settlement Risks in Spot, Forward, and Nondeliverable Forward Deals

Credit risk may be divided into counterparty (credit) risk and instrument (credit) risk. They, in turn, are subdivided into delivery and pre-delivery risks.[1] *We will study all of them in respect to options and underlying assets.*

The concept of credit risk depends on regulatory rules in each country. This is especially true for netting. Therefore, evaluation of credit risks should be based on a legal opinion of the country's law.

SPOT DEALS

Suppose you are traveling from the United States to Switzerland. To exchange $100 into an equivalent sum in CHF, you go to an office of American Express. This is an example of a typical spot transaction. It is called "spot" because the deal is done "on the spot" at the moment of exchange.

Similar transactions are done on the over-the-counter market (OTC)—also known as the interbank market. There spot transactions settle not on the date of a deal, but on the second business day called "delivery/settlement date."

Each financial instrument has its own conventional delivery date; for instance, Eurobonds or stocks settle on the third business day. Let's consider credit risk in spot deals.

Trade Date

Suppose you sold $1 million against CHF at 1.4000. This means that you exchanged $1 million for 1.4 million of CHF ($1 million × 1.4000).

Delivery Date, also Known as Settlement Date

In case of settlement, you will have to deliver $1 million, while your counterparty will deliver 1.4 million of CHF.

On the FX market, spot delivery takes place on the second business day (with the exception of USD/CAD deals, which settle in one day). It is important to remember that a number of business and calendar days may differ. This means that a delivery for a Monday deal takes place on Wednesday (two business as well as two calendar days). A Tuesday deal will settle on Thursday. However, if a transaction takes place on Thursday:

- its settlement takes place on Monday (two business, but four calendar days);
- and, if Monday is a holiday, its settlement moves to Tuesday (five calendar days).

Similarly, if Friday is a holiday, a Wednesday transaction will be settled on Monday (five calendar days).

Credit Risk of a Spot Deal

While on delivery date we send to a counterparty USD 1 million, our client may fail to deliver CHF 1.4 million. That means that spot deals have a delivery risk. The settlement term of two days seems to be insignificant, but in critical situations every additional day of risk is of great value. The importance of this concept is demonstrated by the history of Baring Brothers Bank. It became bankrupt during a weekend. Another example was the decision of the Russian government in August 1998 to declare technical default on a Monday. Banks often have to wait until the end of a bankruptcy procedure to collect payments owed to them by an insolvent counterparty.

FORWARD DEALS

A forward contract is an obligation to buy/sell an asset on a certain date at a previously agreed exchange rate.

Suppose that today (January 1, 2004) you agreed to sell USD 1 million for CHF at 1.4000 expiring on February 1, 2004.

Delivery Risk

A spot deal has the same delivery risk as a forward contract. On February 1, we will have to deliver USD 1 million, and our counterparty will have to deliver us CHF 1.4 million.

Predelivery Risk (Forward Risk)

In a period between a deal and its delivery, the counterparty may become insolvent. The moment this happens, he effectively cancels his obligations to you; that is, his deals become invalidated. That means that after the default announcement, the unrealized profit/loss on the transaction becomes realized.

Example Suppose that on January 15 our counterparty declares bankruptcy. At that moment, USD/CHF is at 1.3500. To replace the canceled deal, we have to sell USD 1 million at 1.3500 (a lower rate). That is, the bankruptcy will cost us CHF 50,000 (USD 1 million × (1.4000 – 1.3500)).

Thus, at the moment of bankruptcy a forward deal exposes us to a risk to the extent of profit/loss, rather than to its total amount.

Thus, both spot and forward transactions have predelivery and delivery risks. The difference is that forward/predelivery risk on a spot deal is short term: between the deal date and the settlement/delivery date. The longer a forward deal's term, the higher its delivery risk. Both spot and forward transactions result in a currency exchange equal to a full amount of a deal, that is, mutual delivery.

For low-volatility markets delivery risk is substantially higher than forward risk. For instance, it is unlikely that the USD will double in respect to the euro. On the other hand, prices on hi-tech shares may double and triple within a relatively short period of time. It means that their predelivery risk may exceed delivery risk.

NETTING

Netting agreements allow counterparties to offset claims during bankruptcy. Thus, instead of settling on a deal-by-deal basis, they exchange a netting payment that settles differences between payments. This is important because in absence of such an agreement, the obligations of a bankrupt are paid according to the seniority of debt holders. At the same time, obligations to a bankrupt have to be paid in full. In other words, netting allows substantial increase in amounts of dealing with a counterparty with the same credit risks.

Bankruptcy legislation is territorial, meaning that it is very different from jurisdiction to jurisdiction. Moreover, in some jurisdictions (for instance, in Russia) some concepts (like netting) are not illegal, but they are not applied by courts in practice.[2] For these two reasons, a court may decide not to adhere to a netting agreement.

Example

On different trading dates, you have made two forward transactions with Barclays Bank for the same settlement date. On that date, you are to deliver USD 1 million against CHF at 1.4100, and Barclays Bank is to deliver you USD 1 million against CHF at 1.4000.

If there is no netting agreement between the banks,

- you are to deliver USD 1 million to Barclays Bank, while Barclays will deliver you CHF 1,410,000,
- under the second contract Barclays is to deliver to you USD 1 million, and you will deliver CHF 1,400,000.

This settlement scheme will require four money transfers and have a high credit (delivery) risk.

If the banks *do have* a netting agreement, the delivery amount equals the difference between sums of the second (domestic) currency (in this example CHF). Thus, Barclays is to deliver you only CHF 10,000 (1,410,000 – 1,400,000).

NONDELIVERABLE FORWARDS (NDFs)

NDFs appeared as a solution to the problem of settlements and credit risks of low creditworthy counterparties. They reduce settlement risk to predelivery risk. On expiration, there is no exchange of a contract face value. Similar to netted trades, only profit/loss on the deal is exchanged.

Although NDFs seem similar to netted obligations, some differences exist. NDF settlement is done on a basis of an FX rate fixed by a local central bank (or other fixings). The fixing rate is the rate taken at a certain time of the day (e.g., in the gold market the daily London fixing price is used). Thus, payment equals the difference between the original spot rate and a fixing of central bank on the delivery date. A settlement rate of an ordinary forward is established at the moment of a deal. Thus, there is no need for a price in a central bank fixing.

For example, on January 1 you buy a one-month USD 10 million NDF against BRL at 2.8700. The contract states that on February 1 settlement will be based on fixing by the Central Bank of Brazil (ptax—the Central Bank of Brazil fixing rate calculated as an average commercial rate of the day (last day of a month) in the spot market used for NDF and futures).

Suppose that on February 1 ptax equals 2.9700. Your counterparty is to deliver BRL 100,000 (USD 10 million × (2.9700 – 2.8700)) or USD 33,6700 (BRL 100,000:2.9700).

Note: a predelivery risk and a delivery risk are limited to the difference between contract price and fixing, and are normally much lower than a contract's face value.

When we talk about predelivery and delivery risks, we imply risks up to the delivery date! For a forward deal, both predelivery and delivery risk stop simultaneously on the delivery date. The same is true for spot and option deals.

QUESTIONS

1. On March 10 (Wednesday), a client bought from a bank a EUR/USD forward expiring on May 10 (Thursday). Between which dates does the bank have a predelivery risk? On what day does it have a delivery risk?
2. A client has a netting agreement with a bank. On March 9, she sold to the bank €1 million face of a EUR/USD forward at 1.000 for delivery on May 11 (Friday). Then, on March 12, she sold $1 million of USD/JPY forward for delivery on May 11. How many dollars does she have to deliver on the delivery date?
3. A month ago, a client bought 2 million of USD/EUR forward for delivery in a month and sold USD 3 million against EUR for delivery in three months. This week, he has signed a netting agreement. Did your risk of the client change?
4. Why may delivery risks be lower, or higher, than predelivery risks, depending on the markets' volatility?
5. Which risk does a netting agreement reduce?
6. A bank bought from a counterparty €1 million of EUR/USD forward at 1.2500 for delivery on June 1 (Monday). When does delivery risk appear and for what amount?

ANSWERS

1. Since EUR/USD settles in two days, the risk exists from March 12 (Friday) to March 14 (Monday). Delivery risk goes away on the delivery date.

2. On May 15 (Tuesday), the USD delivery will equal $200,000: under the EUR/USD contract the bank is to deliver $1.2 million (equivalent to €1 million at 1.200) and simultaneously to collect $1 million sold against yen (to sell a forward on USD/JPY means to sell USD (first currency) against JPY (second currency)).

3. The delivery risks are the same whether or not netting exists as the transactions settle on different days. Yet predelivery risks are different. Without netting, the positions are considered separate. With netting, the forward risk during the first month equals EUR 1 (EUR 3 – 2) million. If bankruptcy takes place within the first month, the transactions are netted and closed at the market rates on the bankruptcy declaration date.

4. Market volatility can substantially change an asset value. If a market is stable (cannot depreciate or appreciate more than twofold), the delivery risk is higher than the predelivery/forward risk, and vice versa. This is true for the majority of assets. The problem appears when markets start trending in one direction. The value of yen, which is normally relatively stable, may fall almost twice within a year (as it did in 1996–1997). Internet stocks may depreciate or appreciate several times. Therefore, a credit risk manager should periodically revise delivery and predelivery risks of assets in a portfolio.

5. Netting agreements are aimed at reducing delivery/settlement as well as predelivery risks in case of a counterparty's bankruptcy. Delivery risks per client may be significant even for big trading houses. Very often, several contracts of one client settle the same day. It is obvious that in such situations netting reduces risk.

   A similar situation is true for a predelivery risk. The netting mechanism must be properly stipulated in an agreement. Otherwise, one may face a one-sided contract cancellation on bankruptcy.

6. Delivery risk will appear on the delivery/settlement, which for an FX contract is two business days after a trading date—June 3 (June 1 + 2 days). Delivery risk can materialize, if you send the money to a counterparty, but the latter fails to send the equivalent in the other currency to you. In our example, it equals EUR 1 million, rather than $1,190,000.

FURTHER INFORMATION FOR THE READER

Risk of Settlement (Delivery)

Counterparty risk is the risk that the counterparty won't meet his obligations. But how can you calculate it in trading?

In practice, when determining settlement risk three methods are used:

1. Risk is equal to the amount of money you sent;
2. Risk is equal to the amount of money owed to you;
3. Risk is equal to the amount of money owed to you +/– position revaluation.

Example One month ago, a bank that keeps books in dollars bought EUR 1 million at 0.8300 EUR/USD. Today, EUR/USD is at 1.3500. What is the size of the settlement risk of the bank?

According to the first method, this risk equals $1,230,000: on the settlement date, you will send this sum for EUR 1 million (1,000,000 × 1.2300). What if you send the money and receive nothing in return?

According to the second method (most popular in practice), this risk equals the sum of money you expect under the contract: EUR 1 million.

The problem is that you do not know in advance in which of the first two variants risk is higher. Probability of the dollar's rise equals probability of the euro's appreciation. Thus, the third way of calculation is more complex, and the best one, since the assets owed to you are subject to constant mark-to-market. That is, your settlement risk should account for the amount of revaluation of the expected delivery. That is, it is equal to the initial risk of delivery you expect +/– risk of predelivery.

In our example, the bank's current settlement/delivery risk is higher than the initial one, since it bought EUR 1 million for $1,350,000.

The third method is optimal, but until recently it was rarely used in practice because not all risk management departments have a capability to mark-to-market the credit risk of portfolios. Besides, to avoid the limits' break ups in nonvolatile markets, it is simpler to follow constant settlement values (transaction's face value).

From the analysis above, one can infer that each company has its own preferred method of credit risk calculation.

CHAPTER 26

Risks of Settlement on Option Deals

SUMMARY OF OPTION CLASSIFICATIONS

Let's briefly recall basics discussed in the book.

Options are divided into two styles: *European* and *American*. European option may be exercised only on an exercise day. An American option may be exercised on any day during its life.

European options are also called "vanilla" since they are the best known and most used. Less used are *exotic* options. Exotics can be in the form of *barrier*, *digital*, and *Asian* options.

Vanilla Options

Vanilla options can be in the form of put or *call* options, *deliverable* or *nondeliverable*. A seller of a call is obliged to sell to the option's buyer the underlying asset at a strike price if the latter requires exercising. A seller of a put is obliged to buy from the option's buyer underlying asset at a strike price in case the latter requires exercising. *Deliverable* options, if exercised, are settled by an exchange of an underlying asset. *Nondeliverable* options are cash-settled, that is, cash is paid for the difference between a strike and a spot price.

Options of this type are exercised or expire depending on whether an option is in-the-money or not.

That is, a call option is exercised if on expiration the underlying is higher than the option's strike. A put option is exercised if on expiration its strike is lower than the underlying.

Barrier Options

Most options of this type are exercised or expire like European options, once it is clear whether a trigger or triggers were touched during the contract's life.

The trigger (also knows as the barrier) is a spot level stipulated when a deal is done. Barrier options may have one barrier or a few. The main categories of barrier options are *in* and *out* options.

One-Barrier Options

In (knock-ins) an option is exercised, if spot *traded* at a barrier during option's life.

Out (knock-outs) an option is exercised, if spot did *not trade* at a barrier during option's life.

Double-Barrier Options

In (knock-ins) an option is exercised, if spot *traded* at one barrier during the option's life.

Out (knock-outs) an option is exercised, if spot *did not trade at* barriers during the option's life.

Binary Options

Unlike vanilla or barrier options, a binary may not have a strike but has a barrier. Once the barrier is touched during an option's life, the sellers have to pay buyers a fixed amount of *payout*. If the event doesn't occur, an option's seller pays nothing to a buyer. For different types of options the terms of an option's contract can specify a different trigger event as follows:

1. *At the moment* of the option's exercise spot is *higher* than a strike. This part is similar to a vanilla option but the buyer receives a fixed payout, however much the option is in-the-money, or
2. *At the moment* of the option's exercise spot is *not higher* than some level, or
3. Spot touched a barrier *during* an option's life, or
4. Spot failed to touch a barrier *during* an option's life, or
5. Spot touched one of two barriers *during* an option's life, or
6. Spot touched none of two barriers *during* an option's life.

The options in points 1) to 6) may be European style, that is, a seller pays to a buyer a stipulated amount on the expiration date. Only options 3) and 5) may be American style. Here, a seller pays stipulated sum the moment the spot touches a barrier.

Asian Options

Asian options are often called *average price* or *average strike* options. The first one has a set strike. It is exercised based on an average historical spot price for some period of time.

However, some Asian options are average strike options. Their strikes are not set in contracts. The contract describes a method of strike determination. The following three ways are possible:

1. Strike equals the maximum spot value during an option's life.
2. Strike equals the minimal spot value during an option's life.
3. Strike is determined as the average spot value at stipulated moments. Fixing dates are used for the average-value calculation.

There a few other types of **exotic options** such as:

Choice option Under this sort of arrangement, the type of option (call or put) is not known at the moment of making a deal. A date on which a buyer determines the type of option is stipulated in the contract.

Compound option This is an option on an option. Another option is used as an underlying asset. At the moment of exercising the compound option, its buyer has a right to buy or to sell the underlying option at the strike.

CREDIT RISKS IN VANILLA OPTIONS TRADING

Although predelivery risks for short and long options are different, delivery risks are the same:

- The predelivery risk of sold options equals the amount of premium to be paid by your counterparty. As soon as a seller receives the premium, his predelivery credit risk disappears. The option's buyer is dependent on him for performing according to the contract.
- The predelivery risk of bought options purchase appears when a deal is done. If a seller does not honor his obligations, a buyer loses all the benefits from the option's purchase.
- The delivery risks of sold and bought options are the same. Both a buyer and a seller have to deliver an underlying asset if an option is exercised.

Let's consider these principles in detail.

1. Today, January 1, you bought a six-month European IBM call. This means that you will not exercise it until July 1.

   If during the six-month period, your counterparty goes bankrupt, you will not make money on the option. The predelivery/forward risk of *long* options is equal to the premium to be paid to substitute these options in the market at the moment of counterparty's default. That is, the predelivery/forward risk *on options* is almost identical to predelivery risk *on forwards*.

   On July 1, if shares trade higher than the strike, you will exercise an option and expect a delivery of shares. The option's seller will expect the delivery of money for these shares. In other words, you will have the same delivery risk as in the case of any stock trade.
2. You sold a six-month IBM call. This means that your counterparty will not be able to exercise it until July 1.[1]

   You are not sure whether your counterparty will exercise this option in six months or not. If the counterparty becomes insolvent, the deal may be canceled. This means that you do not face a predelivery risk on short options. To be more correct, you have no predelivery risk after you collected the premium. The delivery risk is the same: you should be ready to exchange stocks, if a buyer exercises the option.

   Whether the option is exercised or not, a buyer faces both predelivery and delivery risks while a seller has only a delivery risk.[2]

RISK OF REVALUATION AND RISK OF DELIVERY IN FORWARDS AND OPTIONS

As we saw, an option delivery risk is similar to a forward delivery risk. If on expiration date an option is exercised, spot/cash has to be exchanged. Unlike in the case of forward, in the case of options we are not sure whether options will be exercised, yet we consider the risk to be equal to the full face value or a part of it.

Predelivery risks in forward and option deals are different. For instance, if a bank buys a $1 million forward, should a predelivery limit of $1 million be reserved for this deal? Probably not!

Are delivery risks in forward/option deals the same for a buyer and a seller?

So far, we have said that delivery risks of forwards/options for a buyer and a seller are equal, but their predelivery risks differ.

Consider an example: in March two American banks made a forward deal: one sold to the other EUR 1 million at 1.3400 with delivery on October 23.

On October 23, EUR/USD spot was 1.0400. The forward's buyer collected EUR 1 million and paid $1.34 million. His loss of $300,000 was the predelivery risk of the transaction. The party delivering a devaluated currency has lower delivery risk!

LOAN-EQUIVALENT RISK

When calculating a predelivery risk, one can use two methods: nominal and loan-equivalent.[3] The first one is used for calculating based on contracts' face value. The other one calculates a predelivery risk based on VaR, that is, based on market risk calculations. The latter is considered equal to 3 to 4 standard deviations from the current contract price.[4]

Loan-equivalent risk is a widely spread concept that helps to measure risks of different instruments. For an FX forward deal, most banks take it as 10% of face value. That means that if the premium for the option is less than 10% (which is often true in practice), the option's risk will be overvalued for the purpose of credit risk calculation, if the option's exposure is considered to be equal to that of a forward for a credit risk purpose.

Example

EUR/USD is trading at 1.1800. You expect the delivery of EUR 1 million at 1.1700 in a month. At that time, you will have to deliver $1,170,000. Under the nominal method, your predelivery risk is equal to EUR 1 million.

Under the loan-equivalent method, your risk equals the current predelivery risk of $10,000 (1 million × (1.1800 – 1.1700)) plus 15% of €1 million. That is, EUR 150,000 + $10,000.

QUESTIONS

1. On March 10 (Tuesday), a client sold to a bank an IBM 100 call expiring on May 10 (Monday). During which period does the client have predelivery risk?
2. On March 10 (Tuesday), a client sold to a bank an IBM 100 call expiring on May 10 (Monday). During which period does the client have delivery/settlement risk?

3. A client bought an American-style IBM 100 call expiring on May 12 (Wednesday) from you. For which day does he have a delivery risk?
4. On April 1, a client, who has a netting agreement with you, bought EUR 1 million of 1.2000 EUR call/USD put expiring on May 10. On May 1, he sold EUR 0.4 million of this option back. What is the delivery risk on the expiration date?

ANSWERS

1. As a rule, the conventions for options' settlement and delivery are almost identical to those of underlying assets: for currencies (excluding CAD) two days; for shares three days.[5] The client's predelivery risk starts on the deal date of March 10 until the delivery date of May 13 (Thursday). Note that buyer's predelivery risk starts on the deal date rather than at the moment of premium payment for the option.
2. The risk of premium delivery (settlement) appears once a deal is done. Once the premium is received, the bank has no delivery risk until the expiration date. If the client becomes bankrupt, he won't have any obligations to the bank. And vice versa, the client has the bank's obligation (the option). If the client exercises the option on the expiration date, delivery risk appears that is equal to the amount of the option's face value.
3. There is a difference between European- and American-style options. European options can be exercised only on the expiration day. American options may be exercised on any date before the option's expiration (inclusive). This means that theoretically delivery can occur on every day of the option's life.

   At the same time, the probability of American options being exercised is very low unless they are deep-in-the-money (with delta above 92). However, even in this case, the probability is not great: in most situations it is not profitable to exercise them. American-style options are exercised, and delivery risk appears, when swaps (forward differential) are greater than time value. In other words, if by exercising an option a client earns financing on the received position in the underlying asset, the probability of exercise increases. Otherwise, an option may be exercised only by mistake. Therefore, only those who do not understand options may want to exercise them prematurely. However, even in this case one can suggest to a counterparty to buy back the option without exercising it, that is, without a delivery risk on the entire face value. Thus, the real delivery risk of the premature exercise of American-style options is rather small.

4. On the expiration date, the two options are netted, and delivery risk is equal to \$0.6 million.

CHAPTER 27

Credit Risk of Option Strategies

In this chapter we are going to study more complex varieties of option strategies.

COMBINATIONS OF OPTIONS

Straddle

Since you buy a call and a put with the same strike, only one of them will be profitable at expiration, since the market will be either above or below the strike.

Example If you bought $10 million of a 130.00 USD call and $10 million of a 130.00 USD put, on the expiration date spot may be above or below 130.00:

- In the first case, you will buy $10 million at 130.00 (exercising the call);
- In the second case, you will sell $10 million at 130.00 (exercising the put).

And what if the market quotes 129.97/130.03; that is, the strike is in the middle of the bid-offer spread?! The straddle is likely to expire worthless, and you will exercise none of your options. If both options are exercised, you will buy at 130.00 and simultaneously sell at 130.00 without any profit!

Thus, a delivery risk of a straddle is equal to a face value of one side *("one leg")*, in our example—$10 million. *However, predelivery risk is calculated for both options*, since in the case of the seller's default the buyer has to replace both the call and the put.

Due to this characteristic, a straddle provides an opportunity to reduce *credit risks*. Suppose that you bought $100 million of a 50-delta (ATM) call. In other chapters, we have explained that an option's type (call or put) does not change performance of a delta-neutral position. That is, a hedged put behaves similarly to a hedged call with the same strike and expiration date. Therefore, our call, if hedged, behaves the same way as a straddle. In other words, the risk/reward of a position where you are long $100 million of an ATM call hedged with a short $50 million of a forward, is *the same* as the profile of $50 million a leg (ATM call and put) of a straddle (you can check it by drawing a chart). In this case, the delivery risk of the straddle is lower than that of the call. In other words, *by substituting a hedged call or put with a straddle, one reduces delivery risks.*

Strangle

This is almost identical to a straddle: only one option can be exercised on the expiration date.

Suppose that you bought $10 million of a 129.00 USD put and $10 million of a 131.00 USD call.

If on the expiration date spot is

- below 129.00, you will sell $10 million at 129.00.
- above 131.00, you will buy $10 million at 131.00.
- in the range of 129.00–131.00, you will let both options expire since they will be out-of-the-money.

Thus, the delivery risk of a strangle is equal to one leg of the strategy as in case of a straddle. However, predelivery risk is calculated for both options similarly to a straddle.

Bull/Bear Spread (Vertical Spread)

You buy $10 million of a 130.00 USD call and sell $10 million of a 140.00 USD call. You carried out this strategy expecting the USD to go above 130.00, but not to reach 140.00. The sale of the 140.00 call finances the purchase of the 130.00 call. Calculation of settlement risk in this strategy depends on whether or not there is a netting agreement between the parties.

With Netting The maximum settlement risk is $10 million:

- If spot is below 130.00, none of the options will be exercised.
- If spot is in the 130.00–140.00 range, you will buy $10 million at 130.00.
- If spot is above 140.00 you will use netting: $10 million × (140.00 – 130.00)/140.00 = $714,285

Without Netting The maximum settlement risk is $10 million + ¥140 billion and the last point on the previous page does not apply.

- If spot is below 130.00, none of the options will be exercised.
- If spot is in the 130.00–140.00 range, you will buy $10 million at 130.00.
- If spot is above 140.00, you will buy $10 million at 130.00 and sell $10 million at 140.00.

Thus, *in case of a bull spread, where you are long a more expensive option*, your maximum delivery risk equals the face value of the long option plus the maximum P/L of the range if you do netting. If the sides are not netted, both sides are added. Predelivery risk equals the maximum P/L of the range between long and short strikes.

If you are *long a cheaper option*, predelivery risk does not exist, since at worst you will owe to the bankrupt buyer (he owes a more expensive option). In the absence of a netting agreement, the delivery risk equals the sum of both legs. If such an agreement exists, the delivery risk equals a nominal value of one leg.

Ratio Spread

The logic for a ratio spread is almost the same as for a bullish (bearish) spread. The difference is in face values of long and short options. For instance, you buy $10 million of a 130.00 USD call and sell $30 million of a 140.00 USD call. Let's consider the examples with netting and without it.

With Netting

- If spot is below 130.00, none of the options will be exercised.
- If spot is in the 130.00–140.00 range, you will buy $10 million at 130.00.
- If spot is above 140.00, you will have to use a combination of netting and delivery:
  1. Your risk will be reduced by the amount of profit from the $10 million long in the range of 130.00–140.00: $10 million × (140.00 – 130.00)/140.00[1] = $714,285.
  2. Long $10 million will be netted with short $30 million, with $20 million to be delivered.
  3. The remaining $20 million you are short will be settled by a spot deal. Thus, your total maximum delivery risk on this deal is: $20,000,000 + $714,285 = $20,714,285.

Without Netting

- If spot is below 130.00, none of the options will be exercised.
- If spot is in 130.00–140.00 range, you will buy $10 million at 130.00.
- If spot is above 140.00, both options are exercised, and you will have to settle them separately. Thus, the total delivery risk is $10,000,000 + $20,000,000 = $30,000,000.

Risk Reversal (also Known as Collar, Cap and Floor, Combo, Fence, Tunnel)

The maximum risk of a risk reversal is the same as in the case of a single call's or a put's purchase. The reason is that a long leg of the strategy does not cover a short one. Therefore, both delivery and predelivery risks of this strategy are calculated for the long leg.

Calendar Spread

Calendar spreads require a more complex calculation method since the strategy's components must be clear in your mind. A spread, where you buy an October option and sell a December one, has a credit risk different from the one when you purchase a December option and sell an October one.

Predelivery Risk If you are long an October option and short a December one, the value of the October position is always lower than that of the December one: assuming the strikes of the options are the same, a longer-dated option always costs more than a shorter-dated one. Thus, if your counterparty goes bankrupt, you won't face a predelivery risk.

In the second case, you have two alternatives: to divide predelivery risks into two periods or to calculate predelivery risk for one leg. In the first instance, until the expiration of the short side (October 1), the predelivery risk equals the difference between premiums on short and long options. After October 1, a predelivery risk calculation takes into account the long side only.

Delivery Risk In the case of a calendar spread, you face a delivery risk for both dates. If the option is exercised on October 1, you will deliver the underlying on October 3. If the option is exercised on December 1, you will deliver the underlying on December 3. Hence, they must be considered separately since you cannot net them.

Short Strategies

A premium delivery risk is relevant only for strategies in which you sell more expensive options. A delivery risk exists on the date of an options' premium settlement and on the date of strategy expiration. We will discuss in further detail other strategies in later chapters.

QUESTIONS

1. You bought $10 of 90 calls and sold $10 of 92 puts. What is your maximum delivery risk, if the asset is not volatile?

2. On May 1 you sold € 1 million of a 1.1900 EUR call expiring on June 3 (Tuesday), and on May 22 you bought €1 million of a 1.1800 EUR call with the same expiration date. What is your maximum delivery risk with and without netting?

3. You bought a 1.1900 straddle and sold a 1.1800–1.2000 strangle (the strategy is called a butterfly). The face value of each of the four options is €1 million. What is your maximum delivery risk without netting? Above/below which level will you have one? What is your maximum predelivery risk with netting?

4. On May 1, you sold €2 million of a 1.1900 EUR call/USD put expiring on June 3 and bought €1 million of a 1.1800 EUR call/USD put with the same expiration date. What is your maximum delivery risk with and without netting?

ANSWERS

1. If at the moment of exercise the underlying is between 90 and 92, both options will be exercised, and $20 will be delivered.

2. Maximum delivery risk is when the price exceeds 1.1900 EUR/USD. In this case, the counterparty will exercise the 1.1900 EUR call, that is, will buy €1 million at 1.1900 from you. Thus, he will deliver (your delivery risk) $1,190,000 (€1 million × 1.1900), and you will deliver €1 million. At the same time, you will exercise the 1.1800 EUR call and deliver to your counterparty $1,180,000 (€1 million × 1.1800), and he will deliver €1 million to you.

Thus, your delivery risk is €1 million plus $1,190,000. If there is a netting agreement, your maximum risk is $10,000 ($1,190,000 – €1,000,000) + (€1,000,000 – $1,180,000).

3. Maximum delivery risk is €1 million, if you exercise the 1.1900 call, plus $1 million as the counterparty exercises the 1.2000 call. It will occur, if at exercise the EUR/USD is above 1.2000. If there is a netting agreement your maximum predelivery risk is $10,000 (1,000,000 × (1.1900 – 1.1800), if the market is below 1.1800.
4. Your maximum delivery risk without netting is when the exchange rate exceeds 1.1900 at exercise: €1 million and $2.18 million. Netting reduces your risk to approximately €1 million.

CHAPTER 28

Credit Risk of Exotic Options

Exotic options are written out on most underlying assets. The term "exotic" dates back to the times when there were no standard models to price them. Nowadays, price calculators for exotic options are a standard feature of financial software. Although the term implies complexity, they are easy to understand. Thus, they are "exotic" only in name.

BARRIER OPTIONS

Knock-in Options (Knock-ins, Reverse Knock-ins, Double Knock-ins)

A knock-in option is a kind of a "dormant" liability. If its barrier is not touched during its life, its owner is unable to exercise the option at the expiration. Since nobody knows whether the barrier will be touched during the option's life, both the buyer and the seller may treat the risk of such options as equal to that of a vanilla option. Its delivery risk is equal to the option's face value: if you buy $1 million of a 130.00 USD call with a 140.00 knock-in, your settlement risk will be equal to $1 million during the entire option's life. However, in practice, since barriers are very often far out-of-the-money, options stop being a real liability especially close to expiration. That is, delivery risk becomes much smaller than for vanilla options, and some degree of discretion is required in evaluating their delivery risk.

Their predelivery risk equals the option's market value.

Knock-outs

Knock-outs should be handled the same way as knock-ins, since they are valid and represent real obligations until the barrier is touched. Their predelivery risk equals the option's market value.

Other Knock-out Options (Reverse Knock-out, Double Knock-out)

Their predelivery risk equals the option's market value. Barriers limit the risk/reward of these positions to the difference between a strike and a barrier. For instance, if you buy GBP 1 million of a 1.8000 call with a 1.9000 knock-out, your maximum risk is: GBP 1 million × (1.8000 – 1.9000) = $100,000.

Delivery risk of these options is equal to their face value (as in case of knock-in and vanilla options). In our example, if on expiration GBP/USD is 1.8500, we will have to deliver GBP 1 million.

BINARY OPTIONS

Once you hear the term "payout," you should understand that you are dealing with binary options. As always, a predelivery risk is between the trade date and a premium's settlement date. The maximum risk cannot exceed the payout set in the contract. Thus, maximum predelivery and delivery risks equal maximum possible payout (think of a lottery: once you win, you worry whether the organizers will pay the prize).

A seller's delivery risk is equal to the premium, since there is no currency exchange on delivery.

Some other types of exotic options include double knock-outs and double knock-ins (calls and puts with two barriers), double touch options and double no-touch options (their payout depends on two barriers), and many others discussed in the previous chapters. To calculate the credit risk of these options, one should answer the question: what are the maximum predelivery and delivery risks?

QUESTIONS

1. You bought EUR 1 million of a 1.2000 EUR put/USD call with a 1.0000 knock-out. What's your maximum risk for:
   a. predelivery risk?
   b. delivery risk?
2. You sold a one-month "no touch" option for $10,000 with a 1.1900 barrier and the 1:4 payout.
   a. On what date will you have delivery risk?

If you bought this option:

b. On which date will you have delivery risk? What is its amount?
c. How will you calculate predelivery risk during the option's life?

3. You bought EUR 1 million of a 1.1700 EUR call/USD put with a 1.2200 knock-in. What's your maximum:
   a. predelivery risk?
   b. delivery risk?

ANSWERS

1. This is a barrier option, which becomes invalid (expires), if EUR/USD touches 1.0000 at least once during the option's life.
   a. \$200,000. Maximum predelivery risk equals the difference between the strike and the knock-out barrier (1,200,000 × (1.2000 – 1.000)).
   b. \$1 million. Maximum delivery risk in this case (and most often) equals the option's face value of \$1 million, but not euros. When exercising the put, you will sell (and deliver) €1 million, and your counterparty is to deliver \$1 million to you.
2. Option settlements take place on the same date as for their underlying assets. Since in our example the asset is EUR/USD, the settlement takes place on the second business day.
   a. Your settlement (delivery) risk is equal to the premium. Suppose you sold the option on Wednesday. Then settlement risk falls on Friday.
   b. The delivery (settlement) risk date is unpredictable: the market may touch a barrier (1.1900) at any time during the option's life. In this case, the seller will have to pay you \$40,000 (\$10,000 × 4).
   c. Your predelivery risk is \$40,000. To mark-to-market your predelivery credit risk, you can use standard software. In other words, the same software normally revalues exotic options as vanilla options.
3. This is a barrier option, which becomes valid (becomes a real liability) if EUR/USD touches 1.2200 at least once during the option's life.
   a. Predelivery risk of this knock-in option is equal to its mark-to-market. Theoretically at the beginning it is the same as of the ordinary (vanilla) 1.1700 EUR call/USD put. The reason is that, if a trigger is touched, the option turns into a regular vanilla option.

b. The settlement (delivery) risk of this knock-in option is also similar to the risk of the vanilla 1.1700 EUR call/USD put. This assumes that once the barrier is touched and the option becomes "inspired" (valid), it turns into a vanilla option. However, in practice, if the option is close to expiration and the trigger is far out-of-the-money, this risk is very insignificant.

CHAPTER 29

Credit Risk of Combined Positions: Option-Spot/Forward

In this chapter we will cover credit risk management of combined optional spot/forward positions.

DELTA HEDGING

Delta of a vanilla option is a portion of an option's face value. If an option position is delta-hedged, this means that delta is bought or sold against the option. The value of the total (option + forward) position should be indifferent to a forward price fluctuations within a narrow range.

For example, a client bought from you a December 113.00 USD call/JPY put. To hedge, he sells a spot or a forward USD against the option.

- If USD/JPY moves up, the client makes money on the option, but loses on the spot he sold.
- If USD/JPY moves down, the client makes money on the spot hedge he sold, but loses on the option.

Once a P/L of the combined spot option position equals 0 on a 1 b.p. spot move in either direction, the position is called *delta-neutral*.

Delta-hedging is the basic risk management requirement for market makers. To calculate the size of a hedge, one uses delta. The parameter is calculated by standard options software. The term "20 delta option" means to hedge the option, one should buy/sell 20% of its face value.

However, delta changes as an option's expiration approaches and the underlying price moves. Therefore, one makes a number of spot transactions against an option (either bought or sold) in order to adjust the position back to delta-neutral.

Delta Hedging with Forwards

Options should be hedged with forwards, because the purpose of hedging is to hedge options until their expiration. However, most traders hedge with spot/cash since the spot market is more liquid and it is easier to trade there. If a spot hedge is done and it is not swapped into a forward, it should be daily financed on an overnight money market until the option's expiration. Spot hedging often results in unplanned[1] costs as well as in unplanned profits. This happens because the original option price was calculated using a specific interest rate differential embedded in the forward price during the option pricing. The sum of the spot overnight financing costs normally differs from the original interest rate differential used in the original option pricing. A risk manager should keep financing risks in check. *In other words, even if a client hedges his option with you through spot, his risk limit should be set in terms of the forward market.*

This is an important caveat for long-term positions, because many clients sell options against their position in the underlying. As a result, they end up in a hedged option position but still with unhedged forwards.

Positions with Netting

In the case of netting, predelivery and delivery risks are equal. Calculation of forward risk of a combined spot/forward/option position is very similar to calculation of forward risk on spreads. *If a client's maximum profit exceeds maximum profit on your position you don't have a forward risk.* For instance, the client bought $2 million of a forward at 135.00. This means that if the option is exercised on the day he declares bankruptcy, you owe him $2 million at 130.00 and he owes you $2 million at 135.00.

- If spot on the bankruptcy date is 136.00 (above 135.00), you will owe him more than he owes you.
- If spot on that date is 132.00 (in the 130.00–135.00 range), you will have to sell him at a price lower than the market price and to buy above the market price. In other words, he depends on you performing your contract obligations.
- If spot on that date is below 130.00, he won't exercise the call. The only remaining position will be his obligation to buy $2 million at 135.00. Since you will have to buy from him above the market price, he also depends on you.

Let's now discuss credit risks of hedging ATM and OTM options.

Selling Forward against In-the-Money Options

For example, a client buys $2 million of a December 130.00 USD call/JPY put and now wants to sell $2 million of a USD/JPY forward at 134.00. How does the forward change the current credit risk? Some companies calculate risk as a sum of two transactions rather than a combined position. However, the combined position has lower risk, if held by the client until expiration:

- If the option is exercised on December 21, he will buy $2 million at 130.00. This $2 million will be netted against $2 million of the short 134.00 forward. That is, a settlement risk will be lower because risk of the netted delivery of option and forward is less than of the two separate positions;
- If on December 21 the option is not exercised, the settlement risk will be equal to the forward's face value.

For instance, **to hedge an ITM option with a forward,** *a client* transacts with you a forward on the underlying at a price higher/lower than the strike of the call/put she bought. That reduces *your* predelivery risk because if the position is exercised at expiration, she will have a positive P/L. That is, you will owe her some money! At the same time, face values will be netted. Thus, trading forwards against options may reduce credit risks.

Selling Forward against Out-of-the-Money Options

Suppose that on November 1 a client delta-hedges $2 million of a 130.00 USD call/JPY put by selling $400,000 of a forward at 125.00. It settles on the same date as the option's expiration.

On expiration date a bank will be obliged to settle:

- $400,000, if the option is not exercised;
- $1,600,000, if the option is exercised.

What is the bank's predelivery risk on the combined position? Unlucky hedging of OTM options may exacerbate a loss of premium by a loss on delta between a spot price and a strike, increasing your predelivery risk. When the client sold $400,000 at 125.00, his forward position was out-of-the-money. The bank's maximum forward risk equals the difference between the forward price and the strike: $400,000 × (130.00 – 125.00) = ¥2,000,000, or approximately $15,385: ¥2 million/130.00. Yet, as explained earlier, a hedge reduces delivery risk, if an option is eventually exercised.

Positions without Netting

Without a netting agreement with the client, the credit risk of a combined spot/forward/option position is almost the same as the risk of call/put-spreads. *Delivery risk* is equal to the sum of face values of all (long and short) option-spot-forward positions. *Predelivery risk* equals the sum of revaluations of each strategy separately. *But as an alternative, we can consider a situation when predelivery risk on an option-forward position is equal to a maximum loss on a position you bought from a client.*

Delivery (Settlement) Risk

Let's continue the abovementioned example when the client is long $2 million of a 130.00 USD call and short $400,000 of a forward at 125.00. The settlement risk of her position is approximately $2.4 million = $2 million + $0.4 million. To be more precise, if the option is exercised, one delivery will be in USD, the other in JPY.

If at expiration spot is above 130.00, the option is in-the-money. The client will exercise the option and buy $2 million from you, and you will have to deliver $2 million. At the same time, he will deliver $400,000 sold beforehand to you, and you will deliver ¥600 million to him ($400,000 × 125.00). That is, the *settlement risk* almost equals the sum of the option's and forward's face values.

TRADING IN FORWARDS AGAINST OPTION

What if the client has several forward positions against one option position? Then, you should determine an average price of the forwards. For instance, he sold $400,000 at 125.00, $400,000 at 130.00, and $1,200,000 at 135.00. The average exchange rate on the total position of $2 million is 132.00 ((0.4 million × 125.00 + $0.4 million × 130.00 + $1.2 million × 135.00)/$2 million). This approach works if a netting agreement is in place. Otherwise the credit risk will be equal to the sum of all the hedges.

QUESTIONS

1. On March 2 you sold €1 million of the 1.1900 EUR call/USD put expiring on April 3 (Wednesday). On March 22 (Monday), you bought

€1 million of a forward at 1.1800 settling on the same date. Both transactions were with the same client.

a. If instead of the forward you bought spot, would your risk increase?
b. What's your maximum delivery risk?
c. Does a netting agreement with the client change the delivery risk?
d. What's the maximum predelivery risk, if there is a netting agreement?

2. You sold €10 million of a 1.2000 put and bought €10 million of a 1.2200 call. To hedge the position, you sold €10 million of a forward at 1.2100 with the same settlement date as the options.

a. What's the maximum *delivery* risk without netting?
b. What's the maximum *delivery* risk with netting?
c. What's the maximum *predelivery risk* without netting?
d. What's the maximum *predelivery risk* with netting?

3. You bought €2 million of the 1.1900 straddle (€1 million "a leg" (a side)). Two days later you bought €1 million of the forward at 1.1800. A week later you sold €2 million of the forward at 1.200. All deals settle on the same date.

a. What's your maximum delivery risk without netting?
b. What's your maximum predelivery risk with netting?
c. Answer the two previous questions if you hedge with spot instead of forward.

ANSWERS

1. Let's recall that EUR/USD trades settle in two business days. Trades done on April 3 (Wednesday) should settle on April 5, Friday (both the forward and the option, if it is exercised).

a. Unlike a forward, spot settles on March 24. Settlements of the option and spot will take place on two different dates and won't be netted. Thus, in the case of netting the substitution of spot for forward increases settlement risk. Yet, if there is no netting agreement, settlement risk falls, since it will be divided between two dates.[2]
b. €1 million + $1,190,000: (you bought €1 million at 1.1800) + (if the 1.1900 call you sold is exercised, you are to receive €1,000,000 × 1.1900).
c. Maximum delivery risk is €1 million, if spot closes below 1.1900.
d. In the case of netting, maximum predelivery risk equals delivery risk. It is $10,000, if on the settlement date EUR is above 1.1900: €1 million you bought is netted with €1 million to be delivered if the short

option is exercised. While the netted euro amounts are equal 0, the $10,000 settlement risk remains, since $1,190,000 (€1,100,000 × 1.1900) should be netted with $1,180,000.

2. In this case the option strategy is risk reversal. The hedge is needed to cover the risk that spot EUR may drop against the USD. Then, you will lose on the short put and earn on the short spot. If the EUR appreciates (spot moves upwards), you will lose on the spot and earn on the call.

   a. If there is *no netting* agreement three scenarios are possible:

      - If on the options' expiration date spot is between the strikes, none of the options will be exercised and the delivery risk will be $12.1 million (€10,000,000 × .1.2100).
      - If the put is exercised at 1.2000, you will have to buy €10 million (*above* the market) plus $12.1 million (on the forward).
      - If you exercise the 1.2200 call, you will buy €10 million (*below* the market) plus $12.1 million (on the forward).

      That is, you have to deliver under the forward in any case. Plus, if one of the options is exercised the delivery risk increases, because you will have to deliver under both the forward and option contracts.

   b. If there is a netting agreement:

      - If you exercise the 1.2000 put, your delivery risk is 0: EUR nets out and on USD you will have to deliver $12,100,000 and collect $12,000,000. That is, you owe more and, therefore, your risk is 0.
      - If the 1.2200 call is exercised, your delivery risk is $100,000. Explanation is reverse of the previous one.
      - If on the options' expiration spot is between the strikes, none of the options will be exercised and delivery risk will be equal €10 million. This is the maximum risk scenario.

   c. Predelivery risk without netting increases. In case of the client's bankruptcy, his debt to you is considered unsecured. Most likely, you will be paid back only a portion of it. At the same time, you will not receive the entire amount the bankrupt client owes you, because after debt restructuring lenders get paid back only a portion owed to them. On high-volatility markets, predelivery risk may exceed delivery risk. Most currency markets are not very volatile. Therefore, the maximum predelivery risk may be considered equal to the sum of face values of the greatest possible deliveries. Keep in mind that the 1.2000 put and the 1.2200 call can't be exercised simultaneously.

Since there is no netting agreement, if a client owes you \$10,000 and you owe him \$8,000, the forward risk would be the \$10,000 that he owes you.

d. If there is a netting agreement, your maximum risk equals the maximum delivery risk (\$100,000) since your debts are netted.

3. This situation is typical for market makers trading situation. They delta-hedge their positions (buy and sell spot/forward against options) in order to have a delta-neutral portfolio.

a. Your delivery risk without netting is: €1 million at \$1.1800 plus \$2.36 million (€2,000,000 × 1.1800) and plus:

- €1 million, if you exercise the 1.1900 call;
- \$1,990,000 if you exercise the 1.1900 put.

b. Two scenarios are to be considered:

On the expiration date, spot is *above* 1.1900. In this case, your predelivery risk is \$30,000: €2 million sold at 1.2000 through the short forward are netted with €1 million through the long forward you bought at 1.1800 and €1 million you purchased through the exercise of the 1.1900 call. Altogether, €1,000,000 × (1.2000 – 1.1900) + €1,000,000 × (1.2000 – 1.1800).

If at expiration spot is *below* 1.1900, your risk is \$20,000: €1 million from €2 million, sold at 1.2000, is netted against €1 million bought at 1.1800 (€1,000,000 × (1.2000 – 1.1800)). The risk can also be calculated using the "loan-equivalent risk" concept. Then, it is equal to 10% of 1,990,000 plus \$20,000.

c. If hedging is done with spot, then:

Delivery risk *without netting*:

- On the settlement date, delivery risk will be the sum of €1 million at USD 1.1800, and \$2.4 million (€2,000,000 × 1.2000), plus

  €1 million—if you exercise the 1.1900 call;
  \$1,190,000—if you exercise the 1.1900 put.

Since British law recognizes netting of transactions with different expiration dates, the risk with netting is as follows:

- *Before* the spot settlement date: according to British law predelivery risk remains \$20,000: €2 million sold at 1.2000 are subject to netting against €1 million you bought at 1.1800 (€1,000,000 × (1.2000 – 1.1800);

- *After the spot settlement date and before the options settlement date*, theoretically predelivery risk is infinite! Suppose the price on the euro in dollar terms goes up hundred times and the client refuses to sell you €1 million at 1.1900 when you exercise the 1.1900 call. In this case, you will lose millions of dollars. But we should return to the loan-equivalent risk concept once again—the risk will comprise 10% to 15% of €1 million plus $1,190,000 plus $20,000.[3]

Question 3 illustrates several already mentioned points:

In practice predelivery risk of options on low-volatile assets is determined under the method of loan-equivalent risk. It is equal to a current predelivery risk plus a portion of face value (15%) for the markets where a probable market move is relatively small in respect to face value. Nevertheless, this percent should change to take into account that:

- The longer the maturity, the higher is the probability of changes as large as an options face value;
- Credit sensitivity of markets with implied volatility of 10% and 80% should be treated differently. It is obvious that the greater the volatility, the higher the probability of changes close in size to an option's face value;
- Loan-equivalency has to take into account peculiarities in netting definitions and in court practice of different countries,
- Besides, one should determine the threshold value for revising the previously established risk. Even a low-volatile asset may change price by 15% within six months. In this case one should revise predelivery risk on long-term contracts made beforehand (similar to the variation margin concept on exchanges).

To put these ideas in a more practical format:

- For a credit manager responsible for low-volatility assets such as hard currencies, the idea of "infinite" risks may seem unnatural because credit (predelivery) risk on these markets is a small portion of face value (loan-equivalent risk).
- Yet share price of dot.com companies did fall from hundreds of dollars to under 10 dollars within a half of a year! Hence, one has to be much more sensitive to credit risks.

- Emerging currency traders remember the sevenfold devaluation of the Indonesian rupiah and triple devaluation of the Russian ruble. It is difficult to recommend any risk calculation method in such situations. However, during periods of stability, the risk of these markets is closer to that of hard currencies, and predelivery risk may be considered as 10% to 15% from face value. Once devaluation risk appears, risk methodology should obviously become more conservative.

PART Seven

Market Risks Management

The process of evaluating market risk of options works differently in different organizations. Moreover, these processes depend on the mandate of trading desks. Risk-management approaches differ for hedged and unhedged, long-gamma and short-gamma positions, and so on.

The list of credit and operational risks to control and monitor is impressive: basis risk, concentration risk, correlation risk, hedging risk, modeling risk, reinvestment risk, risk of tax legislation change, interest rate risk, credit risk, currency risk, legal risk, and operational risk.

Nowadays, analysis of the Greeks and VaR are the accepted risk management tools. VaR (value-at-risk) is a method of risks analysis that uses asset volatility and correlation between different assets in a portfolio.

Our general advice for a risk manager whatever method she may choose, is to ask herself every time there is a problem: "Won't this method force traders to pay real money for theoretical/virtual risks?"

CHAPTER 30

Typical Mistakes of Options Risk Control

LIMITS BASED ON THE PREMIUM PAID FOR DELTA-NEUTRAL PORTFOLIO[1]

This dangerous fallacy stimulates option selling. The slogan of such managers is "Premium equals profit!" Unfortunately, this sort of options position demonstrates erratic P/L as periods of collecting time decay are interrupted by violent losses when the market moves against the short options positions.

Overall such an approach ignores put/call parity, that is, the core concept of options. Risk profiles of a *hedged* put and a *hedged* call with the same strike and expiration date are the same. In a delta-neutral portfolio (where options are hedged by an underlying asset), the difference between calls and puts disappear.

Let's compare two portfolios. The first one consists of a long 100 call and a delta-equivalent of spot sold on hedge. The second one contains a long 100 put and a delta-equivalent of spot bought on hedge. That is, the options in the portfolios are with the same strike and expiration date, but with different "names."

Let's observe the portfolios' behavior during their life period. If the spot goes up,

- delta of the call expands, and to keep the portfolio risk free you should sell additional spot.
- delta of the put declines, and to keep the portfolio risk free you should . . . also sell additional spot.

That is, both *hedged* portfolios behave absolutely the same way during the option's life.

At exercise, either the call or the put will be exercised depending on which will be in-the-money.

Thus, at the moments of the option's inception/expiration, its "name" is really important. However, during its life hedging and P/L profile are the same. *That's why an 80-delta call and a 20-delta put* (e.g., a 1.2200 call and a 1.2200 put) with the same strike and expiration *will be sold at the same implied volatility.*

In this example, the price of the 1.2200 call may exceed that of the 1.2200 put several times. One of them may be deep-in-the-money, while the other one may be out-of-the-money, yet they have *the same risk*. This example demonstrates that risk profile of a hedged position doesn't depend on the size of an option's premium.

DIFFERENT LIMITS FOR PURCHASED AND SOLD OPTIONS BASED ON THEIR FACE VALUE

It seems trivial to say that the risk of sold options is infinite and of purchased ones is limited. However, when determining limits, one has to think again about what this statement means.

Firstly, this concept is difficult to control: sale of options with the same face value has different consequences depending on the strike and expiration date. For instance, within the 100–120 range short $1 million of a 100 call is likely to lose more than short $2 million of a 110 call!

Secondly, like unsuccessful sales, unsuccessful purchases of options may waste investments. Effectively, risks of short and long positions are almost the same. On exchanges, a client's position is closed once there is no more money left to support a margin on a short position or to buy a new option.

Interestingly, leverage allows traders on low-volatile instruments to get to the level of risk of unleveraged position in high-volatility instruments. Therefore, a theoretical assumption of "better" risk has to be "adjusted" to the realities of trading.

INFLEXIBLE VEGA LIMITS FOR SHORT-TERM PERIODS

Vega measures influence of volatility changes on the price of options/option portfolio. Vega of long-term options is higher than vega of short-term ones with approximately the same delta. For instance, vega of a three-month ATM option is roughly twice as much as vega of a one-month ATM option. This means that having sold 2 million of one-month ATM option and bought 1 million of three-month ATM option, you get a vega-neutral position.

However, a vega-neutral position doesn't mean that change in volatility won't cause the portfolio value to alter. To continue our example, suppose that the volatility of the one-month option fell and the volatility of the three-month option remained stable. In this situation, the position has made money, since it was short the one-month option.

Only simultaneous and parallel shifts of volatility curve leave the value of a vega-neutral position unchanged. Since volatility of options with different maturities rarely moves in similar ways. Thus, vega constantly changes P/L. To cope with the risk, risk managers determine limits for the total position as well as for periods (e.g., up to three months, from three to six months, from six months to one year and for the total portfolio). That is, they "basket" maturities into groups.

However, there are some problems with this method. For example, a risk manager may specify vega limit by month rather than by a "basket" of maturities. This results in an uncontrollable book for at least two factors: a) software-specific interpolation vegas and b) spot/forward movement.

Software's Interpolation of Options' Vegas

Suppose you bought a 10-week option. To which maturity should this option be referred: two- or three-month? As a rule, the system will split it between the two periods: one part will be in a two-month segment, the other part in a three-month segment. Thus, vega limits per short periods can be easily broken because of software peculiarities.

Movement of Spot (and Forwards)

Options' vega changes on every substantial spot move. It causes changes in the ratio between the options' vegas for different maturities. You can see as a long one-month ATM option quickly moves out-of-the-money, losing vega in the process, while a long two-month OTM option goes in-the-money on the same move. On the whole, the one/two month basket is within a limit, while the one and two month vega limits may be broken. That is, the same position may be within a limit in the morning, but end up breaking it in the evening. If limits are divided by month, a trader should constantly adjust his position. That is expensive and ineffective. To avoid transaction costs, vega should be "basketed" into longer time periods.

ADDITIVE LIMITS FOR POORLY CORRELATED ASSETS

Imagine a situation in which a trader deals in options on several assets with similar "names": USD/CHF, EUR/CHF and USD/CAD. Average volatility of the USD/CHF curve is 12%, EUR/CHF 4%, and USD/CAD 4%. Inexperienced managers often establish limits on a basket of USD/CHF and EUR/CHF, because they view USD as a common currency.

Is it possible to hedge USD/CHF vega by EUR/CHF vega? For example, to sell EUR/CHF vega and to buy USD/CHF vega? Yes, it is possible, but it won't have any practical effect, since the level of correlation is too low. Suppose that EUR/CHF moved 1.5% overnight. It is a very substantial move for the asset trading at 4% volatility. We can expect vega of the position to move sharply. Since vega of EUR/CHF and USD/CHF is managed within the same basket limit, the move will necessarily require an adjustment in the USD/CHF position. Such a limit is not helpful in controlling risk. In fact, it is damaging. Similarly, EUR/CHF and USD/CAD do not hedge each other.

However, a limit on a basket of USD/CHF and EUR/USD makes sense because their dynamics are similar, although liquidity differs greatly.

LIMITS FOR OPTION PREMIUM AMORTIZATION (THETA)

Suppose two hours before today's closing spot makes a sharp move and stops at the strike of an option expiring tomorrow. Suddenly, theta (premium amortization) becomes very high since it is at maximum exactly at a long strike. The option's owner ends up over the theta limit. The only way out is to sell the option. But very often there is no market for overnight options in the evening. In other words, in order to avoid such situations traders should sell all short-term options prematurely! It makes no sense to force traders to close such "short-term" positions. Therefore, an inflexible theta limit reduces the position's mobility and increases a chance of losses.

LIMITS FOR AN UNEXPECTED SPOT MOVE

When determining acceptable losses caused by a spot move one chooses an acceptable maximum loss. Normally, this is measured based on a maximum loss for three to five standard deviations. For instance, losses should not reach $1 million, if spot suddenly moves five standard deviations.

Such limits are necessary. However, one should remember that a maximum loss is possible, only if the position is not spot-hedged as the spot moves. That is, the maximum loss will occur only if spot opens with a five-standard deviation gap. In practice, a trader has an opportunity to do intermediate delta-hedging to protect his position from losses.

The logic of some risk managers, who try to prevent their company from possible losses beyond 4% standard deviations, is very interesting. Such managers ask themselves: what will happen to the market if the U.S. President is killed? Since nothing of this kind has taken place for 40 years, it is difficult to forecast a market reaction. It may be awful, but it is senseless to limit everyday activity on the basis of similar hypothetical risks.

One should also remember "pin risk"—the risk of an option exercise today. Suppose the limit restricts losses on a 5% spot move. You are short a large face value option 5.2% away from the current price. Two hours before the market closing, the price moves 0.5%. The option turns out to be in the range covered by the limit. Suddenly, the maximum loss exceeds the acceptable level! What should you do? You can immediately hedge it by spot or buy back the option.

In the first case when spot backs off, you will lose real money on hedging the considerable but unlikely risk. In the second case, you also lose money by paying premium for a useless option. Despite the extremely low probability of the option's exercise, market makers don't sell options at a price lower than 3 ticks ($3,000 for $1-million of face value). Thus, again a flexible procedure of temporary risk limits is required.

USING SMILES[2]

A smile is a premium for OTM options over ATM option with *the same expiration date*, expressed in volatility terms. As a rule, such a premium is paid for options in the price direction in which greater volatility is expected. For instance, on S&P a volatility increase accompanies the market fall. That's why prices of OTM S&P puts in volatility terms are higher than of ATM puts. For instance, a 20-delta put trades at 14.5 volatilities, while an ATM put trades at 14 volatilities. In dollar terms, the volatility premium will translate so that an October 1,100 put is at 6 cents, rather than 5 cents, which corresponds to 14%. That is, the trader "earns" 1 cent. "Earns" is in quotation marks because the profit is theoretical and will materialize only on the option's expiration. If OTM options trade at discount to ATM, traders call such a volatility curve "smirk."

In the case depicted in Figure 30.1, the amount of premium in volatilities over an ATM price is different for options with different deltas. Thus, the premium of a 20-delta put is 0.5% over the ATM price. The premium

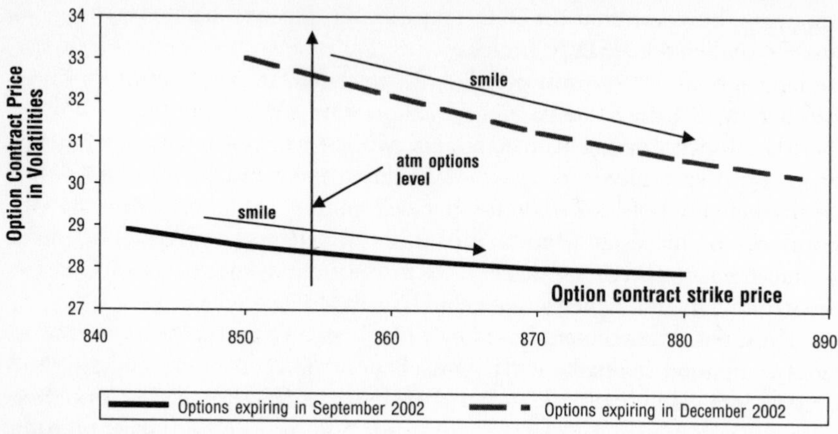

FIGURE 30.1 Options Premiums

of a 30-delta put is 0.4% over the ATM price. Options premiums for each delta are defined by the term "smile." (See Figure 30.1.) In most situations, the market's supply/demand determines a smile.

Most market makers use smiles in managing position risks. Sometimes, traders abuse risk management with this concept. Since the volatility of ATM options often differs from the volatility of OTM options, traders oversell OTM options. Mark-to-market of a position is based on prices of ATM options. Having sold OTM options at a higher volatility, traders collect "theoretical" profit on the amount of difference between volatilities of ATM and OTM options.

To impede this practice, a more complex risk management system was introduced. It revalues volatility of each delta separately, rather than on the basis of 50%-delta (ATM) options volatility. For instance, if volatility of a 20-delta option is higher than the volatility of a 50%-delta option, it'll be revalued on basis of its own volatility.

Although helping to mend the revaluation process, the approach creates other problems. First, the process changes the portfolio's delta since an option priced at different volatilities has a different delta. Additionally, gamma becomes unpredictable. If an option is valued at an ATM volatility, a one-point spot move changes delta in a definite proportion. In case of different volatilities corresponding to different deltas, an extra gamma curvature appears, because it is influenced not only by a spot move, but also by a volatility smile. Thus, the two methods of revaluation have different hedging requirements.

One of the main assumed advantages of smile is that it reflects the market's forecast of the volatility level, if spot reaches a certain price level.

It appears, however, that the forecasting ability of smiles is overrated. Suppose that when the USD/JPY spot is at 115.00, volatility of a three-month 50-delta option is 14% and volatility of a 20-delta 106.00 option is 15%. In other words, the 20-delta option trades with a 1% volatility premium over the 50-delta one. This means that the options market expects volatility to rise if spot moves down. Suppose that afterwards, within a month, the market slowly falls to 106.00 and the volatility of what is now a two-month option trades at 13%. In this case, if the market maker had initially revalued this option at 14%, the book's revaluation fluctuations would be lower. Now, he will have to reduce vols from 15% to 13%.

Thus, risk management based on volatility smile gives a risk manager a better evaluation of results when a deal is done. On the other hand, the distortions in hedging increase, and predictability of results suffers. And once again the risk manager faces the question "Will this method make his employer to pay real money for theoretical/virtual risks?"

QUESTIONS

Detailed explanation of formats used by traders for position management was introduced in Part Four.

1. In Table 30.1, a spot move from 0.8725 to 0.8825 influences the position's vega.

TABLE 30.1

	Vega Exposure @ 0.8725	Vega Exposure @ 0.8825
August	–3,000.00	–3,200.00
September	2,000.00	3,200.00
October	1,000.00	2,000.00
November	1,500.00	500.00
December	–50.00	–800.00
January	–3,000.00	–3,500.00
February	2,900.00	3,200.00
March	0	0
April	200.00	–700.00
May	0	0
June	0	0
July	0	0
Total:	1,550.00	700.00

What should a trader do with the volatility position at 0.8825, if

- maximum monthly limit is ± $3,000.00?
- maximum two-month basket limit is ± $3,000.00?
- maximum three-month basket limit is ± $3,000.00?
- the spot moves back to 0.8725?
- What's the probability of a substantial price fall of one period without a substantial price fall of the following period?

2. See Table 30.2 for the following questions.
   a. If the daily loss limit is $45,000, how should a trader react to potential loss at 0.9250?
   b. If today spot closes 75 pips below the current level, will the limit remain broken?

TABLE 30.2

Spot	0.85	0.8575	0.865	0.8725	0.88	0.8875	0.895	0.925
Delta	–2,000,000	–1,500,000	–1,000,000	0	500,000	2,000,000	1,000,000	–20,000,000
Gamma	–500,000	–500,000	–1,000,000		500,000	1,500,000	–1,000,000	–19,000,000
P/L	–26,450	–13,325	–3,950	–200	1,675	5,850	12,725	–58,675

3. Table 30.3 demonstrates the behavior of a hedged one-day 122.00 USD call. What should the trader do with the position if:

TABLE 30.3

118.10	$+144,835	118.34	$+132,743
118.71	$+114,573	118.95	$+102,545
119.32	$ +84,631	119.56	$ +72,679
119.32	$ +55,107	120.17	$ +43,418
120.53	$ +26,857	120.78	$ +16,374
121.14	$ +3,234	121.39	$ –3,622
121.75	**$ –9,366**	**122.00**	**$ –10,139**
122.36	$ –6,861	122.61	$ –2,012
122.97	$ +7,373	123.22	$ +15,080
123.58	$ +26,691	123.83	$ +35,187
124.18	$ +47,151	124.44	$ +55,737
124.79	$ +67,602	125.05	$ +76,158
125.40	$ +87,873	125.66	$ +96,388

   a. the time decay loss limit is less than $10,000?
   b. spot closes at 121.85?

c. it goes to 121.25 30 minutes before the session closing?
d. if there is a chance to sell the entire overnight option at a loss?
e. minimal trading lot is $10 million?

ANSWERS

1. a. With spot at 0.8825, the trader will have to buy August and January options and sell September and February options. That is, he has to make four transactions.
   b. The trader will have to buy options in December–January and to sell in February–March. That is, he has to make two transactions.
   c. The trader will also have to buy options in the November–December–January period. That is, he has to make one transaction. (See Table 30.4.)

TABLE 30.4

	Vega exposure @ 0.8825
August	–3,200.00
September	3,200.00
October	2,000.00
November	500.00
December	–800.00
January	–3,500.00
February	3,200.00
March	0
April	–700.00
May	0
June	0
July	0
Total:	700.00

   d. Depending on the limit, the trader should carry out four transactions, or two, or one. The difference in transaction fees is very sizable. Moreover, if spot returns to the initial position, the trader has to pay the full amount of spread to reverse his position. The unnecessary transaction fees become very expensive.
   e. In general, correlation between the price levels of neighboring periods is very high.

2. a. It is obvious that in the 0.8950–0.9250 range there is a considerable pin risk (around €20 million). This happens when an option expires the next day. What should the trader do tonight seeing that his worst-case scenario exceeds the limit? Should he be allowed to go over the limit temporarily, or hedge the potential loss with an option or a spot deal?

   In the first case, the trader takes the risk of a sudden price gap from .8725 to .9250 during which he won't be able to delta-hedge. Therefore the pin risk will be left hedged. Such cases happen very rarely— once or twice a year. Therefore, the risk is bearable.

   The second alternative will require the trader to pay for a buyback of an improbable risk that happens once a year at best. Since temporary violations of limits occur often, lack of a limit adjustment mechanism will demoralize the trader and result in losses.

   The third approach will require the trader to purchase some spot at the current level. That will equalize losses at both extremes of 0.8500 and of 0.9250. At least, it will put losses at 0.9250 under the limit. However, the position would no longer be delta-neutral at the current spot level. That will increase chances of losses in the most probable price range—near the current price. That is, you will substitute an improbable risk with the real one for the sake of keeping within unrealistic limits.

   b. No, it will not. The example demonstrates how a strict interpretation of limits may miss a market reality. Small spot moves in the center of a wide price range may result in a substantial increase of improbable maximum losses at the range's extremes.

3. The example demonstrates the importance of a flexible approach to limits. It is obvious that fluctuations within a 25 pip range shouldn't result in sharp changes in the management of the position. Currently, the trader is within the limit. Perhaps he can sell a portion of the option without a considerable loss, but before the market closing it may be difficult to find a buyer. Moreover, since a minimal lot (minimal face value of transaction) equals the option's face value, it is unlikely that he'll manage to sell a part of the option.

   A way out may be to sell a different short-term option. He can also manipulate the estimated time decay by setting up the spot 10 pips further from the strike or reducing volatility. Both methods will result in transferring a portion of tomorrow's estimated losses to the today result; that is, the total risk will be the same but within limits for each day. Such tricks distract traders' and controllers' attention and are dangerous in the long term. It is better if risk managers grant exemptions in these situations to keep the overall system of risk management respected by traders.

CHAPTER 31

Recommended Approach to Risk Management Methodology

The main purpose of risk management is to prevent problems, not business! The more comfortable the risk manager feels on a certain market, the more often he uses simplified limits based on experience. However, he must also be able to understand and use VaR,[1]—a method of accounting for a variety of risk parameters.

SIMPLIFIED APPROACH TO LIMITS

Today, VaR is a standard instrument of risk control. In addition, some of the following methods of risk control, which evolved historically, can also be helpful:

- limit of maximum daily losses
- limit of maximum monthly losses
- limits on position's vega
- limits on vega for a basket of periods
- limits on forward position
- limits on losses in case of a volatility neutral directional spot move
- limit on a number of open positions (unmatched strikes)

The idea of limits on *maximum daily losses and on maximum monthly losses* is clear. This is a guiding directive to be followed by a trader in addition to forecasts based on all the Greeks.

The limit on vega assumes the total amount of a position's vega for all periods. *Limits on vega for a basket of periods* assume limits by a basket of time periods. One can choose to limit vega by baskets of periods, rather than by a month—for instance, to basket periods by quarters: expiration in up to three months, in up to six months, and in up to one year.[2]

Limits on losses on a directional spot move restrict losses in case of an abrupt spot move by three to four standard deviations without accounting for volatility changes.

A limit on the forward position (or interest rate position for options on stocks or bonds) is essential because hedging the options position is done with spot (cash in the case of stocks and bonds). However, the position may consist of long-term and short-term options, which should be hedged with forwards of the corresponding periods. The spot (cash) hedge distorts forward (financing) risks. For instance, a total spot hedge for a portfolio that consists of three-month and one-year options is long $10 million. To hedge a three-month position, one should buy $20 million of a three-month forward[3] and sell $10 million of a one-year forward. Therefore, the spot hedge does not fully protect the position from the risk of moves in the interest rates. To hedge this risk, one should sell $10 million on spot, purchase $20 million of three-month forward and sell $10 million of one-year currency forward.

A limit on the number of unmatched strikes is very useful for hedged portfolios. For instance, in the book you have a hedged 100 call and a hedged 100 put for the same date. Thus, the 100 strike is matched. The lower the number of unmatched strikes, especially short-term ones, the easier to manage the position! Although the author has not heard of this limit being applied by banks, it is very helpful. As a rule of thumb an active market maker with a mid-size position shouldn't have in his book more than 300 open (unmatched) strikes, excluding minor deals. The number of small options may be unlimited, since they do not have a major influence on hedging decisions.

VaR-BASED LIMITS[4]

Given that an option has a curvilinear response surface, the simple application of static partial derivatives and cross partials (the Greeks) is inadequate to this task, and must be supplanted by numerical modeling to determine the range of values that the option will have under various market conditions. This applies *a fortiori* when we consider the effect of market changes upon a book or portfolio of options.

The concept of *value at risk (VaR)* is significant here. Value at risk is the maximum amount of loss predicted for the position:

- Over a given period of time (target horizon)
- For a given confidence level
- For the current market
- Assuming no changes in the position

For example, let's assume that our book consists of one short call with the following parameters: Underlying = 100.0, Strike = 100.0, Maturity = 30 days, Volatility = 19.1%; Greeks: Delta = 0.5109 (~0.50).

A volatility of 19.1% implies that for a one-day *target horizon*, a trading range will be approximately + /– 1%. Thus, assuming a normal distribution, the underlying will move up or down by 1% for two-thirds of the days we see. In other words, we have a *one-day standard deviation in the underlying of 1%*.

How many standard deviations should we use to compute VaR? We have found that in practice, a good number for extreme value is four standard deviations. Why four standard deviations? Well, this is an empirical question. Most beginning students of statistics learn the Gaussian-normal probability distribution by heart, and know that 2.32 standard deviations correspond to 99% of the action, if the world were distributed normally.

But markets are not distributed in a Gaussian normal fashion. It turns out that 4 standard deviations correspond to a 98% confidence interval for a Student-t distribution with three or four degrees of freedom (which most markets seem to fit for small target horizons). Thus, we should move the underlying up or down four standard deviations and determine the equivalent options valuations and delta-equivalents at those points (96.15, 104), as shown in Table 31.1.

However, the underlying is not the only value that can change within the target horizon. Options' *implied* volatility can go up and down, and therefore we must also test the model for different implied volatility levels. We have found that as a practical matter, change in volatility can generally be bounded by 15% relative. This means that if the current volatility is 19.1%, the tomorrow volatility will most likely be within the bounds of (16.61%, 21.97%). Let's use this simple option book within these bounds as well, as shown in Table 31.2.

TABLE 31.1 Change in the Option's Price (See the Example) as the Underlying Asset Price Moves (In One Day)

Price of the Underlying Asset	–4 Standard Deviations = 96.15	Initial Value = 100.00	+4 Standard Deviations = 104.00
Price of the option (delta)	0.74 (–25)	2.18 (–51)	4.76 (–77)

We assume constant volatility of 19.1%.

TABLE 31.2 Change in the Option's Price as Volatility Moves (In One Day)

Volatility	19.1 · (1/1.15) = 16.61%	Initial Value = 19.1	19.1 · 1.15 = 21.97%
Price of the option	1.89	2.18	2.50
(delta)	(–51)	(–51)	(–51)

We assume constant price of the underlying = 100.00.

Putting this all together, we can do a *parametric grid search* that determines the values of the option book at intervals from unchanged to the extremes at the time horizon (in one day), as shown in Table 31.3.

Subtracting the current value of the option book from these results gives us a series of revaluations, shown in Table 31.4.

Revaluation showing the largest loss (–2.81) is our VaR for a one-day period with a 99% confidence level (with 104-point price of the underlying and 21.97% volatility).

This technique is called *parametric value-at-risk*. It does not require masses of historical data, elegant and expensive Monte-Carlo simulations, and reams of specialists. Rather, it is a common-sense approach that allows you to cheaply and simply compute numerical scenarios from the existing data, and to determine how much your position is likely to hurt you:

a. within some target horizon;
b. within some confidence level;
c. for existing markets;
d. with no change in the position.

Now, some refinements. Many products have not only spot, but forward curves as well. These forward curves can also fluctuate, even if spot stays constant. In foreign exchange, for example, the forward curves are the

TABLE 31.3 Revaluation of the Option as Both Price of the Underlying and Volatility Move

	–4 Standard Deviations = 96.15		Initial Value = 100.00		+4 Standard Deviations = 104.00	
16.61%	0.54	(–22)	1.89	(–51)	4.54	(–80)
19.10%	0.74	(–25)	2.18	(–51)	4.76	(–77)
21.97%	1.00	(–27)	2.50	(–51)	5.02	(–74)

TABLE 31.4 Change in the Option's Price and Delta as Both Price of the Underlying and Volatility Move

Volatility \ Spot	–4 Standard Deviations = 96.15		Initial Value = 100.00		+4 Standard Deviations = 104.00	
16.61%	+1.67	(–22)	+0.32	(–51)	–2.33	(–80)
19.10%	+1.47	(–25)	+0.03	(–51)	–2.55	(–77)
21.97%	+1.21	(–27)	–0.29	(–51)	–2.81	(–74)

product of the interest rate ratios of the two counter-currencies. In commodities futures, the forward curves are the product of expectations for tightness of supply when these expectations exist (backwardation), and cost of carry when tightness does not exist. Apart from forward curves (term structure of prices) for the underlying, there are also forward curves for the volatility (term structure of volatility).

For a very simple parametric value-at-risk calculation, we recommend modifying each forward price by its *associated* parametric standard deviation (the option's volatility for that option expiration). Most computer programs do not do this, but rather do parallel shifts (or ratio parallel shifts) in the forward curve as you measure spot deviations, thus ignoring the measure of second-order risk in the forward curves. For a start, this is adequate, but the risk of changes in slope in the curve should be taken into account as well, as you develop your methodology.

Similarly, we recommend varying the volatility along its forward curve in ratio form. Thus, for example, if we have one-month volatility at 19.1% and two-month volatility at 18%, a simple volatility revaluation grid would look like Table 31.5.

For commodities markets, we would move the underlying up or down by one-day movements that correspond to the forward term, as shown in Table 31.6.

TABLE 31.5 An Example of Volatility Revaluation Grid for Two Terms of Option Expiration

Volatility	–15%	–5%	Unchanged	+5%	+15%
1 Mo.	16.61%	18.19%	19.1%	20.06%	21.97%
2 Mo.	15.65%	17.14%	18.0%	18.9%	20.70%

TABLE 31.6 An Example of Underlying Asset's Price Revaluation Grid for Two Terms of Option Expiration

Underlying	–4 Standard Deviations	–1 Standard Deviation	Unchanged	+1 Standard Deviation	+4 Standard Deviations
1 Mo.	96.15	99	100	101	104
2 Mo.	96.37	99.1	100	100.9	103.8

Combining these underlying and volatility curves, we have a simple grid search for underlying, based on its volatility and the forward curves.

VaR FOR PORTFOLIO

Now, this parametric VaR method works rather well for a single commodity pair, such as ATT in dollars, or EUR/USD. When we combine commodity pairs into an overall portfolio (such as a simple FX book consisting of EUR/USD and GBP/USD), the situation gets more complex. Several methods of handling this combination exist. The most widely used includes deploying a Pearson correlation-coefficient matrix. The techniques for this are beyond the scope of this book, but we would still like to express our reservations about trusting correlation overmuch. Correlation is often the first coefficient to break down, even during normal market movements, and should not be trusted overmuch as a means of bounding risk. It is far better for the beginner to look at each individual underlying on its own; indeed, the options dealer must do so in order to understand the component response surface of his book.

STRESS TESTS

A stress test is a measure of "how bad could things be"—a nightmare scenario. In interviews with many (former (!)) risk managers from Russian banks regarding the 1998 crisis, one theme that came out time and time again was that the "stress tests" that were run, totally understated the amount of risk that ultimately was realized with the default. As a result, the managements of many banks were insufficiently worried and failed to close risky positions. For stress purposes, it is generally better to err on the side of conservatism, and overstate the risk scenario.

VaR is a measure of how bad things can get over a given period of time (target horizon), for a given confidence level, for the current market, assuming no changes in the position. *In stress tests, we do not look at an awful move given the current market, but make up* stress scenarios *that look for an absolutely awful markets*. Moreover, in a normal VaR study, we assume an empirically derived level of correlation among different positions in the book. Under a stress test scenario, we may break these correlations down (by increasing correlation coefficients), resulting in maximum predicted damage.

Similarly, under a normal VaR study we take a 99% (or other) confidence level. This means that for a one-day time horizon, we would expect to see losses of the given position, exceeding VaR, twice or less a year. A stress test, whether conducted along fundamental scenario or extreme statistical lines (for example, 10 standard deviations + 100% correlation) should give us a result we expect to see very rarely, or not at all. *The VaR does not answer the question, "how bad can it get?"—the stress test does.*

QUESTIONS

Refer to Table 31.7 for the following questions.

1. Suppose a forward limit on a three-month baskets is no more than + $1 million. Are there periods in which a trader has to change his position?
2. At which spot level would you expect maximum theta (premium time decay)?
3. Suppose in accordance with the limits, daily losses may not exceed $15,000. At the end of the business day, a risk manager realizes that a would-be overnight loss from the premium time decay will be $23,000. Is this a signal of a probable limit breaking?
4. Suppose €10 million of short 0.8480 put hasn't been revalued. What will happen to the maximum risk limit (maximum loss of $50,000 with a 1.5% spot move), if spot falls by 50 pips on closing? (To answer this question you should predict the trader's hedging actions at closing level.)
5. An example of simple VaR is shown in Table 31.8. Changes in spot are placed horizontally, changes in volatility vertically.
   a. In which scenario are the losses maximum?
   b. If VaR shows the risk increase as volatility rises, should one correct the vega position by selling/buying long or short options?

TABLE 31.7 Chapter 31, Question 1 Position's Sensitivity to Spot Moves

Currency: **Euro/Dollar**

Date: 08.08.01 **Spot on revaluation:** 0.8800
Time: after New-York **Step:** 0.0075

Spot	**0.85**	**0.8575**	**0.865**	**0.8725**	**0.88**	**0.8875**	**0.895**
Delta	−2,000,000	−1,500,000	−1,000,000	0	500,000	2,000,000	1,000,000
Gamma	−500,000	−500,000	−1,000,000		500,000	1,500,000	−1,000,000
Result	−26,450	−13,325	−3,950	−200	1,675	5,850	12,725

put – 3.5M @ 0.8900
call 1M @ 0.8850

VEGA			*Forward's* EURO	Dollar
August	−3,000.00	August	−1,000,000	−872,500
September	2,000.00	September	200,000	174,500
October	1,000.00	October	100,000	87,250
November	−2,500.00	November	475,000	414,438
December	−500	December	−2,000,000	−1,745,000
January	−4,000.00	January	3,200,000	2,792,000
February	3,500.00	February	75,000	65,438
March	0	March	125,000	109,063
April	200	April	0	0
May	0	May	0	0
June	0	June	0	0
July	0	July	0	0
Total:	−3,300.00	Total:	1,175,000	1,025,188

TABLE 31.8 Chapter 31, Question 5

VaR on USD/JPY Position

Spot/Volatility	**12.30**	**12.15**	**12.00**	**11.45**	**11.30**
124.38	−95,780	−98,176	−100,571	−102,967	−105,361
123.59	−66,010	−68,345	−70,678	−73,008	−75,336
122.79	−32,670	−34,907	−37,139	−39,366	−41,588
122.00	4,205	2,098	−1,000	−2,090	−4,172
121.21	44,514	42,566	40,628	38,702	36,789
120.41	88,128	86,357	84,602	82,860	81,135
119.62	134,880	133,300	131,738	130,194	128,670

c. If VaR shows the risk increase as spot moves, should one correct the gamma position by selling/buying long or short options?
d. What can you say about the book's sensitivity to spot moves?
e. What can you say about the book's sensitivity to volatility changes?

ANSWERS

1. The trader should change his November–January position. It's easier to do a swap: to buy €2 million with delivery on December and to sell €2 million with delivery in January. In case there is only one transaction in each period (e.g., standard date of options' exercise on exchange), the swap's dates should correspond to the options' dates of payment. If the portfolio contains options with different expiration dates, the swap is done for any date of the month.

2. Maximum negative theta (loss) is most likely to be at the spot level, where the strike of the largest long option expiration for tomorrow is. In this example, it is at 0.8850 where €1 million of a long call is settled. The largest profit will be at the spot level, where the strike of the largest short option expiration is. In this case, it is at the level of 0.8900 (settlement of €3.5 million of a short put).

3. No doubt that high time decay may forebode losses over the established limit. However, one should remember that:
   - The concepts of time decay and theta are different, although they are usually used as synonyms. Time decay equals theta ± time decay of forwards. Most software products *do not* separate them. If they *do*, one should remember that often the time decay of forwards is very significant, especially over weekends. Let's remember that in FX the delivery period for the deals done on Thursday is two business but four calendar days. Hence funding is charged for four days and appears normally on the Thursday P/L, (i.e., is charged up front). Very often funding is a significant sum and it balances high theta.
   - See Question 3 in the previous chapter and Question 2 for this one. High time decay may be a result of the strike's closeness.
   - In any case, spot seldom remains at the same level over a day, and chances for the position to cover a part of a would-be loss are very high.

   Therefore, one should wait till the options' expiration and make sure of the results. Certainly, if time decay exceeds the limit greatly, one should receive explanations from traders.

4. It will turn out that the limit is broken significantly. This question demonstrates the conditional character of limits, especially if we take a range that greatly exceeds a likely daily price move due to improbable events. If a trader is forced to follow the limit, he has two alternatives. First, he can buy back the option by paying real money for the improbable risk. Second, he can sell spot, making the position locally unhedged, that is, locally increasing the risk in order to hedge against an improbable risk far away.

5. Current volatility is 12.00; current spot is 122.00

   a. In case volatility falls to 11.30 and spot rises to 124.38.
   b. We have discussed that vega risks should be corrected by long-term options. Their prices react to changes in volatility to a greater extent than prices of short-term options.
   c. We have discussed that to change position's gamma, one should use short-term options (with maturity up to one month). Their prices react on spot moves to a greater extent than prices of long-term options.
   d. It is obvious that with a downward move the result is positive, and with an upward move—negative. This happens when the position is *not* delta-neutral: it is short spot. If the current position is delta-neutral, the report shows that USD calls were sold and USD puts were bought.
   e. At 12.30 (high volatility), the result is as follows:

      - at 119.62, the result is better than at the current volatility. Therefore, the position is long long-term options with strikes below the current spot level.
      - at 124.38, the result is also better than at the current volatility. Therefore, although the position is short gamma (and spot), it is long long-term options with strikes above the current spot level.

   However we have just said (point d) that the calls were sold (to be more precise, the calls and the puts with the strikes above the current spot level (see put-call parity)). Doesn't this conflict with the last statement?

   The answer is no. In points b) and c) we said that short-term options are more sensitive to spot moves due to high gamma, while long-term options are more sensitive to volatility changes (vega). This position contains many sold short-term options with strikes above the current spot. However, it also has bought long-term options. Therefore, the total gamma above the current spot level of the short- and long-term options is negative. This causes risk of losses when spot appreciates. The total vega is positive.

The previous discussion demonstrates how by means of one table one can get a complete description of a complex position.

PART
Eight

Psychology of Trading

The cemetery is full of traders whose last words were: "I've never seen this before."

—Wall Street proverb

CHAPTER 32

Personal Factors in Risk Evaluation

To make a correct evaluation of risks, one must filter classical statistical factors through a personal risk profile.

In classical statistics, risk is defined as the standard deviation from the mean. To some extent, this basic concept governs the minds of most decision makers, including investors. Let's rephrase this concept: a decision that differs from the one an average person would make in a given situation carries a risk equal to "the deviation from the average person's decision." Of course, it is anybody's guess as to what the average person's point of view is. Consequently, one cannot know for sure how far away one is from the average. Therefore, there is an incongruency between a generally acceptable conceptual framework and the real-life behavioral aspects of decision making. In other words, decision makers tend to forget that the concept of risk is always individual in nature, which makes their decisions riskier.

The fact that different people (and companies) evaluate the risks of a particular situation differently does not require an explanation. This is similar to fitting a suit: although it is tailored to your size, it may not fit well when you actually put it on. In other words, all other things being equal, people treat risk differently. In this sense, statistical measures often do not help. For example, the risks associated with a small child's crossing a road are higher than those involving an adult, although objectively they are on the same road and may be hit by the same car.

The same applies to investment: most market participants have the same access to market information and trading methodologies, but there are huge discrepancies in results. The core reason for such discrepancies is the individuality of all decision makers. Therefore, the ability to adapt common knowledge to personality is one of the most important characteristics of a successful investment manager.

THEORETICAL APPROACH TO RISK PERSONALIZATION

In financial theory, risk personalization is achieved by classifying investors as risk averse, risk neutral, and risk positive. But this remains theory. A decision maker discovers to which class he belongs by testing real events and observing how others react to them. After determining one's place in this classification, one can define the most suitable risk niche. In turn, this reduces nervousness and, consequently, enhances rationality.

For example, imagine that a person decides to gamble. By understanding one's fit within a certain category, one can limit actions according to the appropriate feeling in a given situation. Suppose that this person limits the size of a single bet to $5 and the total loss to $500. With these limits, one can build an action plan and play rationally, *without emotions*.

In practice, such recipes do not work, because categorization among the three groups is abstract (like other academic concepts) and is only tangentially applicable to most people. Most of us assume a different approach vis-à-vis the risk of various financial instruments and situations. That is, the same person can be risk averse to driving cars and risk acceptant to stock picking. Likewise, a sick person can have less stamina with regard to risk as opposed to when he is healthy. In other words, a person fits different categories of risk preference under different circumstances.

PERSONAL PSYCHOLOGY AND ATTITUDE TO REALITY

Why is an individual's psychology one of the determining factors for success? The answer is that psychology is not a subject one can touch and feel, and therefore it is difficult to identify and control. As a result, very few of us have a grasp of it. In other words, it is a rare monopolistic-like advantage that makes some people more successful than others. According to the ancient Chinese strategist Sun Tse, "One who knows his enemy is strong, one who knows himself is unbeatable." What he probably meant is that without a precise evaluation of your own resources, one cannot attain success, even with correct information about external goals.

An investor capable of acquiring better quality information compared to others enjoys an advantage. However, if this person is unrealistic in self-evaluation or ignores the environment in which one operates (e.g., the reaction of a supervisor to losses), one will not fully benefit from the most precise forecast.[1]

The importance of individual psychology in risk evaluation is not a trivial observation. It is easier to illustrate the difficulty of correctly evaluating personal abilities by comparing our physical and psychological abilities. In fact, everything that lacks a physical component leaves us in the world of highly personal estimates rather than "reality."

With any physical activity, one's strengths and weaknesses (limitations) become evident almost immediately, and there is a relatively clear plan of action to change the situation. For example, if one decides to lift a weight and fails, he will know that he cannot do it. In other words, tests of physical ability are relatively objective. This is not so with psychology. The risks one take are based on one's abstract estimates. Because of that, they are highly imprecise. *In statistical terms, one can say that a given risk estimate is a point (most likely not the mean) within a random distribution (not necessarily a normal distribution).*

DECISION MAKING AS OVERCOMING YOURSELF

A given decision maker is a dynamic system with emotional, informational, conscious, and subconscious inputs. That may sound a bit philosophical, and it is! Still, in talking to long-time investors, one may find that most of them are unique, because they clearly understand their own risk profile and their place in relation to common knowledge or mainstream thinking. The knowledge of themselves is the cornerstone of their common sense.

To achieve stable success, an investor or trader must have a fair evaluation of the limitations of one's psychology as well as a system of self-control. Otherwise, in the long term, even the most efficient mechanism of analysis and execution will fail to yield positive results.

QUESTIONS

1. Based on the article about General Electric you read over the weekend, you have decided to sell its stock on Monday. But the stock opened higher. Having talked to your friends you concluded that the market has not digested the published information. Emotionally, would it be easier for you to sell if the market opened lower, higher, or at the Friday closing price?

2. To continue the case described in Question 1: you decided to hold on. But the market continues moving upwards. You consult your colleagues but they don't understand what's going on. What is the psychology behind the market action?

3. You have discovered a technical signal, which is very profitable for FX trading. Looking through the commodity markets charts, you notice an almost identical pattern in the oil market. You test the signal for historical profitability and its efficiency is confirmed. Can you force yourself to take the same size position in currencies? If you cannot what prevents you from that?

4. The market is rising. You believe that it has reached the top. You would "sell into strength" a short-term low-delta call, but everybody around is amazed at the market strength and the general admiration makes you nervous. Will you be able to sell, if the
   - last two days you have been losing when going short?
   - last two days you have been losing money?

ANSWERS

1. Probably, it is easier when the market is a bit higher than the closing on Friday, especially, if it has risen to a strong technical resistance level. If the market activity makes it uncomfortable to execute the original decision, a good decision is to divide the would-be position into several parts and sell them when planned execution levels are reached.

2. If you and everybody around agree that this stock should go down but it moves up, there are two alternatives. The first one is driven by a liquidity consideration: everybody had sold the stock prior to the article. The market is moving up on stop-losses, squeezing the early bears out. The other one is information-related: the new information was "priced in" (reflected in price), and the market fluctuates, expecting the new one. Of course, it is possible that the majority of players are not yet aware of the new information, but most of the time this reason does not work since news becomes known to the market in real time.

3. If you are a technical trader, you must be indifferent to a product you trade as long as the signal is the same albeit the efficiency of the same signal for different instruments is different. However, even if it is as

good for other instruments, traders still can rarely force themselves to take the same risk in new products as in known products.

4. You will hardly be able to make a rational decision. "Rationally" in this situation means independently from previous results. Actually, there are two contradicting pieces of advice. The first one is to continue trading but take a smaller position. The other one is to have a break: when stressed out, you'd better leave the market and return to trading after some rest. The latter assumes a recuperation of internal resources and only then can you restart trading lower volumes to regain confidence.

CHAPTER 33

Self-Control of Psychological Factors when Investing

Time always separates the moment of decision making from the moment of implementation. It is said that the truth cannot exist separately from time: each new period has its own perceptions different from the cornerstone "truths" of the past.

The same is true of risks. At the moment a decision is made, investors base their choices on particular outlooks regarding market developments. Although at that moment a scenario may look very likely, it rarely occurs in the expected shape or time frame.

IMPACT OF TIME ON RISK EVALUATION

Let's consider an example that illustrates how time transforms our outlook. Suppose we place a stick in a pool of water: the new environment completely changes the stick's shape. From straight, it becomes crooked. In effect, the water is a prism through which we observe a subject known to us.

Similarly, time is a prism that alters our current outlook. As a result, one can say that our comprehension of the world is linear, whereas reality is curvilinear. When making forecasts, we assume the stability of current processes (as well as the stability of variation intervals within which the processes fluctuate). Of course, we build feasibility studies that account for possible changes, and based on these we derive some desirable course of action. In other words, any decision is based on some fixed assumptions. In reality, the process of implementing decisions normally resembles a discrete curve, since most processes tend to accelerate, decelerate, or substantively change at some point in the future. Ignoring "the curvelinearity of the future" leads to misrepresentation of present initial risk.

A colleague who normally traded delta-neutral strategies once decided to try directional positions in options. At that point, the USD/JPY rate had been trading within a range of 101.20–105.20 for almost three months. Moreover, concerted intervention by the Fed and the BOJ at one point prevented it from going lower. To benefit from the range, he applied a 1-by-2 premium-free yen call/dollar put spread, which would lose should the spot on expiration trade below 100.60.

Once the author learned of the strategy, he advised his colleague to substantially reduce the size of his position. The reasoning was simple: it is difficult to predict one's own behavior if one has not done similar things in the past. Therefore, it is very difficult to protect oneself from one's own unpredictable reaction to an event that does not fit the original scenario.

The night before the option was due to expire, an unexpected statement was made in Japan. At 3:00 A.M. the trader received a call that the USD/JPY rate was trading below 101.00. At around 5:00 A.M he closed the position at a substantial loss. Ironically, at expiration time the USD/JPY rate was trading back at the maximum profit level of the strategy!

This example illustrates a few points. First, the initial scenario analysis did not help. Although he was ready to lose at the beginning, his attitude changed by the end of the period. Second, he did not appreciate the fact that the holding power of untested strategies is less than that for tested ones. Third, he thought he was prepared for the negative scenario, but his mind merely focused on the fluctuation range established during the *preceding* three-month range.

Such an inability to follow an initial plan dominates the world of investment. Most of the famous traders interviewed in Jack Schwager's book *Market Wizards* called discipline factor number one in succeeding in the market! Note the emphasis on discipline, not technical or fundamental knowledge.

With regard to derivatives, realization of the curvlinearity of our psychology is increasingly important due to the curvilinear responses of P/Ls, which depend on the Greeks (i.e., the risk management parameters of option positions).

To summarize, always control your comfort level by adjusting your own forecasts. In fact, you will always be overly optimistic if you do not discount your ability to forecast.

WRONG ANALYTICAL BASIS FOR FORECASTING

In order to move to the mean of one's risk tolerance band (i.e., make a risk estimate more realistic), one must keep in mind the practical aspects of implementing decisions.

When most of us buy a stock, we decide upon an appropriate stop-out level. But after the trade occurs, most of us reevaluate both the previous stop-loss and profit-taking levels. This happens for many reasons, such as new information, changes in physical and emotional health, and the consequences thereof. For example, imagine you hear that a similar stock dropped as a result of lower-than-expected earnings, and at that particular moment you are in bad mood due to a toothache and a recent fight with your spouse. If that wasn't bad enough, you are now losing money on your investment. In such a situation, you are very likely to close your position before it reaches the stop-loss level.

Another example is the so-called hope factor when executing a stop-out. If the stock we are long goes down and reaches the predetermined stop-loss level, we hope that it will reverse direction. But when it goes even lower, we hope that it will return to the higher stop-out, at which point we would cut the loss, and so on. In other words, during implementation our initial understanding of risk changes.

To summarize, risk considered during decision making can often be referred to as "theoretical" risk.

ADVICE OF THE WISE PYTHON KHAA: "BE CAREFUL LEAVING THE SKIN—IT WILL BE DIFFICULT TO PUT IT ON AGAIN"

A significant pitfall for risk evaluation lies in the ratio of the time required to identify a trend to the time horizon of a forecast. Most people tend to consider a short period of analysis and then derive a long-term forecast. For example, after two or three weeks of market inactivity, investors begin selling three-month options to collect a premium, since they expect volatility to stay low that long.

A law in cybernetics requires just the opposite—that the term used for trend analysis be three times longer than the term for which we forecast! In our example, the investor should have sold a one-week option because he analyzed a three-week tendency.

THE SIMPLER, THE SAFER; THE MORE INTERESTING, THE RISKIER

Another assumption in our risk perception is an immediate adjustment of our mind to situational change. For example, after a while one learns enough about oneself to make an appropriate risk evaluation, and then suddenly the situation changes. This happens when the market changes direction or becomes range-bound. Alternatively, a trader may move to another company with a different information (order) flow or level of management involvement in decision making. This can also occur when one shifts into a very similar but different field (e.g., from interbank trading to fund management). To summarize, once the market or exterior environment changes, it takes a while to tune in and readjust. In the meantime, one's attitude toward risk must be much more cautious.

The author has encountered another curious and widespread psychological trap. This can be referred to as a vertical, or multilayer risk. Let's consider path-dependent options. These financial instruments make money if, for example, the price of a given asset on the option's expiration day is higher than, say, 100, but never reaches 110 during the option's life. Such instruments have been popular among institutional investors and serve best in demonstrating convoluted risk evaluation practices.

Let's pause for a moment. Most of us have a hard time guessing the market's direction. Trying to figure out when the market will move in a particular direction is extremely difficult (remember, being at "the right entry level at the right time" is a trader's version of another common expression). But in addition to this, one must be correct regarding how far/low the asset must go in order to make money (path dependence).

The probability of each event occurring is much less than 100%, and the joint probability is impossibly low. However, this does not stop many investors: since they feel they are getting great odds per trade, they will take four times as many positions to get the same risk/reward as a simple position!

The moral is to stay away from enticing psychological traps involving multiplying risks. One must stick to simple risks that the human mind can handle. As a side note, it seems that different cultures have different appetites for "intellectually challenging" risks. For example, Asians seem to enjoy them noticeably more than, say, Europeans or Americans. Traders or investors with creative personalities are also more likely to appreciate such sophisticated and intellectually challenging investment concepts.

A lack of understanding of such multiplying (as well vertical) risks is common outside the realm of investment management. For example, in their military memoirs, generals frequently blame failures on an underestimation of time required for troops to learn how to handle new technologies (tanks, artillery, etc.). This mistake leads to an excessive reliance on technological factors before they yield the expected benefits. In turn, this leads to substantial human casualties, which in turn leads to nervousness of command and even more irrational decision making.

In conclusion, it is worth mentioning that it is easy to notice these mistakes when others make them. After a while, one realizes that everybody makes the same mistakes. Once that happens, after noticing somebody else's error, one begins reviewing one's own actions to determine when similar errors were made. Those who learn not to repeat the same errors usually survive in the market, and those who learn from the errors of others stand an even better chance of survival.

The key in survival/success tactics is the dilemma of time and money versus self-management expertise. The less time or money one has to learn these skills, the more cautious one must be. Yet the more cautious one is, the more difficult it is to refine decision-making process! In order to resolve this dilemma, one must continuously balance the emotions of greed and fear.

QUESTIONS

1. Your colleague bought call options on EUR/USD. His logic is simple: when NASDAQ goes down, investors sell USD and buy EUR. Since he believes that NASDAQ will continue falling, he expects EUR to increase. Using the concept of multilayered risks, what advice can you give him?
2. The stock market has been already falling for three weeks and is approaching a very important support level. You expect that before today's closing bears will close a part of their positions. To make money, you can buy a knock-out call, which will expire if the market goes down and touches the knock-out barrier. Alternatively, you can buy futures on the index. What is the better way to realize the idea, if in general you expect the continuation of the downward trend?
3. Unbelievable, but you have found the short-term technical algorithm to predict copper futures! It has worked for the three last times and you want to increase the position since you are absolutely sure in the indicator's efficiency. To what extent should you increase the position?
4. A new client has given you money to manage. You are known to take high-risk positions aimed to maximize profit, but the client expects stable performance. How should you alter your investment strategy?

ANSWERS

1. It is a widespread situation. Since traders lack either limits or conviction to execute their views in a certain asset, they realize them in other assets. A typical example: a trader predicting lower interest rates, takes positions in stocks or currencies, rather than interest rates themselves. However, stocks or currencies are influenced by many different factors in addition to interest rates. Therefore, even if the rates come down, traders can lose money for the other reasons. If you forecast certain dynamics in one product, take a position in that rather than in the second-best to minimize the influence of other factors, on which you do not have an opinion.
2. Since you have short-term expectations, you should take a short-term position. Even if you guess the barrier level, your option's position should be a medium-term one, rather than a short-term punt. Besides, taking it through options you'll have to pay two spreads (for entrance and for exit). As you know, option spreads are wider than those of futures.
3. You can increase your position two- or threefold depending on the signal's strength and accumulated profit. Generally, it is difficult even to double a position, if the trade goes wrong. The pitfall is that until you test your level of comfort with losses from this signal, any increase is not "scientifically tested."
4. Stability of profits is a very-difficult-to-achieve concept. It greatly differs from the goal of maximizing absolute results. You will have to reduce position sizes and stop using high-risk strategies such as exotic options. Therefore, you should warn your client that until you adjust your style, performance on his portfolio would significantly differ from results on other portfolios you manage.

FURTHER INFORMATION FOR THE READER

Advice to Beginners

The following recommendations may help you to build-up internal protection against failures in trading:

(Continued)

FURTHER INFORMATION FOR THE READER *(Continued)*

1. *Never blame the market for losses, always blame yourself.* Anyone who blames the market de facto admits that he can't predict it or cope with it. However, his subconscious mind knows the truth. In critical moments, his internal discomfort overwhelms consciousness and suppresses the decision-making ability. That is, internally you know that you are doing things you should not do, and that makes you incapable of handling crises. The longer you ignore your weaknesses, the more you undermine your faith in your own success. Weak self-confidence is difficult to overcome, in effect by not facing the real reasons for losses one dooms himself.
2. *Never let the trading losses injure your psyche.* At any moment remind yourself that you need a small success to strengthen your sense of confidence. And you need all your confidence to defend yourself against temporary misfortunes.
3. *Create "light" conditions for your psyche.* At crisis moments avoid conflicts in private life and provide yourself with additional rest: "In a healthy body, a healthy mind."
4. *"Morning is wiser than evening."* This is an old Russian proverb. It is a biological fact that the crisis of confidence and faith usually takes place between 2:00 and 5:00 A.M. This time corresponds to the hiatus of the moon cycle. Disproportionate number of deaths, and heart and asthma attacks occur during this time. Don't let yourself forget that the decisions taken during the night hours will be too pessimistic.
5. *"When it rains, it pours."* A trader facing a misfortune should be prepared that "everything will go against him." One loss can knock the trader down, and cause a few more bad decisions. Sometimes, such periods are long and people call bad decisions "bad luck." The trader should promptly understand that he is unable to control the situation and step back for a while.
6. *Please yourself.* Do something that will distract you from the market problems.
7. *Always believe in your luck.* Everybody faces hard times. However, *for those who remember that winds change, hard times remain just hard times while those who lose hope go mad.*
8. *Improve your trading skills.* Work at your skills, and never make the same mistakes—correcting mistakes strengthens your faith in better results in the future.

CHAPTER 34

Problems with Standard Methods of Risk Minimization

Of course, there are well-known remedies that seek to reduce risks. Some of the most popular ones involve expert advice and information as well as portfolio diversification.

INVESTMENT ADVISORS: THE BLIND LEADING THE BLIND

Investors are surrounded by the expert opinions of advisors and financial publications. Additionally, most traders and investors exchange opinions. Frequently, such opinions are not even sought, but still end up being taken into consideration by a decision maker. Although problems regarding the reliability of their outlooks are always in the back of our minds, it takes some time to evaluate their true magnitude. One must distinguish between real information and the personal views of an advisor. For example, when the author's family immigrated to the United States, we discovered the advisor problem the hard way. Most of the advisors were recent immigrants themselves and promoted their views based on personal short-term experiences in the United States. In following their advice, we were certain to fail, because what applied to them did not apply to our situation or they themselves misread the information.

It's easy to find examples of those who have provided reliable information and yet made wrong market calls. The author's experience with salespeople from one of the largest banks in Singapore is particularly memorable. The bank had an exclusive client franchise, and its salespeople saw tremendous client flows and orders. This notwithstanding, their interpretations and predictions were wrong day after day for years. In fact, such consistency was useful: upon listening to their advice, one had to position himself in the opposite direction.

Most of us understand the pitfalls of listening to others. Still, all of us go through the daily routine of collecting expert opinions from brokers, newspapers, newsletters, economic advisors, and so on. In doing so, it should be remembered that in evaluating risk, one must be very demanding about receiving unbiased information.

Second, one must learn to heed individuals whose advice can be implemented. For example, what is the purpose of listening to somebody who is a breakout trader if you are a contrarian? There is a great difference between the mode of thinking and the defense of trading techniques. The same is true of fundamental traders who start trading on technical signals. Their inherent level of comfort with the new method is very low, which makes sustainability to market volatility very low.

INFORMATION: DOCTOR OR KILLER?

But what if you base trading decisions exclusively on official announcements? In this case, one would think, the bias that comes with the personal interpretations of your advisors should be reduced to zero. Yet you encounter another painful problem with information: it takes years for one to understand which of the many pieces of information is important for a particular risk evaluation.

The informational requirements for risk evaluation depend heavily on the cultural background of a particular decision maker. Based on the author's observations, Anglo-Saxon-based cultures require less information, whereas those in continental Europe require much more. One of the reasons for this is that most education in continental Europe is based on the French or German models. The former emphasizes the availability of scientific calculations, whereas the latter focuses on in-depth comprehension of a particular subject. Their mixture results in a person who has learned from an early age that there is something mechanical, calculable, or at least comprehensible underlying the world. Since they exist, one must find "real" mechanisms before making decisions.

On the other hand, an Anglo-Saxon education is based on an imprecise humanitarian education. Somebody with such an education is much less liable to demand full information before making a decision.

There is another, even more hidden rift, and this is again psychological in nature. Readers of *New Market Wizards* were probably shocked by psychologists who argue that many people make decisions that are based on subconscious motives rather than rational calculations. If one were to ask what the purpose of information is on a personal level, one of the top three answers is that it creates comfort in decision making. In other words, information often serves as a weapon against the fear of risk rather than a means of preparing for decision making.

Most people subconsciously need as much information as possible to evaluate risk *as a means of countering fear*. When teaching seminars on options, the author discovered that individuals with math/accounting backgrounds tried to learn more than they really needed. Pushing them to trade (make decisions) was an impossible task because they were debilitated by the need to learn all the aspects related to a particular issue. However, they would go to another extreme once they liked a given set of information. They would not change their mind even if the market went against them: the "right" information served as psychological protection against the fear of risk rather than guiding them toward a better risk evaluation! They did exactly the opposite to what Henri Bergson suggested: "Think like a man of action and act like a man of thought."

Let's look at the utility of information in conjunction with timing. We all know that once all information is priced in, the market becomes rangebound. A priori, this means that we must force ourselves to trade with less than comfortable proof of our correctness. In other words, we must feel discomfort with every decision we make! Which is exactly the opposite to our nature. That is why learning to accept risk with a minimum of information is one of the key skills for a decision maker.

DIVERSIFICATION: POISONOUS ANTIDOTE

Diversification is a highly popular means of combating risk. As with other truisms, this method is of limited utility. Originally, it was devised based on an analysis of the historical behavior of a market portfolio comprised of a huge number of stocks. In other words, it is impractical, since a real-life trader or investor cannot own so many stocks. This method also discounts human emotion, since historical data lacks a personal emotional component. Those two issues may help explain why most mutual fund managers underperform their benchmarks.

Peter Lynch, Fidelity's famous mutual fund manager, called it di*wors*ification. The reason is that it is very hard to properly (without emotions) manage more than a handful of different risks. In order to serve its purpose, diversification should be personalized to fit the informational and emotional make-up of the decision maker. For example, if three out of your five stocks go down, will you be able to think rationally about the remaining two? If not, this means that your psychological potential for risk evaluation is not geared to handle five stocks. "What if market volatility increases—will you be able to stay rational with your chosen diversification," is the question that can help you optimize the number of stocks in your portfolio.

By the way, general management also includes a concept governing the efficiency of managerial structures. It is claimed that a manager cannot run a team of more than five or six associates efficiently.

ALTERNATIVE APPROACH

The real way to reduce risk involves a combination of horizontal and vertical diversification. The author has yet to encounter such a distinction in literature, so let's explain it. Horizontal diversification takes place across assets (e.g., buying a few different stocks). Vertical diversification involves splitting the risks of a given decision (position) within one instrument/asset. For example, instead of buying the entire amount at one level, you can buy varying amounts at varying levels. Vertical diversification not only assumes different entry levels, but also different exit levels, different amounts at different levels, and a combination of instruments used.

For example, in order to reduce risk, one can enter in a position at three levels rather than one. To determine them, charts can be used, and thereafter one can ascertain the proportion of the total amount at each entry level. However, if the overall potential loss of such a position is too high, one can use options at the first and second levels of entry.

Once the entry strategy is decided, one must decide on the exit strategy. The exit should be structured as well. Exits (stop-outs) can be linear (based on price levels) as well as nonlinear (based on volatility ranges). Exits can also be facilitated through different instruments. For example, one can buy options to protect or optimize a position (i.e., to switch from the underlying asset into an option on the underlying asset in the preferred direction.). In effect, exiting becomes its own science.

By the way, it seems that the structuring of exits takes place less frequently than the structuring of entries. For example, the other day a colleague became upset after he got stopped out just before the market did what he had anticipated. This was a typical situation: he put a stop on a short S&P position above a certain technical level. The market overshot that level, he got stopped out and the market went down 30 figures. That was just unlucky. Yet the stop would not have been fatal had he split it into three levels with the same overall maximum loss.

In that case, he would have been stopped at the first two levels (one below the original level and one at the original level), but the market would not have reached the third level (above the original level), and he would have made money on the overall position. There was no extra risk involved in such a strategy, and indeed it was diversified!

The problem with vertical diversification is that it implies a significant internal struggle between greed and fear. When one likes a particular idea, one naturally does not want to miss the potential upside. At this point, he must force greed to respect fear.

When the market does go to the second entry point and the initial portion is losing money, doubts about the correctness of the original view appear. At this point, one must force fear to respect greed.

In other words, the fewer intermediate decisions we make, the simpler our life becomes. Our psychology is tuned toward a simple binary outcome—win or lose. Yet to survive, we must live in a cumbersome nonlinear world of multiple outcomes that imply multiple decisions for every trade. The success of the process lies in internal comfort with the idea and trust in one's own judgment. Both of these are impossible if the analysis is not done solely by the trader/investor. At this point, one's psychological strength undergoes survival tests, and all third-party ideas that were not thoroughly adjusted by the decision maker turn out to be seriously destabilizing.

To conclude, decision making assumes a conflict between opposing concepts. At some point, one must be disciplined, whereas at another the smartest thing to do would be to call it quits. There are moments when it is better not to take a position until all information is available and the market reaction is clear. Yet, if one waits too long to join the market, the action turns into a runaway trade.

Finding a balance between these truisms is a highly individual process. Someone who has tested her ability to withstand pressure from repeatedly taking stops will be disciplined when encountering multiple cuts. Yet, somebody who is emotionally affected by stops must learn to stay away from emotional (irrational) renewals of her positions.

That is why Sun Tse's belief that "one who knows his enemy is strong, one who knows himself is unbeatable" best summarizes the importance of honoring the personal dimensions of risk.

QUESTIONS

1. Last week you started studying the technical analysis method called "Japanese candles" and it appeared to be exceptionally efficient for your type of trading. You have been earning quite a bit using other signals (e.g., moving averages crossovers). Today "candles" gave a signal to buy, but the averages remain "silent." What should you do?
2. You have just returned from vacation. Your colleague advises you to take on an interesting trade. Now it is more expensive than when he entered. You colleague has never given you any advice before. What will you do?
3. The market is very volatile and reaching a substantial resistance level. You are sure that it'll bounce back from this level eventually as long as it does not break through the resistance in the short term. The market tests this level for the third time, and you still hope it holds. How can you structure the position?
4. The night before yesterday a broker woke you up and informed that your stop order was executed. Yesterday, the market fluctuated the entire night, and you barely slept. Normally, you do not take more than five positions. Now, three positions are opened, should you "enter" two more?

ANSWERS

1. As a rule, new methods confuse traders: they hamper the use of the previous ones since new methods provide slightly different signals and "stops." In other words, a new method will divert your internal compass. That's why it is recommended to observe new signals for a while until you find a way to use them, either in conjunction with the old ones or separately. Otherwise, when changing methods of analysis or consultants, one suffers massive losses.
2. If you haven't worked with the consultant, you'd better not follow his advice, since you are not aware of his risk preferences! The consultant may have a different stop-out methodology; for example, he may have a much higher stop-loss threshold than you. That is, not only is the idea important, but the conformity of trading styles is as well. In general, it is a bad idea to start trading the day after a vacation when you have not followed the market for a while.

3. Your view can be executed through a put-spread. Since volatilities increase near important technical levels, buying outright puts may not be as beneficial as a spread. The short leg will not only finance the long one, but also provide you with a hedge when volatilities come in. Such a combination will give you an opportunity to stay in the position longer and to be less dependent on guessing "the top." The staying power is important, since very often the market hovers on critical levels and moves in another time zone. If you execute your view by shorting the underlying, your stops may be misplaced, and you can be shaken out of the position on a false breakout. If after taking the stops out the market starts falling again, you'll have no opportunity to reenter.

   To prevent the latter while trading the underlying, you'd better tier the entry and stop-out orders and place them at three levels. For example, the first stop-out under the resistance, the second one at the resistance and the third one above the resistance. In this case, your maximum loss won't exceed the planned one, and a chance to remain with a position increases. By the way, traders with high risk appetite sell a call option at the breakout levels while the implied volatility is very high.

4. If the market has been disturbing you for two or three days, it most likely upset your working routine. Your ability to react to several markets and, the most difficult, not to extend the mood from one position to another will be sharply reduced. Therefore, you'd probably better not open more positions.

FURTHER INFORMATION FOR THE READER

Trading Psychology in Fables, Quotes, and Proverbs

Once a wise man bought a bird at a market. He was about to enter his house when the bird opened its wings, stared at him, and spoke in a human voice. "Don't panic," it said. "I'm a very cultured bird. The wise man of the birds, so to speak. Tell me, if I teach you three valuable truths, will you set me free?" The wise man thought for a second and agreed.

"The first one is, never believe nonsense, particularly if common sense tells you that something can't be true. Secondly, soberly evaluate

(Continued)

FURTHER INFORMATION FOR THE READER *(Continued)*

your abilities. Never undertake anything if your chances of success are slim. And thirdly, never regret the good deeds you have done."

Having heard this, the wise man let the bird go. No sooner had it perched on the branch of a tree than it started teasing him. "Yesterday I swallowed a diamond! Had you killed me, you would have found it and become a rich man!" After hearing that, the wise man became very angry and tried to climb the tree to grab the bird. But, being old, he slipped from the tree and fell to the ground. The bird hopped onto his head and said in a strict tone, "Wise man, you seemed to have listened to and appreciated my advice, but you failed your very first exam miserably! Stop and think for a moment: What are the chances of a bird swallowing a diamond? And, at your age, did you really think you could still climb trees? Finally, you started having second thoughts about the good deed as greed consumed you!" Having said that, the bird flew away.

The Bird's First Lesson This story demonstrates several truisms that traders and investors nevertheless find hard to learn. Enticing ideas flow from various sources—as well as talking to consultants and brokers, traders talk to each other, and read numerous publications. Informational pollution leads to an ongoing need to weed out various opinions before making a decision.

One of the easiest types of opinion to transfer is the expectation of a major "inevitable" market move. Very often, technical analysis[1] results in predictions of a technical breakthrough. However, in reality, markets fluctuate within ranges 70% of the time and trend only the remaining 30%.

Addiction to the belief in miracles are inherent in human nature. Within the past 30 years, investors have lost huge sums of money on fads such as emerging markets in the 1980s, biotech in the early 1990s, and TMT over the past three years. In other words, greed and fear block common sense with frightening regularity.

Clearly, most investors possess the same information and consider similar risks. As a result, they simultaneously "jump on the trend." If a prediction does not materialize immediately, the "weaker hands" soon start doubting their own actions. This explains why historical graphs exhibit market overextensions, as well as immediate sharp reversals.

FURTHER INFORMATION FOR THE READER *(Continued)*

Floor traders track and bully those expecting a miracle. When at the critical technical level[2] they sense a decline in trading volumes of new orders and an increase in a number of recently opened positions, they know that exchange clients are anticipating high reward-to-risk trades. In other words, short-term traders suddenly identify a technical level—points that if not broken, would force the market back into a certain range. However, once broken, the market would then start to trend in the direction of a breakout. Beyond the technical level, traders establish a trade stop-out level and give the order to close a position once that technical level is crossed. (See Figure 34.1.)

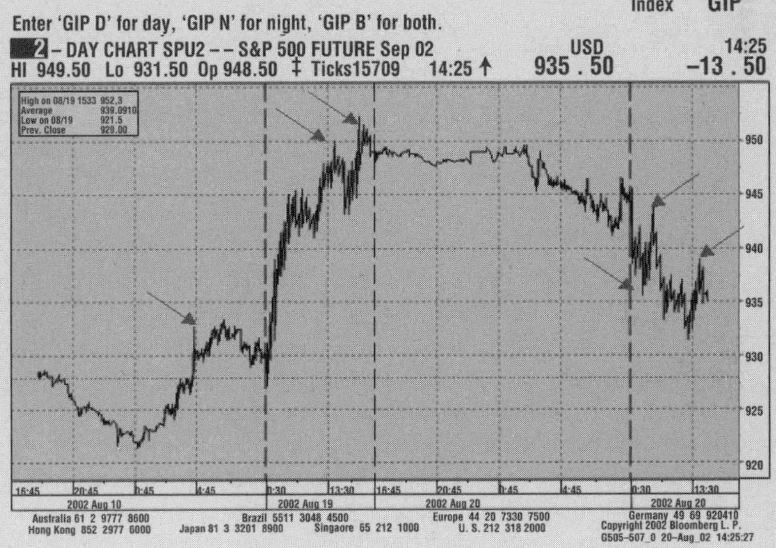

FIGURE 34.1 The arrows on the one-minute chart point at the moments when the exchange players "go through the clients' stops."
Source: Bloomberg, L.P.

(Continued)

FURTHER INFORMATION FOR THE READER *(Continued)*

A few times a day, once enough stops have built up at what is considered a "key level," floor traders force the market through it. By doing so, they squeeze clients through the stop-levels (see Figure 34.1) and earn a few points as the market goes through the stops. After triggering the stops, they reestablish their own positions, and the market returns sharply to the direction the unfortunate miracle seekers so fervently hoped for just a few moments earlier. The moral of the story is that once an investor senses the desire to believe in miracles (such as high risk reward trades), she should make a U-turn.

The Bird's Second Lesson According to one rather coarse French proverb, "One must have the stomach, and make sure it is his." It is common for investors to forget that their financial resources are finite and invest in just one idea. The pain of those who held their Individual Retirement Annuities in Enron stock exemplifies one possible outcome of such behavior. Always leave yourself a chance to return to the market.

When an investor takes on a large position, the first significant move in the market can throw her out of it—she simply cannot handle this amount of risk. To determine the best comfortable position, the reader may try the following rule of thumb: determine the smallest position one would hold under any circumstances, given the expected level of risk, and then take a position one-half that size. The gains will not be extraordinary, but you will stay in the game.

The Bird's Third Lesson Of course, the fable in the beginning of this section was not made up solely for traders. After all, try to find a trader who would perform a good deed free of charge! Rather, the third lesson highlights the importance of the ability to control your greed: "It is better to be out of the position wishing you were in, than in one wishing you were out." Subconscious realization of excessive risk leads to uncontrolled fear or the loss of faith in one's judgment and ability to succeed. As a result, the holder of a position becomes uncomfortable with it. At that point, bereft of psychological comfort, he is highly unlikely to succeed.

Therefore, when implementing chosen strategies, investors should never forget "the rule of the pyramid" used by floor traders: the smallest portion of the position comes at the worst price, and the largest one, at the best. For example, however advantageous a price may be,

FURTHER INFORMATION FOR THE READER *(Continued)*

investors should buy only a fraction of the position. Should the market stick to a downward trend, they will still be able to buy a larger piece at a better price. Of course, this rule works best when the market stays in range. That is, the rule applies over 70% of the time, as the market tends to be range-bound.

However, what happens if the range is broken? By that time, an investor has bought (or sold) at two or three different levels, and the range breakout is causing substantial losses. When the market switches from being range-bound to trending, the rule is "When you panic, panic first." If the market appears to be on the threshold of a new trend, investors must order their brokers to follow it and double the position in the opposite direction.

Although somewhat dramatic, such a depiction is entirely appropriate. Any range breakout results in prices that have not been seen in a long time. At that moment, the reasons underlying the market's changed behavior are still unknown, while the whole trading community continues to hope that comfortable levels will return. Although it is initially intimidating to stand alone in the market, once the move has been confirmed, the winner ends up with a position secured at an advantageous price. He can then build up its size with less fear, despite the residual possibility that the breakout proves to be false. "The trend becomes your friend," and exhausting efforts at the beginning start to pay off. Therefore, don't be afraid to panic, just pick the right moments to do so!

According to a classic saying on Wall Street, "Trees do not grow to the skies." This proverb became popular at the beginning of the last century, and it reminds people that nothing lasts forever, even if the trend seems endless. When it is unclear about what to do with either a profitable or losing position, the investor should heed a poker oldie: "When in doubt, do a half." Any discussion of discipline and greed is never complete without two more proverbs: "Bulls make money, bears make money, pigs get slaughtered." Quite explicitly, this is a reminder to remain levelheaded and follow a plan. The second is an action plan championed by Will Rogers: "If I buy and the market goes up, I sell. If it goes down, I sell as well."

The tale of the bird also warns against repeating previous mistakes. However, we often fail to avoid them and chastise ourselves

(Continued)

FURTHER INFORMATION FOR THE READER *(Continued)*

afterwards. Nowadays, everybody tries to memorize as much as possible, and the necessity to purge your mind of superfluous thought is neglected. Imagine that you have been losing money for the first four days of a week. By Friday, you are worn out and distressed. It is surely difficult to force yourself to take on a new position, since the losing streak has exhausted you. The skill of being able to forget cleanses your mind of euphoria as well as panic. Release the worries of your past—even the most recent ones. "Focus on your consequent steps," was another piece of advice from Tudor Jones.

Finally, markets always outsmart even the smartest investors. Remember: "Those of us who were lucky were born smart, but those who were smart chose to be born lucky." The winners only rarely explain how they made money, whereas losers have much to account for. But then again, everybody has a natural right to make dumb mistakes, ones that were undoubtedly made by many well before our time. That is why proverbs dealing with standard situations serve as useful reminders.

Conclusion

Options are a field arguably different from any other one in sales and trading. The main driving factor in trading options as in trading other assets is the direction of prices. In addition to that, options trading is greatly affected by the factors of *time* and volatility. During an option's life, one puts up with unpredictability of direction volatility and time.

The time factor is especially important. One has to remember that market and management views change dramatically over time. Without reminding oneself about limits of one's forecasting abilities, one is doomed to make mistakes and suffer losses.

Another peculiarity of options is their variety. As we have seen, even options on the same underlying asset with various deltas and expirations behave differently. It is personal comfort that will tell you which segment of options suits you better. For example, once you work with different delta options, you may choose to focus on one-month 20-delta options, "sensing" their dynamics the best. Furthermore, to learn your personal optimal style of portfolio management is even more difficult. The combination of Greeks, their dependence on time, liquidity, and other market variables are different for different markets.

Third, options enable one to create flexible strategies adapted to one's objectives and market views. Once you link their flexibility and your experience, you can achieve amazing results.

Fourth, options are not measured in absolute terms of "expensive" and "cheap." Premium of long-term options seems expensive but amortize slowly and secure the time necessary to reach your objectives. That is, they have many advantages that compensate for the "expensiveness in monetary terms." Low-delta options are cheaper than at-the-money options, but their chance to earn is lower. In view of the balance of advantages and disadvantages of different options, it makes no sense to search for riskless profit: pricing models balance price, risk, and profit probability. Yet understanding the differential features of different options is one of the keys to success in this field.

In other words, options make users respect risk. They require operational procedures that make you and your company comfortable. In return, they provide you with flexible instruments for realizing you plans.

In summary, the book has familiarized you with an interesting and diverse sphere of financial options. We described a number of obvious and hidden problems of this class of instruments. We considered the key techniques used by different market segments. The suggested methods may be equally effective for short-term as well as for long-term hedging and investment programs. We hope that this book will not only help you avoid expensive mistakes, but secure your success.

Good luck, my dear readers!

APPENDIX A

Options: Mathematical Models

Options are valued and options' positions are managed based on formulas mentioned earlier in the book. By learning them the reader will gain psychological confidence because filling some gaps in his knowledge will help to avoid obvious errors in trading. However, one should not overestimate importance of the formulas. Work on financial markets is a real art, which includes many components. Knowledge of financial mathematics is only one of them. Although it is psychologically important to get to know the formulas, the majority of experts will agree that knowledge of formulas is not the essential part of success.

BASIC TERMS: DERIVING A CALL OPTION FORMULA

Let's begin by considering the standard European-style call option. This is a contract that gives its owner the right to buy a certain asset at a definite price (strike) at a certain moment (expiration date).

An option contract provides the owner with a right but does not put him under an obligation. If the owner believes that it's unprofitable for him to exercise the option at the price stipulated in the contract (strike price), he can simply let the option expire worthless.

Current option's price (C) depends on the following factors:

T—time left to the expiration (settlement!) date

S—current spot price of the underlying asset

K—strike price

r—continuously compounded risk-free rate

$S(T)$—the underlying asset spot price on expiration

σ—volatility of the underlying asset price

Let's examine these parameters.

Time (T) is annualized (measured in years). If D days are left until the option's expiration date, then T is calculated by the following formula:

$$T = D/365;$$

The Black-Scholes model was the first model to value options on equities. The model[1] assumes that at the expiration date price of the underlying asset is distributed lognormally. In other words, the lognormal distribution assumes that the logarithm of the ratio between current underlying asset price and the one at expiration is normally distributed. This assumption is supported by the actual data. Lognormal distribution enables us to determine the asset's future value at present moment as well as an average asset price and probability of its rise above a certain level.

The Black-Scholes model takes into account the previously mentioned parameters: time to option expiration, the current underlying asset price, the continuously compounded risk-free rate and volatility of the asset σ that characterizes the variability of asset price.[2] The price of a high-volatility stock changes more than the price of a low-volatility stock. The model assumes it to be constant during an option's life even though in practice, the volatility of an asset changes over time.

Let's consider the relationship between asset price and the strike price at the expiration date:

1. $S(T) > K$, i.e., the underlying asset price is higher than the strike. In this case, the payoff from the option's exercise is $S(T) - K$ (the asset is bought at K and immediately sold at $S(T)$).
2. $S(T) \leq K$, i.e., the underlying asset price is lower than the strike. In this case, it makes no sense to exercise the option since it is cheaper to buy the stock at the current price. Thus, the payoff equals 0.

Therefore, for any level of the asset price $S(T)$ payoff of the call option is

$$\max[0, S(T) - K]$$ [3]

The expected profit from the option's exercise *today* is

$$\max[0, S(T) - K] \times e^{-rT},$$

where e^{-rT} is a discount factor that represents cost (interest rate) of money from today until the expiration date. The expected profit equals the intrinsic value multiplied by the discount factor.

Since the asset price $S(T)$ is a variable, the current option's price or premium equals the mean of the distribution of the expected payoff:

$$C = E\{e^{-rT} \times \max\,[0, S(T) - K)]\}$$

The Black-Scholes formula for the European call option on the stock without dividends (*ex-dividend*) can be derived after the integration assuming lognormal distribution of $S(T)$:

$$C = \underbrace{S \times N(d1)}_{\text{return}} - \underbrace{K \times e^{-rT} \times N(d2)}_{\text{expense}}$$

Here, $N(x)$ is a distribution function of standard normal variable. It may be found in table of standard normal distribution.

$d1$ and $d2$ can be calculated from the following equations:

$$d1 = [\ln(S/K) + (r + \sigma^2/2) \times T]/[\sigma \times \sqrt{T}\,];$$

$$d2 = [\ln(S/K) + (r - \sigma^2/2) \times T]/[\sigma \times \sqrt{T}\,] = d1 - \sigma \times \sqrt{T}$$

$N(d2)$—probability of the option exercise. Then:

$K \times e^{-rT} \times N(d2)$—present value of expected expenses caused by the option's exercise;

$S \times N(d1)$—present value of expected stock price at the moment of the option's exercise.

OPTION PRICE PARAMETERS

According to the Black-Scholes formula, the option's price depends on a number of parameters:

r—the continuously compounded risk-free rate

T—time to expiration

S—current stock price

K—the option's strike

σ—the volatility of the underlying asset price

Let's evaluate how each parameter affects the call option's price. To do so, consider the changes of each parameter assuming that the others remain constant.

Underlying Asset Price

The higher the stock price, the better the chance that the call will be in-the-money on expiration date. Therefore, the price of the call option increases with the increase of the asset price.

Distance from Spot to Strike Price

The lower the strike price of a call option is the higher is its price, since a call option with a lower strike provides an opportunity to buy the asset at a more favorable price. Probability of exercise of such a call is higher as well.

Volatility

The higher the σ, the greater the stock price fluctuation. Gain on a call is unlimited, and loss is limited to the premium paid. Therefore, a higher-volatility option should cost more than a lower-volatility option.

Time Remaining until Expiration Date

The time to an option's expiration influences the stock price similarly to volatility. Actually, the more time remains until expiration, the higher the probability that the stock price will increase and the greater the chance to make money on exercise. Therefore, as its expiration approaches, the option's price declines. The discount rate, which reduces future profit to its present value, declines as well, partially compensating the decline in the option's value.

Risk-Free Interest Rate

An increase in a risk-free rate leads to an appreciation of the future price of the underlying asset. Therefore, a call option becomes deeper in-the-money and appreciates as the risk-free rate increases.

DIVIDENDS

Let's derive the price of a European call on a stock that pays dividends. On the ex-dividend date, the stock price falls. We expect it to fall by the amount of the dividends. Therefore, when valuing an option on this stock, we must take future reduction of its price into account. Let's assume that the stock price consists of the risk-free and risky components.

The *risk-free component* is a present value of all dividends to be paid before the expiration date. *Risky component* can be calculated after subtracting risk-free component from the current stock price. The price of an option is calculated as the price of the option on the risky component. Thus we should substitute stock price S with risk component in the Black-Scholes model. If the DVD is the present value of dividends paid on the stock during the option's life, the risk component equals S – DVD.

While pricing options on indexes we may assume with a high degree of accuracy that dividends are paid continuously, because a dividend is paid on one of the stocks included in an index quite often. Suppose that we need to calculate the price of a European call on AAA stock, subject to continuous dividend payment (q—dividend rate, S_1—the current spot). At the time T the expected price of AAA will be $e^{(r-q)T} \times S_1$ not e^{rT} (as in case of no dividend stock).

Let's consider the price of a European call on a similar stock BBB. BBB pays no dividends and the current spot of BBB is $S_1 \times e^{-qT}$. At the time T the expected price on the BBB stock will be $S_1 \times e^{-qT} \times e^{rT} = S_1 \times e^{(r-q)T}$.

Since AAA and BBB stocks are similar the standard deviation of their stock prices from the mean will also be the same. That is, both the mean and the volatility are the same. Thus options on AAA and BBB stocks with the same strike price will result in the same payoff.

Thus we can derive the Black-Scholes formula for a dividend-paying stock by substituting $S_1 \times e^{-qT}$ for S.

Then C_1—price of a call on stock with dividends—is as follows:

$$C_1 = \underbrace{S_1 \times e^{-qt} \times N(d1)}_{\text{return}} - \underbrace{K \times e^{-qt} \times N(d2)}_{\text{expense}}$$

$d1$ and $d2$ are calculated from the following equations:

$$d1 = [\ln(S_1/K) + (r - q + \sigma^2/2) \times \sqrt{T}]/[\sigma \times T]$$

$$d2 = [\ln(S_1/K) + (r - q - \sigma^2/2) \times \sqrt{T}]/[\sigma \times T] = d1 - \sigma \times \sqrt{T}$$

PRICE OF A PUT OPTION: THE PUT/CALL PARITY FORMULA

So far we have studied only call options. Now let's consider put options. The owner of a put option has the right to sell the asset at a certain (strike) price at the expiration date. As in the case of the call option, the owner is not obliged to exercise the option.

To derive the formula for the put option, one can use the put/call parity. The parity represents the relationship between the premiums on put and call options on the same underlying asset, with the same strike K and time to expiration (T).

To derive the parity let's consider two portfolios. The first portfolio consists of one call and $K \times e^{-rT}$ dollars that we deposit at r interest for T period of time. The second portfolio consists of one put and one share. Let's consider the value of the portfolios at the moment of the options' exercise at different share price levels $S(T)$.

The First Portfolio

$$S(T) > K$$

In this case, after exercising the option we collect profit $S(T) - K$, and the $K \times e^{-rT}$ dollars that we deposited at the beginning of the period will increase to K dollars. Therefore, the value of the portfolio equals

$$S(T) - K + K = S(T)$$

$$S(T) < K$$

In this case, exercising the option is not profitable. Therefore, the value of the portfolio equals K.

The Second Portfolio

$$S(T) > K$$

In this case, it is not profitable to sell the stock at price K, since the current price is higher and put option will not be exercised. The value of the portfolio equals the value of one share $S(T)$:

$$S(T) = K$$

Payoff of the put option will be $K - S(T)$. Thus value of the portfolio equals K.

It is easy to notice that at the expiration date both portfolios worth the same regardless of the stock price. In arbitrage-free markets both portfolio should cost the same at the present moment, that is,

$$C + K \times e^{-rT} = P + S$$

Here

S—current share price
K—options' strike
C—value of the call option
P—value of the put

This equation is called *call/put parity*. On its basis we derive the formula of a put option on stock with no dividends:

$$P = K \times e^{-rT} \times N(-d2) - S \times N(-d1),$$

where $d1$ and $d2$ are the same as in the formula for the price of the call option.

If the stock expects a dividend payment q, the price of a put option is:

$$P_1 = K \times e^{-rT} \times N(-d2) - S \times e^{-qT} \times N(-d1),$$

where $d1$ and $d2$ are the same as in the formula for the price of the call option with continuous dividend payment.

In other words, the higher q is, the higher the put price and the lower the call price.

QUESTIONS

1. Consider a stock that is subject to continuous dividend payout $q = 5\%$. Current stock price is \$50, volatility—60%, the continuously compounded risk-free rate—7%. What is the probability that a three-month European call on this stock will be exercised when its strike is a) \$40 and b) \$60?

2. An investor purchased five six-month European calls on a no-dividend stock. Determine investor's average costs on exercising the call if we know the following:
   - Current stock price is \$50;
   - Options' strike is \$60;
   - Volatility is 70%
   - Risk-free rate is 8%.

3. Consider a three-month call on a no-dividend stock. The stock trades at \$50, the option's strike is \$49, and risk-free rate is 5%. How much does

a three-month put on this stock with the same strike cost if the call costs \$5? If a three-month call on this stock costs \$5, what is the price of the put with the same strike and expiration?

To determine the value of $N(1.17)$, let's find the line marked "1.1" in Table A.1 and the column marked "0.07." Desired value (0.8790) we are looking for is where they meet. For values $x < 0$: $1 - N(-x)$.

TABLE A.I Function Table

X	0.00	0.01	0.02	0.03	0.04	0.05	0.06	0.07	0.08	0.09
0.0	0.5000	0.5040	0.5080	0.5120	0.5160	0.5190	0.5239	0.5279	0.5319	0.5359
0.1	0.5398	0.5438	0.5478	0.5517	0.5557	0.5596	0.5636	0.5675	0.5714	0.5753
0.2	0.5793	0.5832	0.5871	0.5910	0.5948	0.5987	0.6026	0.6064	0.6103	0.6141
0.3	0.6179	0.6217	0.6255	0.6293	0.6331	0.6368	0.6406	0.6443	0.6480	0.6517
0.4	0.6554	0.6591	0.6628	0.6664	0.6700	0.6736	0.6772	0.6808	0.6844	0.6879
0.5	0.6915	0.6950	0.6985	0.7019	0.7054	0.7088	0.7123	0.7157	0.7190	0.7224
0.6	0.7257	0.7291	0.7324	0.7357	0.7389	0.7422	0.7454	0.7486	0.7517	0.7549
0.7	0.7580	0.7611	0.7642	0.7673	0.7704	0.7734	0.7764	0.7794	0.7823	0.7852
0.8	0.7881	0.7910	0.7939	0.7969	0.7995	0.8023	0.8051	0.8078	0.8106	0.8133
0.9	0.8159	0.8186	0.8212	0.8238	0.8264	0.8289	0.8315	0.8340	0.8365	0.8389
1.0	0.8413	0.8438	0.8461	0.8485	0.8508	0.8513	0.8554	0.8577	0.8529	0.8621
1.1	0.8643	0.8665	0.8686	0.8708	0.8729	0.8749	0.8770	0.8790	0.8810	0.8830
1.2	0.8849	0.8869	0.8888	0.8907	0.8925	0.8944	0.8962	0.8980	0.8997	0.9015
1.3	0.9032	0.9049	0.9066	0.9082	0.9099	0.9115	0.9131	0.9147	0.9162	0.9177
1.4	0.9192	0.9207	0.9222	0.9236	0.9251	0.9265	0.9279	0.9292	0.9306	0.9319
1.5	0.9332	0.9345	0.9357	0.9370	0.9382	0.9394	0.9406	0.9418	0.9429	0.9441
1.6	0.9452	0.9463	0.9474	0.9484	0.9495	0.9505	0.9515	0.9525	0.9535	0.9545
1.7	0.9554	0.9564	0.9573	0.9582	0.9591	0.9599	0.9608	0.9616	0.9625	0.9633
1.8	0.9641	0.9649	0.9656	0.9664	0.9671	0.9678	0.9686	0.9693	0.9699	0.9706
1.9	0.9713	0.9719	0.9726	0.9732	0.9738	0.9744	0.9750	0.9756	0.9761	0.9767
2.0	0.9772	0.9778	0.9783	0.9788	0.9793	0.9798	0.9803	0.9808	0.9812	0.9817
2.1	0.9821	0.9826	0.9830	0.9834	0.9838	0.9842	0.9846	0.9850	0.9854	0.9857
2.2	0.9861	0.9864	0.9868	0.9871	0.9875	0.9878	0.9881	0.9884	0.9887	0.9890
2.3	0.9893	0.9896	0.9898	0.9901	0.9904	0.9906	0.9909	0.9911	0.9913	0.9916
2.4	0.9918	0.9920	0.9922	0.9925	0.9927	0.9929	0.9931	0.9932	0.9934	0.9936
2.5	0.9938	0.9940	0.9941	0.9943	0.9945	0.9946	0.9948	0.9949	0.9951	0.9952
2.6	0.9953	0.9955	0.9956	0.9957	0.9959	0.9960	0.9961	0.9962	0.9963	0.9964
2.7	0.9965	0.9966	0.9967	0.9968	0.9969	0.9970	0.9971	0.9972	0.9973	0.9974
2.8	0.9974	0.9975	0.9976	0.9977	0.9977	0.9978	0.9979	0.9979	0.9980	0.9981
2.9	0.9981	0.9982	0.9982	0.9983	0.9984	0.9984	0.9985	0.9985	0.9986	0.9986
3.0	0.9987	0.9987	0.9987	0.9988	0.9988	0.9989	0.9989	0.9989	0.9990	0.9990
3.1	0.9990	0.9991	0.9991	0.9991	0.9992	0.9992	0.9992	0.9992	0.9993	0.9993
3.2	0.9993	0.9993	0.9994	0.9994	0.9994	0.9994	0.9994	0.9995	0.9995	0.9995
3.3	0.9995	0.9995	0.9995	0.9996	0.9996	0.9996	0.9996	0.9996	0.9996	0.9997
3.4	0.9997	0.9997	0.9997	0.9997	0.9997	0.9997	0.9997	0.9997	0.9997	0.9998

ANSWERS

1. a. First of all let's consider an option with the \$40 strike. The probability of its exercise is $N(d2)$.

$$d2 = [\ln(S/K) + (r - q - \sigma^2/2) \times T]/[\sigma \times \sqrt{T}\,] =$$
$$= [\ln(50/40) + (0.07 - 0.05 - 0.36/2) \times 0{,}25]/[0{,}6 \times 0{,}5] =$$
$$= [0.223 - 0.04]/[0.3] = 0.61$$
$$N(d2) = N(0.61) = 0.7291.$$

b. For K = \$60 we have:

$$d2 = [\ln(S/K) + (r - q - \sigma^2/2) \times T]/[\sigma \times \sqrt{T}\,] =$$
$$= [\ln(50/60) + (0.07 - 0.05 - 0.36/2) \times 0{,}25]/[0{,}6 \times 0{,}5] =$$
$$= [-\,0.182 - 0.04]/[0.3] = -0.74$$
$$N(d2) = N(-0.74) = 0.2269.$$

2. If the investor exercises the options, he will have to spend 5 × \$60 = \$300 to buy the stock. If the options are not exercised the investor's costs will equal 0. Average costs (AC) will equal the costs of exercising the options multiplied by the probabilities of the exercise.

$$AC = 300 \times N(d2)$$

In this example:

$$S = 50;$$
$$K = 60;$$
$$r = 8\% = 0.08;$$
$$\sigma = 70\% = 0.7;$$
$$T = 0.5;$$
$$d2 = [\ln(S/K) + (r - \sigma^2/2) \times T]/[\sigma \times \sqrt{T}\,] =$$
$$= [\ln(50/60) + (0.08 - 0.49/2) \times 0{,}5]/[0{,}7 \times 0{,}707] =$$
$$= [-0.182 - 0.083]/[0.495] = -0.54$$
$$N(d2) = N(-0.54) = 1 - N(0.54) = 0.2946.$$
$$AC = 300 \times 0/2946 = 88.38$$

3. From the put/call parity formula,

$$P = C + K \times e^{-rT} - S = 5 + 49 \times e^{-0.05 \times 0.25} - 50 = 5 + 48.39 - 50 = 3.39$$

APPENDIX B

"Greeks"—Parameters Used in Portfolio Management

"Greeks" are essential in management of portfolio that consists of options and underlying asset. In this appendix we introduce major Greeks and explain their meanings. We consider call option on stocks that are subject to continuous dividend payment at q rate. Similar formulas can be derived for other assets using summary table at the end of Appendix C.

DELTA

Delta demonstrates to what extent the option's value will change, when the stock price moves one point (one cent, one dollar, etc.):

$$\text{delta} = dC/dS$$

Delta is measured in percentage points. It allows creating a portfolio insensitive to changes in the asset rate with the *small* share price move. Such a portfolio is called delta-neutral. For example, it may consist of two sold 50(%)-delta calls and one bought share (2 options × 50%) = one share. Here one share hedges two options from losses.

If the stock price rises by one cent value of two calls will also increase by one cent (1 cent × 2 × 50%). If the two calls were sold, your losses would be one cent. The loss would be compensated by profit on the stock, which appreciated by one cent. In other words, the total position value stays the same.

Delta used by market makers. It allows them to buy or to sell options positions and immediately hedge the position in the underlying asset market.

The following formula is true for delta:

$$\text{Call delta} = e^{-qT} \times N(d1)$$

THETA

Theta is time derivative of an option's price. It shows how the option's price changes in time. Theta of European options is always negative. The following formula is true for theta:

$$\text{Call theta} = e^{-qT} \times [(-1) \times S \times n(d1) \times \sigma/(2\sqrt{T}) + q \times S \times N(d1)] - r \times K \times N(d2) \times e^{-rT}$$

where $n(x) = \exp\{(-1) \times x^2/2\}/\sqrt{2\pi}$—density of standard normal distribution.
Based on the formula we can say that:

- the higher the q and the lower the r, the smaller the option's price depreciation per day;
- the higher the volatility, the greater the option's price decline with every passing day.

Theta is a very important indicator. It represents the cost of holding the option's position. Investors might hold an option position expecting a favorable move of the underlying position. While executing this strategy they should be very attentive to theta.

GAMMA

Gamma is the second-order derivative of an option's price C with respect to underlying asset price S. If delta is a car's speed, gamma is its acceleration.

Gamma shows the change in delta as S moves. The lower the gamma the less sensitive the delta to the price moves. Let's return to the concept of delta-neutral portfolio: its value stays the same regardless of *small share price move*. If the move is more than small, some adjustments in the hedge should be made. The number of shares should be increased or decreased in order to maintain the portfolio risk-free.

The following formula is true for gamma:

$$\text{Call gamma} = [n(d1) \times e^{-qT}]/[S \times \sigma \times \sqrt{T}]$$

Let's suppose that dS is the asset price change within comparatively short period of time dT, and $d\sigma$ is the corresponding portfolio value move. Then for delta-neutral portfolio

$$d\sigma = \text{theta} \times dT + \text{gamma} \times dS^2/2$$

The owner of portfolio with positive gamma (bought options, "long gamma") earns profits on large share price fluctuations and loses on small ones.

The owner of portfolio with negative gamma (sold options, especially short-term ones) loses more as the price fluctuations increase. Therefore, it is profitable to hold a positive-gamma position for an assets environment. In case of low-volatility assets it is better to hold a negative-gamma position.

GREEKS PARITY

Delta, gamma, and theta are interrelated. If C is the option's price and S is the asset price then

$$\text{theta} + (r - q) \times S \times \text{delta} + (\sigma^2/2) \times S^2 \times \text{gamma} = r \times C$$

Parity demonstrates that one cannot optimize all "Greeks" at once. Improvement in one will cause deterioration in the other.

VEGA

So far we've assumed that volatility of the asset stays constant. In reality that isn't so. That's why it makes sense to consider vega—option's price derivative with respect to volatility change. Vega is measured in percentage points and shows how sensitive the option's price is to the asset volatility changes. Typically vega is calculated for a 1% volatility move.

Vega's value may be determined with the following formula:

$$\text{Call vega} = S \times \sqrt{T} \times n(d1) \times e^{-qT}$$

Vega is very important for market makers. Even if the portfolio is delta-neutral they can lose or make money from volatility changes. If a market maker believes that volatility will increase, she should create long-vega portfolio and vice versa. If she doesn't have a view on vega, it warrants a vega-neutral portfolio (i.e., portfolio insensitive to volatility change). Such a portfolio may be achieved only by buying/selling options.

RHO

Rho shows sensitivity of the option's value with respect to the interest rate.

For a European call option on stock paying no dividends rho is determined by the following formula:

$$\text{Call rho} = K \times T \times e^{-rT} \times N(d2)$$
$$d2 = [\ln(S/K) + (r - \sigma^2/2) \times T]/[\sigma \times \sqrt{T}]$$

For a put option:

$$\text{Put rho} = -K \times T \times e^{-rT} \times N(-d2)$$

If the stock pays dividends at q rate, $d2$ is determined by the following formula:

$$d2 = [\ln(S/K) + (r - q - \sigma^2/2) \times T]/[\sigma^2 \times \sqrt{T}].$$

From the formulas it follows that a European call's price rises as the interest rate increases. And conversely, the price of a put falls as the interest rate increases.

QUESTIONS

1. Data in the table use formulas derived in this appendix. Calculate theta/premium ratio. What conclusion can you make regarding relationship of theta/premium and delta?

Strike	Premium	Delta	Theta
1.9	109.52	87%	0.46
2.0	39.96	52%	0.9
2.05	19.83	32%	0.82
2.1	8.48	17%	0.57

2. Data in the table use formulas derived in this appendix. Calculate vega/premium ratio. What conclusion can you make regarding relationship of vega/premium and delta?

Strike	Premium	Delta	Theta
2	183	59%	7.6
2.1	139	49%	7.8
2.3	75	32%	7.0
2.5	38	19%	5.36

3. An investor sells $N = 1{,}000$ of three-month European calls on share that are subject to continuous dividend payment at the rate $q = 5\%$. Current stock price $S = \$50$, annual volatility = 60%, continuously compounded risk-free interest rate $r = 7\%$, option's strike $K = \$60$. How many shares should the investor purchase so that the value of his portfolio doesn't substantially fluctuate with small price changes?
4. The investor's position consists of $N = 1{,}000$ of bought three-month European calls on shares ex-dividend. Current stock price $S = \$40$, annual volatility = 40%, continuously compounded risk-free interest rate $r = 6\%$, option's strike $K = \$45$. Determine by how much the position's value will fall in a day if the market does not move.
5. Returning to Question 3, to which extent a strong stock price move will influence the value of the portfolio?

ANSWERS

1. Low-delta options have higher theta/premium ratios.
2. Low-delta options have higher vega/premium ratios.
3. Investor needs to delta hedge position. Delta of investor's option position equals

$$\text{delta} = -e^{-qT} \times N(d1) \times N$$

where $d1 = [\ln(S/K) + (r - q + \sigma^2/2) \times T]/[\sigma^2 \times \sqrt{T}\,]$

Consequently:

$$d1 = [\ln (50/60) + (0.07 - 0.05 + 0.36/2) \times 0.25]/[0.6 \times 0.5]$$
$$= [-0.182 + 0.2 \times 0.25]/[0.3] = -0.13$$
$$N(d1) = N(-0.13) = 1 - N(0.13) = 1 - 0.5517 = 0.4483$$
$$\text{delta} = -e^{-0,05 \times 0,25} \times 0,4483 \times 1{,}000 = -443$$

Therefore, to make delta of the portfolio equal 0, the investor should buy 443 shares in the market.

4. Theta of the investor's position equals

$$\text{theta} = -N \times [(S \times n(d1) \times \sigma)/2 \times \sqrt{T} + r \times K \times e^{-rT} \times N(d2)],$$

where $n(x) = e^{-x2/2}/\sqrt{2\pi}$

$$d1 = [\ln(S/K) + (r + \sigma^2/2) \times T]/[\sigma \times \sqrt{T}]$$

$$d2 = d1 - \sigma \times \sqrt{T}$$

Consequently:

$$d1 = [\ln(40/45) + (0.06 + 0.16/2) \times 0.25]/[0.4 \times 0.5] =$$
$$= [-0.118 + 0.035]/[0.2] = -0.42$$
$$n(d1) = e^{-0.176/2}/2.5 = 0.366$$
$$d2 = -0.42 - 0.4 \times 0.5 = -0.62$$
$$N(d2) = N(-0.62) = 1 - N(0.62) = 1 - 0.7291 = 0.2709$$
$$\text{Theta} = -1{,}000 \times [(40 \times 0.366 \times 0.4)/2 \times 0.5 + 0.06 \times 45$$
$$\times e^{-0.06 \times 0.25} \times 0.2709] = -1{,}000 \times [5.856 + 0.72] = -6{,}576$$

Thus, in one day the value of the position will fall by theta/365 = \$18.

5. Since the investor sold the options, the total gamma of the portfolio will be negative. It means that a strong price move in either direction will cause losses.

APPENDIX C

American Options: Options on Futures, Currencies, Commodities, Equities, and Bonds

AMERICAN-STYLE OPTIONS

Unlike a European option, which may be exercised only on the expiration date, an American option can be exercised at any moment before its expiration date.

The most popular model to value an American options is the Cox-Ross-Rubinstein model that uses a binomial trees. Consider an American call option on stock. For simplicity assume that stock pays no dividends.

Let's divide the option's lifetime into short time periods of a dT length. Suppose that in each period the stock price may either rise to Su with p probability, $u > 1$, or fall to Sd with $(1 - p)$ probability, $d < 1$, where S is the current stock price. Assuming that $u = 1/d$, consecutive price moves upward and downward should compensate each other.

Values of u and p are determined based on probability. According to the Black-Scholes model $S(t + dT)$ stock price at the time $t + dT$ is a lognormal variable with parameters $(\ln S + (r - \sigma^2/2) \times dT, \sigma \times \sqrt{dT})$, where S—current stock price. Thus mean of $S(t + dT)$ variable equals to $S \times e^{r \times dT}$ and dispersion equals to $S^2 \times e^{2r \times dT} (e^{\sigma 2 \times dT} - 1)$.

A binomial model assumes that $S(t + dT)$ variable is equal to Su with p probability or Sd with $(1 - p)$ probability. Its mean is $pSu + (1 - p)Sd$ and variable is $pS^2u^2 + [(1 - p)S^2d^2 - S^2(pu + (1 - p)d)]$. (See Figure C.1.)

To derive p and u we need to equal mean and dispersion of binomial approximation to the parameters of lognormal distribution.

$$p = (e^{r \times dT} - d)/(u - d)$$

$$u = 1/d = e^{\sigma \times \sqrt{dT}}$$

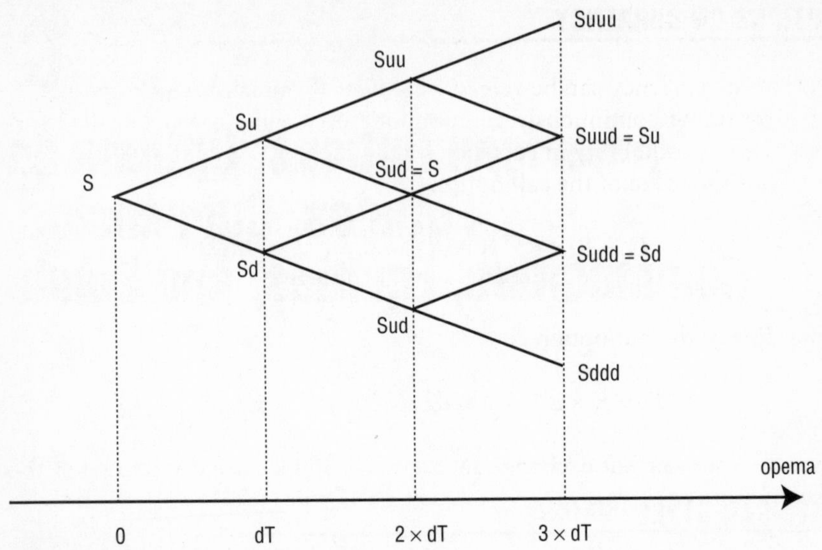

FIGURE C.1

Knowing u and d, one can build up the tree that describes the probable share price trend for the option's lifetime.

The left point of the binomial tree corresponds to the current time when stock price is S. The i tier of the tree corresponds to $i \times dT$ time and has $i + 1$ nodes. Stock price at the node j equals to $S \times u^j \times d^{i-j}$, $j = 0, \ldots, i$.

Suppose that we have already calculated the option's price at *Suu* and *Sud* points. It is X and Y respectively. At *Su* point the option's buyer has two alternatives: to exercise the option immediately and collect the profit $A = \max(Su - K, 0)$ or to hold the option. In the former case after the dT time period the option will cost X with p probability and Y with $(1 - p)$ probability. Thus present expected value of the option is $B = e^{-r \times dT} \times (p \times X + (1 - p) \times Y)$. Since the option's buyer is aimed at maximizing the profit he will certainly choose the most profitable variant because the option's price at *Su* point will equal $\max(A,B)$.

Share prices at the moment of option's exercise are easy to calculate; thus the option's value at expiration is: $\max[(S(T) - K)]$. To calculate the option price today we will move from the top tier to the zero tier using the above algorithm.

To calculate an option's value with a good degree of accuracy, the market practitioner typically use 100 steps in the binomial tree.

OPTIONS ON CURRENCY

Options on currency can be valued by similar formulas as stock options after substituting continuously compounded dividends (q) on so-called foreign rate of profitability in currency – r_f.

Thus the value of the call option is:

$$C_2 = \underbrace{S_2 \times e^{-r_f T} \times N(d1)}_{\text{receipts}} - \underbrace{K \times e^{-rT} \times N(d2)}_{\text{expenses}}$$

The value of the put option is:

$$P_2 = K \times e^{-r_f T} \times N(-d2) - S_2 \times e^{-r_f T} \times N(-d1)$$

Here S_2 is the current exchange rate, and $d1$ and $d2$ are determined in the following way:

$$d1 = [\ln(S_2/X) + (r - r_f + \sigma^2/2) \times T]/[\sigma \times \sqrt{T}]$$

$$d2 = [\ln(S_2/X) + (r - r_f - \sigma^2/2) \times T]/[\sigma \times \sqrt{T}] = d1 - \sigma \times \sqrt{T}$$

There is an additional "Greek" value using to hedge currency options against moves of the foreign rate called phi.

Phi is calculated by the following formulas:

$$\text{For call options: Phi} = -T \times e^{-r_f T} \times S_2 \times N(d1)$$

$$\text{For put options: Phi} = -T \times e^{-r_f T} \times S_2 \times N(-d1)$$

OPTIONS ON FUTURES

Pricing formulas for calls (puts) on a futures contract can be derived from formulas on options on stock by taking into considerations formulas for forward price of the asset.

The resulting formulas are:

$$C = e^{-rT} \times [\underbrace{F \times N(d1)}_{\text{receipts}} - \underbrace{K \times N(d2)}_{\text{expenses}}]$$

The value of a put on futures equals

$$P_3 = e^{-rT} \times [K \times N(-d2) - F \times N(-d1)]$$

Here F is the current price of the futures, and $d1$ and $d2$ are determined the following way:

$$d1 = [\ln(S_2/X) + \sigma^2/2 \times T]/[\sigma \times \sqrt{T}]$$
$$d2 = [\ln(S_2) + \sigma^2/2 \times T]/[\sigma \times \sqrt{T}] = \mathrm{d}1 - \sigma \times \sqrt{T}$$

SUMMARY TABLE

The following table summarizes option formulas on shares, bonds, precious metals, base metals, and oil base metals.

Underlying Asset	Call	Put
Shares ex-dividend	$S \times N(d1) - K \times e^{-rT} \times N(d2)$	$K \times e^{-rT} \times N(-d2) - S \times N(-d1)$
Shares with dividend	$S_1 \times e^{-qT} \times N(d1) - K \times e^{-rT} \times N(d2)$	$K \times e^{-rT} \times N(-d2) - S1 \times e^{-qT} \times N(-d1)$
Futures, bonds, oil, metals	$e^{-rT} \times [F \times N(d1) - K \times N(d2)]$	$e^{-rT} \times [K \times N(-d2) - F \times N(-d1)]$
Currency	$S_2 \times e^{-rfT} \times N(d1) - K \times e^{-rT} \times N(d2)$	$K \times e^{-rT} \times N(-d2) - S2 \times e^{-rfT} \times N(-d1)$
Gold*	$G \times e^{-r1T} \times N(d1) - K \times e^{-rT} \times N(d2)$	$K \times e^{-rT} \times N(-d2) - G \times e^{-r1T} \times N(-d1)$

*In the case of options on gold we use the model for currency options, the only change being that we use so-called **lease rate—r_1** instead of profitability in currency.

In this table:

- K—option's strike;
- S, S_1—share price;
- S_2—currency rate;
- F—futures' price on share, bond, oil, metals;
- G—price on gold;
- r—risk-free profitability rate;
- q—continuous dividends' rate;
- r_f—rate of profitability in currency;
- r_1—lease rate;
- $d1$, $d2$—are determined for each type of options by corresponding formulas.

Notes

CHAPTER 2 Drawing Option Charts

1. Risk profile is a graphic representation of a strategy risk.
2. The Black-Scholes Model is described in Chapter 20.

CHAPTER 4 Put/Call Parity

1. Arbitrage profit is a riskless profit received from arbitrage (arbitrage operations) by means of a simultaneous purchase and sale of the same asset. That is, a trader having a client's order to purchase a share at 11 points buys it on the market at 10 with no risk that the trade will lose money.
2. The portfolio that consists of a long K call and a short K put is effectively (synthetically) equal to a long K spot.
3. In all the above examples, the option premium is assumed to equal 0.
4. The term "spot" in currency operations is analogous to the term "cash" on stock and bond markets.

CHAPTER 5 Basic Option Strategies

1. If you deal in currencies, you should calculate the breakevens based on the second currency pips (CHF pips for $/CHF, USD pips for GBP/$, etc.) If your premium is expressed otherwise, you should transform it into pips at the current exchange rate.
2. The EUR call is the same as the USD put: in currency pairs when one appreciates, the other depreciates. That is why you can often see currency options expressed as "EUR call/USD put." In fact, dealers prefer talking in terms of the second currency. For instance, they would say "EUR/USD, 25 delta call." That would mean the 25 delta **USD** call.
3. A "naked" option is an option without a hedge. Another funny term is the "Texas hedge"; when options and their "hedges" have the same direction. Such a "hedge" doubles the position's risk rather than protects it.
4. One pip equals 0.0001. 100 pips = 1 figure. Thus, the price of 454 CHF pips is expressed mathematically as 0.0454. For example, the breakeven point of 1.4200 call will be at 1.4200 + 0.0256 = 1.4456.

5. Pay attention to the currency pair format: the result is calculated in the second currency terms. If USD/JPY appreciates from 100 yen per $1 (100.00) to 110.00 yen per $1 (110.00), the owner of $1 will gain 10 yen. If GBP/USD appreciates from 1.5000 to 1.6000, the owner of 1,000 pounds will gain $100.
6. One contract on the "Merc" equals CHF 125,000, JPY 125,000, etc.

CHAPTER 6 Complex Option Strategies

1. If you are a net payer, the strategy is called a "*debit strategy*," where you "*pay debit*." If you are a net receiver, the strategy is called a "*credit strategy*," where you "*earn credit*."
2. Gray color marks the text to which a special attention should be paid.

CHAPTER 7 Practical Steps in Creating and Designing Strategies

1. "Support" is a term used in technical analysis. It stands for a price level at which there is a great number of buyers. As a result, the market shall have difficulty breaking below it.
2. Until now we considered OTM and ATM *spot* strikes. It is more precise to say OTM and ATM *forward* strikes. We will discuss this topic later in the book.
3. Asian options are also called Average Price options, since their strike is determined on the basis of an average price of a certain time period. They are generally used by industrial hedgers and are not covered in this book.

CHAPTER 8 Delta

1. Delta is expressed in percentages: 20 delta means 20% of the face value. In publications, you can find the following delta expression: 0.2; 20% or 20 delta.
2. Hedge is an insurance of an asset value.
3. We shall use different terms for this strategy to accustom the reader to them.
4. To prevent the contracts from expiring on weekends, a certain weekday per month is fixed as an expiration date.
5. The "year" for the most currencies consists of 360 days. For GBP, AUD, NZD, and some other currencies in the new markets, it equals 365 days.
6. Credit risk of swaps is lower than of futures since these are counter obligations.
7. Buyers and sellers are defined in terms of the fixed leg. The seller is the party who sold the fixed leg of a swap (is a receiver of fixed payments), and the buyer is a party who bought the fixed leg of a swap (is a payer of fixed payments).
8. One can choose other floating rates; for example, the six- or nine-month LIBOR rate.

9. 0.25% discounted by three-month LIBOR at that time.
10. When the rates of both currency deposits are equal, there is no interest rate differential (swap points equal 0), and the current and future FX rates are the same.
11. The calculation is the same for options and forwards.

CHAPTER 9 Spreads

1. Jan XYZ 100 120, 1:3 call stands for a ratio spread on XYZ stock where one face value with 100 strike is bought/sold and three face values with 120 strike are sold/bought.

PART THREE Risk Parameters of Options

1. At the heart of the modern industry of options, there are a number of important formulas, most of which were published for the first time in the following articles:

   F. Black and M. Scholes, "The Pricing of Options and Corporate Liabilities," *Journal of Political Economy* 81 (1973): 637–659;

   J. Cox and S. Ross, "The Valuation of Options for Alternative Stochastic Processes," *Journal of Financial Economics* 3 (1976): 145–166;

   J. Cox and M. Rubenstein, "Option Pricing: A Simplified Approach," *Journal of Financial Economics* 7 (1979): 229–263;

   M. Garman and S. Kolhagen, "Foreign Currency Option Values," *Journal of International Money and Finance* 2 (1983): 231–237.

CHAPTER 11 Introduction: Volatility and the "Greeks" (Theta, Vega, and Gamma)

1. Statisticians denote volatility with the Greek letter sigma. However, the term "sigma" is rarely used in options.
2. The definition sounds difficult, but we will not use it later on. Thus, there is no need to remember it.
3. Traders prefer to call theta "time decay." Theoretically, this is not correct, since time decay = theta ± daily funding.
4. "Tick" in different markets is equal to a different mathematical value. On the FX market, the tick equals 10 basic points (pips). On exchanges, the tick stands for a minimum contract step. E.g., in a copper contract on COMEX, the tick equals 5 basic points.
5. This logic doesn't correspond to the options theory, but it explains in lay terms how strategies with different directions may have the same financial result.
6. This holds true only if the interest rates on both currencies are the same.
7. Peter L. Bernstein, *Against the Gods: the Remarkable Story of Risk* (Moscow: CJSC Olimp-Business, 2000), pp. 327–335.

CHAPTER 12 Volatility

1. Technical analysis is a method of market analysis. It uses historical graphs or mathematical analysis of prices to identify historical price patterns, which are used to predict future behavior.
2. For calculations of volatilities for a period other than 1 day, instead of 16 we use the formula $\sqrt{365/N}$, where N is the number of periods in the year. E.g., for a weekly volatility, we use $\sqrt{52}$, because there are 52 weeks per year.
3. One may finetune the formula to one's own style since the number of business days fluctuates from country to country and from year to year. Therefore, it is different depending on the year and the underlying. However, the net result will not differ very much *if the number of days is applied consistently*.
4. In terms of statistics, a 55-pip daily range means that we expect a daily high-low price range of 55 pips or less for two trading days out of each three, a price range 2×55 or less will occur 19 days out of 20, and for only one day out of 20 will we expect a change in excess of 2×55. It is unlikely you will ever use this concept in trading, but it is widely used by risk managers in setting up trading limits.
5. In calculating volatility for the period other than one day, daily high/lows are to be replaced with the corresponding period's high/lows. Such calculations are reported by analysts, but not used for trading.
6. Generally, markets treat the options with expiration within a month or less as short-term.
7. Annualized time is used (see Chapter 14).
8. The term "two-week volatility" stands for the implied volatility of an option expiring in two weeks.

CHAPTER 14 Theta

1. Time value changes not only because of the time left to expiration, but also because of volatility changes.
2. Traders prefer to call theta (and amortization) *time decay*.
3. For ITM and OTM options, this observation does not hold.
4. The terms "week" or "month" are used *only in forward market terminology*: 30 days from spot delivery date till forward delivery date rather than from the spot dealing date until the option expiration date. For example, a one-week USD/CHF option is purchased on Thursday, June 30 (dealing date). Under ordinary circumstances, the premium settlement date is July 4 (the second business day). Since July 4 is a U.S. bank holiday, the second business day is July 5. Now, we add a week to July 5 and realize that the forward settlement date is July 12 (Tuesday). Now, count down two business days to find that transactions done on July 8 (Friday) settle on July 12. That is, if the option is exercised on Friday, July 8 it will be settled on July 12. Therefore, in this case one week will be eight days long—from Thursday, June 30 till Friday, July 8, although the period between delivery is seven days.

5. Most advisors argue that if you buy low-delta options, your position's time decay is small. They never explain that this is true for the face value comparison rather than the comparison on the basis of investment size. That causes a lot of confusion and losses!
6. See observation 2 in Chapter 18: Opening the Short-Term and Long Term Positions.
7. See Chapter 17: Dynamic Option Hedging.
8. Here, we assume no influence of interest rates and dividend rates, which are discussed later.
9. That is the reason why traders call it time decay rather than theta: they see a cumulative number of theta + swaps (funding).

CHAPTER 15 Gamma

1. An intentional mathematical discrepancy: one cannot add up speed and acceleration.

CHAPTER 16 Impact of Interest Rates on Options Pricing and Strategies

1. In Chapter 4, we assumed interest rates and dividends to equal 0, which allowed use of spot (cash) instead of forward.
2. The actual formula is: $Call\ (K) - Put\ (K) = Spot \times e^{-RfT} - K \times e^{-RdT}$; where
   Rf—compound interest rate of the first currency (foreign);
   Rd—compound interest rate of the second currency (domestic).
   Since $Forward\ (F) = Spot \times (e^{-RfT}/e^{-RdT})$, the parity formula may be transformed into
   $Call\ (K) - Put\ (K) = (F - K) \times e^{-RdT}$.
3. This is true for European-style options. In the case of American-style options, the face value of the forward hedge may exceed the option's face value.
4. Also known as equivalent positions. A synthetic position is a combination of instruments that has the same risk/reward profile as another combination comprised of different instruments.
5. For the FX market, the differential between the foreign and domestic rates. For stocks, the difference between dividend and financing rates.
6. In the FX options market (OTC) price is requested for "an ATM option." In the absence of clarification, a request implies an ATM option with a strike at **forward** rate level. In the Eurobond options, a request for "an ATM option" stands for an ATM option with a strike at a current cash price.
7. FX traders also call it swaps or swap-points.
8. Any currency option is simultaneously a call on one currency and a put on the other. In this case, a call on the currency with the lower interest rate is simultaneously a put on the currency with the higher interest rate.
9. This is true for ATM options.

10. This discussion is subject to those currencies in which USD is the foreign (rather than the domestic) currency, e.g., USD/JPY. For GBP/USD, the reverse logic applies. That is, it is important to know the difference between "foreign" and "domestic" currencies.
11. A strike of an *ATM spot* option is fixed at a *spot* level at the moment of transaction. A strike of an *ATM forward* option is fixed at a *forward level* at the moment of the deal.

CHAPTER 17 Dynamic Option Hedging

1. For more details, see Chapter 25, the section on options' portfolio management.
2. Volatility changes cause P/L changes as well.
3. The forward differential is assumed to be equal to 0. If you'll have to pay (or collect) forward points to support your short position, these payments will reduce (or increase) your profit.

CHAPTER 18 Summing Up

1. When an investor asks for an option price, a dealer calculates the size of a forward hedge. Without knowing the client's position, he adds up a spread on spot, a spread on forward, and a spread on implied volatility.
2. Spreads reduce impact of volatility changes on strategy prices.

CHAPTER 19 Introduction to Exotic Options

1. The term *trigger* in the case of exotic options is synonymous with *barrier*. If as a result of the market's reaching the price level the option "comes to life" or "inspires" this level is called "knock-in"; if, as a result of contact with a given price level, the option "dies off," this level is called "knock-out."
2. In some situations, actual payments are made only at expiration of the options.
3. The terms "validated," "knocked in," "triggered in," "inspired" are interchangeable as well as terms "invalidated," "knocked out," "triggered out," "expired."

4 "+"—option is bought; "–"—option is sold.

PART FOUR Market Support (Market Making)

1. Traders on exchanges are also called specialists.

CHAPTER 21 Market Making: Price Support of the Market

1. At a given moment on the Merc (CME), there are no more than five expiration dates for almost all instruments. The number of strikes is initially limited as

well. If spot deviates considerably from the initial range, the exchange introduces new strikes.

2. 1.3825 (so many Swiss Francs per dollar) is the European format of FX. It is used by OTC traders. Exchange traders use American price format in trading: *72.33* (1/0.7233 = 1.3825). Both forwards and futures are contracts on future prices of instruments, but futures expire once a month and forwards can expire on any day of month. Forwards trade on OTC while futures trade on exchanges.
3. The signs "+" and "–" means that a value is a bit higher or lower than stated.
4. The expiration date is determined by an exchange. CME-listed FX options expire on the first Friday of each month.
5. Options with settlement:
   in January, February, March use as an underlying March futures and trade on the basis of March futures price,
   in April, May, June—of June futures price,
   in July, August, September—of September futures price,
   in October, November, December—of December futures price.
6. Gamma of a short-term option improperly predicts change in delta when spot moves. This happens because gamma of short-term options spikes in the area of 50 delta and is very low for OTM and ITM strikes. In other words, there is a lack of smoothness in gamma's rise/fall. Moreover, it is concentrated on a small segment of the spot. In conjunction, these two factors prevent the use of gamma of short-term options to predict a change of delta.
7. There are several formats for making ("showing") prices. The author suggests this format as the simplest. It assumes a "choice" price on a more expensive option and a bid/offer on the cheaper one.
8. E. Derman and I. Kani, "Riding on a Smile." *RISK* (February 1994).

CHAPTER 22 Introduction to Options Portfolio Management

1. In the case of OTC currency options, the exercises take place in Tokyo and London/New York time (as a rule the latter ones coincide).
2. In a risk-free (delta-neutral) portfolio, options are hedged by an underlying asset. Thus, the difference between calls and puts disappears. Let us review the material covered in detail in Chapter 17 "Dynamic Option Hedging." Consider the following example. Step 1: you buy a 0.0850 *call* and hedge it by *selling* a delta-equivalent of the spot. If instead you bought a 1.2850 *put*, you would *buy* delta-equivalent of the spot. Step 2: spot goes up, the call's delta increases, and to retain the portfolio risk-free (delta-neutral) you should sell more spot. To hedge puts on the rising market you should . . . also sell spot as the put's delta falls. *That is, during the option's life the difference in hedging calls and puts with similar strike and expiration disappears.* Step 3: in exercising your actions for puts and call differ.

That's why an 80-delta call and a 20-delta put (for example, 0.8200 call and 1.2200 put) with the same strike and expiration date trade at the same volatility: their risk profiles and cost of hedging is the same in a flat forward curve environment.

3. Assumption of delta's proportional increase simplifies the explanation, but it is incorrect: for every range of any portfolio the dynamics are a bit different. On average, in the case of direct gamma it is more correct to say that deltas and gains due to the spot appreciation on the first two-thirds of the range equal to those on the last one-third of the range.
4. In theory, the forward interest rate differential determines the forward exchange rates. In practice, traders look at the exchange rates to see the forward interest rate differential between periods.
5. Resistance level is a difficult-to-break upward price level. It is calculated based on history of a given asset. Support level is an analogue of resistance level, but on the bottom of the range.
6. See previous paragraph.
7. When spot drops to a "support," the smile (a volatility premium for OTM puts above ATM) increases. Similarly a calls' premium increases when the spot rises to a "resistance." In other words, at technical levels the market is nervous: if they are "broken," volatility increases until the underlying price "finds" a new range.
8. Remember a simplified definition of delta: a chance that an option will be in-the-money on an exercise date. The higher the volatility, the greater is the chance and vice versa. That is, when volatility decreases, delta of OTM puts falls.
9. Remember that delta's change due to a change in volatility is much smaller than due to a spot change.
10. This is simplified logic: as a rule, theta is paid off about halfway through the first interval, rather than the first 10 pips as here.
11. "Today" for a currency options trader in Europe and America begins at 10:00 (NY time) and is over at 10:00 (NY time) the next day. Summarizing it for the market in general, a "day" is measured from the previous expiration until the following one. Expirations of currency options occur at 10:00 (NY time) and at 15:00 (Tokyo time). Therefore, for a trader dealing in options in Tokyo time, "today" will differ from that for those dealing on other continents.

CHAPTER 23 Hedging with Options

1. A strategy is a combination of options and underlying assets put together to reflect the hedger's market view.
2. For simplicity's sake, in the example we use a European-style option. In practice, oil is generally hedged with Asian-style options.
3. In Chapter 4, we discussed three types of options: out-of-the-money (OTM), at-the-money (ATM), and in-the-money (ITM). An OTM option has a little chance to be exercised, e.g., if the market trades at 100, a 150 call is OTM and is un-

likely to be exercised. An at-the-money option has a 50:50 chance to be exercised, e.g., if the market trades at 100, a 100 call is ATM. An ITM option has a significant chance to be exercised, e.g., if the market trades at 100, a 70 call is ITM and is unlikely to be exercised.

4. Source: Internet site of Morgan Stanley Bank.

CHAPTER 24 Advanced Hedging Strategies

1. The options with barriers are called "barrier options" and are part of an extended family of "exotic options."
2. Notice that the strikes of these options are equidistant from the forward rate rather than from the spot.
3. Clients like risk reversals and albatrosses since these hedging strategies are free or very cheap.
4. In equity options, one stock option is written on 100 shares.
5. Some readers may read this chapter without knowing that an option's premium is comprised of time and intrinsic value (see Chapter 4). With this knowledge, the previous statement has to be corrected: "Opportunity loss on the long stock position will be only partially compensated by the *time value portion of* the option's premium."

   For example, the IBM stock price is at 100, and you sell a 90 call for 15 dollars. If the buyer immediately exercises the 90 call, he buys the shares at 90 from you. Now, he can sell them at the current price of 100 collecting back 10 dollars out of 15 he spent on premium. Thus, "intrinsic value" is the portion of option's premium, which can be collected by immediately exercising the option. "Time value" is a difference between premium and intrinsic value. In our example it equals $5 (15 – (100 – 90)).

   In other words, the extent to which the option's premium compensates opportunity losses on the stock price increase is $5, that is, the option's time value.
6. A sale of options is a sale of opportunities, that is, time value. That's why it is better to sell ATM options, since their time value is higher than that of ITM options, and if the rate remains stable, you will earn more.
7. This is a barrier option often called "up-and-in" or "reverse knock-in"; 107.00 is called a "barrier" or a "trigger."
8. This relationship holds ideally for the situation of relatively flat volatility and interest rate curves.
9. Swap points reflect the difference in interest rates. Spot + Swap points = Forward.
10. In options on other underlyings, the standard meaning of the term "at-the-money" may be the opposite: an option's strike is at the current spot level. This is true for the options on emerging market Eurobonds.
11. You may recall that equidistant strikes are calculated around forward prices rather than spot prices.

CHAPTER 25 Forward and Settlement Risks in Spot, Forward, and Nondeliverable Forward Deals

1. Operational risks under DVP (Delivery Versus Payment) and safe settlement (advanced settlement/delivery) contracts are not discussed.
2. Russian law permits netting of similar liabilities, e.g., FX transactions in the same currency pair for the same delivery date. Under English law, netting covers a universe of contracts described in a netting agreement.

CHAPTER 26 Risks of Settlement on Option Deals

1. This statement is true for European options. Since nowadays they make up 99% of all operations with options, we will not go into details of American-style options.
2. However, there is a predelivery risk until the premium is paid: the counterparty may fail to pay the premium, and then you will have to void the option.
3. H. Riehl and T. Heffernan, "Pre-Delivery Credit Risk on Distant-Date Financial Contract," *Annual Report of the Foreign Exchange Committee* (1989): 26–29.
4. Due to software limitations, most banks estimate the risk to be equal 15% of the contract face value instead of an everyday adjustment according to VaR calculations.
5. There are some exceptions. For example, Eurobonds settle in three days, while Eurobond options settle in two days.

CHAPTER 27 Credit Risk of Option Strategies

1. The USD/JPY exchange rate used to translate P/L in the range between the strikes into USD is equal to the exchange rate at expiration, presumably 140.00 or higher.

CHAPTER 29 Credit Risk of Combined Positions: Option-Spot/Forward

1. Options are priced using a set of interest rates. Such pricing assumes hedging with forwards to an expiration date. If one hedges with spot and refinances spot hedge overnight, the interest rate risk remains unhedged.
2. In any case between March 24 and April 5 there is a market risk if spot changes.
3. *The answer is a bit different depending on whether the investor (bank) measures the results in dollars or in euros! The calculations are correct for results in dollars. If calculations are carried out in euros, each result in dollar terms should*

be converted at a current EUR/USD exchange rate. That is, the result in euro-equivalent fluctuates until it is "fixed" by an FX translation.

PART SEVEN Market Risks Management

1. Charles M. Cottle, *Options: Perception and Deception* (Chicago, London, Singapore: Irwin Professional Publishing, 2002), p. 36.

CHAPTER 30 Typical Mistakes of Options Risk Control

1. The concept makes sense in the case of investing in options but without hedging the latter.
2. E. Derman and I. Kani, "Riding on a Smile," *RISK* (February 1994).

CHAPTER 31 Recommended Approach to Risk Management Methodology

1. VaR means "Value at Risk."
2. Basketing recommendations differ depending on the underlying asset.
3. Let us recall that a forward is a contract to transact in future at a price, established today. A swap consists of two transactions: spot and forward in the reverse directions. Forward price is calculated as spot price multiplied by the difference between the interest rates of both currencies.
4. Paragraphs 2–4 are written by Phil Halperin, a head of Risk-Management Department in Alfa-Bank.

CHAPTER 32 Personal Factors in Risk Evaluation

1. This observation is at the core of the problems with mechanical trade systems. Backtesting of the models is normally positive. However, learning in practice how to use the system is a challenge. Interventions in the decisions suggested by the systems reduce the systems' efficiency.

CHAPTER 34 Problems with Standard Methods of Risk Minimization

1. Technical analysis is a method of forecasting based on the history of price behavior. Paul Tudor Jones once said, "To be a great trader you have to be a great price historian."
2. Technical level is the price level a specific asset should have difficulty breaking; such a level is determined through technical analysis.

APPENDIX A

1. This material is written by the staff of *eGAR Technology* and edited by the author on the basis of the following articles and the company's own works:
   Fischer Black and M. S. Scholes, "The Pricing of Options and Corporate Liabilities. *Journal of Political Economy* 7 (1973): 54.
   Robert C. Merton, "The Theory of Rational Option Pricing." *Bell Journal* 4 (1973): 183.
   Fisher Black, "The Pricing of Commodity Contracts." *Journal of Financial Economics* 3 (1976): 79.
   J. Cox, S. Ross, and M. Rubinstein "Option Pricing: A Simplified Approach." *Journal of Financial Economics* 7 (1979): 263.
   M. B. Garman and S. W. Kohlhagen, "Foreign Currency Option Values." *Journal of International Money and Finance* 2 (1983): 37.
2. Initially we'll consider shares without dividends (ex-dividend).
3. Let the yearly volatility σ of some AAA share equal 20%. Its current spot is \$100. On the basis of these data, one can make a forecast that in a year the stock price with 0.66 probability will be in the range of $\$100 \times (1 - 0.2)$ to $\$100 \times (1 + 0.2)$ or \$80 to \$120. One can also predict the stock price behavior on the basis of other time periods. To realize it, one should determine the stock price volatility in that period. For example, $\sigma_{3\text{-month}} = \sigma \times \sqrt{3 \text{ months}/1 \text{ year}} = \sigma \times \sqrt{0.25} = \sigma \times 0.5 = 10\%$. That is, in three months the stock price with 0.66 probability will be in the range of \$90–\$110.
4. max $[0, S(T) - K]$ is the intrinsic option's value at the moment of the option's exercise. In this case, the option's time value equals 0.

Glossary

albatross This strategy consists of options in the same direction (only calls or only puts). For instance, long $1 million of a 1.2800 call, short $2 million of a 1.2900 call, long $1 million of a 1.000 call. All the options have the same expiration date. The P/L of the strategy is limited by the strikes.

American option An American-style option provides the buyer with a right to exercise the option at any time before the contract's expiration

arbitrage See **arbitrage profit.**

arbitrage profit Risk-free profit from an arbitrage deal where the same underlying asset is bought and sold simultaneously with profit. For instance, a trader buys a stock at 10 on an exchange and sells it to a client at 11.

Asian option There are two types of Asian-style options: average rate and average strike options. The strike of an average strike option is determined on the basis of the underlying asset's average price over the option's life. The strike of an average rate option is determined in advance but the option is exercised based on the average price for the period. Asian options are mainly used for hedging by commodity producers.

At-the-money (ATM) option An option with a strike equal to the current forward level. Its premium equals the option's time value. In some markets the term "at-the-money option" applies to an option with a strike equal to the current spot level.

ATM See **at-the-money option.**

AUD Australian dollar.

back spread A combination of a ratio spread and a horizontal spread. That is, the spread combines long and short options with different strikes, different expiration dates, and different face values.

barrier option Knock-in and knock-out, reverse knock-in and reverse knock-out, double knock-in and double knock-out are some types of barrier options. These are *European* calls and puts with barriers. A barrier (also known as a trigger) is a certain price level. Depending on a type of a barrier option, once a barrier is touched the option becomes "inspired" (becomes validated) or "expires" (becomes invalidated).

bearish spread A spread that consists of a long put with a high strike and a short put with a low strike. A spread can also consist of a short call with a low strike and a long call with a high strike. Both options in either combination have the same face value and expiration date.

bearish strategy A strategy that makes money if a price of the underlying asset declines.

binary option An option contract defined by the amount of payouts. Many types of binary options do not have strikes and face values. Instead they have barriers and amounts of payouts.

breakeven (breakeven point) A price level of the underlying asset at which the P/L of an option strategy is 0. For instance, if a $110 call costs $1, the breakeven is $111: at this point the option premium is recovered, and only above $111 does the option become profitable.

bullish spread A spread that consists of a long call with a low strike and a short call with a high strike. A spread can also consist of a short put with a high strike and a long put with a low strike. Both options in either combination have the same face value and expiration date.

bullish strategy A strategy that makes money if a price of the underlying asset increases.

butterfly A speculative strategy based on an expectation of a price staying between the strikes. It consists of a long (short) straddle and of a short (long) strangle. All the options expire on the same date. P/L of the strategy is limited.

calendar/horizontal spread Assumes purchase and sale of calls (puts) with the same strikes and face values, but different expiration dates.

call option (call) A contract that provides a buyer with a *right* (but not an obligation) to *buy* a stipulated amount of the underlying asset on a certain date at a certain price (definition for European-style options). A seller of a call is *obliged* to *sell* the underlying asset at an option buyer's request, even if the price is unfavorable to him.

call spread A strategy that consists of long and short call options with different strikes but the same expiration date; for example, long a 100 call and short a 110 call with the same expiration date and face value.

cap and floor See **risk-reversal.**

cash A deal with stocks and bonds that settles on the current settlement date. The term is equivalent to the term "spot" on the FX market.

CHF Swiss franc.

choice option At the moment of transaction, the type of the option (call or put) is not defined. The contract specifies the date on which the buyer is to determine the option's type.

combo See **risk-reversal.**

compound option An option that provides its buyer with a right to buy another option, that is, the underlying asset of a compound option is another option.

contract size See **face value.**

Cost of carry Cost of funding a position.

currency swap Consists of two deals done simultaneously: buy/sell (sell/buy) of a spot contract and sell/buy (buy/sell) of a forward contract. In this case, the same amount of the *first* (foreign) currency is sold and bought for different dates and different amounts of the second (domestic) currency.

delivery date See **settlement date.**

delta (hedge ratio) One of the Greeks—a parameter that measures the sensitivity of the option price to changes in the price of the underlying asset. A portion of an option's face value known as delta or hedge ratio should be sold or bought against the option position in order to make the position indifferent to small market changes.

delta-neutral position (risk-neutral position, hedged position) A position at which P/L of the combined position (option + forward or option + option) equals 0 as the price of the underlying moves by 1 b.p. (pip) in either direction.

diagonal spread A combination of vertical and horizontal spreads that consists of two options with different expiration dates and strikes, but with the same face values.

digital option A type of binary option that combines conditions of vanilla and "touch" options. For instance, €10 million of November 1.2000 call (as in the case of a vanilla option) with a 400-pip pay-out (as in the case of a one-touch option). In other words, if the option is exercised, a buyer collects 400 pips irrespective of the fact of whether spot is at 1.2005 or 1.2800 at the moment of exercise.

directional strategy Strategies, such as long (short) call or put or risk reversal, that bets on a certain market direction.

domestic rate An interest rate that is used in FX option pricing and paid for deposits in a country whose currency is in the numerator (e.g., JPY in the USD/JPY). It is equivalent of a risk-free rate used for pricing stock options.

double-barrier option An option with two barriers.

dynamic hedging A process of maintaining a delta-neutral portfolio. It assumes rehedging it as the underlying asset price and the Greeks change.

equivalent position See **synthetic position.**

EUR euro.

EUR/USD (USD/JPY etc.) An exchange rate of EUR to USD (or USD to JPY).

exchange market A market traded on exchanges.

expiration date A date when an option contract expires. On this date, an option is either exercised or expires worthless.

expire The term has two meanings: The common one is that an option expires if not exercised on the expiration date. In the case of a barrier or digital option, this term means an option's expiration when spot touches a barrier. If spot touches a barrier during the option's life, the option expires worthless and cannot be exercised, even if it is at-the-money.

face value (notional value, nominal amount, contract size) The amount of a contract.

FOREX (foreign exchange, FX) Currency market.

forward See **forward contract.**

forward contract (forward) A contract on the delivery of the underlying asset at a certain date in the future at a price fixed at the moment of the deal.

forward differential See **swap points.**

gamma One of the Greeks—a parameter that measures delta's sensitivity to underlying asset price changes. The higher gamma, the greater delta changes when the underlying asset price moves. That is, gamma is an *acceleration of delta* (acceleration of premium changes) as the underlying asset price moves (the second derivative of the option premium in respect to the price of underlying).

Greeks Parameters that measure the option's risk. Each type of risk has a corresponding letter in the Greek alphabet. The most widely used Greeks are *delta*, *gamma*, *theta*, and *vega*.

hedging A process of asset value protection similar to insurance.

"horizontal" diversification A classical diversification that is achieved by increasing a number of managed assets with corresponding reduction of risk on each asset.

inspire (to become validated, to be knocked in) A barrier option inspires when spot touches a knock-in barrier. If spot doesn't touch a barrier during the option's life, the option expires worthless, even if it is in-the-money.

in-the-money (ITM) option A call with the strike below a current market forward price; a put with the strike above a current market forward price.

intrinsic value A portion of premium equal to the profit if the option is exercised before expiration. For example, if the stock price is 110 and you own a 100 call, the intrinsic value of the option equals 10, because if you were to exercise the call before expiration, your profit would be 10 (110 – 100).

ITM See **in-the-money (ITM) option.**

JPY Japanese yen.

knock-in option An option that inspires (becomes valid) being out-of-the-money. See **barrier option.**

knock-in See **trigger.**

knock-out See **trigger.**

knock-out option An option that expires (becomes invalidated prior to the expiration date) if the market touches a trigger while the option is out of the money. See **barrier option.**

leg One part of a strategy. For example, in a straddle "$5 million-a-leg" means that both the call's and the put's face values equal $5 million.

leverage Using a loan for purchase of an asset. Leverage is used to increase risk in order to receive greater profits from investments. For example, a fivefold leverage assumes purchase of an asset with a down payment of 20%. A broker lends the remaining 80%. If the initial value of the asset is $100, then with a $5 asset price increase (to $105) return on the capital will be 25%. The lower the leverage, the lower the profitability and the risk.

LIBOR (London Interbank Offered Rate) An average interest rate on short-term deposits in a group of London banks with the highest credit rating.

liquidity Informal market parameter that describes the ability to exchange a certain instrument or portfolio into cash and vice versa.

long (bullish) position (long strategy) A portfolio in which you bought some commodity or financial instrument to benefit from the market growth. For example, Long $1 million of USD/JPY—a position in which $1 million is bought and an equivalent amount of yen is sold.

long gamma See **long gamma position.**

long gamma position A hedged option position that appreciates as spot moves in either direction.

long vega See **long vega position.**

long vega position A position that makes money as the *implied* volatility rises.

mio Million.

naked option An option that is unhedged with an underlying asset.
nominal amount See **face value.**
notional value See **face value.**
no-touch option See **touch option.**
option A financial contract that confirms the buyer's right and the seller's obligation to buy or to sell a stipulated notional amount during a defined period or on a certain date at an agreed price(s) or for a certain fixed payment. A contract may fix not only the date, but also the time of expiration, price levels at which it becomes invalid or comes into effect, and so on.
option exercise Complete or partial presentation of an option contract for exercise by a buyer to a seller.
option expiration An option contract that is not presented for exercise by a certain hour on the date of expiration, and expires worthless.
option with rebates An option with several barriers. For example, if you invest $1,000 and USD/JPY is in the range of 105.00–110.00 for three months, you receive $2,000. However, if the market touches either 105.00 or 110.00, you have a right to receive the invested premium back as long as the market doesn't touch 103.00 or 112.00. If deals at any of the latter barriers take place on the market, you will lose the premium as well.
OTC (over-the-counter) A market of interbank trading.
OTM See **out-of-the-money (OTM) option.**
out-of-the-money (OTM) option A call with the strike above a current market forward price; a put with the strike below a current market forward price. The premium of an OTM option equals the option's time value.
participating forward A simultaneous purchase (sale) of a call and sale (purchase) of a put with the *same strike and expiration date.* As a result you have an option strategy in which P/L and risks are equivalent to an ordinary forward. That is why the term "participating forward" is interchangeable with "synthetic forward."
payout/payout ratio A term that defines the amount of profit (loss) to premium paid (received). It is an attribute of binary options (e.g., "no-touches").
P/L, P&L (profit and loss statement) A financial result of trading.
portfolio See **position.**
position (book) A combination of instruments and products that compose an investment portfolio.
premium A price that is paid or collected for an option.
premium time decay (theta) See **theta.**
put/call parity formulas describing the relationship of prices of put and call options.
put option (put) A contract that provides a buyer with a *right* (but not an obligation) to *sell* a stipulated amount of an underlying asset on a specified date at a certain price (definition for European-style options). A seller of a put has an *obligation* to *buy* the underlying asset at an option buyer's request, even at unfavorable price.
put spread A position that consists of long and short puts with different strikes, but the same expiration date (e.g., purchase of a 90 put and sale of an 80 put with the same expiration dates and face values).

range-bound strategy A position is oriented on a price staying within a range. Strangles and straddles are examples of such strategies.

ratio spread A combination of a long and a short same type options (calls or puts) with the same expiration date, but different face values. For instance, 1.1800–1.1900 1 by 2 call-spread (to buy/sell $1 million of 1.1800 call and to sell/buy $2 million of 1.1900 call).

release Announcement of some economic or political information.

resetting forward An exotic strategy. For instance, if USD/JPY spot has reached neither 107.00 nor 117.00 during the option's life and is above 110.00 on the expiration date, a buyer can exercise the 110.00 call (buy dollars at 110.00). However, if USD/JPY has reached either 107.00 or 117.00 during the option's life, he will have to buy dollars at 113.00.

resistance A term used in technical analysis that stands for a price level at which there is a great number of sell orders that may stop or delay appreciation of the underlying.

revaluation level (reval level) the level of spot/cash, and volatilities and interest rates at which the report of option position is calculated.

reverse knock-in A barrier option that *inspires* (is validated, is knocked in) when *in-the-money*. A knock-in trigger of a call is higher than its strike. A knock-in trigger of a put is lower than its strike.

reverse knock-out A barrier option that *expires* (becomes invalid) when it is in-the-money.

risk-neutral position See **delta-neutral position.**

risk profile A graphic presentation of a strategy's risk.

risk-reversal (combo, cap and floor, range forward, tunnel, collar) This strategy includes purchase of a call (a put) and sale of a put (a call) with the same face value and expiration date, but different strikes.

settlement date (delivery date) Date when a payment or an asset is received (paid/transferred).

short (bearish) position (short strategy) A portfolio aimed at collecting profit on market falls.

short gamma See **short gamma position.**

short gamma position A hedged option position that loses value when spot moves in either direction.

short vega See **short vega position.**

short vega position A position that loses money when *implied* volatility rises.

spot (cash) A deal that settles on a spot delivery date. The spot delivery date for currencies is two business days from the trading date. "Spot" is a term used in the FX and precious metals markets. It is similar to the term "cash" used on the stock and bond markets. The spot settlement date may be different for each currency.

straddle A strategy that consists of a call and a put *with the same strike and expiration date*. For instance, a combination of a November 1.1900 put and 1.1900 call.

strangle A strategy that consists of two options: an OTM call and an OTM put with different strikes, but the same expiration date (e.g., a combination of a

November 1.1900 put and a 1.2000 call). The strategy is applied similarly to a straddle, but it is cheaper.

strategy A combination of financial instruments that implements a market forecast.

strike (strike price) An underlying price stipulated in the option contract, at which a buyer of a call (put) can buy (sell) the underlying asset, upon presenting the option to a seller for exercise.

support A term used in technical analysis that stands for a price level at which there is a great number of buy orders which may stop or delay depreciation of an underlying asset.

swap The term has a different meaning for FOREX (see **currency swap**) and for other markets. On securities and commodities markets a swap is an "exchange" of a floating rate contract for a fixed rate contract. An owner of the fixed portion receives (or pays) compensation to an owner of the floating portion for deviations of initial difference of fixed price from current (floating) market price. For example, the price of a swap of six-month LIBOR on five-year fixed rate is 300 bps. A buyer of the fixed leg (the five-year rate) pays or receives compensation quarterly upon update of the six-month LIBOR rate.

swap points (forward differential) A difference between spot and forward rates. The term is used on the FX market.

synthetic forward See **participating forward, synthetic position.**

synthetic position (synthetic strategy) A strategy that combines options as well as the underlying asset that has the risk profile and P/L equivalent to other options and the underlying assets strategies. For example, the profile of a sold forward is similar to a combination of long put and short call with the same strikes and expiration dates as the forward. P/L of the forward and of the options strategy is the same, which is why this strategy is also called a "synthetic forward."

technical analysis A method of price forecasting based on past price behavior. It requires studying charts of historical market behavior.

Texas hedge This is an ironic term. An underlying position is taken in the same direction as the option position, leading to the option position risk doubling rather than edging.

theoretical profit (paper profit) An unrealized profit of an option position.

theta (decay, time decay) One of the Greeks—a parameter that measures sensitivity of the option premium to changes in the time remaining until the option expiration. The higher the theta, the faster the amortization of the option premium. To be more precise, theta measures sensitivity of the *time value component of the option premium* to the shortening of the period remaining until expiration. Theta is high for short-term options and in the high *implied volatility* environment.

tick A step in the underlying asset price. The term stands for different values on various markets. On the FOREX market, a tick equals 10 b.p. (10 pips). On exchanges, a tick stands for a minimal contract step. For example, in the case of the COMEX copper contract a tick is equal to 5 b.p.

time decay Traders substitute this term for theta. Theoretically, this substitution is incorrect, because *time decay* = theta ± *interest carry*.

time value A portion of an option's premium equal to the difference between the option premium and its intrinsic portion. Time value is sensitive to changes in the time remaining until the option's expiration and in *implied* volatility. For example, the stock price is $110; you buy a $100 call for $12. The option's intrinsic value equals $10, because if you immediately exercise the call, the cost of the position will be $10 ($110 – $100). The remaining $2 ($12 – $10) is the option's time value.

touch option (one-touch option) A type of binary option; the option contract specifies conditions similar to those of a lottery: if you invest $1,000 and spot trades at 1.1800 during the option's life, you will earn $4,000.

trigger See **barrier option**. The term is used for exotic options.

underlying asset This is a product that serves as a reference asset. Anything can be an underlying asset: shares, currencies, coffee, gold, and even weather!

USD U.S. dollar.

Value-at-Risk (VaR) A method that measures risk of investments depending on market volatility and an underlying price move.

vanilla option A commonly used term, a synonym for European-style option.

vega One of the Greeks—a parameter that measures sensitivity of option prices to changes in *implied* volatility. The higher the option's vega, the greater the option's price changes as the implied volatility changes.

vertical diversification A method of managing a single-asset position in order to increase chances of making money and reduce chances of losses. It assumes (1) multiple entrance and exit levels in and out of a position, (2) various sizes per entries/exits at different levels, (3) various instruments and methodologies.

vertical spread All bullish and bearish spreads are referred to as vertical spreads: long call (or a put) and short call (or a put) with different strike, but the same expiration date. In this case both options have the same maturity and face value.

Bibliography

Articles

Black, F. "The Pricing of Commodity Contracts." *Journal of Financial Economics* 3 (1976): 167–179.

Black, F., and M. Scholes. "The Pricing of Options and Corporate Liabilities." *Journal of Political Economy* 81 (1973): 637–654.

Cox, J., and S. Ross. "The Valuation of Options for Alternative Stochastic Processes." *Journal of Financial Economics* 3 (1976).

Cox, J., S. Ross, and M. S. Rubenstein. "Option Pricing: A Simplified Approach." *Journal of Financial Economics* 7 (1979): 229–263.

Derman, E., and I. Kani. "Riding on a Smile." *Risk* (February 1994).

Garman, M., and S. Kolhagen. "Foreign Currency Option Values." *Journal of International Money and Finance* 2 (1983): 231–237.

Merton, R. "The Theory of Rational Option Pricing." *Bell Journal* 4 (1973): 141–183.

Books

Caplan, David L. *The New Options Advantage.* Chicago: Probus Publishing, 1995.

Connolly, Kevin B. *Buying and Selling Volatility.* Chichester, New York: John Wiley & Sons, 1997.

Cottle, Charles M. *Options: Perception and Deception.* Irwin Professional Publishing, 2000.

Cox, John C., and Mark Rubinstein. *Options Markets.*

Derosa, David F. *Options on Foreign Exchange.* Wiley Series in Financial Engineering, John Wiley & Sons.

Eng, William F., Ed. *Options: Trading Strategies That Work.* Dearborn Financial Publishing, Inc., 1992.

Fabozzi, Frank J. *Valuation of Fixed Income Securities and Derivatives.* 3rd Ed. FJF, 1998.

Hull, John C. *Introduction to Futures and Options Markets.* 3rd Ed. Englewood Cliffs, NJ: Prentice Hall, 1997.

Levich, Richard M. *Can Currency Movements Be Forecasted?* AIMR Conference Proceedings: Currency Risk in Investment Portfolios, June 1999.

Natenberg, Sheldon. *Option Volatility & Pricing: Advanced Trading Strategies and Techniques.*

Niederhoffer, Victor. *The Education of a Speculator.*

Pettis, Michael. *The Volatility Machine, Emerging Economies and the Threat of Collapse.* Oxford University Press, 2001.

Riehl H., and T. Heffernan. *Pre-Settlement Credit Risk on Distant-Date Financial Contracts.* 1989 Annual Report of the Foreign Exchange Committee, 1989.

Schwager, Jack D. *Market Wizards: Interviews with Top Traders.* New York: HarperBusiness, 1993.

Sparandeo, Victor. *Trader Vic II—Principles of Professional Speculation.* New York: John Wiley & Sons, 1994.

Taleb, Nassim. *Dynamic Hedging: Managing Vanilla and Exotic Options.* New York: John Wiley & Sons, 1997.

Treat, John Eltting, Ed. *Energy Futures: Trading Opportunities for the 1990s.* PennWell Books, 1990.

Index